Hiking Southern Oregon

Hiking Southern Oregon

A Guide to the Area's Greatest Hiking Adventures

Art Bernstein and Zach Urness

FALCONGUIDES

GUILFORD, CONNECTICUT
HELENA, MONTANA

AN IMPRINT OF GLOBE PEQUOT PRESS

FALCONGUIDES®

Copyright © 2014 by Morris Book Publishing, LLC.

FalconGuides is an imprint of Globe Pequot Press.
Falcon, FalconGuides, and Outfit Your Mind are registered trademarks of Morris Book Publishing, LLC.

Maps: Alena Joy Pearce and Daniel Lloyd © Morris Book Publishing, LLC.
Project editor: Julie Marsh
Layout: Sue Murray

Library of Congress Cataloging-in-Publication Data

Bernstein, Art.
 Hiking Southern Oregon : a guide to the area's greatest hiking adventures / Art Bernstein and Zach Urness.
    pages cm
 Includes bibliographical references and index.
 ISBN 978-0-7627-8481-3
 1. Hiking—Oregon—Guidebooks. 2. Trails—Oregon—Guidebooks. 3.
 Oregon—Guidebooks. I. Urness, Zach. II. Title.
 GV199.42.07B48 2014
 796.5109795—dc23
                                                    2014010772

5578 4549
9/14

Printed in the United States of America

10 9 8 7 6 5 4 3 2 1

Contents

Acknowledgments x
Introduction 1
How to Use This Guide 6
Backcountry Regulations.. 12
Zero Impact 13
All about Hiking: Safety and Hazards 14
Trail Finder... 18
Map Legend 21

Southeast Oregon...23
Steens Mountain Area
  1. Wildhorse Lake.. 24
  2 Big Indian Gorge 27
  3 Little Blitzen Gorge 30
  4 Pike Creek Canyon.. 33
High Desert
  5 Crack in the Ground.. 36
Hart Mountain Antelope Refuge
  6 DeGarmo Canyon 39
Gearhart Mountain Wilderness
  7 Gearhart Mountain 43
  8 Blue Lake 46
Klamath Falls Area
  9 Crater Lake Pinnacles.. 49
Cascades—North of Crater Lake
  10 Mount Thielsen 52
  11 Mount Bailey.. 55
  12 Thielsen Creek Meadows... 58
North Umpqua River
  13 Wolf Creek Falls 62
  14 Yellowjacket Loop 65
  15 Fall Creek Falls 69
  16 Twin Lakes 72
  17 Pine Bench 75
  18 Toketee Falls 78
  19 Watson Falls 80
  20 Dread and Terror / Umpqua Hot Springs.................................. 83
  21 Lemolo Falls 86
  22 Miller to Maidu Lake... 89

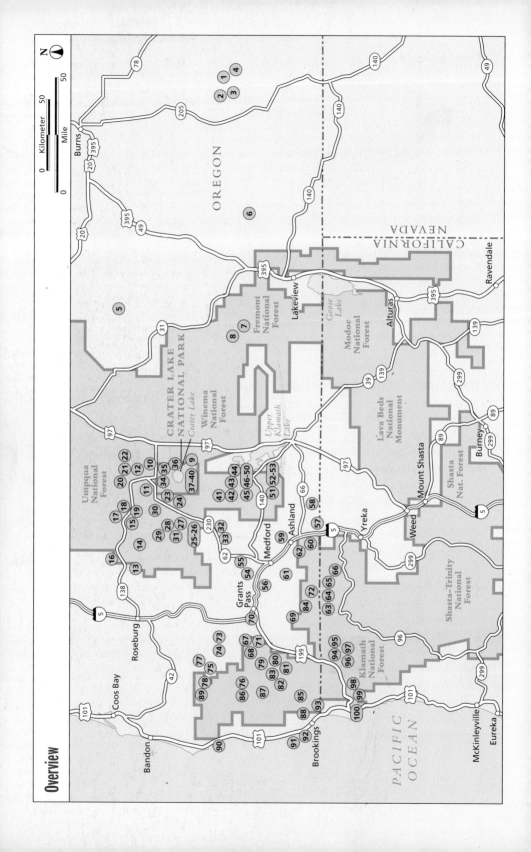

Overview

Upper Rogue River

23 Upper Rogue Canyon / Rough Rider Falls 92
24 National Creek Falls 96
25 Natural Bridge / Farewell Bend 98
26 Takelma Gorge 102
27 Golden Stairs 105

Rogue-Umpqua Divide Wilderness

28 Cliff Lake / Grasshopper Mountain 108
29 Fish Lake 111
30 Rattlesnake Mountain 114
31 Abbott Butte 117

Lost Creek Lake Area

32 Viewpoint Mike 120
33 Mill Creek Falls 123

Crater Lake National Park

34 Boundary Springs 126
35 Cleetwood Cove 129
36 Mount Scott 131
37 Garfield Peak 134
38 Annie Creek Loop 137
39 Union Peak 141
40 Plaikni Falls 145

Sky Lakes Wilderness

41 Middle Fork Rogue River 147
42 Seven Lakes Basin—West 150
43 Seven Lakes Basin—East 154
44 Devil's Peak 158
45 Blue Canyon Basin 162
46 Badger Lake 167
47 Squaw Lake 170
48 Nannie Creek / Puck Lake 173
49 Lower Sky Lakes 176
50 Upper Sky Lakes 180
51 Mount McLoughlin 184

Mountain Lakes Wilderness

52 Clover Creek 187
53 Varney Creek 190

Bear Creek Valley

54 Lower Table Rock 194
55 Upper Table Rock 197
56 Rogue River Greenway 200

Cascade-Siskiyous

57 Pilot Rock.. 203
58 Hobart Bluff / Pacific Crest Trail.............................. 206
59 Grizzly Peak 210
60 Mount Ashland Meadows / Pacific Crest Trail 212
61 Tunnel Ridge / Sterling Mine Trail 215
62 Wagner Butte.. 218

Red Buttes Wilderness

63 Tanner Lakes.. 221
64 Frog Pond.. 225
65 Azalea Lake.. 228
66 Red Buttes / Pacific Crest Trail.................................. 232

Grants Pass / Rogue / Siskiyou Area

67 Taylor Creek.. 236
68 Briggs Creek.. 240
69 Kerby Peak 243
70 Dollar Mountain.. 246
71 Limpy Creek Botanical Loop 249
72 Grayback Mountain.. 251
73 Rainie Falls.. 254
74 Rogue River Trail—Grave Creek to Foster Bar............ 257

Wild Rogue Wilderness Area

75 Rogue River Trail—Marial to Paradise Bar Lodge........ 263
76 Bear Camp Prairie 267
77 Mount Bolivar 270
78 Hanging Rock Trail.. 272

Kalmiopsis Wilderness Area (Illinois Valley)

79 Illinois River—East.. 275
80 Little Falls Loop.. 279
81 Babyfoot Lake.. 282
82 Magic Canyon.. 285
83 Eagle Mountain.. 289

Oregon Caves National Monument

84 Big Tree Loop.. 292

Kalmiopsis Wilderness Area (Pacific Coast)

85 Vulcan Lake 295
86 Illinois River—West 298
87 Windy Valley.. 301

Coast Ranges and Coast

88 Loeb State Park / Redwood Nature Loop...................... 304
89 Coquille Falls 306
90 Humbug Mountain.. 308
91 Boardman Scenic Corridor—Indian Sands.................... 310
92 Boardman Scenic Corridor—Cape Ferrelo 313
93 Oregon Redwoods 315

Siskiyou Wilderness

94 Black Butte 317
95 East Fork Illinois River 321
96 Raspberry Lake 325
97 Devil's Punchbowl 329

Northern California Redwoods

98 Stout Grove 332
99 Boy Scout Tree Trail 336
100 Hatton Trail 339

Appendix A: Hiker's Checklist 341
Appendix B: References 344
Appendix C: For More Information 345
Hike Index 347
About the Authors 349

ACKNOWLEDGMENTS

The authors are hugely indebted to Vic Harris, administrator of the Josephine Country Forestry Department in Grants Pass. At age 55, Vic still competes regularly in
mountain ultra-marathons. He's also one of the nicest people you'll ever meet. More
to the point, the authors figured they knew just about everything there was to know
about Southern Oregon trails, but Vic put them both to shame. (Thanks for your help,
Vic. We owe you one.)

The authors also wish to thank Gabe Howe and the Siskiyou Mountain Club of
Ashland. Despite a shoestring budget, Howe and the group he cofounded have kept
trails in the Kalmiopsis Wilderness open despite the devastation wreaked by the 2002
Biscuit Fire. Without their work, the trails to many spectacular places might have
disappeared forever.

Finally, the authors wish to thank the employees of the federal agencies that
administer the lands and trails described in this book. In most cases, they bent over
backwards to be helpful and provide information.

The Rogue River Trail tightropes along the canyon walls in some stretches (hike 74). ZACH URNESS

INTRODUCTION

Among natural regions in the United States, Southern Oregon ranks near the top on just about anybody's list, not only in scenic magnificence but also in the abundance of hiking trails from which to admire that magnificence. Within the vast and diverse region between the Idaho state line and the Pacific Coast, and from an east–west line drawn through the City of Roseburg, south to the California line (and perhaps just a tiny bit beyond), it may be possible to hike every weekend for thirty or forty years and never run out of interesting and beautiful trails. Nineteen federal wilderness areas, eleven national forests, two national parks, two national monuments, and six national wildlife refuges await trail enthusiasts.

For this book, the authors chose an assortment of the region's best pathways, sadly limited to one hundred. Just remember that trail selection is highly subjective, so if your favorite was omitted, the authors apologize. An attempt was made to not only include the best but also provide a range of trail lengths and degrees of difficulty. The selection is heavily weighted toward the Cascades and Siskiyous because those areas have the most trails and the most people.

About the Region

The Oregon High Desert

East of the Cascades, from the Idaho state line to the city of Klamath Falls, lies a vast, lonely, and beautiful region referred to locally as the High Desert or Eastern Oregon. Narrow, north–south oriented fault-block mountain ranges typify the area, with desert in the valleys. Major fault-block ranges include the North Warners east of Lakeview, the spectacular Hart Mountain ridge, and spectacular 9,700-foot Steens Mountain.

Note: Some geologists contend that what has historically been called the "Steens Mountains" is actually a single mountain. As a result, an attempt was made to change the name from the "Steens Mountains" to "Steens Mountain." The latter is now used on road signs, maps, and the Steens Mountain Wilderness. The authors, however, believe that "Steens Mountain" is ungrammatical and should be either "Steen's Mountain" or "Steen Mountain," named for Enoch Steen. However, to avoid confusion and remain consistent with what hikers will encounter on the ground, we have chosen to use the conventional spelling.

The region is pocked with small, often spectacular volcanic areas such as Gearhart Mountain, Jordan Craters, and Diamond Craters. The historic Owyhee River canyon flows through extreme southeast Oregon. Part of southeast Oregon (the Harney Basin) belongs to the Great Basin geological province and has no external river drainage.

In the desert areas, look for sagebrush, rabbitbrush, and bitterbrush in the vast valley areas. On slightly upland or somewhat moister slopes, you'll see western junipers scattered here and there.

The ecology of the southeast Oregon mountain ranges is similar to the Cascades except the trees are a little smaller and farther apart and there is a much higher percentage of pines (ponderosa and lodgepole).

Wildlife is also similar to the Cascades, with two major exceptions. Instead of Columbian black-tailed deer, they have mule deer. Also, from time to time you might spot a herd of pronghorns, a beautiful antelope-like desert dweller. And if you're really fortunate, in the low elevations around the Steens, you just might encounter part of the Kiger mustang herd, a sight you'll never forget. The wildlife refuges around Upper Klamath Lake are famous for bald eagles.

The best known native tribes are the Modoc and Klamath. The Modoc are remembered for the Modoc War of 1872, in which twenty-seven tribal members, hiding in a natural fortress of lava rock, held off the US Army for six months.

A memorable pioneer was Jean Baptiste Charbonneau (1806–66), buried near the tiny town of Danner, near Jordan Valley. He was the baby that Sacajawea is always carrying in pictures of the Lewis and Clark Expedition.

Major industries are hay and cattle farming, with large Basque-owned herds of sheep around Jordan Valley, Oregon's most southeastern town.

The Cascades

This majestic range, with its broad, snowy volcanoes, dominates Southern Oregon and the entire Pacific Northwest, from Northern California to British Columbia. The Cascades' string of towering volcanic peaks, culminating in Mounts Rainer and Shasta, form a weather barrier between the verdant western valleys and the eastern deserts. In Southern Oregon, Cascades highlights include Crater Lake, Mount McLoughlin, and the canyons of the upper Rogue and Umpqua Rivers.

The volcanoes of the Cascades are strung out along the Pacific "Ring of Fire" and are fueled by the westward advancement of the North American continent, dating back fifty million years,

The Cascades can be divided into the Western and High Cascades. The much older Western Cascades lie west of the High Cascades and are highly eroded. Bedded rock layers, mysteriously, are all tilted 18 degrees. In Southern Oregon, the Soda Mountain area and the Rogue-Umpqua Divide belong to the Western Cascades.

The major South Cascades volcanoes, such as Crater Lake (Mount Mazama) and Mount McLoughlin, belong to the High Cascades. In Southern Oregon, only isolated remnants of the Western Cascades remain, usually the innermost core of an ancient volcano that has almost completely eroded (such as Rabbit Ears and Pilot Rock).

The primary volcanic event influencing Southern Oregon occurred at 11,000-foot Mount Mazama about 7,000 years ago (it wasn't named Mazama then). Mazama erupted with a fury that sent an ash plume around the world and filled the Rogue River canyon with lava as far away as what is now Shady Cove. The peak's empty innards then caved in, forming a giant, steep-sided crater called a caldera. The pit eventually filled with rainwater and snowmelt to become Crater Lake. The Mountain

Lakes basin, the Medicine Lake Highland near Mount Shasta, and Newberry Crater, near Bend, have origins similar to Crater Lake's.

Plants in the Southern Oregon Cascades mostly fall into the Pacific Northwest and California forest regions. Incense cedar, sugar pine, Douglas-fir, white fir, and Shasta red fir are California species; western red cedar, western hemlock, Pacific silver fir, Douglas-fir (again), and noble fir are Northwest denizens. Most California species fade out at or near the Rogue-Umpqua Divide.

The primary large mammals in the Southern Oregon Cascades are black bear, Roosevelt elk, red fox, and cougar, although you're not likely to run across them. Smaller animals include hundreds of types of songbirds, quail, ground squirrels, gray squirrels, chipmunks, coyotes, and red-tailed hawks.

While there is definitely a human history in the Southern Cascades, there was no gold to be rushed, and native tribes ventured into the area only in summer.

The Siskiyou Mountains and Western Interior Valleys

The Siskiyou Mountains are part of the Klamath Mountains geological province, which extends from Redding, California, to Roseburg, Oregon, and from Medford almost to the coast. Within the province, a number of distinct ranges can be identified, including the Trinity Alps, Salmon Mountains, Marble Mountains, and, in Oregon, the Siskiyou Mountains.

USDA Forest Service maps confine the Siskiyous to the ridge immediately north and west of the Klamath River in Oregon and California (including Mount Ashland, the Red Buttes, and the Siskiyou Wilderness). Most geologists include the entire Klamath system in Southern Oregon as part of the Siskiyous, including everything south of Roseburg, west of the Cascades, and east of the Coast Ranges.

The name Siskiyou is a Cree word meaning "bobtailed horse." The Cree still live in western Canada. An early explorer (possibly Peter Skene Ogden), so the story goes, purchased a bobtailed race horse on a visit to the Cree. In the 1820s, at what is now Siskiyou Summit on I-5, the horse died in a snowstorm.

The most common rock in many areas of the Siskiyous, including the Lower Rogue canyon, is an ancient, partially metamorphosed (chemically altered in place over a long period of time) basaltic lava called greenstone. Greenstone's numerous cracks and fissures are occasionally filled with white quartz. Quartz veins may be accompanied by flakes of gold and silver, giving rise to the region's colorful mining history. Other rock types in the Siskiyous also contain gold-bearing quartz.

Patches of limestone also dot the Siskiyous, some of which has metamorphosed into schist and marble. Occasional marble lenses dissolve along fracture lines to form caves (including Oregon Caves), usually with spectacular flowstone and stalactite formations. There are also areas of granitic rock (lava that solidified deep underground)

Geologists theorize that the North American continent is slowly moving westward and overriding the oceanic crust. Near the surface, the oceanic crust is composed mostly of basaltic lava flows. Deeper down, it is made of types of coarse granite called serpentine and peridotite. Basalt, serpentine, and peridotite have relatively little sodium, potassium, or silica. They contain potentially minable amounts of nickel, copper, chrome, platinum, and magnesium.

Occasionally serpentine finds its way to the surface. There is more peridotite and serpentine in the Klamath Mountains than anywhere else on the continent. The largest single mass is about 15 miles wide and 30 miles long. Vulcan Lake is located on this formation.

Peridotite and serpentine areas have their own special ecosystems because most major forest species will not grow there. Trees that do grow there are small and widely spaced. Ponderosa pine is replaced by Jeffery pine. Serpentine-loving plants include coffeeberry, western azalea, and the insect-eating *Darlingtonia* (cobra lily, or California pitcher plant).

A major geological factor shaping both the Cascades and Siskiyous is glaciation. The most recent North American ice age, between one million and 10,000 years ago, was confined in western North America to the mountains. Evidence of past glaciation can be found throughout the region. Signs of past glaciation include valleys with a U-shaped profile, elongated rubble heaps called moraines, and amphitheater-shaped basins called cirques, marked by a steep horseshoe-shaped cliff with a lake at the cliff's base. The majority of high mountain lakes occupy glacial cirques.

Except for serpentine areas, Siskiyou forests are similar to the Cascades—a mixture of California and Pacific Northwest forest regions. Wildlife is also similar, except that Bigfoot is allegedly common.

Oregon's earliest human settlement, more than 9,000 years old, is believed to be an archaeological site in the heart of the Lower Rogue River canyon. The same area, near Marial, was also Southern Oregon's earliest white settlement.

Tribes of the Rogue River region, the Takelma and Tututni, were called the "Rogue" Indians (*Coquin* in French). Having heard stories about European settlers' efforts to subdue and eliminate native tribes farther east, the Takelma and Tututni did everything they could to make the first European visitors and settlers feel unwelcome. Farther north, the Umpqua were the dominant tribe. Mostly hunters and gatherers, these extremely small tribes lived a quiet life with minimal impact on the land (except for setting occasional forest fires to improve deer habitat).

In 1852 gold was discovered near the Lower Rogue River. This led to a number of skirmishes between miners, settlers, the US Army, and the native tribes. The Rogue Indian Wars of 1855–56 culminated in the Lupton Massacre, in which two soldiers and twenty-seven native women and children perished.

Southwest Oregon was a focal point of the Western gold rush in the 1850s through the 1870s. The region's first two county seats, Jacksonville (Jackson County) and Waldo (Josephine County), began as mining settlements. Gold mining in Southern Oregon, still a popular hobby, is mostly confined to the Siskiyous.

The Coast Ranges and the Coast

High on the list of Oregon scenic wonders is the rocky Southern Oregon Pacific Coast and the adjacent Coast Ranges, with dense, immense old-growth forests (and the northernmost coastal redwoods). These are some of the rainiest places in North America.

The Southern Oregon Coast is more rugged, with more offshore rocks than the central and northern coast (and has a lot more serpentine). According to geological maps, there is supposed to be a distinct line of transition from the Siskiyous to the Coast Ranges on the Rogue River Trail at Big Slide Camp (mile 3.0 from Grave Creek). It is very difficult to see. For the most part the transition is gradual and indistinct.

Botanically the area is similar to the Siskiyous except that grand fir replaces white fir. Right along the coast, a whole new ecosystem takes over, consisting mostly of Sitka spruce and shore pine, a stunted, windswept version of lodgepole pine. Like lodgepole, shore pine can grow in sand.

Historically the native tribes of the Pacific Northwest coast are considered the most culturally and technologically advanced of any nonagricultural North American tribe. Living off salmon, deer, elk, and huckleberries, the tribes built permanent villages and had highly developed art and communities.

The Southern Oregon coast and Coast Ranges marked the southernmost extent of the Northwest coast culture. The primary south coast tribe is the Coquille (French for "shell"). No Southern Oregon tribe was as advanced as the more northerly Oregon coastal tribes such as the Salish and Tlinkit. The Coquille were eventually displaced by European settlers and forced to share a reservation with the Siletz tribe, located in the Coast Ranges west of Salem.

The California Far North

Included in this guide are a few Northern California trails that either begin in Oregon or are far more easily accessed from Oregon. Directions are given from Oregon. Trails are located in the Red Buttes Wilderness, the northern portion of the Siskiyou Wilderness, and the Stout Grove area of Jedediah Smith Redwood State Park. All three are within or near the Siskiyou Mountains.

With the exception of the redwoods near the coast, forest communities in the Siskiyou Mountains and Coast Ranges of California Far North are virtually identical to those of Oregon. The uniquely California ecosystems don't begin until you travel a little farther south and a little higher up in elevation, when trees such as digger pine, blue oak, redbud, and, at high elevations, foxtail pine, begin to appear.

As in Oregon, directly along the coast, expect to encounter mostly Sitka spruce and shore pine. The redwood zone begins slightly inland from the Sitka spruce zone and follows low-elevation river canyons upstream and uphill, as they say, "as far as the fog reaches." Principal redwood associates are western hemlock and tanoak. Look also for redwood sorrel, a giant clover with a bright red underside. Away from the redwoods, sorrel has a green underside. Moving inland and upstream, the redwoods are replaced by vast Douglas-fir forests.

The human history of the California Far North is also similar to the Oregon Coast and Siskiyous except the native tribes are Hoopa, Karuk, Yurok, and Chimariko. As in Oregon, early European settlement was mostly driven by gold mining at first and then by logging. In the Red Buttes, you might encounter some abandoned World War II–era chromite mines.

HOW TO USE THIS GUIDE

Trail Jurisdictions

Of the one hundred primary hikes described in this book (plus another one hundred optional and "extra" hikes), thirty-six lie mainly on land administered by Rogue River–Siskiyou National Forest, headquartered in Medford, Oregon. Twelve hikes lie mostly within Fremont-Winema National Forest, headquartered in Lakeview. Fifteen hikes fall under the jurisdiction of Umpqua National Forest, headquartered in Roseburg. Eight hikes are mostly located within Crater Lake National Park. Twelve hikes are on land administered by the US Bureau of Land Management (BLM). One hike sits on property owned by The Nature Conservancy. One hike falls under the jurisdiction of the Rogue River–Bear Creek Greenway Commission. One hike is owned by a private timber company. One hike lies within Oregon Caves National Monument, administered by the National Park Service. Of the hikes in California, three are in Six Rivers National Forest, one is in Klamath National Forest, and three are in Jedediah Smith State Park, a component of Redwood National and State Parks.

Much labor has gone into designing and maintaining these trails, and the responsible agencies are to be commended and thanked. The best way to repay their efforts is to treat the land with respect.

Fees, Hours, Bicycles, and Pets

Although there are numerous forest service, BLM, and national park fee parking areas in the rest of Oregon, they are being phased in slowly in Southern Oregon; parking remains free at most trailheads (for now). Some sections of Crater Lake National Park require an entrance free and some do not. Oregon Caves National Monument charges for cave tours but not for entry. The Redwood National and State Park System is free. Parking is also free at most Southern Oregon national wildlife refuges. Many Oregon state parks have self-service day-use fees or toll booths; others do not. Valley of the Rogue State Park charges only for campground use.

Day-use parking at federal fee sites generally costs a few dollars. In self-service areas, if you have an annual Golden Eagle Pass or lifetime Senior Pass, display it in your window to avoid the fee (but remember that the cards may melt in direct sunlight). Fee sites that accept the Northwest Forest Pass are rare in Southern Oregon and much more common farther north.

Hours are simple to figure out. National forest and national park trails are open 24 hours a day, seven days a week. The same is true of trails managed by BLM and most other agencies. Most Oregon state parks close at dusk, but Valley of the Rogue State Park also has a 24-hour freeway rest area. The paved greenway path that runs through the park is open 24 hours.

Pet regulations are also pretty standard. On forest service and BLM trails, pets must be either on a leash or under voice command. In Oregon state parks and the Bear Creek Greenway, they must be leashed at all times. In national parks and monuments, pets are not permitted on backcountry trails because they disrupt wildlife. They are permitted, on leash, only in developed areas. Pets are not permitted on the Table Rock trails, but they are at Mill Creek Falls.

Unless otherwise posted, bicycles are permitted on most forest service and BLM trails. They are not permitted on national park trails or in wilderness areas. Motorized dirt bikes and ATVs are permitted, with many restrictions, only on the Golden Staircase Trail.

Pacific Crest Trail (PCT)

The Pacific Crest Trail (#2000) follows the crest of the Sierra Nevada and Cascade ranges for 1,800 miles from the Mexican border to the Canadian border. It is considered America's most challenging trail, and hiking its entire length is a worthy accomplishment.

About 90 miles of the PCT traverse the Southern Cascades and Siskiyous. This book features the best hikes of those 90 miles. Readers desiring more information on the PCT will find several publications with mile-by-mile narratives.

In this guide the PCT is described as it crosses Mount Thielsen, Crater Lake National Park, Devil's Peak, the Sky Lakes Basin, Mount McLoughlin, Brown Mountain, the Soda Mountain area, the back side of Mount Ashland, and the Red Buttes Wilderness. Less-scenic sections, such as the 30-mile stretch across the Dead Indian Plateau, which mostly follows old logging roads, are omitted.

For those lacking the inclination to hike the entire PCT, taking in the highlights is the ideal way to experience this national treasure. PCT day hikers should bear in mind that (1) one person's highlight may be another person's lowlight, and (2) you can never predict when an unheralded highlight will appear out of nowhere. A good example is the junction of the Pumice Flat and Pacific Crest Trails in Crater Lake National Park. The lead-in routes leave much to be desired, but the actual junction—in a tiny grass-and-wildflower basin surrounded by white-rock ledges—is exquisite.

Winter Access

There are downhill ski areas in the Southern Cascades at Pelican Butte, near Klamath Falls, and at Mount Bailey, near Diamond Lake. Both are accessible via commercial snowcat and have no lifts. The nearest ski areas with lifts are at Mount Ashland, near Ashland (in the Siskiyou Mountains), and the small but beautiful Warner Canyon, north of Lakeview. Diamond Lake, north of Crater Lake, has a rope-tow hill for inner tubes and snowboards.

Established cross-country ski trails (plus a few snowmobile trails) may be found in Crater Lake National Park and the surrounding national forest, but only five main roads are kept open in winter in the Southern Oregon Cascades: Oregon Highways 140, 62, 66, 138, and 230. OR 140 continues to Lakeview, crossing into Nevada near the Sheldon National Antelope Range (where a young couple with a baby famously became lost in the snow several years ago and had a movie made about them). There are numerous snow zones on OR 140.

Side roads in the snow zones can become buried under as much as 20 feet of snow. To park in a cleared snow zone in Oregon, including ski resorts, an annual Sno-Park Permit is required, available at any forest service, BLM, or Department of Motor Vehicle office or at ski areas.

No snow zone roads in the Siskiyou Mountains are maintained in winter. The Happy Camp Road, out of Cave Junction, is cleared to the Page Mountain Winter Sports Area, a cross-country ski site. OR 199, from Grants Pass to Crescent City, California, crests at Collier Tunnel (just over the California line), barely brushing the snow zone.

Snow Country Driving (This Is Important!)

When traveling in winter over mountain passes, it is critical to check the weather forecast and road conditions. Go to tripcheck.com for all highway cams in Oregon. No matter where you are (but especially on remote forest and desert roads), if there is deep snow on the road surface, if it begins snowing heavily and the road is heading uphill, or if it begins snowing and you're not sure where the road goes, TURN AROUND and go back the way you came! People become lost, stranded, and occasionally die because they continued forward in snow on an unfamiliar road. Remember: The best "shortcut" is usually the main highway. Unpaved forest roads may be interesting and scenic, but they are rarely shortcuts.

Trail Selection

The hikes chosen for this guide lead to significant natural features, such as a lake, a mountaintop, a free-flowing creek or river, or a waterfall. They were selected over dozens of other perfectly good trails. Some trails were omitted because they lead only from one random point to another; others too closely paralleled roads, led to places where you can drive, or followed the shores of reservoirs.

The following information is included in each trail description:

Overview. This short description of each hike includes those special natural features for which it was chosen, as well as any other aspects that make the trail outstanding.

Type of hike. Hikes fall into the following categories: "Day hikes" are usually less than 6 miles one-way. These trails may lack water or suitable camping sites. "Backpack hikes" require spending at least one night in the backcountry (depending on how fast you hike). "Loop trails" start and finish at the same trailhead, with at least a portion of the route not retracing the same path on the return route. Loops include shapes such as figure eights and lollipops. Completing a loop may require a short walk on a dirt road to get back to the trailhead. On an "out-and-back" hike, you travel the identical route coming and going. A "shuttle hike" is a point-to-point trip that requires two vehicles (one left at each end of the trail) or a prearranged pickup. One effective way to manage a shuttle hike is to arrange for a second party to start at the other end of the trail and hike toward you. When you meet, you simply trade keys.

Distance. This figure gives the total distance hiked. In an out-and-back hike, the number is twice the length of the trail. Since the advent of Global Positioning System (GPS) devices, measuring trail distances has become fairly accurate; all primary trail routes described in this book were measured using GPS and include GPS coordinates.

Most wilderness trail signs do not include distances, and when they do, they are often just somebody's best guess. Forest service signs round the posted trail length to the nearest 0.5 mile. Because of the accuracy of GPS readings, this guide may give mileages that differ from forest service trail signs.

Keep in mind that "distance" only indicates map distances. Since maps reflect only the horizontal, a trail that's listed as "1 mile" but climbs a steep slope is actually longer than 1 mile. Most hikers average about 2 miles per hour, although a steep 2-mile climb on rocky tread can take longer than a 4-mile stroll through a gentle river valley.

Note: Mileages in chapters that are continuations of other hikes are given from the beginning of the described hike, not from the trailhead where you parked your car.

Difficulty. Difficulty ratings are inherently flawed. What's easy for you might be difficult for someone else. Still, such ratings offer a useful approximation of a hike's challenge. Remember to factor in your own fitness level when interpreting the rating and planning your trip.

In general, a gradient of less than 300 feet per mile is considered "easy" and a gradient over 600 feet per mile is considered "strenuous." Everything in between is "moderate." A rating may be modified by the presence of steep sections on an otherwise easy trail and by the trail's overall length. It's hard to call any trail less than 1 mile "strenuous" unless it climbs more than 1,000 feet. On the Fish Lake Trail, rated "moderate," the average rise is only 250 feet per mile over 4 miles, but the climb is concentrated into 1.5 strenuous miles while the rest is virtually level. The Union Peak Trail is rated "easy" for 4.4 miles and "strenuous" for 0.5 mile.

RATING THE HIKES

Longest
74. Rogue River Trail–Grave Creek to Foster Bar

Highest
51. Mount McLoughlin

Most Difficult–A Three-Way Tie
10. Mount Thielsen
51. Mount McLoughlin
82. Magic Canyon

Most Scenic
1. Wildhorse Lake

Most Unusual
5. Crack in the Ground

Best Hike Overall
1. Wildhorse Lake

Best months. Winter snow in Southern Oregon is usually confined to areas above about 3,000 feet, while trailhead elevations range from 50 feet at the Oregon coast to 9,400 feet at Wildhorse Lake in the Steens. Trailheads above 4,000 feet are usually accessible by mid-May but have been known to remain inaccessible until late July after especially harsh winters.

This guide's highest trail segments (over 9,000 feet) usually do not become passable until late June or July, sometimes even later. Snowfall varies greatly from year to year, and storms can temporarily bury even the lowest elevations. In spring, even when the snow at lower elevations has melted and the trail is clear, swollen creeks and rivers may block your way.

Summers are fairly mild in the mountains, so heat and humidity usually aren't problems. When it's 100°F in Medford, it is 20 degrees cooler at 5,000 feet. A few low-elevation trails, including river canyons, are best avoided when the temperature in Medford or Grants Pass is over 90°F because of high humidity and lack of air circulation.

Summer highs in Medford average between 85°F and 105°F. Rain is rare in valley areas in summer, but terrifying localized thunderstorms, with lots of lightning and even hail, may occur in the mountains. These happen three or four times a year and may touch off dozens of forest fires. Do not hike on a trail if there is any possibility whatsoever of coming near an active forest fire. If you do find yourself anywhere near a fire, turn around immediately. People have died because they failed to follow this advice. If the flames don't get you, heat and smoke might.

Winter highs in Medford average in the 40s and 50s. The first snowfall usually shows up some time in November, with a snowpack developing by mid-December.

Maps. This section lists the applicable US Geological Survey (USGS) 7.5-minute topo map (or maps) for each hike, plus agency and wilderness area maps. Forest service and BLM maps are generally outstanding, and most wilderness maps include topographic contour lines.

While USGS topo maps are amazingly detailed, forest service wilderness maps cover a larger area. Forest service and BLM maps are available at outdoors stores and chamber of commerce offices and at any forest service or BLM office. Maps may also be ordered online. Each national forest has its own website (see Appendix C).

Map insets for each chapter are based on GPS tracks. Although these maps are fairly accurate, the authors recommend always carrying a second map source, which would also be a backup source for the trailhead directions in case you get lost or come from a different direction.

Parking and trailhead facilities. This section tells you where to park, how much room you're likely to find for your vehicle, and what amenities are offered (such as camping and vault toilets).

Special considerations. Readers may want to know if they might run into heavy horse traffic, huge mosquito swarms, or bears; if they should bring extra water; or if there are pet restrictions or parking fees. This section tells what to expect.

This small blue wildflower can be found on Pine Bench in the Boulder Creek Wilderness.
Zach Urness

Finding the trailhead. Directions for all trails are given from the nearest city in Oregon: Burns, Lakeview, Klamath Falls, Medford, Grants Pass, Roseburg, Brookings, or Gold Beach. Burns is not quite in Southern Oregon, but it is the nearest city to Steens Mountain and Jordan Valley areas.

If coming from a different directon, modify the book directions accordingly using a state road map and a forest service or BLM Map. The primary purpose of "Finding the trailhead" is to assist the reader in locating the route on a map prior to the trip. It is not advisable to use the section as your sole source of directions. The heading also describes points where markings on the ground may be ambiguous.

Miles and Directions. This includes all trail junctions, even if the hike does not turn there. It also gives major landmarks. Mileages are given within 0.1 mile based on GPS tracks. The designations "go right," "go left," or "go straight," indicate either a change of trails or the direction to go if the route is unclear.

Options. These may be alternate routes leading to the same destination as the main hike, a short side trip, or a nearby trail of interest. Just because a hike is optional does not mean it is less desirable than the main hike, because everybody's taste is different. The Wizard Island Trail at Crater Lake may be the most scenic hike in Southern Oregon, but it is shown as optional because it is extremely difficult and expensive to reach.

BACKCOUNTRY REGULATIONS

❏ Wilderness permits are not required in Oregon.

❏ Trailhead parking fees may be required in Oregon.

❏ Camp only in appropriate places.

❏ Stay on trails (where possible), and don't create shortcuts.

❏ Dispose of human waste in a cat hole at least 200 feet from all water sources and campsites.

❏ Dispose of bathing water and dishwater well away from water sources.

❏ Use camp stoves rather than cooking fires when possible, or eat cold meals.

❏ Carry out all trash. If you packed it in, you can pack it out.

❏ Limit group size to ten or fewer.

❏ Suspend food out of reach of animals.

❏ Do not feed or in any way disturb wildlife. Do not leave behind food scraps.

❏ Do not operate any motorized vehicle in a Wilderness Area.

❏ Do not destroy, deface, disturb, or remove from its natural setting any plant, rock, animal, or archaeological artifact.

Robyn Orr makes her way through Big Indian Gorge in Steens Mountain as viewed from the big rock overlook (hike 2). ZACH URNESS

ZERO IMPACT

Most wilderness users want to walk softly, but some aren't aware that they have poor manners. Their actions may be dictated by past generations of campers who cut green boughs for evening shelters, built campfires with fire rings, and dug trenches around tents. In the 1950s these practices may have been acceptable. But they leave long-lasting scars and are unacceptable today.

Because wild places are becoming rare and the number of backcountry visitors is mushrooming, a new code of ethics is emerging. Today we all must leave no clues that we were there. Enjoy the wild, but leave no trace of your visit.

Three FalconGuide principles of zero impact:

❏ Leave with everything you brought in.

❏ Leave no sign of your visit.

❏ Leave the landscape as you found it.

Most of us know better than to litter—in or out of the backcountry. Be sure you leave nothing along the trail or at your campsite. Pack out all items, no matter how small, including orange peels, flip-tops, cigarette butts, and gum wrappers; and do your best to pick up any trash others leave behind.

Follow the main trail. Avoid cutting switchbacks and walking on vegetation beside the trail. Don't pick up souvenirs, such as rocks, antlers, or wildflowers. The next person wants to see them too, and collecting them violates many regulations.

Avoid making loud noises on the trail (unless you are in bear country) or in camp. Be courteous—sound travels easily in the backcountry, especially across water.

Carry a lightweight trowel to bury human waste 6 to 8 inches deep at least 200 feet from any water source. Pack out used toilet paper.

Go without a campfire. Carry a stove for cooking and a flashlight, candle lantern, or headlamp for light. For emergencies, learn how to build a no-trace fire.

Camp in obviously used sites when they are available. Otherwise, camp and cook on durable surfaces such as bedrock, sand, gravel bars, or bare ground.

Leave no trace—and put your ear to the ground and listen carefully. Thousands of people coming behind you are thanking you for your courtesy and good sense.

Details on these zero impact principles for specific outdoor activities can be found at the Leave No Trace website, www.LNT.org.

ALL ABOUT HIKING: SAFETY AND HAZARDS

The Boy Scouts of America have been guided for decades by what is perhaps the single best piece of safety advice: Be prepared! On a hike, especially if you plan to spend the night, this means carrying survival and first-aid materials, proper clothing, a compass, and a topographic map—and knowing how to use them.

Perhaps the second-best piece of safety advice is to tell somebody where you're going and when you plan to return. Pilots must file flight plans before every trip, and anybody venturing into a blank spot on the map should do the same. File your "flight plan" with a friend or relative.

Water. Always carry water, even on short hikes in cool weather. A couple bottles of store-bought water or a reusable bottled filled with tap water, stashed in a light day pack, will usually keep you quenched on day hikes. Should something unexpected happen and you find yourself stranded, extra water could save your life. Remember that nearly every bad thing that can happen on a trail is made worse by dehydration. One sign of dehydration is bright yellow urine.

The consensus among hiking experts is that it is never safe to drink untreated water directly from lakes, creeks, or even springs. Carry either a filter or purification tablets that can kill giardia.

Mosquitoes. Mosquitoes are worst near standing water and snowmelt patches (they breed in puddles). As the season dries up, they tend to become less of a pest.

Clothing. Dress comfortably and according to your personal taste. In "hypothermia weather" (any season other than summer), loose and layered clothing traps heat better than tight clothes. Rain gear and fleece/down can be invaluable in helping retain body heat in hypothermia weather. Always bring a jacket, no matter what—if you have to unexpectedly spend the night, you'll need it even in summer. Shoes should be comfortable. For most trails in this book, a heavy hiking boot is unnecessary, although a sturdy high-top boot can help prevent a sprained or broken ankle.

Sun Protection. In summer, hats, sunglasses, and sunscreen are essential in open areas. Sunburn is not a trifling matter. It is very dehydrating and energy-sapping, and multiple sunburns increase your risk for melanoma, which can be fatal.

Bears and Cougars. Bears and cougars can get aggressive, but your chance of seeing one on these trails is remote. The rangers' advice? Don't leave food in your car that is visible through the window.

While hiking, make some noise once in a while, especially just before rounding a bend. Just a little noise will do—you don't want to bothers other hikers. (See "Zero Impact.") If the animals hear you coming, they'll probably be long gone by the time you arrive.

When camping, clean up when you're done eating, and wash all plates, utensils, and cans. Bring a nylon rope so that you can hang packs containing food from a tree limb and out of reach of bears. Do not keep food in your tent.

Food. The best trail foods are high in carbohydrates and water content. Avoid foods that are difficult to chew and that require lots of saliva (steak and peanut butter are out) and foods that are difficult to digest (such as fried eggs). Sliced fruit is fantastic (less chewing uses less energy). So are nuts, trail mix, power bars, juice, thinly sliced cheese, thinly sliced meat, Gatorade, and the usual assortment of traditional trail foods.

Overheating and Hypothermia. Two lurking dangers on any hike are over- and underheating. Overheating can lead to heat exhaustion and heat stroke; under- heating can lead to hypothermia. For heat exhaustion (headache, dizziness, nausea, breathlessness, profuse sweating), rest, get out of the sun, and drink water until you feel better. For heat stroke (headache, dizziness, fever, and very little sweating), imme- diate medical attention is required, although the first-aid treatment is similar to heat exhaustion. With heat stroke, the body loses its ability to produce perspiration and regulate its temperature. Ideally, you will get out of the sun, rest, and take a drink long before either condition develops.

Hypothermia occurs when the body's heat core begins to cool. The main symp- tom is uncontrolled shivering. Extreme cold can cause this, but so can moderate temperatures combined with a breeze and perspiration. Always wear a jacket or rain gear to hold in your body heat when it's cool out, even if it's a little uncomfortable to do so.

Children. Taking your children hiking is a great educational and family bonding experience that can produce cherished memories, but it should be done with caution. For a child under age 6 or so, keep the hikes short and safe (nature trails, etc.). On longer hikes with older children, be aware that children can't pace themselves very well, get bored easily, can wander off, and can do foolish and dangerous things when you aren't looking. They may be more interested if a friend comes along. Above all, be patient and flexible.

Toxic Plants. Identifying poison oak should be the first thing any West Coast hiker learns. Even if you've never reacted to poison oak before, the allergy can develop without warning and make you uncomfortable or ill for days. The plant is most toxic when the leaves first come out. Stinging nettles can also cause redness, pain, and swelling, but they go away fairly quickly. The authors saw nettles on only one trail in this guide, but the plant can be difficult to spot because it is usually mixed in with a jumble of other plants.

Snakes. You might see a rattlesnake on the trail, but don't count on it. You'll almost always hear the telltale rattling noise first, but never step into or over anything without first checking for rattlers. The standard first aid for snakebites is to get to a doctor within two hours if possible. If not, try to slow your metabolism by resting so that your kidneys can detoxify the poison faster. Snakebites are not usually life- threatening, except in children, the elderly, and people with heart conditions.

Bugs. Yellow jackets, bumblebees, bald hornets, and scorpions can all give you a nasty sting that swells up and hurts like the blazes, but the reaction usually doesn't last long. If you are allergic to stings, however, be sure to carry an EpiPen, antihistamine, or inhaler. Scorpions (the Oregon variety is small and black) live under rocks and rotted wood. Ticks are nasty little armor-plated arachnids that drop onto you from overhanging branches or reach out from grasses. Their bite can cause Lyme disease. Always check yourself (and your pets) for ticks after a hike.

Lightning. There are occasional lightning storms in the Oregon mountains during summer, usually in late afternoon or early evening. Standing in an open area or under an isolated tree at such times is not advised. Even indirect lightning strikes can be fatal. Thunder and lightning close up can be terrifying and deafening—and can possibly knock you over or cause injury. If you run into a storm, try to keep warm and, if you can, find a safe shelter. If you can't, take cover in a thick forest or, in an emergency, squat (do not lie down) in a deep depression until the storm passes.

First-aid Kit. It's always a good idea to have one with you; if nothing else, carry a few Band-Aids and some sterile pads. You might never use them, but they can be incredibly helpful if you get a blister between your toes. "Moleskin" bandages are fantastic for blisters and chafed spots on the feet but can be painful to remove

Communications and Direction Finders. Cell phones are unlikely to work in remote areas, but you never know; if you break a leg, a cell phone could save your life. Two-way radios can also come in handy if you get separated from your group. If you get lost, a compass might or might not help (you need to know in which direction the trailhead lies). A GPS unit is much more helpful, provided you know how to use it to guide yourself from point to point. The best safety tip: Always let someone know where you are going and when to expect you back.

Maps. Always bring a map (and this guidebook), even if it is not your first time on a trail.

Intoxicants. When hiking, strive to be as alert and as physically "ready" as possible. Hiking when your reasoning, perception, and reflexes are impaired is foolish and dangerous.

Conditioning. Hiking can help you get in shape, but it also helps to already be in shape. If you are not in good condition, make sure your doctor approves of hiking as an activity for you, and don't overdo it, especially in summer at low elevations. If you get out of breath, stop and rest. And remember that while uphill gradients are cardiovascular stressors, downhill gradients are orthopedic stressors. You are more likely to trip, sprain an ankle, or develop a blister on the downhill.

Personal Security. Although there is no reason to believe that any hike in this guide is unsafe, a couple of security precautions can never hurt. First, hiking after dark and hiking alone are not advised. Although night hiking is allowed on most national forest and BLM trails, there is an increased chance of bear or cougar encounters. Day or night, if you feel unsafe, consider bringing a friend or a dog or carrying pepper or bear spray or a Taser. (Check regulations before carrying the latter.)

Weather. Check the weather forecast. Be careful not to get caught at high altitude by a bad storm or along a stream in a flash flood. Watch cloud formations closely so you don't get stranded on a ridgeline during a lightning storm.

From the viewpoint at the end of the featured hike here, the view spread all the way to the headwall of Little Blitzen Gorge (hike 3). ZACH URNESS

Common Sense. A little common sense can help ensure a safe, enjoyable hike:

❑ Study basic survival and first aid before leaving home.

❑ Before you leave for the trailhead, find out as much as you can about the route, especially the potential hazards.

❑ Avoid traveling alone in the wilderness, and always try to keep your party together.

❑ Don't exhaust yourself or other members of your party by traveling too far or too fast. Let the slowest person set the pace.

❑ On day hikes, know what time it gets dark, and turn back with plenty of time to spare.

❑ Don't wait until you're confused to look at your maps. Follow them as you go so that you'll have a continual fix on your location.

❑ If you get lost, don't panic. Sit down and relax for a few minutes while you check your topo map and compass or GPS device. It's often a good idea to retrace your steps until you find familiar ground, even if it might lengthen your trip. Lots of people get temporarily lost in the wilderness and survive—usually by dealing with the situation calmly and rationally.

❑ Stay clear of all wild animals.

❑ Make sure your survival kit includes a compass, whistle, matches in a waterproof container, cigarette lighter, candle, signal mirror, flashlight, fire starter, aluminum foil, water purification tablets, space blanket, and flare.

Trail Finder

Authors' Top 11

1. Wildhorse Lake
5. Crack in the Ground
7. Gearhart Mountain
36. Mount Scott
44. Devil's Peak
51. Mount McLoughlin
66. Red Buttes/Pacific Crest Trail
75. Rogue River Trail—Marial to Paradise Bar Lodge
85. Vulcan Lake
97. Devil's Punchbowl
99. Boy Scout Tree Trail

Wilderness Trails

1. Wildhorse Lake
2. Big Indian Gorge
3. Little Blitzen Gorge
4. Pike Creek Canyon
7. Gearhart Mountain
8. Blue Lake
10. Mount Thielsen
12. Thielsen Creek Meadows
22. Miller to Maidu Lake
28. Cliff Lake/Grasshopper Mountain
29. Fish Lake
30. Rattlesnake Mountain
31. Abbott Butte
42. Seven Lakes Basin—West
43. Seven Lakes Basin—East
44. Devil's Peak
45. Blue Canyon Basin
46. Badger Lake
47. Squaw Lake
48. Nannie Creek/Puck Lake
49. Lower Sky Lakes
50. Upper Sky Lakes
51. Mount McLoughlin
52. Clover Creek
53. Varney Creek
63. Tanner Lakes
64. Frog Pond
65. Azalea Lake
66. Red Buttes/Pacific Crest Trail
74. Rogue River Trail—Grave Creek to Foster Bar
75. Rogue River Trail—Marial to Paradise Bar Lodge
77. Mount Bolivar
78. Hanging Rock Trail
79. Illinois River—East
81. Babyfoot Lake
82. Magic Canyon
85. Vulcan Lake
86. Illinois River—West
94. Black Butte
96. Raspberry Lake
97. Devil's Punchbowl

Riverside Trails

3. Little Blitzen Gorge
13. Wolf Creek Falls
15. Fall Creek Falls
18. Toketee Falls
20. Dread and Terror/Umpqua Hot Springs
23. Upper Rogue Trail/Rough Rider Falls
25. Natural Bridge/Farewell Bend
26. Takelma Gorge
33. Mill Creek Falls
34. Boundary Springs
41. Middle Fork Rogue River
56. Rogue River Greenway
73. Rainie Falls
74. Rogue River Trail—Grave Creek to Foster Bar
75. Rogue River Trail—Marial to Paradise Bar Lodge
79. Illinois River—East
80. Little Falls Loop
86. Illinois River—West
89. Coquille Falls
95. East Fork Illinois River

Trails to Lakes

1. Wildhorse Lake
8. Blue Lake
14. Yellowjacket Loop
16. Twin Lakes
22. Miller to Maidu Lake
28. Cliff Lake/Grasshopper Mountain
29. Fish Lake
35. Cleetwood Cove
42. Seven Lakes Basin—West
43. Seven Lakes Basin—East
45. Blue Canyon Basin
46. Badger Lake
47. Squaw Lake
48. Nannie Creek—Puck Lake
49. Lower Sky Lakes
50. Upper Sky Lakes
52. Clover Creek
53. Varney Creek
63. Tanner Lakes
65. Azalea Lake
66. Red Buttes/Pacific Crest Trail
81. Babyfoot Lake
85. Vulcan Lake
96. Raspberry Lake
97. Devil's Punchbowl

Trails to Summits

1. Wildhorse Lake
10. Mount Thielsen
11. Mount Bailey
14. Yellowjacket Loop
30. Rattlesnake Mountain
31. Abbott Butte
36. Mount Scott
39. Union Peak
44. Devil's Peak
51. Mount McLoughlin
57. Pilot Rock
58. Hobart Bluff/Pacific Crest Trail
59. Grizzly Peak
62. Wagner Butte
69. Kerby Peak
70. Dollar Mountain
72. Grayback Mountain
77. Mount Bolivar
83. Eagle Mountain
90. Humbug Mountain

Waterfall Trails

6. DeGarmo Canyon
13. Wolf Creek Falls
15. Fall Creek Falls
18. Toketee Falls
19. Watson Falls
20. Dread and Terror/Umpqua Hot Springs
21. Lemolo Falls
23. Upper Rogue Canyon/Rough Rider Falls
24. National Creek Falls
40. Plaikni Falls
71. Limpey Creek Botanical Loop
73. Rainie Falls
80. Little Falls Loop
89. Coquille Falls

Trails with Paved Road Access

2. Big Indian Gorge
3. Little Blitzen Gorge
10. Mount Thielsen
12. Thielsen Creek Meadows
13. Wolf Creek Falls
15. Fall Creek Falls
18. Toketee Falls
19. Watson Falls
23. Upper Rogue Canyon/Rough Rider Falls
25. Natural Bridge/Farewell Bend
32. Viewpoint Mike
33. Mill Creek Falls
36. Mount Scott
37. Garfield Peak
38. Annie Creek Loop
39. Union Peak
40. Plaikni Falls
54. Lower Table Rock
55. Upper Table Rock
56. Rogue River Greenway
67. Taylor Creek
70. Dollar Mountain
73. Rainie Falls
74. Rogue River Trail—Grave Creek to Foster Bar
76. Bear Camp Prairie
84. Big Tree Loop
86. Illinois River—West
88. Loeb State Park/Redwood Nature Loop
90. Humbug Mountain
91. Boardman Scenic Corridor—Indian Sands
92. Boardman Scenic Corridor—Cape Ferrelo
100. Hatton Trail

Best Kid-Friendly Trails

9. Crater Lake Pinnacles
15. Fall Creek Falls
16. Twin Lakes
40. Plaikni Falls
60. Mount Ashland Meadows/Pacific Crest Trail
61. Tunnel Ridge/Sterling Mine Trail
71. Limpy Creek Botanical Loop
80. Little Falls Loop
88. Loeb State Park/Redwood Nature Loop
98. Stout Grove

Map Legend

Transportation

≡⟨5⟩≡ Interstate Highway

≡⟨199⟩≡ US Highway

≡⟨138⟩≡ State Road

≡⟨3703⟩≡ Local/County Road

= = = = Unpaved Road

├──┼──┤ Railroad

Boundaries

— ⋅ — ⋅ — State Boundary

▬▬▬▬ National/Wilderness

———— State Park

Water Features

Body of Water

Marsh

River/Creek

Intermittent Stream

Waterfall

Spring

Trails

- - - - - - Featured Trail

- - - - - - Trail

Symbols

)(Bridge

■ Building/Point of Interest

▲ Campground

——— Dam

P Parking

)(Pass

▲ Peak/Elevation

⊞ Picnic Area

•—•—• Powerline

▲ Primitive Campsite

Restroom

Scenic View

⟨20⟩ Trailhead

○ Town

Optional Hiking Opportunities in Southeast Oregon

Although no "official" hikes are listed in this book for Oregon's extreme southeast corner, several spectacular locations are classified by the BLM as containing "hiking opportunities." That means there are no developed trails or trailheads but there are suggested cross-country routes (with no forests, you can often see a very long way) or seldom-used jeep or ATV roads. None of these meet the FalconGuide standard for a "trail."

The following are especially noteworthy:

Succor Creek State Park is an immense, steep-sided canyon of yellow rock with a beautiful creek running down the middle. The park is 21 miles down a 41-mile dirt road between Nyssa and Jordan Valley. The park lists the main hiking opportunity as the ATV road from the campground.

Leslie Gulch lies a few miles past Succor Creek and then down an extremely steep, unpaved side road. The side road, through the gulch, is famous for its amazing red rock spires. The access road dead-ends in the Owhyhee Canyon near the upper end of Owyhee Lake.

Jordan Craters is a jet black, 7-mile by 3-mile lava flow in the desert near Jordan Valley, accessed by a 26-mile, frequently muddy dirt road off US 95 north of Jordan Valley. The flow's obvious source is a big hole in the hillside, at Coffeepot Crater. The road's final mile to Coffeepot Crater requires four-wheel drive. A fantastic trail leads to the top of Coffeepot Crater, but it's only about one-eighth of a mile long.

Three Forks. A few miles west of Jordan Valley, a 37-mile dirt road takes off across the sagebrush desert to Three Forks. The road touches the rim of the Owhyhee Canyon at mile 16 and again at mile 36, where it drops abruptly down into the gorge in which the three forks of the Owyhee merge. There is an excellent hiking opportunity here. If you cross the river and follow an old, extremely rough jeep road upstream for 1.5 miles, it leads to a little hot spring.

◀ *Thielsen Creek rolls below the steep narrow spire of Mount Thielsen a few thousand feet overhead from Mount Thielsen Creek Meadow (hike 12).* Zach Urness

1 Wildhorse Lake

An amazingly beautiful lake in a treeless glacial-cirque basin near the summit of Steens Mountain. The drive to the trailhead follows the highest and possibly most spectacular road in Oregon.

Distance: 2.6-mile out and back
Difficulty: Moderate to strenuous
Elevation loss: 1,100 feet
Best season: June–Oct
Maps: USGS Wildhorse Lake; BLM Burns District (south); Steens High Desert Country
Trail contacts: BLM Burns Office: (541) 573-4400; Frenchglen Historic Hotel: (541) 493-2825

Parking and trailhead facilities: The mountaintop parking area has room for about eight cars. There are stunning views, but not much else.
Special considerations: Although a road goes nearly all the way to the summit, the fact that you're hiking above 9,000 feet means you should take extra precautions. Bring extra water, make sure you have plenty of time, and only attempt this hike when the weather is clear.

Finding the trailhead: Reaching the trailhead for Wildhorse Lake is an adventure in itself. It follows Steens Mountain Loop Road—the highest road in Oregon—past overlooks into massive gorges and the desolate Alvord Desert. From the tiny hamlet of Frenchglen, turn onto gravel Steens Mountain Loop Road and continue a total of 22 miles up the mountain to a junction with a sign for Steens Summit / Wildhorse Lake. Go left and follow a rough and bumpy road 2 miles to a mountaintop parking area and one of Oregon's famous viewpoints. If you're making the trip in late June or autumn, call the Burns District Office to make sure the snow gate, which allows access to Steens Mountain Loop Road, is open.
Trailhead GPS: N42 38.483' / W118 34.794'

The Hike

Everything about Wildhorse Lake and the Steens Mountain summit is spectacular, starting with the drive to the trailhead. Although this chapter focuses on Wildhorse Lake, make sure to visit the mountain's 9,733-foot summit, an easy trek from the parking area (see "Options").

The trail to Wildhorse Lake begins at a mountaintop parking area and heads downhill on an old road to an overlook of almost unbelievable beauty. The lake shimmers in a multicolored basin with massive, jagged cliffs dropping thousands of feet onto the desert floor just beyond the lake.

The real hike begins at that overlook. A trail skirts the edge of the rock face and zigzags down into the basin. There are two sets of very steep switchbacks. Gradually the trail becomes easier and follows a small creek into a basin blossoming with wildflowers in colors of orange, yellow, purple, and blue. The rocks and meadows make nice places to explore. The surrounding cliffs feature no lack of wonderful nooks and crannies.

Wildhorse Lake sits in a stunning glacial basin near the summit of Steens Mountain in southeastern Oregon. Picture taken from trailhead overlook. ZACH URNESS

Miles and Directions

0.0 Begin at the summit parking area.

0.2 Arrive at the overlook and trailhead. Follow the narrow trail downhill.

1.3 Reach Wildhorse Lake; return the way you came.

2.6 Arrive back at the trailhead.

Options

Steens Mountain summit: Reaching a 9,733-foot summit usually requires an exhausting climb. Steens Mountain, despite boasting Oregon's ninth-highest summit, is very easy. From the mountaintop parking area—the same place the Wildhorse Lake Trail begins—simply hike uphill on the gated road. Continue 1.0 mile up and back to the summit, which showcases views of the Alvord Desert a vertical mile below. The

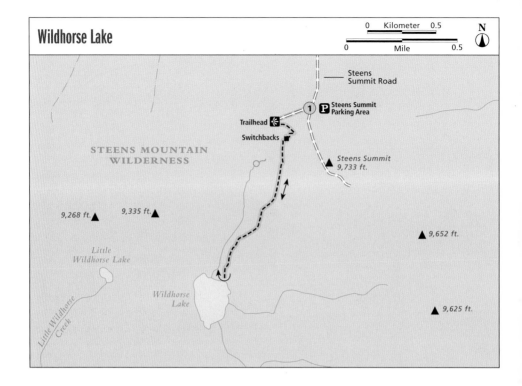

peak isn't quite sublime, however; you'll be sharing it with cell phone and radio towers, along with propane tanks. Still, how often can you climb a 9,733-foot mountain without breaking a sweat?

South Steens Road: This isn't a hike but it is worth noting that the drive from Wildhorse Lake to South Steens Campground on South Steens Road is one of the more spectacular in Oregon. Huge canyons, sweeping viewpoints, and high elevation plateaus can all be found on a road like no other place on the West Coast.

2 Big Indian Gorge

The most visually stunning of the accessible gorges in the Steens Mountain area. Home to a wonderful campsite among cottonwood trees. Longer option to headwall.

Distance: 13-mile out and back
Difficulty: Moderate
Elevation gain: 1,660 feet
Best season: June–late Nov
Maps: USGS Fish Lake; BLM Burns District (south); Steens High Desert Country
Trail contacts: BLM Burns District Office: (541) 573-4400; Frenchglen Historic Hotel: (541) 493-2825

Parking and trailhead facilities: South Steens Campground features 36 campsites and running water.
Special considerations: Three creek crossings are required to enter the canyon, which can be hazardous in spring and early summer. Sagebrush can be brutal on your legs, so wear long pants while hiking.

Finding the trailhead: From Frenchglen head south 10 miles on OR 205 toward Fields. Turn left onto Steens Mountain Loop Road (the south entry point), and follow the gravel road 19 miles to South Steens Campground. The trailhead is in the back of the family campground in a parking area.
Trailhead GPS: N42 39.381′/W118 43.388′

The Hike

The gorges of the Steens Mountain region are among its most defining characteristics. Carved by snow and glaciers, these massive chasms are 2,000 feet deep and over time have become incubators for trees, wildlife, and even a few small trout.

Big Indian is the most impressive of the accessible gorges and popular among hikers, backpackers, and equestrians. Those seeking an easy day hike often stop at a large rock that provides an impressive view into the canyon, while backpackers head for Cottonwood Camp. Adventure seekers occasionally travel all the way to the canyon's headwall, where hidden waterfalls can be found (see "Options"). Some even scramble 2,000 feet up the headwall cliffs into Wildhorse Lake basin.

Wearing long pants is essential, because the sagebrush—always a slight annoyance on high-desert trails—would make this a miserable trek in shorts.

From the trailhead the route passes a registration box and runs 1.9 miles on an old road, through grassy meadows and below wide-open sky, to the first of three stream crossings. The crossings should not be taken lightly during spring and early summer. They are 10 to 15 feet wide and require careful footwork even during autumn.

Beyond the crossings, the scenery improves as the trail swings east into the mouth of a canyon. The entire gorge sweeps out in a massive U-shaped landscape carpeted with sagebrush, aspen, and juniper. At mile 4.1, a massive boulder provides views all the way to the headwall and makes a nice turnaround or lunch spot.

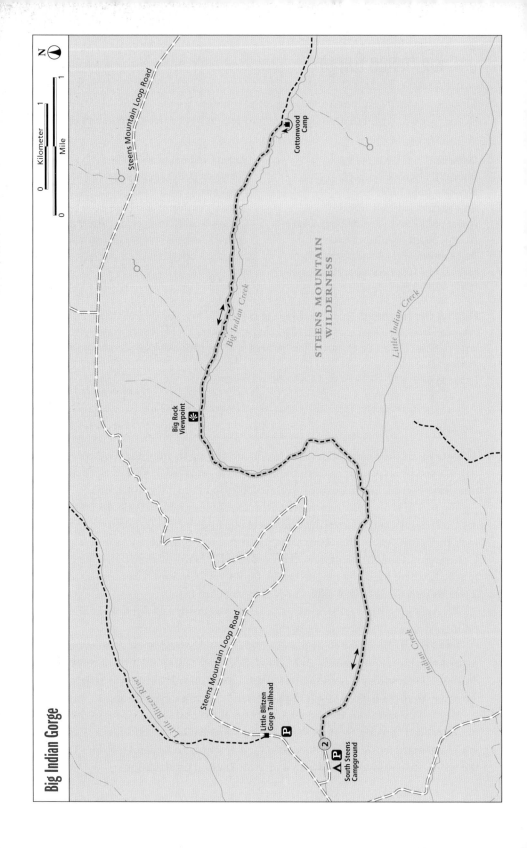

Big Indian Gorge

Cottonwood Camp is a perfect goal and a nice place to spend the night in Big Indian Gorge in southeast Oregon's Steens Mountain. ZACH URNESS

The trail becomes increasingly scraggly during the next 2.0 miles, but the views stay sublime. At mile 6.5, a well-established trail veers off the main route toward Cottonwood Camp, a nice spot along the creek that's perfect for those staying the night.

Miles and Directions

0.0   Begin at the South Steens Campground Trailhead.

2.0   Cross Indian Creek.

2.2   Cross Little Indian Creek.

3.1   Cross Indian Creek again.

4.1   Arrive at the big rock viewpoint (an optional turnaround).

6.5   Veer right from the trail to Cottonwood Camp; return the way you came.

13.0   Arrive back at the trailhead.

Options

Headwall: The trail becomes increasingly rough to follow beyond the junction to Cottonwood Camp, but it does travel 8.5 total miles near a headwall where Steens Mountain's summit looms above. Those interested in off-trail exploration will find waterfalls tucked into both the right and left corners of the canyon's headwall. Some hikers even test themselves with a 2,000-foot scramble up through the rocks. A scramble trail in the left side of the headwall leads up to the Steens Mountain Loop Road; a scramble route on the right heads to Little Wildhorse and Wildhorse Lake basins. Both routes are very difficult and should be attempted only by experienced hikers or rock climbers.

3 Little Blitzen Gorge

A richly colored canyon with swimming holes, sweeping views, and many backcountry camping options. Quicker and easier access than Big Indian. Options to headwall.

Distance: 10-mile out and back
Difficulty: Moderate
Elevation gain: 1,513 feet
Best season: June–late Nov
Maps: USGS Fish Lake; BLM Burns District (south); Steens High Desert Country
Trail contact: Burns District Office: (541) 573-4400; Frenchglen Historic Hotel: (541) 493-2825

Parking and trailhead facilities: Parking for up to 10 cars. South Steens Campground is less than 0.5 mile down the road and features 36 campsites and running water.
Special considerations: A creek crossing can be treacherous in spring and early summer. The trail can be rocky, slippery, and steep in sections. Because of sagebrush and overgrown sections of trail, be sure to wear long pants.

Finding the trailhead: From Frenchglen head south 10 miles on OR 205 toward Fields. Turn left onto Steens Mountain Loop Road, a fairly bumpy gravel road, for 21 miles (past South Steens Campground) to a parking area on the right marked LITTLE BLITZEN TRAILHEAD. The official trail begins just up the road on the left.
Trailhead GPS: N42 39.814' / W118 43.285'

The Hike

Almost as scenic as its neighbor Big Indian, the canyon of Little Blitzen River features better autumn colors, fewer people (though not by much), and easier access to the canyon proper.

The actual trail doesn't start at the parking area. Hikers must follow the road 0.2 mile more to where the trail begins on the left. It's easy to find.

The trail starts with a 0.5-mile downhill drop to a river crossing. This can be a difficult crossing in spring and early summer. Beyond the crossing the trail swings right and passes through a field of sagebrush before entering the narrow passageway into the canyon, at the base of 1,000-foot walls.

The hiking becomes a bit tougher as the trail follows Little Blitzen River through groves of aspen and juniper, over a sometimes rocky and steep landscape. In autumn the forest is ablaze with every autumn color imaginable.

At mile 2.5 the river features wonderful swimming holes between large silver boulders, perfect for hot summer days. Just past mile 3.0, the canyon opens up into a wide meadow blooming with wildflowers during spring and summer.

Many nice campsites dot the next mile. At mile 4.7 you'll pass a grove of aspen, and at mile 5.0 a rock cairn marks a side trail leading uphill to an excellent vista of the headwall in the distance. This makes a great place to stop, since the trail

The canyon walls rise up as the trail enters Little Blitzen Gorge in southeastern Oregon's Steens Mountain. ZACH URNESS

becomes increasingly ragged beyond this point and eventually gives out as it reaches the headwall.

Miles and Directions

0.0   Begin at the parking area.
0.2   Reach the actual start of Little Blitzen Trail.
0.9   Cross Little Blitzen River.
3.1   Pass swimming holes.
3.5   Pass meadows and camping spots (optional turnaround).
5.0   Arrive at a trail junction and viewpoint; return the way you came.
10.0 Arrive back at the trailhead.

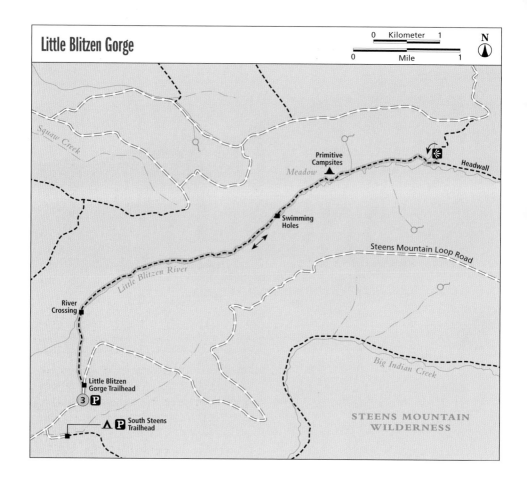

Little Blitzen Gorge

0 Kilometer 1
0 Mile 1

N

Squaw Creek

Primitive Campsites

Meadow ▲

Headwall

Swimming Holes

Steens Mountain Loop Road

Little Blitzen River

River Crossing ■

Big Indian Creek

Little Blitzen Gorge Trailhead

3 P

South Steens Trailhead

▲ P

STEENS MOUNTAIN WILDERNESS

Options

Headwall: The trail continues along the river a total of 8.0 miles before almost disappearing into the sagebrush. Bushwhack 1.0 mile farther and you'll eventually enter a massive bowl of wildflowers in spring and summer and, at the far end, find a waterfall.

4 Pike Creek Canyon

A narrow, multicolored canyon in the sheer eastern face of Steens Mountain. A stunning drive to the trailhead.

Distance: 8.2-mile out and back
Difficulty: Moderately strenuous
Elevation gain: 2,180 feet
Best season: May–Nov
Maps: USGS Wildhorse Lake; BLM Burns District (south); Steens High Desert Country
Trail contacts: Burns District Office: (541) 573-4400; Frenchglen Historic Hotel: (541) 493-2825

Parking and trailhead facilities: Park either along East Steens Road or at the end of the rough access road.
Special considerations: This area is popular among hunters September through November at the campsites along the east face.

Finding the trailhead: Locating this remote trailhead on a rough, unsigned road can be a challenge, but the hike and drive are worth it. The route takes you below the sheer eastern face of Steens Mountain along the edge of the Alvord Desert.

From Burns: Drive east on OR 78 for 65 miles past the town of Crane. At mile marker 65, turn right onto East Steens Road, which has sections of both pavement and gravel, for 38.5 miles, following signs for Fields. The road to the trailhead is unmarked but can be identified by a yellow cattleguard on the right. The road is roughly 3.7 miles past the Alvord Ranch. The road to the trailhead is very rough but only 0.5 mile, so people in passenger cars should consider parking near the yellow gate and adding 0.5 mile to the hike. If you have a high-clearance vehicle, continue 0.5 mile down the bumpy road to where the road forks. Park in a little pullout on the right, and follow the left fork of the road to the trailhead at a small camping spot.

From Frenchglen: Drive OR 205 south for 50 miles. Turn left onto gravel East Steens Road for 24 miles and look for a rough road on the left marked by a yellow cattleguard. If you pass the Alvord Ranch, you've gone too far.
Trailhead GPS: N42 34.558'/W118 31.833'

The Hike

Half the fun of exploring this rich and brightly colored canyon is simply finding it. Unlike the trails to Big Indian and Little Blitzen Gorges, this trail begins near the vast Alvord Desert and knifes into the mountain's sheer eastern face.

The hike is not only remote but is also narrow, rocky, and steep. But don't let that discourage you—the trail is surprisingly well maintained.

The route begins at the parking area where the road splits, 0.5 mile past the yellow cattle gate. Follow the split to the left toward an unimproved campsite and large stack of rocks that marks the trailhead near Pike Creek. Hop across the creek onto its left side and follow the trail, past a registration box, into what seems little more than a crack in the mountain. Spectacular views of this narrow canyon begin immediately.

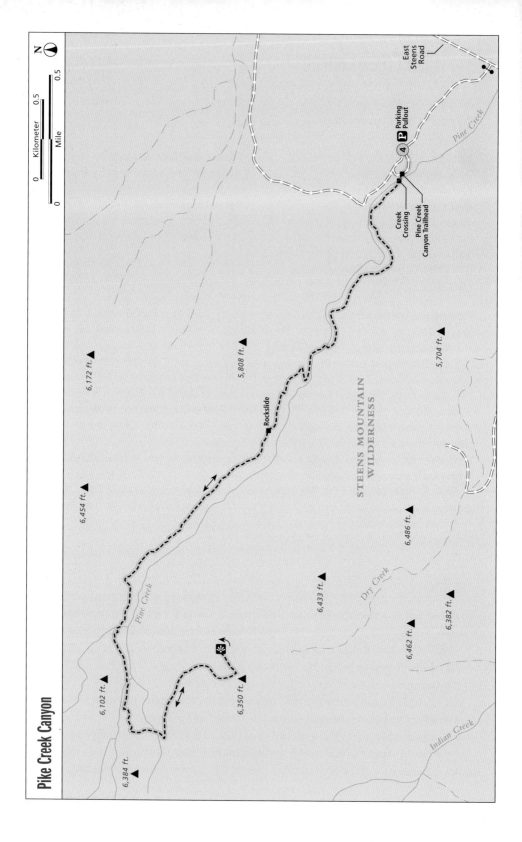

Pike Creek Canyon

N

Kilometer
0   0.5

Mile
0   0.5

East Steens Road

Pine Creek

Parking Pullout

4 P

Creek Crossing

Pine Creek Canyon Trailhead

5,808 ft. ▲

6,172 ft. ▲

Rockslide

STEENS MOUNTAIN WILDERNESS

5,704 ft. ▲

6,454 ft. ▲

6,486 ft. ▲

6,102 ft. ▲

Pine Creek

6,433 ft. ▲

Dry Creek

6,384 ft. ▲

6,350 ft. ▲

6,462 ft. ▲

6,382 ft. ▲

Indian Creek

Although Pike Creek Canyon is a mostly rocky, barren place, there is some vegetation and trees along the creek. ZACH URNESS

Colors of red, pink, orange, and dark blue highlight the rock as the trail undulates through a landscape of towering formations and lush creekside pockets of trees and brush. After 1.0 mile, a sign marks the boundary of the Steens Mountain Wilderness. Near the sign are the wooden remains of a uranium mine with a small wooden shack you can walk into (sort of).

The trail gets steeper beyond the mine, climbing 400 feet in 0.7 mile to a rock-slide with a wonderful view of the canyon. You'll encounter rocks here that sound as though you're walking on glass when you cross over them. (**Note:** It's probably just light shavings of rock.)

Beyond the rockslide, the trail only gets steeper, providing excellent views in every direction before crossing the creek and heading into the only real forested patch on the entire hike.

Finally, the trail swings to the left, crosses the creek a final time, and then climbs to an open overlook at 6,393 feet. To the west is the thick headwall of Steens Mountain; to the east you peer down into the canyon you just ascended and view the vast desert beyond.

Miles and Directions

0.0 Begin at dirt road parking pullout (follow left fork of road).
0.1 Arrive at true trailhead.
0.2 Cross Pike Creek.
1.0 Pass wilderness boundary.
1.7 Arrive at large landslide (optional turnaround).
4.1 Arrive at overlook; turn back.
8.2 Arrive back at trailhead.

5 Crack in the Ground

In the Christmas Valley desert, a trail runs along the bottom of this exquisitely beautiful, 2-mile-long crack in an immense, nearly level field of lava rock. The recommended route enters on the bottom of the crack and forms a loop by returning along the ridge.

Distance: 1.2-mile lollipop
Difficulty: Moderate
Elevation gain: Less than 100 feet
Best season: May–Nov
Maps: USGS Crack in the Ground; Lakeview
(The two sides of the loop, along the bottom and top of the crack, are difficult to see on the map or GPS track because they're only a few feet apart.)

Trail contacts: BLM Lakeview District (North)
(The BLM refers questions about trails to their Seattle Regional office, which is limited to very general information.)
Parking and trailhead facilities: A developed BLM trailhead has a vault toilet and parking for 15 cars.
Special considerations: The rim can get very hot in midsummer. The road is snowed over in midwinter and can get muddy in spring.

Finding the trailhead: From the Christmas Valley Store, head east on paved CR 5-14 (Christmas Valley–Wagontire Road) for 1 mile to Crack in the Ground Road. The junction is well marked. Turn left and follow the new road for 8 miles to the well-marked parking area. The new road runs out of pavement at about mile 4.
Trailhead GPS: N43 19.971'/W120 40.561'

The Hike

The trail from the parking area crosses a sandy sagebrush desert for 0.3 mile before dropping down to the crack entrance. The portion inside the crack is also only 0.3 mile, but it is exquisite. The nearly straight crack runs for 2 miles along a nearly level flow of basaltic lava. The crack averages 10 to 20 feet wide and maybe 40 feet deep.

The contrast between inside and outside the crack is dramatic. Inside can be 20 to 30 degrees cooler, which makes for excellent summer hiking. The vegetation is also completely different. Outside the crack, look for western juniper, sagebrush, and a few ponderosa pines. Inside the crack is much greener and moister.

The crack wall of basaltic lava forms many beautiful shapes and patterns. The bottom is mostly soil, but the trail crosses several large piles of broken lava rock, which very much slows you down and increases the difficulty.

At mile 0.6 the trail exits the crack and climbs up to the rim. The trail through the upper portion of the crack begins here at an immense rockfall. Leave the crack by

Entrance to Crack in the Ground, a 2-mile lava fissure in the Central Oregon desert.
The trail follows the bottom of the fissure and returns along the rim. ART BERNSTEIN

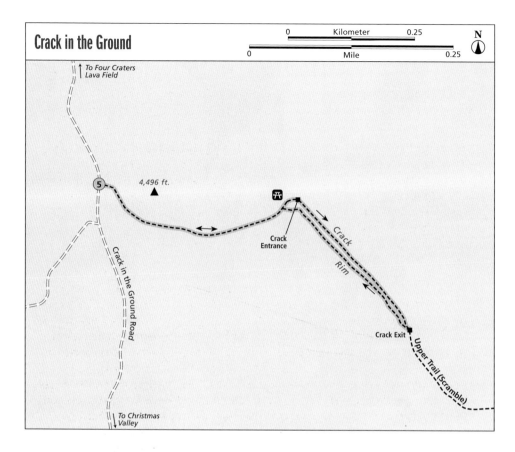

bearing to the right, and head back along the west side rim to the entrance. The rim segment is much hotter but also much faster than inside the crack.

Miles and Directions

0.0 Begin at the trailhead parking area.

0.3 Enter the crack, on the right.

0.6 The trail exits the crack. Bear right and head back along the west side rim toward the trailhead.

0.9 The loop segment ends near the crack entrance. Bear left to return to the trailhead.

1.2 Arrive back at the parking area

Options

The upper trail, beginning where the trail exits the crack at the far end, continues for another 1.4 miles. The path is much less distinct, and there are several side cracks to explore. Other natural features in the vicinity are the Christmas Valley Dunes, Fossil Lake (very interesting but difficult to find), and Lost Forest. On Klamath Marsh Road near Silver Lake, a sign points to the Hager Mountain Trail. This is supposedly a nice little trek, but you can reach the same spot by car.

6 DeGarmo Canyon

A high-desert trek through a canyon in the Hart Mountain National Antelope Refuge leads to an unexpected waterfall and a fun, challenging optional loop.

Distance: 1.6-mile out and back
Difficulty: Easy
Elevation gain: 400 feet
Best season: Late Apr–Nov
Maps: USGS Hart Mountain
Trail contacts: Friends of Hart Mountain National Antelope Refuge; US Fish and Wildlife Service: (541) 947-2731

Parking and trailhead facilities: Small dirt area with room for 5 or 6 cars
Special considerations: This area is popular among hunters from September through November.

Finding the trailhead: From Lakeview follow US 395 north 4.7 miles. Turn right (east) onto OR 140 for a total of 15.6 miles. Veer left off the highway onto Plush Cutoff Road (CR 3-13) and follow it 18.6 miles into the tiny hamlet of Plush, home to a gas station, a small supply store, and a really interesting rock store specializing in Oregon sunstones. Continue through town and turn right onto Hart Mountain Road. Make a second right to stay on the pavement after 2 miles and continue past Hart Lake toward the massive fault block of Hart Mountain overhead.

From the turnoff in Plush, continue 8.6 miles to the DeGarmo Canyon access road. Keep your eyes peeled once the road straightens out below Hart Mountain. A very small wooden sign marks DeGarmo Canyon on the right. When you see it, turn right onto a very rough road. This might not be suitable for low-clearance passenger cars; if you're driving one, park here and continue on foot. Follow the rough road 0.5 mile to a parking area and trailhead at the road's end.
Trailhead GPS: N42 28.735' / W119 47.372'

The Hike

A narrow crack into the belly of this fault block mountain, DeGarmo Canyon is among the very few developed trails in the Hart Mountain National Antelope Refuge. It's an excellent spot to explore this unique and rugged landscape amid red rock walls and aspen trees.

The drive alone is well worth the effort, passing the tiny town of Plush before winding past Hart Lake and below the jagged escarpment of the mountain's steep western face. The trailhead is unmarked and a challenge to locate, but as with many southeastern trails, the journey is part of the fun.

There are two distinct hiking options: Either hike the easy 1.5-mile out-and-back route to a waterfall, or take a sometimes steep and rough scramble trail to turn the hike into a more adventurous 2.8-mile loop (see "Options").

Either way, the trail starts by crossing DeGarmo Creek. The crossing can be dangerous in spring or early summer. Instead of crossing where the trail leads, consider inching your way along the rock ledges to the right until you find an easier crossing.

The trailhead of DeGarmo Canyon requires some rough driving into southeastern Oregon's Hart Mountain. Zach Urness

Beyond the creek, the trail leads through a narrow, red-rock canyon entrance and emerges at an open meadow of sagebrush and aspen. The most noticeable landmark is a rock the size of an SUV. The trail continues upstream just 0.8 mile to the base of a trickling waterfall. The official trail is short, so enjoy each step if you're planning on hiking right back out.

Miles and Directions

0.0 Begin at the DeGarmo Canyon Trailhead.

0.1 Cross DeGarmo Creek.

0.7 Pass the loop junction (see "Options").

0.8 Arrive at the base of the waterfall; return the way you came.

1.6 Arrive back at the trailhead

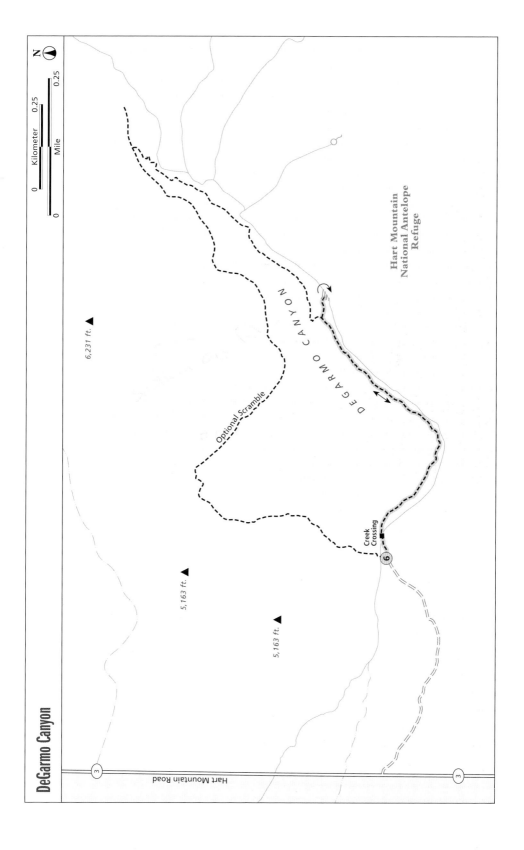

DeGarmo Canyon

N

Kilometer
0   0.25

Mile
0   0.25

6,231 ft. ▲

5,163 ft. ▲

5,163 ft. ▲

Optional Scramble

DEGARMO CANYON

Creek Crossing

6

Hart Mountain Road

3

3

Hart Mountain
National Antelope
Refuge

Options

For those up for greater adventure, head back 0.1 mile from the base of the waterfall to an obvious scramble trail leading steeply uphill. From the top of that first scramble, the trail straightens out and heads 0.2 mile to another steep uphill scramble, and then flattens out again at a wonderful creekside spot surrounded by trees.

Follow stacked rock cairns along an increasingly faint trail through a gap in the rocks, always up and to the left, gradually moving uphill for 0.4 mile until you reach a ridgeline with a well-established trail going in both directions.

To the right, the trail continues into the refuge, all the way to Warner Peak before giving out. To complete the loop, head left and follow this former cattle drive route above the canyon past sweeping views of the high desert and a trio of lakes—Swamp, Anderson, and Hart—in the distance.

The upper trail heads above the canyon and then gradually downhill back to the parking area to finish the loop. The trail becomes difficult to follow toward its end, but at that point you'll be able to spot your car below. Bushwhacking downhill through the sagebrush is quite easy as long as you're wearing long pants.

7 Gearhart Mountain

Bizarre and beautiful pearl-white lava formations. A short hike to the Palisades or a longer trek to a cliff-walled meadow.

Distance: 11-mile out and back
Difficulty: Strenuous
Elevation gain: 2,041 feet
Best season: July–Oct
Maps: USGS Gearhart Mountain; Fremont-Winema National Forest
Trail contacts: Bly Ranger District: (541) 353-2427

Parking and trailhead facilities: Room for around 10 cars at the trailhead. Corral Creek Campground is a free campsite with picnic tables and a vault toilet.
Special considerations: This area is popular among hunters from September through November. Mosquitoes are thick until the end of July.

Finding the trailhead: From Klamath Falls follow OR 140 east for 55 miles to the tiny hamlet of Bly. About 1 mile past Bly, turn left onto Campbell Road for a quick 0.5 mile, then turn right onto Road 34, following the sign for the Gearhart Mountain Wilderness. Follow the paved road 16 miles toward the mountain, and turn left at the sign for Corral Creek Campground (Road 212). Follow this increasingly rough gravel road, past the campground, a total of 1.5 miles to the trailhead. The final 0.5 mile is rough and may be difficult for low-clearance passenger cars.
Trailhead GPS: N42 27.637' / W120 48.061'

The Hike

Oddball geology, high-desert features, and a truly stunning cliff-walled meadow make this trail into the heart of Gearhart Mountain Wilderness one of Oregon's true hidden treasures.

The trail traverses a forest of sagebrush, pine, and aspen, but the rocks are the main attraction. Formations of ancient lava stand in hulking, layered towers and odd shapes along a trail that's good for either a day hike or backpacking trip.

You reach the most famous rock formation just 0.7 mile up the trail at the Palisades. A collection of stratified towers, the largest rocks resemble Stonehenge without the organization, while smaller rocks have the appearance of squat dwarfs running around below.

Beyond the Palisades, the trail climbs through a forest without many views for the next few miles. At mile 2.8, the hulking monolith of The Dome rises above the trees; more formations follow, including a steep slab of rock that cuts into the distance like a massive white wall.

After 4.6 miles and a climb of 1,959 feet, you arrive at a pass where views spread in every direction. The path then drops 200 feet in 1.0 mile, crosses Dairy Creek, and enters a stunning meadow below cliffs that shoot straight overhead. The meadow is a wonderful place to camp or rest before turning around to hike back out.

Gearhart Mountain

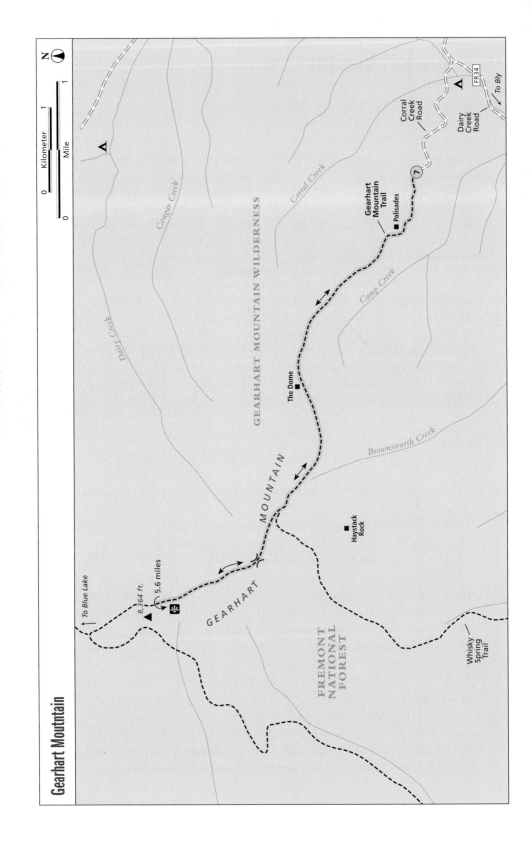

The Palisades are an odd collection of rocks located a short trip down the trail at Gearhart Mountain. Zach Urness

Miles and Directions

0.0 Begin at the Gearhart Mountain Trailhead.

0.4 Pass the wilderness boundary.

0.7 Arrive at the Palisades (optional turnaround).

2.8 Pass below The Dome.

4.6 Cross the pass.

5.5 Reach Gearhart Meadow; return the way you came.

11.0 Arrive back at the trailhead.

Options

Past the meadow to Blue Lake: The Gearhart Mountain Trail is 15 miles one-way and, beyond the meadow, continues to Blue Lake and then to the Blue Lake Trailhead. However, the trail can be very difficult to follow beyond the meadow, as it drops through a dusty, burnt patch of dead and fallen trees. Hikers traversing the entire trail should be prepared for some navigating and difficult hiking.

8 Blue Lake

A pretty hike along the North Fork Sprague River through aspen forest to wide, aptly named Blue Lake. Fishing opportunities.

Distance: 6.0-mile out and back (optional 1.0-mile trail circles the lake)
Difficulty: Easy to moderate
Elevation gain: 850 feet
Best season: July–Oct
Maps: USGS Lee Thomas Crossing; Fremont-Winema National Forest
Trail contacts: Bly Ranger District: (541) 353-2427

Parking and trailhead facilities: The trailhead is located in a small campground by an extremely pretty meadow and creek. There is parking for 20 cars.
Special considerations: This is among the more popular hikes in the Gearhardt Wilderness, though typically not crowded.

Finding the trailhead: From Klamath Falls follow OR 140 east for 55 miles to the tiny hamlet of Bly. About 1 mile past Bly, turn left onto Campbell Road for a quick 0.5 mile, then turn right onto Road 34, following the sign for the Gearhart Mountain Wilderness. Follow the paved road 20 miles, past a sign and turnoff for Corral Creek Campground, to a major four-way junction.

Turn left onto FR 3428, following the sign to Lee Thomas Campground. Five miles farther, past a little shady canyon, arrive at a turnoff to the left. A badly faded, almost impossible-to-read sign says Blue Lake. Continue for 3 miles on the side road, through a large burn and logging area, to the trailhead.

Trailhead GPS: N42 33.496' / W120 50.482'

The Hike

Between the two featured hikes in the Gearhart Wilderness, the Blue Lake Trail is the easier and more surprising. Unlike the full Gearhart Mountain Trail, the route to popular Blue Lake doesn't feature dramatic cliff faces or sweeping mountain vistas.

What it does have is a much easier hike through a beautiful forest of quaking aspen trees draped in lichen, with pink stones along the North Fork of the Sprague River. Autumn brings brilliant yellow color to the aspens.

Blue Lake is circular body of water in a forested setting offering plenty of campsites and fishing opportunities.

The first 2.0 miles require two crossings on the river—along with a third one, closer to the lake—that may be somewhat difficult during spring and early summer, but they're not something that should stop progress.

After 3.0 miles on this wide and well-traveled trail, Blue Lake comes into view among the trees. In spring, wildflowers can be found near the lake's marshes.

Blue Lake is surrounded by dense forest at the end of a 3-mile trail in the Gearhart Mountain Wilderness in southeastern Oregon. ZACH URNESS

Miles and Directions

0.0   Begin at the Blue Lake Trailhead.

0.7   Arrive at the first North Fork Sprague River crossing.

1.4   Make the second North Fork Sprague River crossing.

3.0   Reach Blue Lake; return the way you came.

6.0   Arrive back at the trailhead.

Options

Lake loop: A 1.0-mile loop trail circles the lake and provides access to a few primitive campsites.

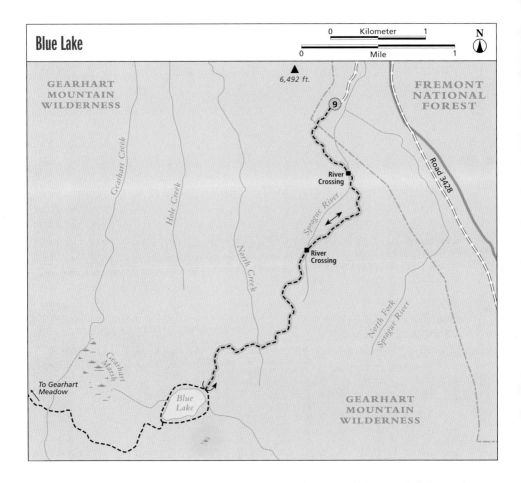

Blue Lake

GEARHART
MOUNTAIN
WILDERNESS

6,492 ft.

9

FREMONT
NATIONAL
FOREST

Gearhart Creek

Hole Creek

North Creek

Sprague River

River
Crossing

River
Crossing

North Fork Sprague River

Road 3428

To Gearhart
Meadow

Gearhart
Marsh

Blue
Lake

GEARHART
MOUNTAIN
WILDERNESS

Beyond Blue Lake, a very steep and sometimes hard-to-follow path follows the Gearhart Mountain Trail, reaching a stunning meadow and the mountain's summit in 4.0 miles before emerging at the Corral Creek Trailhead. The combined trails total 15 miles.

9 Crater Lake Pinnacles

A short, fascinating route to the Pinnacles area of Crater Lake National Park from the opposite direction.

Distance: 1.6-mile out and back
Difficulty: Easy
Elevation gain: Less than 100 feet
Best season: May–Oct
Maps: USGS Sun Pass; Fremont-Winema National Forest; Crater Lake National Park
Trail contacts: Chiloquin Ranger District: (541) 783-4001; Crater Lake National Park: (541) 594-3000

Parking and trailhead facilities: Parking is on the shoulder, with room for maybe a dozen cars. There are no facilities.
Special considerations: Pets are not allowed on any trail in Crater Lake National Park. Access to the trailhead is easier from the national park end and is entirely paved. However, if you start from the national forest end, you will save the park entrance fee, see a bunch more pinnacles from the car—and be the only one there.

Finding the trailhead: From Klamath Falls, follow US 97 north for 21 miles to the junction with OR 62 to Crater Lake. Turn left and continue for 12.5 miles to Sun Mountain Road, then bear right while OR 62 veers left. It's 2.4 more miles to Jackson Kimball State Park, where the pavement ends, and about 8 more miles, over Sun Pass, to FR 2304, on the left. Continue about 3.4 miles on the gravel FR 2304 to the well-marked trailhead.
Trailhead GPS: N42 50.874' / W121 59.673'

The Hike

The drive up FR 2304 to the trailhead is pretty interesting. It follows Sand Creek and passes a small, unmarked turnout with pinnacles that park visitors will not see rising out of the steep creek bank.

The Pinnacles are very tall, narrow spires formed when escaping gas hardened columns of the surrounding loose volcanic ash; the unhardened ash later eroded away, exposing the spires. They are very impressive.

From the trailhead, the path enters Crater Lake National Park almost immediately. The route used to be the paved East Entrance to the park, but the road was closed in the 1970s and all traces of it removed. All that remains is the huge stone entrance sign, sitting forlornly in the middle of nowhere.

The path follows the rim of a steep-banked gorge with pink pinnacles jutting up everywhere. Eventually Sand Creek turns away and the route ends up following Lost Creek to the Pinnacles parking area inside the park.

The Crater Lake Pinnacles rise out of the soft volcanic ash alongside Lost Creek. LYNN BERNSTEIN

Miles and Directions

0.0 Begin at the trailhead.

0.1 Enter Crater Lake National Park at the old entrance sign.

0.8 Reach Pinnacles parking area; return the way you came.

1.6 Arrive back at the trailhead.

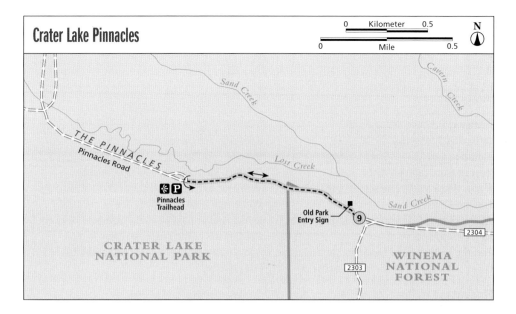

Crater Lake Pinnacles

0   Kilometer   0.5

0   Mile   0.5

N

Sand Creek

Cavern Creek

THE PINNACLES

Pinnacles Road

Lost Creek

Pinnacles Trailhead

Old Park Entry Sign

9

Sand Creek

2304

CRATER LAKE NATIONAL PARK

2303

WINEMA NATIONAL FOREST

Options

There are many excellent trails in the Klamath Falls/Chiloquin Area. An old rail-road bed is now a trail that runs from Klamath Falls to Bly (over 30 miles). The Yamsay Mountain Trail ascends an old volcano near Klamath Marsh. The trailhead is unmarked, and the trail is an old road. The area is considered sacred by the Klamath tribe (which could be why the author fell and cut his face).

10 Mount Thielsen

A challenging climb to the 9,182-foot, frighteningly narrow spire of the "Lightning Rod of the Cascades."

Distance: 9.6-mile out and back
Difficulty: Strenuous
Elevation gain: 3,732 feet to summit
Best season: Late July–Oct
Maps: USGS Mount Thielsen; Umpqua National Forest
Trail contacts: Diamond Lake Ranger Station: (541) 498-2531
Parking and trailhead facilities: The trailhead accommodates 30 cars. There is excellent camping at South Diamond Lake, less than 2 miles from the trailhead.
Special considerations: Above the PCT (#2000) junction, this hike is extremely strenuous and dangerous, with loose scree slopes and rock scrambling. The summit can be reached without climbing gear, but hikers attempt this at their own risk. There is no water. Horse travel is not allowed above the PCT junction.

Finding the trailhead: From Medford: Take OR 62 north from Medford to Union Creek. Past Union Creek, where OR 62 swings right toward Crater Lake (at milepost 57), continue straight on OR 230 toward Diamond Lake. In 24.5 miles, at the junction with OR 138, turn left and proceed 1.5 miles to the well-marked trailhead parking area on the right.

From I-5 in Roseburg: Take exit 124 off I-5, marked Diamond Lake/City Center, and follow signs through downtown Roseburg for Diamond Lake. Follow OR 138 east from Roseburg for 81 miles, past the Diamond Lake turnoff, to a large trailhead on the left.

Trailhead GPS: N43 08.768' / W122 07.659'

The Hike

The ascent of towering Mount Thielsen, whose tilted spire has earned it the nickname "the Lightning Rod of the Cascades," is probably the most difficult in this guide. With its rarefied elevations and precipitous gravel slopes, Mount Thielsen Trail soars almost 1,800 feet in its final mile and is like scaling the side of a bell, with every step steeper than the last. The final 150 feet is a considered a Class 4 scramble—meaning a fall could easily be fatal—with an over-the-top sense of exposure that requires pulling yourself up a steep rock spire.

From the trailhead, the Thielsen Trail (#1456) climbs steadily but gently into a forest of Shasta red fir, mountain hemlock, and western white pine. After 1.6 miles it passes the Spruce Ridge Trail (#1458) junction. The Thielsen Trail comes around a point 0.5 mile beyond, and the looming avalanche basin that forms the peak's west face emerges in all its glory.

The summit remains in view for most of the route beyond this first vista point as the forest thins, the terrain grows rockier, the trail steepens slightly, and high-elevation species such as subalpine fir and whitebark pine begin to turn up.

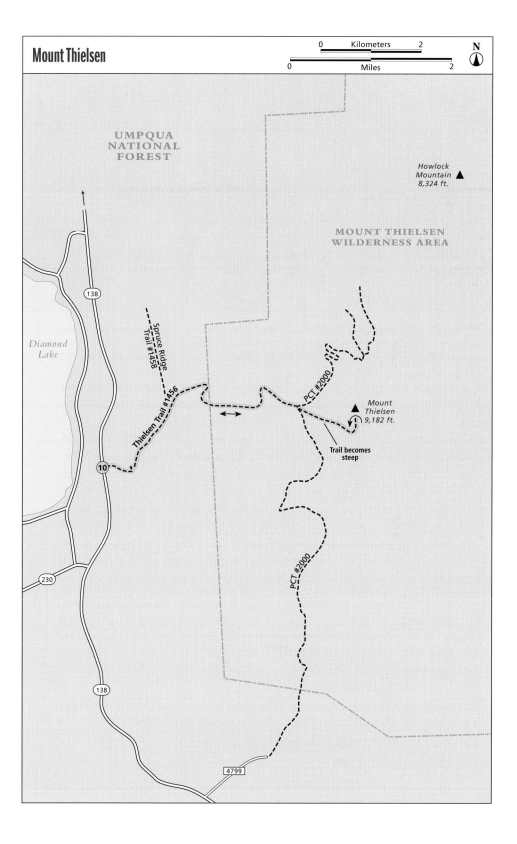

Zach Hausken of Corvallis looks up at the summit spire of Mount Thielsen from the west ridge in a flat area just before the steep climb up the screen patch. ZACH URNESS

The Pacific Crest Trail crosses the Thielsen Trail at mile 3.9, with an outstanding vista. You may wish to either turn around here or content yourself with exploring a couple of miles of the PCT. Northward, the PCT winds through the avalanche basin; to the south it makes its way among emerald meadows and multihued rock formations.

Above the PCT crossing, the Thielsen Trail gradually becomes a faint scramble route, inching up the ridge on loose rock, or scree. The easiest route involves staying left, as close to the ridge as you feel comfortable (since it's a long, long way down).

Eventually the ridge peters out and you hit a sheer rock wall towering above the rim. A little scrambling takes you to the area's only flat spot, Chicken Point.

Technical gear isn't necessary to ascend the final 150-foot spire to the summit, but don't feel bad if Chicken Point lives up to its name. Not everyone feels comfortable clinging to narrow ledges above 2,000-foot drop-offs. Never attempt the spire alone, and watch out for people below you.

Miles and Directions

- **0.0** Begin at the Mount Thielsen Trailhead.
- **1.6** Pass the Spruce Ridge Trail junction.
- **1.9** Cross the wilderness boundary.
- **3.9** Reach the PCT junction (popular turnaround point). Continue uphill on a less-distinct trail.
- **4.7** Arrive at Chicken Point; begin to climb toward the summit.
- **4.8** Reach the summit of Mount Thielsen; return the way you came.
- **9.6** Arrive back at the trailhead.

11 Mount Bailey

A spectacular hike to the top of an 8,368-foot volcanic dome rising directly above popular Diamond Lake.

Distance: 9.6-mile out and back
Difficulty: Strenuous
Elevation gain: 3,196 feet
Best season: Late June–Oct
Maps: USGS Diamond Lake; Umpqua National Forest
Trail contacts: Umpqua National Forest, Diamond Lake Ranger District: (541) 498-2351

Parking and trailhead facilities: Parking at Fox Spring is ample (at least 10 cars), and there are several well-developed campgrounds nearby at Diamond Lake.
Special considerations: There is no water on this trail.

Finding the trailhead: Take OR 62 north from Medford to Union Creek. Past milepost 57, where OR 62 swings right toward Crater Lake, continue straight on OR 230 toward Diamond Lake for 24.3 miles. Just before the stop sign at OR 138, look for FR 6592 along the Diamond Lake south shore. Turn left; proceed for 1 mile and then turn left again onto FR 4795. Follow FR 4795 for 2 miles. Just past Silent Creek, turn up Spur 300. The trailhead is 0.4 mile up, at Fox Spring.
Trailhead GPS: N43 07.614' / W122 09.689'

The Hike

Not quite as overwhelming as neighboring Mount Thielsen, 8,377-foot Mount Bailey is a favorite among Southern Oregonians. The two giant volcanoes, Thielsen and Bailey, rise up on opposite sides of Diamond Lake, just north of Crater Lake. Mount Bailey is the one seen from the Diamond Lake Resort. A major, if underrated, Cascade Peak, Bailey is only 800 feet lower than Thielsen, with a beautiful and challenging summit trail.

Originally named Mount Baldy because of its domed profile, the peak became Bailey as a result of a cartographer misreading a surveyor's handwriting.

From the trailhead, the Mount Bailey Trail (#1451) begins in a lodgepole pine stand typical of Cascade volcanic regions and works its way into Shasta red fir, mountain hemlock, and western white pine. Over the forested summit of Hemlock Butte (6,027 feet) at mile 2.7, down a slight dip, and beyond the wooded flat at Spur 380 (which is usually closed to traffic), the route steepens and breaks out into the open, passing tree-line clusters of subalpine fir and whitebark pine.

Most of the stretch between Spur 380 and mile 5.3 snakes up a south-facing facet, with views of the Crater Lake rim to the south. Occasionally the path bumps a sharp rim, revealing panoramas to the northeast of Diamond Lake and Bailey's dizzying avalanche bowl. Beginning 0.5 mile before the false-summit overlook, things become quite steep; be sure to bring water.

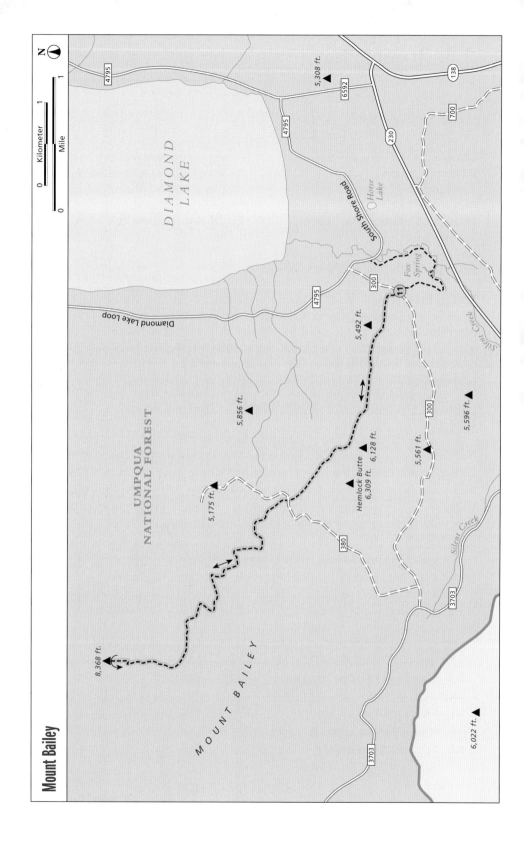

Mount Bailey

UMPQUA NATIONAL FOREST

DIAMOND LAKE

MOUNT BAILEY

Diamond Lake Loop

South Shore Road

Silent Creek

Fox Spring

Horse Lake

8,368 ft.
5,175 ft.
5,856 ft.
6,309 ft.
Hemlock Butte
6,128 ft.
5,492 ft.
5,561 ft.
5,596 ft.
6,022 ft.
5,208 ft.

4795
4795
4795
6592
138
230
700
300
300
380
3703
3703

N

0   Kilometer   1
0   Mile   1

Mount Bailey is an immense volcano rising from the southwest shore of Diamond Lake. The trail also begins at Diamond Lake. VIC HARRIS

Technically the trail ends at the false summit. The true summit lies 0.5 mile north at the end of a precarious way trail (never formally constructed). The route drops briefly and then follows the base of a vertical rock wall on the right, with loose gravel shooting downhill a couple of thousand feet on the left. Eventually the wall ends; the route starts back up and then peters out. From there, scramble back up to the ridge crest (a couple hundred feet). It's a relatively easy walk along the ridge, around a couple more small outcrops, to the lookout base capping the flat peak.

Miles and Directions

0.0 Begin hiking west (right) from the Spur 300 (Silent Creek) Trailhead.

1.4 Cross the summit of Hemlock Butte.

2.0 Cross Spur 380.

4.7 Arrive at the false summit overlook.

4.9 Arrive at the true summit and turn around.

9.8 Arrive back at the trailhead.

12 Thielsen Creek Meadows

A hike along a bubbling creek to a meadow directly below Southern Oregon's second-highest peak. Options to further explore the Pacific Crest Trail (PCT).

Distance: 11.2-mile out and back
Difficulty: Strenuous
Elevation gain: 1,943 feet
Best season: Late June–Oct
Maps: USGS Mount Thielsen; Fremont-Winema National Forest
Trail contacts: Diamond Lake Ranger Station: (541) 498-2531; Diamond Lake: (541) 793-3333

Parking and trailhead facilities: This large trailhead has room for 20 to 30 cars. It is surrounded by horse stalls and a place where guided trail rides begin. Many good camping spots can be found around Diamond Lake.
Special considerations: Mosquitoes are an issue into early August. Horse riders frequent the first stretch of this trail and can make the trail dusty.

Finding the trailhead: From Medford: Take OR 62 north to Union Creek. Where OR 62 swings right toward Crater Lake (at milepost 57), continue straight on OR 230 toward Diamond Lake for 24.5 miles. At the junction with OR 138, turn left; proceed 4.3 miles to signs for Diamond Lake Recreation Area and turn left. Follow Corral Road for 0.4 mile to the Howlock Mountain Trailhead, which is directly across from the Diamond Lake gas station.

From I-5/Roseburg: Take exit 124 off I-5 for Diamond Lake/City Center and follow signs through downtown Roseburg for Diamond Lake. Follow OR 138 east of Roseburg for 78 miles to a Diamond Lake Recreation Area sign and turn right. Follow Corral Road to Howlock Mountain Trailhead, with a large sign on the left, which is directly across from the Diamond Lake gas station. **Trailhead GPS:** N43 11.013'/W122 07.994'

The Hike

Mount Thielsen is a spectacular sight from any direction, but the view from the grassy alpine glen of Thielsen Creek Meadows is second to none. The mountain's narrow spire shoots thousands of feet above a creek winding through an open meadow.

The journey to this magic spot does require some work, traversing Howlock Mountain Trail for 3.2 miles before swinging onto Thielsen Creek Trail (#1449). The meadows themselves offer a stunning camping or lunch spot just off the trail near the PCT.

The main drawback on this hike is mosquitoes, which stay thick and bloodthirsty into mid–August.

The trail begins alongside Diamond Lake at the Howlock Mountain Trailhead, where a commercial outfitter offers guided equestrian rides. Hike 0.2 mile to a tunnel below OR 138 and then 0.6 mile on a wide and dusty trail to an unmarked junction, where hikers veer right.

Thielsen Creek rolls below the steep narrow spire of Mount Thielsen a few thousand feet overhead from Thielsen Creek Meadows.
ZACH URNESS

The first real point of interest is Timothy Meadows at mile 2.7, the first place you'll come into contact with the crystal water of Thielsen Creek in a grassy oasis of lodgepole pines and a few wildflowers. A side trail explores this wonderful spot.

Just beyond, a sign marks the wilderness boundary, where you'll cross over Thielsen Creek. Follow Thielsen Creek Trail #1449, which takes off on the right.

The trail climbs 2.2 miles and 953 feet through mountain hemlock and stands of true fir along the creek as the narrow point of Mount Thielsen looms above.

Thielsen Creek Meadows—also known as Thielsen Creek Camp—is located on the right, just off the trail. Multiple stacked rock cairns and scramble trails lead downhill to the beautiful vistas alongside the creek.

The Thielsen Creek Trail ends at a junction with the PCT just beyond, offering a few more potential adventures.

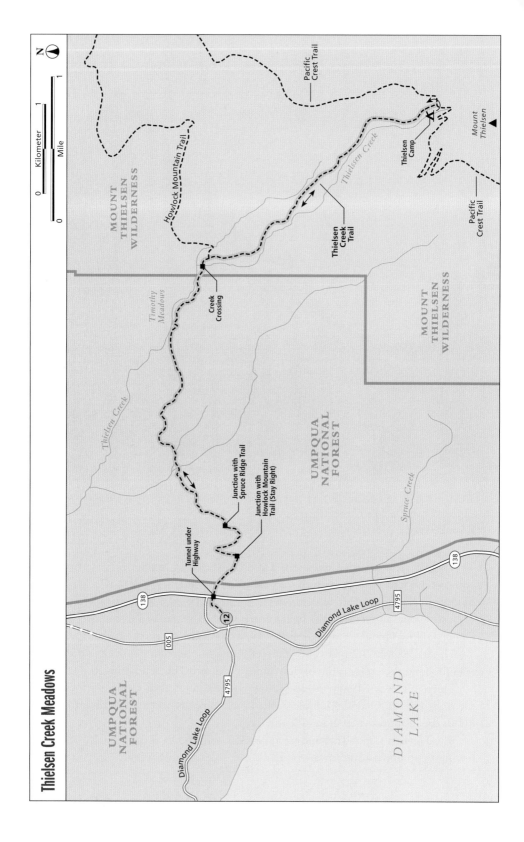

Thielsen Creek Meadows

Miles and Directions

0.0 Begin at the Howlock Mountain Trailhead.

0.2 Pass through a tunnel under the highway.

1.1 Pass the Spruce Ridge Trail junction.

2.7 Arrive at Timothy Meadows, on the left.

3.2 Cross over Thielsen Creek and turn right on Thielsen Creek Trail (#1449).

5.5 Arrive at Thielsen Creek Meadows on the right, just off the trail.

5.6 Reach the PCT junction; return the way you came.

11.2 Arrive back at the trailhead.

Options

Howlock Meadows: There are a number of options from the PCT junction for those looking for either a very long day hike or a backpacking trip. Follow the PCT left (north) and you'll reach Howlock Meadows and the Howlock Trail you followed in from Diamond Lake. Combining Howlock Mountain Trail, Thielsen Creek Trail, and the PCT makes an almost 16-mile loop.

Mount Thielsen summit: If the view of Mount Thielsen gets too tempting, and you simply have to climb it, turn right at the PCT junction and head south 2.0 miles to the Mount Thielsen Trail.

13 Wolf Creek Falls

A hike through quiet, secluded forest to an upper and lower waterfall that drops a total of 125-feet. Options for four other waterfall hikes.

Distance: 2.4-mile out and back
Difficulty: Easy
Elevation gain: 350 feet
Best season: Year-round
Maps: USGS Illahee Rock; Umpqua National Forest

Trail contacts: North Umpqua Ranger District: (541) 496-3532
Parking and trailhead facilities: The parking area is a pullout on the side of the road with room for 6 to 8 cars.

Finding the trailhead: From I-5 in Roseburg, take exit 124 for the North Umpqua River and OR 138. Follow signs for Diamond Lake through downtown Roseburg and continue on OR 138 to the town of Glide at milepost 16. From Glide, turn right onto Little River Road and follow it 10.8 miles to a trailhead sign and parking pullout on the right side of the road.
Trailhead GPS: N43 14.024' / W122 57.074'

The Hike

Although the North Umpqua River canyon is famous for waterfalls—and sees the most traffic—a small tributary to the south called Little River has its own claims to fame.

There are four stunning waterfalls in the Little River area (see "Options"), but Wolf Creek is the best. The trailhead is easy to find and open year-round, even when the area receives a few inches of snow. The waterfall drops in upper and lower tiers of 75 and 50 feet, respectively, and the trail winds through a quiet forest, following the stream.

The trail begins by crossing over Little River on a scenic wooden footbridge. After just 0.1 mile, you'll pass below a truly massive boulder and cross another footbridge.

After 0.7 mile the canyon tightens, the trail gets steeper, and the sound of falling water can be heard as the lower stretch of Wolf Creek Falls comes into view.

A difficult and potentially dangerous scramble trail leads downhill for a better view of the lower falls; the main trail ends at a viewpoint of the upper falls sliding down a slab of thick basalt.

Miles and Directions

0.0 Begin at the Wolf Creek Falls Trailhead by crossing a large footbridge.
1.2 Reach Wolf Creek Falls; return the way you came.
2.4 Arrive back at the trailhead

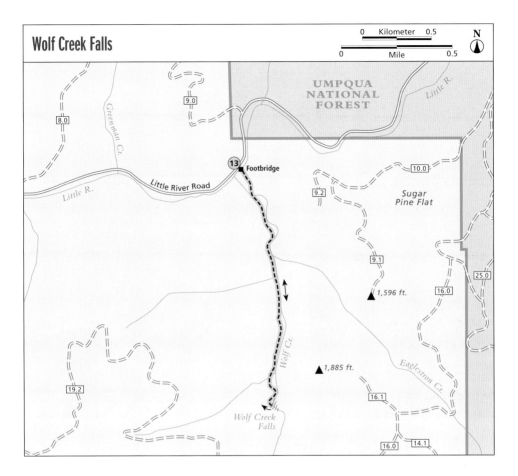

Options

The waterfalls featured below are not open during winter, since most start at around or above 3,000 feet. The best time to visit is May to late November. Call the North Umpqua Ranger District (541-496-3532) to check conditions.

Shadow Falls: This triple-descent waterfall has eroded its way through a rock fracture to form a narrow, natural grotto after a 100-foot plunge. The trail totals 1.6 miles. From Glide, follow Little River Road 6.6 miles. Turn right at the covered bridge on Cavitt Creek (Road 82B) and continue 11.6 miles on Road 82B and FR 25 to the trailhead. Follow Trail #1504 to the falls.

Grotto Falls: The shimmering waters of this waterfall plunge along Emile Creek. Visitors can walk into the grotto behind the falls, but be careful; it's slippery. The hike is 0.6 mile round-trip. From Glide, take Little River Road (CR 17, becoming FR 27) for 16.1 miles to Road 2703 across from Coolwater Campground. Turn left onto Road 2703 for 4.5 miles and stay left on a turnoff for Road 2703-150 for another 2 miles to a trailhead just over a bridge. The route is marked with Grotto Falls signs.

The Wolf Creek Falls Trail is open year-round, even when a bit of snow hits the ground. It crosses a number of wooden footbridges over the creek. ZACH URNESS

Hemlock Falls: Rocks, ferns, and trees surround this 80-foot falls along Hemlock Creek. The hike is 1.2 miles round-trip. From Glide, follow Little River Road (CR 17, becoming FR 27) for 25.8 miles to Lake in the Woods Campground. The final 7 miles are gravel. Trailhead parking is at the campground entrance. Access to Hemlock Falls Trail is near Campsite 1.

Yakso Falls: Little River drops 70 feet among protruding rocks that spread the water flow out like a silver fan. The hike is a round-trip of 1.4 miles and also begins at Lake in the Woods Campground. Follow the same directions as to Hemlock Falls (above) and park in the campground. The trailhead is just across FR 27 from the campground.

14 Yellowjacket Loop

A beautiful loop, beginning at a lake and winding through forest, mountaintop, and multiple meadows.

Distance: 5.3-mile loop
Difficulty: Moderate
Elevation gain: 1,150 feet
Best season: June–Oct
Maps: USGS Quartz Mountain; Umpqua National Forest
Trail contacts: Umpqua National Forest: (541) 496-3532

Parking and trailhead facilities: There is parking for 8 cars at the trailhead. A campground with pit toilets is located nearby, and you can fish in the lake.
Special considerations: No potable water despite crossing many wet seeps

Finding the trailhead: From I-5 in Roseburg, take exit 124 for the North Umpqua River and OR 138. Follow signs for Diamond Lake through downtown Roseburg and continue on OR 138 to the town of Glide at milepost 16.

Turn right onto Little River Road (CR 17, becoming FR 27) for 31 miles to Hemlock Lake. The route has 20 miles of pavement and 11 miles of gravel and is well marked with signs. At the Hemlock Lake junction, go right, cross the reservoir's dam, and find a large parking area near the bulletin board and campground registration.
Trailhead GPS: N43 11.269' / W122 42.288'

The Hike

Among the many interesting facets of Yellowjacket Loop—the meadows, wildflowers, and mountain views—the thing you'll likely notice first are the many trail junctions. Although the trail is well marked and easy to follow, it's important to keep an eye out for the signs at various junctions that point you in the correct direction.

From the campground trailhead at the bulletin board, Yellowjacket Loop heads to a large floral meadow crossed by a boardwalk. The meadow, like six other meadows in the next 2 miles, is home to coneflower, spirea, Queen Anne's lace, butterweed, Indian paintbrush, columbine, and, above all, corn lily. At other meadows, you can spot penstemon, bleeding heart, tiger lily, and other wildflower and shrub species too numerous to list here.

Being north of the Rogue-Umpqua Divide, forest trees consist mostly of western hemlock and Douglas-fir at the lower elevations, transitioning to mountain hemlock and noble fir at the higher elevations, with Pacific silver fir at all elevations.

At the first meadow, just before the boardwalk, the Hemlock Creek Trail (#1505) takes off to the right while Yellowjacket Loop begins to the left; go left. After wandering through three successive corn-lily meadows, Yellowjacket Loop hits its only steep stretch on a series of forest switchbacks leading to the junction with the Flat Rock Mountain Trail (#1526), near yet another large meadow.

Yellowjacket Loop crosses an open meadow and heads into the forest to begin the hike.
ZACH URNESS

The sign at Flat Rock Trail junction says FLAT ROCK MOUNTAIN—1 MILE, but it's actually 0.8 mile. Flat Rock Mountain offers a compelling view of Hemlock Lake with the High Cascades rising up behind (see "Options").

Just beyond Flat Rock junction comes Yellowjacket Glade, where the path breaks out of the woods into an immense dry meadow, looks south into the South Umpqua drainage for the first time, and then quickly ascends a ridgetop with a fine view of Flat Rock Mountain to the north.

The highlight here is not Mount Bailey, on the horizon to the east, or Mount McLoughlin, on the horizon to the south, but Quartz Mountain (5,500 feet). Quartz Mountain is marked by steep bluffs, little vegetation, and what looks like volcanic ash deposits from a recent eruption on its flat summit. The "ash" is actually tailings from a quartz mine, one of the few mines in the Cascades that doesn't remove pumice or gravel.

Until a few years ago, the quartz was used in the smelting process in the Riddle Mountain (Hannah) nickel mine in the Siskiyous southwest of Roseburg, the only operating nickel mine in the United States. When the Riddle Mountain mine closed down, they began selling the quartz to a glass manufacturer.

At mile 2.9 from the trailhead, the path reenters the woods and climbs a small forested hillock, the vista point advertised on one of the trail signs. It's not much of

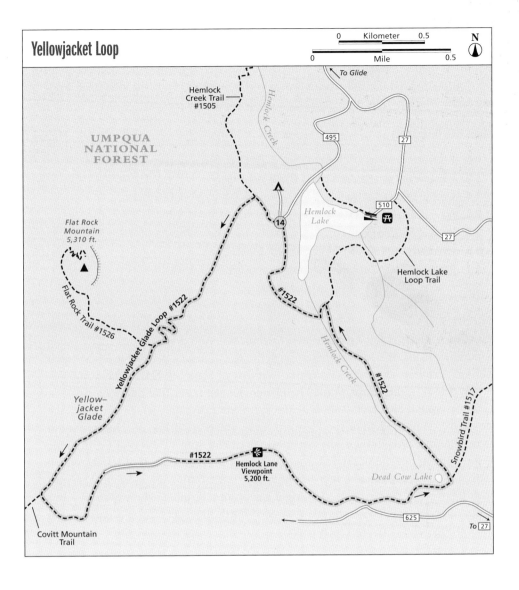

Yellowjacket Loop

0   Kilometer   0.5

0   Mile   0.5

N

To Glide

Hemlock
Creek Trail
#1505

Hemlock Creek

495   27

UMPQUA
NATIONAL
FOREST

510

Hemlock
Lake

27

Flat Rock
Mountain
5,310 ft.

14

Hemlock Lake
Loop Trail

Flat Rock Trail #1526

Yellowjacket Glade Loop #1522

#1522

#1522

Hemlock Creek

Snowbird Trail #1517

Yellow-
jacket
Glade

#1522

Hemlock Lane
Viewpoint
5,200 ft.

Dead Cow Lake

625

Covitt Mountain
Trail

To 27

a vista, but it offers the trail's only view of Hemlock Lake. This is the loop's highest point. At 5,250 feet, it is less than 100 feet lower than Flat Rock Mountain.

Soon after the vista point, the path hits a real road briefly, at mile 3.5. The sign there has been knocked down in the past. If confused, head uphill just left of the road.

The path turns away from the ridgetop at mile 4 and starts downhill through an area of magnificent old growth to Dead Cow Lake. The name "Dead Cow" actually makes this 0.25-acre cesspool sound nicer than it is. The pond resembles a tallow vat where they boil dead animals (including cows) to make candle wax. The water is stagnant and a horrible gray.

The route soon passes the beginning of the Snowbird Trail (#1517), on the right.

The path back to Hemlock Lake is straight, short, and in the woods until you hit bottom at mile 5.0, at the junction with the Hemlock Lake Loop Trail (not numbered).

You then spend 0.5 mile making your way around the huge meadow that drops down into the lake. The loop ends exactly where it started.

Miles and Directions

0.0 Begin at the campground trailhead and go right (counterclockwise) to begin the loop.

1.2 Pass junction with Flat Rock Trail (1.0 mile to summit).

1.4 Arrive at Yellowjacket Glade.

2.9 Arrive at the Hemlock Lake vista point.

3.5 Brush against the road.

3.9 Pass Dead Cow Lake and the junction with Snowbird Trail.

4.7 Reach the junction with Hemlock Lake Loop; go left.

5.3 Arrive at the end of the loop and your starting point.

Options

Flat Rock Trail: If you have time, this 1.0-mile side path is lots of fun. After crossing a meadowy saddle, the path ascends through the woods from 4,800 feet to a 5,310-foot summit. A clifftop aerie offers a dramatic overview of Hemlock Lake and beyond.

Hemlock Lake Loop Trail: The Hemlock Lake Loop Trail offers an easy 2.0-mile trip around Hemlock Lake. It begins at the east boat ramp, which you can reach via car by going straight at the Hemlock Lake junction on FR 27. Heading south (left), the path runs through the meadows south and west of the lake for 0.7 mile before joining the end of the Yellowjacket Loop. Turn right onto Trail #1522, which returns to the campground after 0.5 mile (1.2 miles from the trailhead). The path then follows the campground road (right again) for 0.3 mile to the west boat ramp. From there, the route hugs the lake's wooded north shore for 0.5 mile, returning to the starting point at the east boat ramp.

15 Fall Creek Falls

Lush, mossy canyon full of massive boulders (one of which you walk through) to a doubled-tiered waterfall. Option for a second, almost as spectacular, hike nearby.

Distance: 1.6-mile out and back
Difficulty: Easy
Elevation gain: 429 feet
Best season: Year-round
Maps: USGS Steamboat; Umpqua National Forest

Trail contacts: Umpqua National Forest—North Umpqua Ranger District: (541) 496-3532
Parking and trailhead facilities: Vault toilet and room for about 20 cars
Special considerations: Can be muddy and slippery in winter and spring

Finding the trailhead: From I-5 in Roseburg, take exit 124 for the North Umpqua River and OR 138. Follow signs for Diamond Lake through downtown Roseburg and then follow OR 138 east for 32 miles. Just past milepost 32 is a large and obvious parking area and trailhead on your left. **Trailhead GPS:** N43 18.801' / W122 50.125'

The base of Fall Creek Falls forms a misty grotto. ZACH URNESS

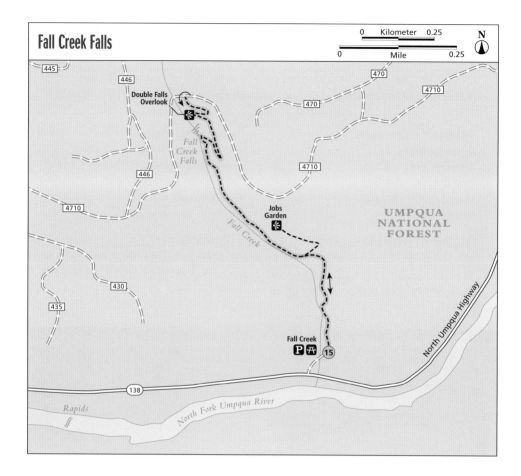

Fall Creek Falls

The Hike

For a short, easy, beautiful waterfall hike, Fall Creek Falls is tough to beat. The trailhead, easy to reach and open year-round, traverses a moss-draped canyon of house-size boulders and encounters an enchanted pool at the waterfall's base before heading uphill to a viewpoint of the fall's double tiers.

The trail begins by crossing a wooden footbridge across Fall Creek, a tributary of the North Umpqua. Not long after crossing the bridge, the trail squeezes into the narrow crack of a massive boulder, so hikers can appreciate how it feels to be inside a rock.

After 0.2 mile the trail passes a junction with Jobs Garden Trail on the right, which leads to the base of a basalt columnar rock outcropping in just a few hundred feet. It's worth checking out on the way back.

The main trail follows the creek upstream for 0.5 mile to the misty pool at the waterfall's base. This is a fine place to stop, but if you follow the trail uphill 0.2 mile more, you'll reach an overlook of the fall's double tier. The trail ends at FR 4710.

Miles and Directions

0.0 Begin at Fall Creek Falls Trailhead by crossing a wooden footbridge.

0.2 Pass the Jobs Garden Trail junction.

0.5 Arrive at the base of Fall Creek Falls.

0.7 Arrive at the Double Falls overlook.

0.8 Reach FR 4710; return the way you came.

1.6 Arrive back at the trailhead

Options

Susan Creek Falls: Since you're in the area, why not check out a hike and waterfall almost as impressive as Fall Creek Falls? The trailhead is at mile marker 28.2 on the left side of OR 138, just across from Susan Creek Campground.

The trail runs 1.6 miles to a 50-foot waterfall dropping into a bowl made of moss-lined cliffs. If reaching the falls isn't enough, a rough and difficult trail continues 0.4 mile to the Susan Creek Indian Mounds. In this spot, Native American boys approaching manhood built stone piles and spent the night in search of a vision from a guardian spirit.

16 Twin Lakes

A wonderful drive in the densely forested mountains above the North Umpqua River, followed by an easy, short hike through meadows, old-growth forest, and an excellent vista point to a pair of beautiful lakes.

Distance: 2.2-mile out and back
Difficulty: Easy
Elevation gain: 237 feet
Best season: June–Oct
Maps: USGS Twin Lakes Mountain and Illahee Rock; Umpqua National Forest

Trail contacts: Umpqua National Forest–North Umpqua Ranger District: (541) 496-3532
Parking and trailhead facilities: There's parking for 10 cars at the trailhead, more on the road shoulder.
Special considerations: This trail is fairly popular. Mosquitoes are very bad until midsummer.

Finding the trailhead: From I-5 in Roseburg, take exit 124 for the North Umpqua River and OR 138. Follow signs for Diamond Lake through downtown Roseburg and follow OR 138 east to milepost 49. The Twin Lakes turnoff is well marked on the right (FR 4770). Continue 10 miles, with occasional outstanding panoramas of the North Umpqua Canyon, to the trailhead, a small but beautiful green opening in the surrounding old-growth Douglas- and noble fir forest.
Trailhead GPS: N43 13.440' / W122 34.726'

The Hike

There is something surprisingly serene about this trail, even with the mosquitoes and the other hikers. Maybe it's the shaded north slope; maybe it's the persistent green; maybe it's the old-growth forests. What the trek lacks in length, it makes up for in emotional pull. The vista point and lake aren't bad either.

From the trailhead, the path crosses a large salal, fern, and forest covered flat and then traverses the side of a steep slope before arriving at a level spot atop a cliff at mile 0.5. The view of Deception Creek and the North Umpqua canyon is memorable.

It's hard to pull yourself away, but it gets better. After crossing a gentle crest at mile 0.7 and brushing a side trail at mile 0.8, the path crosses the Twin Lakes Mountain Trail in the middle of a large open area at mile 0.9.

Big Twin Lake shows up at mile 1.1. There is an old shelter and a picnic table on a little hill above the lake. Big Twin Lake covers 14 acres, is 48 feet deep, and is stocked with brook trout. A network of trails around the lake leads to Little Twin Lake, 6 acres, 30 feet deep, and 0.2 mile away.

Twin Lakes is an easy hike high up in the densely forested mountains above the North Umpqua canyon. Many vistas and two beautiful lakes. LYNN BERNSTEIN

Miles and Directions

0.0 Begin at the trailhead.

0.5 Arrive at an overlook of North Umpqua Canyon.

0.9 Cross the Twin Lake Mountain Trail.

1.1 Reach the picnic table and shelter at East Twin Lake; return the way you came.

2.2 Arrive back at the trailhead.

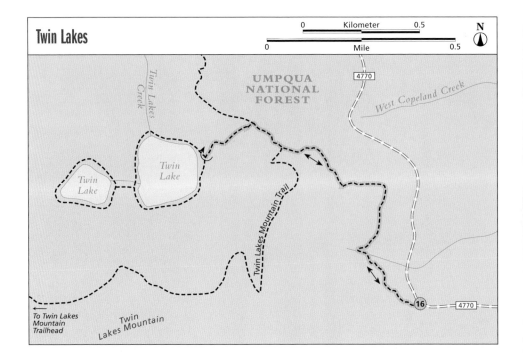

Options

The Twin Lakes Mountain Trail is reached via a 25-mile network of roads from Glide, off OR 138 up the Little River Road. The path drops 800 feet and reaches Big Twin Lake in 2.5 miles.

17 Pine Bench

A steep wilderness hike up an immense river bluff to an enchanted flat, through fire-scorched landscape in the Boulder Creek Wilderness.

Distance: 7.0-mile out and back
Difficulty: Strenuous
Elevation gain: 1,757 feet
Best season: Year-round
Maps: USGS Toketee Falls and Illahe Rock; Umpqua National Forest
Trail contacts: North Umpqua Ranger District: (541) 496-3532

Parking and trailhead facilities: The small parking area has room for about 10 cars along the North Umpqua River.
Special considerations: The bench can become very hot in summer, and there is little shade. While there is plenty of water, purifying it is a good idea. Water from the spring at Pine Bench is delicious. Check for ticks in spring and early summer.

Finding the trailhead: From I-5 in Roseburg, take exit 124 for the North Umpqua River and OR 138. Follow signs for Diamond Lake through downtown Roseburg and continue east on OR 138 to milepost 55. Turn left onto Road 4775. Almost immediately, turn left onto gravel Soda Springs Road, passing the dam and continuing a total of 3 miles to a trailhead at the end of the road alongside the North Umpqua River (you'll pass the Soda Springs Trailhead en route). The final 1 mile is quite rough.
Trailhead GPS: N43 18.299' / W122 31.448'

The Hike

Although this hike traverses much of the area burned during the 1996 Spring Fire, the unusual scenic and botanical interests make it a charmer.

If the scientific side isn't alluring enough, then the mountain views, backcountry camping spots, and hidden swimming holes are worth your time.

The best way to explore the 19,886-acre Boulder Creek wilderness is atop Pine Bench, which can be reached by two different trails: one that starts at Soda Springs Dam and one that begins at the North Umpqua Trailhead.

The authors suggest the North Umpqua Trailhead because the trail's shorter (though a bit longer drive). The hike begins on an old road, but after 0.2 mile you'll turn right at a sign for Boulder Creek Trail 1552 and begin heading up a long series of switchbacks. The trail climbs 1.4 miles and a steep 943 feet to a flat plateau of Pine Bench.

Upon arriving, you'll see ample evidence of the forest fire. In most areas the burn raced through the understory, slightly singing the bases of the conifer trees, which ultimately survived.

A history of repeated fires may be the reason for the abundance of pines at Pine Bench. Ponderosa pine shows up in the rainy North Umpqua valley only on extremely dry, sunny, low-elevation sites that have been burned over or clear-cut.

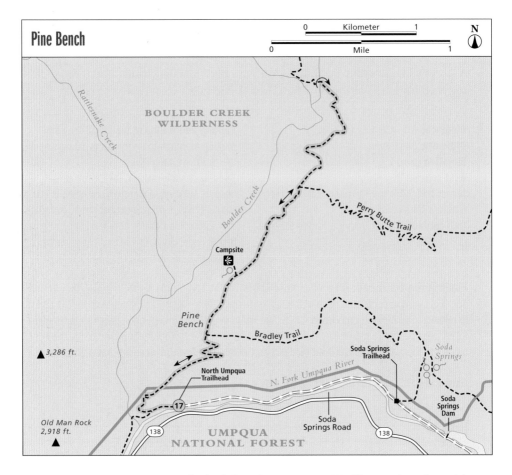

Once you're atop Pine Bench, the hiking becomes easy. You'll pass a junction with Bradley Trail (#1491) at mile 1.3 (see "Options" for a loop). Take the time to admire the area's wildflowers, which include delphinium, wild iris, houndstongue—and lots of poison oak.

For the campsite, spring, and overlook, turn left at an unsigned fork in the trail 0.3 mile from the Bradley–Boulder Creek junction. It's a couple of hundred feet on the side trail to a campsite with a stunning panorama of the Boulder Creek canyon from atop cliffs. The spring is slightly downhill to the left.

This makes a nice turnaround spot, and considering the elevation gain on the way in, the return trip is easy.

If you want to see Boulder Creek itself, venture onward, across more of Pine Flat, until the trail starts dropping downhill. The trail reaches the creek itself at mile 3.5. There's one nice campsite along the creek, and it makes an excellent place for swimming hole hunting.

Pools of glass-clear water between canyon walls can be found with some exploring, and these are heavenly spots on hot summer days (though, again, the forest is mostly burned).

The ponderosa pines for which Pine Bench is named can be found along the trail. ZACH URNESS

Miles and Directions

0.0 Begin at the North Umpqua Trailhead at the road's end.

0.2 Arrive at the junction for Boulder Creek Trail (#1552); turn right.

0.3 Pass the wilderness boundary.

1.3 Arrive at the junction with the Bradley Trail (#1491); continue straight.

1.7 Veer left and arrive at the Pine Bench campsite, spring, and overlook (popular turn-around spot).

3.5 Reach Boulder Creek; return the way you came.

7.0 Arrive back at the North Umpqua Trailhead.

Options

Boulder Creek–Bradley Loop: If you're willing to hike some of the road—or want to save your knees some of the steepness on the way home—an excellent loop is possible. On the way back, instead of dropping down toward the North Umpqua Trailhead, turn left onto Bradley Trail. The trail follows Pine Bench before heading downhill, running a total of 1.5 miles to a junction. At the junction, turn right and follow the trail 0.4 mile to the Soda Springs Trailhead that you passed on the way in. Follow the road 1.5 miles to your car at the road's end.

18 Toketee Falls

A short, easy walk to an unusual and stunningly beautiful waterfall.

Distance: 0.8-mile out and back
Difficulty: Easy
Elevation loss: 27 feet
Best season: Year-round
Maps: USGS Toketee Falls; Umpqua National Forest

Trail contacts: North Umpqua Ranger District: (541) 496-3532
Parking and trailhead facilities: The trailhead has room for 20 cars.
Special considerations: Watch children and pets very closely on the platform.

Finding the trailhead: From I-5 in Roseburg, take exit 124 for the North Umpqua River and OR 138. Follow signs for Diamond Lake through downtown Roseburg and continue east on OR 138 to milepost 59. Turn left onto Toketee Falls/FR 34. Keep left at the first junction and go 0.4 mile to a well-marked trailhead and parking area.
Trailhead GPS: N43 15.842'/W122 25.655'

The Hike

This is an easy path through a dense riparian forest of Douglas-fir, western hemlock, and western red cedar to one of the world's more impressive waterfalls. You hear the falls long before you see them.

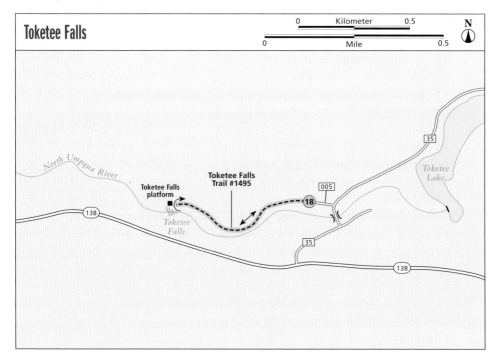

Toketee Falls can be seen from the viewing platform. ZACH URNESS

From the trailhead, the Toketee Falls Trail (#1495) winds through the woods briefly and then comes out atop a rock gorge just upstream from the falls. A series of steps on the trail, some stone and some wooden, lead over a low crest and then down to a viewing platform. There are ample guardrails.

Toketee Falls is a 120-foot plunge on the North Umpqua River. The first 40 feet drop into a collecting pool inside a strange and beautiful bowl of columnar basalt. The water spilling out of the bowl then falls another 80 feet before resuming its journey westward to Roseburg, Reedsport, and the Pacific Ocean.

The viewing platform was rebuilt a few years ago. The old platform perched danger-ously and never quite gave an adequate view. You came away feeling that the best angle for viewing Toketee Falls was from a helicopter in the middle of the river. The new platform offers a better view, accommodates more people, and is more structurally sound.

The North Umpqua Trail misses Toketee Falls because it turns away from the river immediately west (it had been running 0.2 mile inland anyhow) to make its way around Toketee Lake. Toketee Lake and Falls are the last connection either the North Umpqua Trail or the North Umpqua River has with OR 138.

Miles and Directions

0.0 Begin at the Toketee Falls Trailhead.

0.4 Reach the Toketee Falls platform; return the way you came.

0.8 Arrive back at the trailhead.

19 Watson Falls

A short, magnificent hike to Oregon's third-highest waterfall.

Distance: 1.0-mile out and back
Difficulty: Moderate
Elevation gain: 440 feet
Best season: Year-round
Map: USGS Fish Creek Desert; Umpqua National Forest

Trail contacts: North Umpqua Ranger District: (541) 496-3532
Parking and trailhead facilities: There are restrooms, picnic tables beside the creek, and a paved parking lot with room for 50 cars.

Finding the trailhead: From I-5 in Roseburg, take exit 124 for the North Umpqua River and OR 138. Follow signs for Diamond Lake through downtown Roseburg and continue east on OR 138 to milepost 61, then turn right (south) onto FR 37. The trailhead parking lot is just down FR 37.
Trailhead GPS: N43 14.733' / W122 23.493'

The Hike

Magnificent and unheralded, Watson Falls ranks not far behind Crater Lake as a Southern Oregon "must see" scenic attraction. Even if you take your time and savor every step, this enchanted little trail requires less than an hour out of your life. The falls are just off the North Umpqua Highway, 18 miles from Diamond Lake.

At 272 feet, Watson Falls is Oregon's third-highest waterfall. Salt Creek Falls, near Willamette Pass out of Eugene, beats it by a couple feet. Watson and Salt Creek Falls are the highest waterfalls between Multnomah Falls (620 feet) and California's Yosemite Valley (several over 1,000 feet).

The 300-foot-high escarpment responsible for Watson Falls is the nose of a giant lava flow that emanated from the Mount Bailey area some 750,000 years ago. You pass more of the giant cliffs, rising just to the south of OR 138 as you approach the Watson Falls turnoff from Diamond Lake.

The Watson Falls Trail (#1496) begins in the highly developed parking area and gets considerable use. After 200 feet, it crosses paved FR 37 and then takes up a position alongside Watson Creek. Bear left at the beginning of the loop. The path is fairly steep and winding and seems longer than 0.3 mile. It snakes its way around and over giant, moss-covered boulders and countless mini-waterfalls before emerging at a little wooden footbridge with a beautiful view of the plummeting falls. Whoever designed the bridge was very creative.

Above the footbridge, the main loop doubles back to the right. If you head left here, toward the falls on a side trail, you come to a switchback after 0.1 mile with a sign that says To Upper Vista Point. This is not a trail to the top of the cliff, as the name suggests. The fairly steep route ends up atop the moss-covered rubble pile next to the falls after 0.2 mile. By all means, check out this short trail.

Watson Falls drops 272 feet in the North Umpqua River canyon area. ZACH URNESS

At the UPPER VISTA POINT sign, you also have the option of following a rugged little way trail that charges straight ahead to the base of the falls and one of the most enchanting, spiritually uplifting rock grottoes you'll ever see. Just below the falls, a moss-covered boulder field litters the terrain, with the white creek braiding in and out through a dozen channels. Use this route if you want to actually experience the base of the falls. None of these trails is very long, and all are highly recommended.

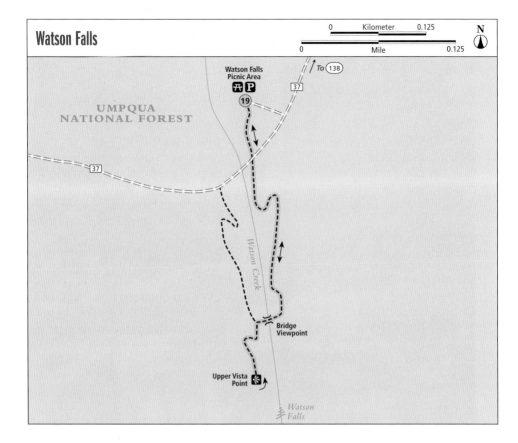

Watson Falls

Watson Falls Picnic Area

UMPQUA NATIONAL FOREST

Watson Creek

Bridge Viewpoint

Upper Vista Point

Watson Falls

To 138

37

19

37

0   Kilometer   0.125

0   Mile   0.125

N

Miles and Directions

0.0 Begin at the Watson Falls Trailhead.

0.1 Cross the paved road, and bear left on the loop.

0.3 Arrive at the footbridge with a view of Watson Falls.

0.4 Reach the loop turnaround. Begin the short uphill trail to the upper vista point.

0.5 Arrive at upper vista point; return the way you came.

1.0 Arrive back at the trailhead.

Options

Loop Trail: Most people who hike to Watson Falls return the way they came instead of completing the loop. If you do stay on the loop, the return leg takes you back to the trailhead a little more quickly than the way you came in, but it lacks the dramatic views of the cascading creek and giant boulders. There is no crosswalk where the far end of the loop trail meets FR 37, so you have to walk along the road for a short distance.

20 Dread and Terror / Umpqua Hot Springs

Two easy hikes in one. A trek past cold waterfalls and old-growth forest, followed by a visit to a natural hot spring and an optional soak. An Oregon classic.

Distance: 4.0-mile out and back
Difficulty: Easy
Elevation gain: Minimal
Best season: Apr–Nov
Maps: USGS Potter Mountain; Umpqua National Forest
Trail contacts: Umpqua National Forest: (541) 496-3532

Parking and trailhead facilities: The Umpqua Hot Springs parking area accommodates 20 cars. There's a pit toilet at the parking area and a couple of campsites.
Special considerations: A sign informs people heading to Umpqua Hot Springs to expect nudity.

Finding the trailhead: From I-5 in Roseburg take exit 124 for OR 138. Follow signs for Diamond Lake through downtown Roseburg and follow OR 138 east for 59 miles. At milepost 59, turn left onto the Toketee Lake turnoff (FR 34) and proceed 2 miles up the paved road. Then turn right onto gravel FR 3401 (Thorn Prairie Road) and follow it 2 miles to a large and obvious parking area on the left.
Trailhead GPS: N43 17.611' / W122 21.901'

The Hike

The Dread and Terror / Umpqua Hot Springs Trailhead provides the chance to explore a truly stunning section of the North Umpqua Trail and then enjoy a soak in open-air hot springs while watching the river roll past. Not a bad way to spend the day.

Start with the North Umpqua Trail's "Dread and Terror" section, a name that comes from a nondescript hill just to the south that evokes neither dread nor terror and isn't even particularly interesting. The name does not come from pioneer encounters with murder or mayhem, sightings of ghosts or monsters, or menacing by crazed or mythical animals. It refers to the whitethorn ceanothus bushes for which Thorn Prairie, the flat between Dread and Terror Ridge and the North Umpqua canyon, is named. Apparently forest workers found the thorns dreadful and terrifying to work in.

The first mile on the Dread and Terror section of the North Umpqua Trail (#1414) may be the most beautiful mile on the entire North Umpqua Trail. After leaving the trailhead, you pass a magnificent campsite on the river's edge, downhill to the left, and a huge gushing spring.

Next comes Columnar Falls, an outcrop of columnar basalt covered with moss. A gentle trickle of water oozes over the 50-foot rock face, weaving in and out of the columns and sending out a pleasant, cooling spray.

At mile 0.5 the path passes an enchanted grotto with a small footbridge and a fairly large waterfall. No matter how hot and muggy the weather, when you pass this

The Dread and Terror stretch of the North Umpqua River Trail travels above the North Umpqua River. ZACH URNESS

falls, the temperature momentarily drops 30 degrees, with a steady wind blowing from the crashing water to your face. It feels like an air conditioner.

The path comes to another footbridge over a beautiful, cascading creek that forms Blue Pool (0.7 mile), a pool that seems to glow an eerie iceberg blue in the midst of the churning and bubbling.

The next mile, and in fact the next 13 miles from Umpqua Hot Springs to the Lemolo Lake Trailhead, passes hundreds of small springs, trickles, seeps, and wet spots. The reason for all this emerging water is that the water table is very close to the surface; when the trail builders dug into the steep hillside, they tapped into frequent underground flows.

Beyond Blue Pool, the scenery settles down somewhat, although the next mile still is a gorgeous walk that occasionally drops down to the river's edge, then climbs 50 to 100 feet up the canyon, only to drop down again soon after.

A good place to turn around is Michelle Creek, just before the 2.0-mile mark, where a spring virtually floods the trail and it's difficult to keep your shoes dry.

When you're done with the chilly springs of Dread and Terror, return to the main parking area and trailhead to take a relaxing dip in the hot springs that sit atop a ledge overlooking the North Umpqua River. These famed pools were visited by the Western writer Zane Grey and require a steep but only 0.3-mile hike.

The springs sit atop a large limestone formation above the river, created by deposits from the calcite-laden water that flows from the spring. A wooden open-air lean-to covers the largest of the three hot-water pools (seating six or eight people). The smaller pools (seating about three each) are completely exposed.

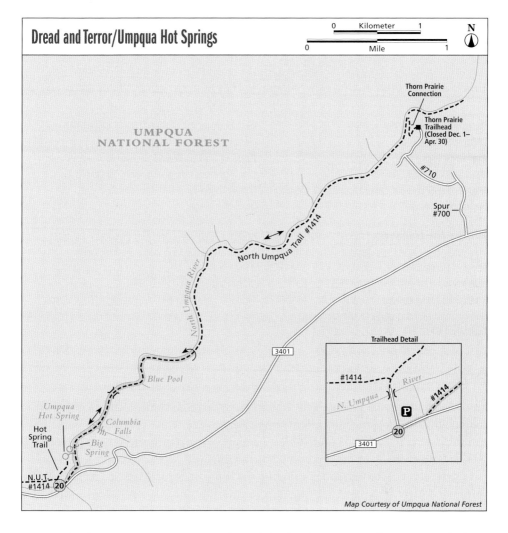

Dread and Terror/Umpqua Hot Springs

0 Kilometer 1

0 Mile 1

N

UMPQUA
NATIONAL FOREST

Thorn Prairie
Connection

Thorn Prairie
Trailhead
(Closed Dec. 1–
Apr. 30)

#710

Spur
#700

North Umpqua Trail #1414

North Umpqua River

3401

Blue Pool

Umpqua
Hot Spring

Columbia
Falls

Hot
Spring
Trail

Big
Spring

N.U.T.
#1414 20

Trailhead Detail

#1414

N. Umpqua

River

#1414

P

20

3401

Map Courtesy of Umpqua National Forest

The hot springs are quite popular. While the forest service has no record of any problems with the large number of visitors, the springs are unattended; bathers use them at their own risk. Anyone hiking to the hot springs should be prepared for nudity, as many folks choose to enjoy the heated water in their birthday suits.

Miles and Directions

0.0 Begin on the North Umpqua Trail's Dread and Terror section, heading north.

0.4 Pass Columnar Falls.

0.5 Arrive at a footbridge, creek crossing, and waterfall.

0.7 Reach a waterfall and Blue Pool.

2.0 Reach Michelle Creek; return the way you came.

4.0 Arrive back at the trailhead.

21 Lemolo Falls

A remote and steep trail to the base of a thundering 108-foot waterfall on the North Umpqua River. Option for a view of Lemolo Falls from the other side of the river.

Distance: 2.4-mile out and back
Difficulty: Moderate
Elevation loss/gain: 582 feet
Best season: Apr–Nov
Maps: USGS Lemolo Lake; Umpqua National Forest

Trail contacts: Diamond Lake Ranger District: (541) 498-2531
Parking and trailhead facilities: The trailhead is a logging landing with room for 3 to 5 cars. Follow the closed-off road, which eventually becomes a trail.

Finding the trailhead: Take OR 138, the North Umpqua Highway, east from Roseburg (or west from Diamond Lake) to milepost 73 and the Lemolo Lake turnoff on FR 2610. Follow this road about 4 miles until you reach gravel FR 3401 (Thorn Prairie Road). As the paved road swings right, veer left on this gravel road for 0.5 mile and turn right onto unmarked Spur 800. Continue on Road 800 for about 1.5 miles to a sign for Lemolo Falls Trail on Spur 840 on the right. This narrow, bumpy road leads quickly to the trailhead.
Trailhead GPS: N43 20.422' / W122 13.434'

The Hike

From the trailhead, the Lemolo Falls Trail (#1468) descends gently along an old road through a partial logging cut (mostly white fir, western white pine, and mountain hemlock). After 0.4 mile the route makes a couple of sharp turns, becomes a genuine trail, and enters the steep canyon of the North Umpqua.

There are lots of rhododendrons in the canyon, which are spectacular in spring and early summer. There are also tons of mosquitoes, especially in spring and early summer,

After a long switchback, the path hits the river and the falls come into view. They're not quite a plunge (free-falling water), since the white liquid hugs the rock surface most of the way down. But the falls are immense—108 feet high, with tremendous water volume much of the year. The path goes to the base of the falls, with its emerald collecting pool, constant cold breeze, and soaring mist. The walk back to your car is much more difficult than the walk in.

Miles and Directions

0.0 Begin at the Lemolo Falls Trailhead.

1.2 Reach the base of Lemolo Falls; return the way you came.

2.4 Arrive back at the trailhead

Lemolo Falls is a massive waterfall on the North Umpqua River and can be reached via a steep but short hike. ZACH URNESS

Options

North Umpqua Trail to top of falls: It's 1.5 miles from the Lemolo Lake Trailhead of the North Umpqua Trail, located on the paved FR 2610 off OR 138, just past the Lemolo Lake Dam (turn left after passing the dam). This is a beautiful walk, although it has a nasty habit of descending to the river, then climbing far up the canyon only to descend again. It does this two or three times in 1.5 miles. The North Umpqua Trail passes several low but impressive waterfalls before skirting the top of Lemolo Falls.

Warm Springs Falls: As long as you're visiting waterfalls near Lemolo Lake, don't miss Warm Springs Falls. They plunge 70 feet over an immense vertical rock face of columnar basalt, much like Toketee Falls but without the rock bowl and upper falls.

To reach Warm Springs Falls, continue on FR 2610 for 2 miles past the Lemolo Lake Trailhead to a paved (briefly) spur road to the left (Spur 680), where FR 2610 swings sharply right. It's exactly 1.7 miles on Spur 680 to the Warm Springs Falls Trailhead, which can be difficult to find. In the middle of a large, level conifer plantation, look for a very small turnout on the right, with the trailhead directly opposite on the left. Spur 680 crosses Warms Springs Creek 0.5 mile later.

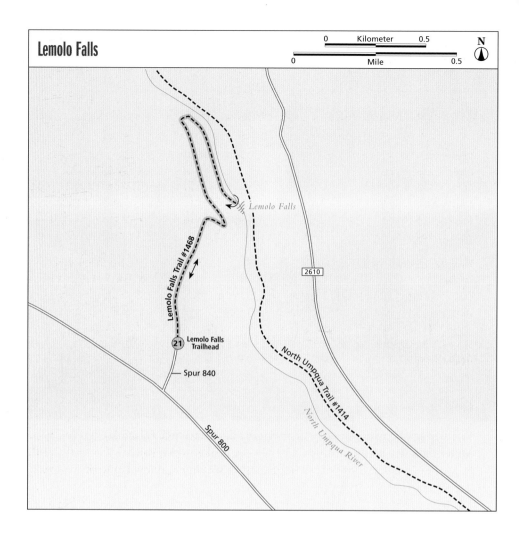

The 0.3-mile (or less), perfectly level Warms Springs Falls Trail (#1499) ends near the top of the falls, which has a huge amount of water for a side creek. For the best view, look for a short, steep, slippery side trail leading to an abrupt ledge directly above the falls. There is no guardrail, so be careful. Back on the main trail, continue another 100 yards to the trail end and a much safer, if less spectacular, vista.

22 Miller to Maidu Lake

A pair of clear blue lakes in the High Cascades and a hike to the source of the North Umpqua River. Great fishing in early summer.

Distance: 7.4-mile out and back
Difficulty: Moderate
Elevation gain: 955 feet
Best season: Late June–Oct
Maps: USGS Mount Thielsen; Fremont-Winema National Forest

Trail contacts: Winema National Forest– Chemult Ranger District: (541) 365-7001
Parking and trailhead facilities: There is a long parking area with room for around 40 cars.
Special considerations: Mosquitoes are thick through July and early August.

Finding the trailhead: From Klamath Falls, head north on US 97 for 70 miles to the town of Chemult, northeast of Diamond and Crater Lakes, and continue north of town for 0.5 mile. Between mileposts 202 and 203, turn left onto Miller Lake Road (FR 9772). Follow this wide gravel road 12.2 miles to Digit Point Campground. Stay left on the entrance road and park at the large parking area along the lakeshore near a picnic area. The trailhead is located on the left edge of the picnic area. (This trailhead marks the very end of the 79-mile North Umpqua Trail.)
Trailhead GPS: N43 13.741'/W121 58.104'

The Hike

The vast majority of people who make the drive to Digit Point Campground and Miller Lake are coming to fish. The 600-acre lake in the volcanic flatlands north of Mount Thielsen is popular among anglers seeking rainbow trout, brown trout, and kokanee.

Explore this area a little more carefully—perhaps with a fishing rod in your hand—by hiking around Miller Lake and up through the glacier-carved basin to Maidu Lake, the source of the North Umpqua River. Beware of a dense mosquito population prior to late August.

From the picnic area trailhead, the path follows Miller Lake's southwest shoreline past a few creeks and groves of wildflowers in summer. After 1.0 mile the trail reaches the upper end of the lake, crosses Evening Creek on a footbridge, and comes to a junction. To the right the route continues on a 5.0 mile loop around the lakeshore (see "Options"). Go left for Maidu Lake and into the Mount Thielsen Wilderness.

The trail follows Evening Creek for a bit before shooting uphill, climbing a few hundred feet, with vistas of Miller Lake in its large basin below.

At mile 2.7 you arrive at the junction with the Pacific Crest Trail (PCT). The best viewpoint of Miller Lake can be found about 0.5 mile to the right, down the PCT. Otherwise, continue 1.0 mile more to the pretty blue shoreline of Maidu

The trail along Miller Lake provides views of the water and offers the chance to do some fishing.
ZACH URNESS

Lake (20 acres, 12 feet deep). A trail circles the lake and provides a view of the North Umpqua River's birthplace, as well as some nice fishing spots.

The Maidu were an indigenous tribe who lived in the central Sierra Nevada in California, in the vicinity of the Feather and American Rivers.

Miles and Directions

0.0   Begin at the Digit Point Campground Trailhead.

1.0   Arrive at Maidu Lake junction. Go left.

1.2   Cross the wilderness boundary.

2.7   Pass the PCT junction.

3.7   Arrive at Maidu Lake; return the way you came.

7.4   Arrive back at the trailhead.

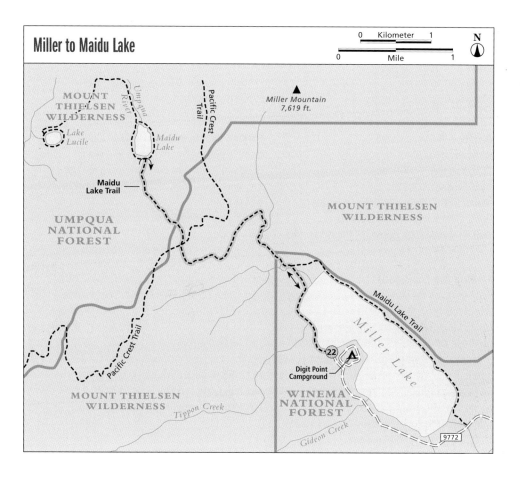

Miller to Maidu Lake

Options

Miller Lake Loop: Many anglers hike or ride their bikes around the 5.0-mile loop of Miller Lake to various fishing spots. To take this route, head right at the Maidu Lake junction. The trail is almost completely level.

   Lake Lucile. If you're up for exploring one more small blue lake, continue past Maidu Lake a little less than 2.0 miles to Lake Lucile. The route provides some of the area's best mountain views.

23 Upper Rogue Canyon / Rough Rider Falls

Fantastic, waterfall-laden canyon cut by the Rogue River into Mount Mazama ash. May be done as a longer one-way shuttle or shorter out-and-back hike.

Distance: 8.4-mile shuttle
Difficulty: Moderate
Elevation loss: 1,800 feet
Best season: June–Oct
Maps: USGS Pumice Desert and Hamaker Butte; Umpqua National Forest
Trail contacts: High Cascades Ranger District: (541) 560-3400

Parking and trailhead facilities: Northern: There is parking for 30 cars in a paved lot. Southern: Eight cars can park along the shoulder. Hamaker Campground is 1 mile away by trail or road.
Special considerations: Narrow side canyons may be clogged with snow long after the area appears to be snow-free. Plenty of water.

Finding the trailheads: Mount Mazama Viewpoint Trailhead (upper): From Medford take OR 62 north to Union Creek. Where OR 62 swings right toward Crater Lake, past milepost 57, continue straight on OR 230 toward Diamond Lake. The northern trailhead is located at milepost 19, at the Mount Mazama Viewpoint Trailhead parking area.
Trailhead GPS: N43 05.446' / W122 13.280'
   Hamaker Campground Trailhead (lower): For the southern trailhead, turn off OR 230 past milepost 12 onto FR 6530. Continue straight on FR 6530 for 1 mile, past the Hamaker Campground turnoff, and proceed to the river crossing. The northbound trail takes off 0.1 mile before the bridge, uphill to the left, a few hundred feet beyond the southbound trailhead.
Trailhead GPS: N43 03.925' / W122 19.448'

The Hike

The shuttle hike from the Mount Mazama Viewpoint Trailhead to Hamaker Campground may be the most scenic segment of the Upper Rogue River Trail. The contrast between the river's crashing roar and the stillness of ash canyons, plus the smell of pine on warm days, is heavenly (though the sound of the highway is an occasional annoyance).

To start the full hike, begin from the Mazama Viewpoint parking area and drop 0.5 mile to the Boundary Spring Trail junction, marked by a small wooden sign on a tree.

Shortly beyond the junction, the trail descends steep ash slopes to the water's edge and then chugs back up to the high plateau.

The next mile is spectacular as the gray ash bluffs soon evolve into a memorable gorge. The loose, barren ash and pumice of the canyon walls shoot downward to a vertical drop-off above the water. A maze of pinnacles and eroded ridges jut from the bottom, while the river courses through narrow crevices and over cascading waterfalls. All this occurs less than 4.0 miles from Boundary Springs, the source of the Rogue.

Rough Rider Falls rumbles through the Upper Rogue River gorge. ZACH URNESS

The trail follows a flat-top bench for 1.5 miles, then dips down to Cascade Creek.

For 2.3 miles beyond Cascade Creek, the path continues along a level bench among Shasta red fir, lodgepole pine, mountain hemlock, and western white pine before a long descent to Rough Rider Falls, the trail's highlight at mile 5.2 (or 3.2 miles from Hamaker Campground Trailhead).

The noise deafens, the spray exhilarates, and the scene enchants as a brilliant green mossy rock face frames the falling water. For a good look, you must leave the trail briefly. It's a wonderful lunch spot.

Past Rough Rider Falls, the route follows a narrow, densely wooded canyon bottom. Douglas-fir, western hemlock, grand fir, white fir, incense cedar, and sugar pine begin to sneak in, along with evergreen chinquapin. Willow and alder brush line the streambanks, as they do from Boundary Springs to the ocean.

Eventually you'll pass a smaller, but still impressive, unnamed waterfall. Past this spot, the trail ascends the much gentler hillside along the river to FR 6530, a total of 8.4 miles from the Mount Mazama Viewpoint Trailhead.

If you do the shorter, out-and-back hike from Hamaker Campground to Rough Rider falls (see "Options" below), the description is the same except in reverse.

Upper Rogue Canyon/Rough Rider Falls

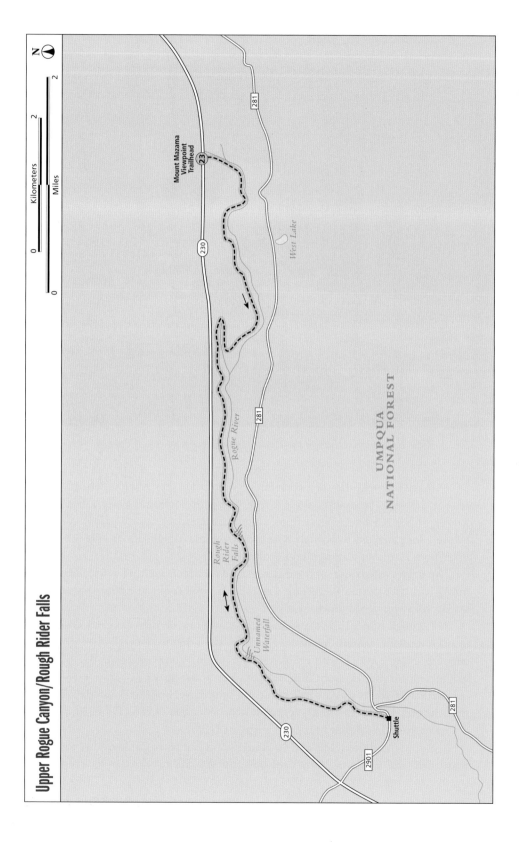

N

Kilometers
0   2

Miles
0   2

230

281

Mount Mazama
Viewpoint
Trailhead

23

West Lake

Rogue River

281

Rough
Rider
Falls

Unnamed
Waterfall

UMPQUA
NATIONAL FOREST

230

Shuttle

2901

281

Miles and Directions

0.0 Begin at the Mount Mazama Viewpoint Trailhead.

0.5 Pass the Upper Rogue Trail / Boundary Spring Trail junction. Go straight.

1.1 Pass the Rogue River access.

2.9 Cross Cascade Creek.

5.2 Reach Rough Rider Falls.

8.4 Arrive at FR 6530, the southern trailhead and end of the hike.

Options

Out and back to Rough Rider Falls: For a shorter hike involving only one vehicle, start at the Hamaker Campground Trailhead on Road 6530 for a 6.4-mile out-and-back trek past two beautiful waterfalls—the second of which is the moss-covered 60-foot cascade of Rough Rider Falls.

24 National Creek Falls

A very short trail to a huge waterfall.

Distance: 1.2-mile out and back
Difficulty: Moderate
Elevation loss: 283 feet
Best season: May–Nov
Maps: USGS Hamaker Butte; Rogue River–Siskiyou National Forest

Trail contacts: Prospect Ranger District: (541) 560-3400
Parking and trailhead facilities: There's room for 10 cars in the gravel parking lot.

Finding the trailhead: From Medford take OR 62 north to Union Creek. Where OR 62 swings right toward Crater Lake, past milepost 57, continue straight on OR 230 toward Diamond Lake. Past milepost 6, take FR 6530 (National Creek Road). The trailhead is 4 miles up, on the right, with lots of signs. Continue 0.1 mile up a spur road to the parking area.
Trailhead GPS: N43 01.905' / W122 20.826'

The Hike

After 1 mile, National Creek Road dips down across the Rogue and then climbs onto an immense plateau, uncharacteristically flat even for an ash deposit, with high

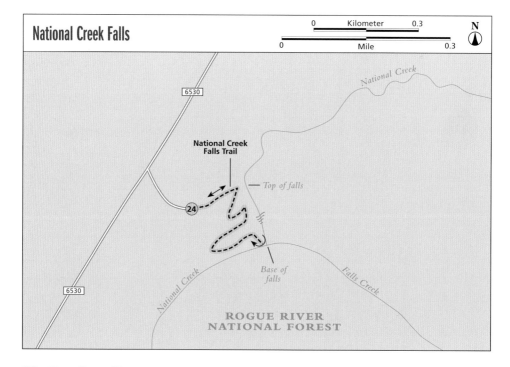

National Creek Falls drops through the forest near the Upper Rogue River. LYNN BERNSTEIN

mountains rising in the background. The arrow-straight road takes you to a parking area in the middle of the flat, where the sign says NATIONAL CREEK FALLS TRAIL—1053. Within a minute you're walking down the steep sides of a narrow, shaded gorge. A glance at the USGS topo map shows that all streams in the vicinity flow through narrow, shaded, steep-sided gorges.

It takes two long switchbacks for the path to drop down through the dense woods to the top of the falls at National Creek, and two longer switchbacks to reach the bottom of the 100-foot tumble. Since it's only 0.6 mile to the bottom, it would be hard to rate this trail as "strenuous," even if it were ten times steeper.

One thing to remember about this country, with its narrow canyons that receive little sunlight, is that the snow lingers in the canyons far longer than it does on top.

On the hike back, be sure to take the short side trail to the top of the falls.

Late spring is a good time to visit, because that's when the water is its most thunderous. However, it's also when the canyon has the most mosquitoes. The falls fan out over a pyramidal rock face with a split flow in the middle, collecting in a large pool. In spring you can't get very close to the falls because of wind and spray, but that dies down somewhat by late summer.

Miles and Directions

0.0 Begin at the trailhead.

0.6 Arrive at bottom of falls; start back toward the trailhead.

0.7 Take the short side trip to the top of the falls.

1.2 Arrive back at the trailhead and parking lot.

25 Natural Bridge / Farewell Bend

Spectacular vistas, rock gorges, and a geological oddity along a secluded path. Popular shorter options.

Distance: 7.2-mile shuttle
Difficulty: Moderate
Elevation gain/loss: 1,187 feet
Best season: May–Nov
Maps: USGS Union Creek; Rogue River–Siskiyou National Forest

Trail contacts: Prospect Ranger District: (541) 560 3400
Parking and trailhead facilities: Natural Bridge Trailhead: Bathroom and campground. Parking for 30 or so cars. Forest Road 6510: Restroom at adjacent campground.

Finding the trailhead: Natural Bridge Campground (southern): From Medford take OR 62 past Prospect to the Natural Bridge Campground near milepost 54. Turn onto the campground road, bearing left after 0.3 mile toward the interpretive sign and parking area (0.2 mile). There's a restroom and parking for 50 cars. Access the northbound trail, to Natural Bridge and beyond, by crossing the bridge.
Trailhead GPS: N42 53.315' / W122 27.889'

FR 6510 trailhead (northern): Continue on OR 62 north from Natural Bridge onto OR 230 toward Diamond Lake. One mile later, turn left onto gravel FR 6510 (to Herschberger lookout). Continue 0.5 mile to the trailhead, on the left.
Trailhead GPS: N42 56.431' / W122 25.572' (Road 6510)

The Hike

This segment of the Upper Rogue Trail passes one of the river's most famous formations, Natural Bridge, where the river briefly disappears before reappearing downstream.

Featured here is a 7.2-mile one-way trek that requires a shuttle to FR 6510. But there is an optional and easy 2.4-mile loop that begins and ends at Natural Bridge Campground. Both are fine choices for enjoying this natural wonder and the surrounding landscape

Both options begin at the large parking area next to Natural Bridge Campground. Over the footbridge, follow the paved Natural Bridge Trail for 0.2 mile to an observation deck overlooking the river's disappearing act. According to the forest service, the river follows a network of underground lava tubes. Such tubes, which riddle volcanic areas, are formed when the outer surface of flowing lava hardens while the still-molten interior continues moving.

Most people turn back here, but why waste a perfectly good day in the woods? Continue on the unpaved Upper Rogue Trail to mile 1.2 and another beautiful spot where the river churns through a narrow canyon and a wooden footbridge crosses

The Rogue River performs an odd trick when it disappears into lava tubes and comes out the other side at a geologic spot called Natural Bridge. ZACH URNESS

to the opposite bank. (**Option:** If you're here for the short loop, cross the footbridge, turn right on the Rogue Gorge Trail, and pass Natural Bridge Campground sites back to the parking area and your car.)

To continue on the featured one-way route through a more secluded section of trail to FR 6510, admire the bridge but don't cross it, and continue upstream.

The next few miles are quite pleasant, crossing Flat Creek via a downed log at mile 2.3 and heading uphill, along another miniature canyon, before the trail veers away from the river at the Rogue Gorge (which you can hear but not see).

After 4.8 miles, Farewell Bend Campground comes into view on a flat across the river. At the actual bend, the spectacular scene reveals a long view up the canyon and a profusion of outcrops, islands, and rapids.

The final 2.4 miles pass through a forest with trickling streams and climbs above and away from the river, which can only periodically be seen below. The sound of OR 230 lets you know when FR 6510 isn't far away.

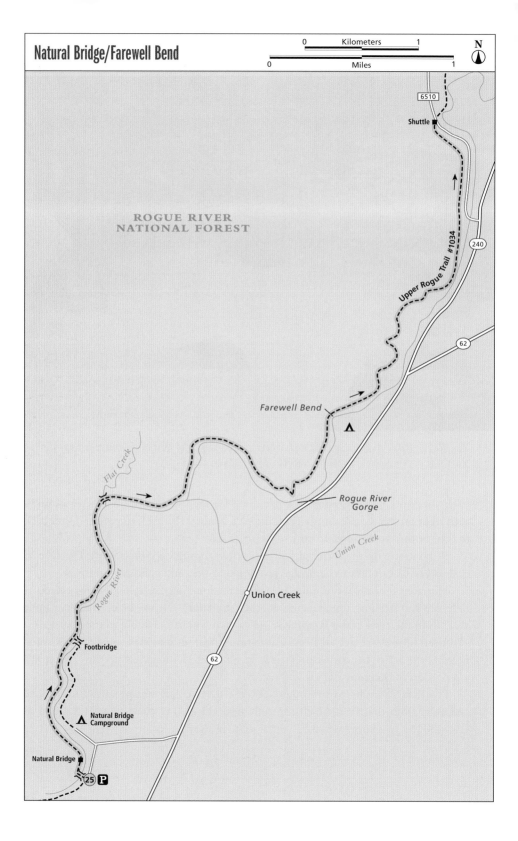

0   Kilometers   1

0   Miles   1

N

6510

Shuttle ■

ROGUE RIVER
NATIONAL FOREST

Upper Rogue Trail #1034

240

62

Farewell Bend

Flat Creek

Rogue River
Gorge

Union Creek

Rogue River

Union Creek

62

Footbridge

Natural Bridge
Campground

Natural Bridge ■

25   P

Miles and Directions

0.0 Begin at the Natural Bridge Trailhead by crossing a footbridge over the Rogue River.

0.2 Pass Natural Bridge Geologic Area and vista (with fence).

1.2 Pass the bridge back to Natural Bridge Campground. (**Option:** Take this bridge to complete the short loop.)

2.3 Cross Flat Creek.

4.8 Pass Farewell Bend Campground, viewed from across the river.

7.2 Arrive at FR 6510.

Options

River within a River: This easy 4.0-mile stretch of the Upper Rogue Trail is adjacent to and immediately north of the Farewell Bend segment. Just look for a trailhead on FR 6510 heading north. The area is marked by frequent meanders where ash filled the original Rogue canyon and the river then recut a channel through them. The far trailhead is at Foster Creek, a large creek that must be forded to reach the parking area.

Knob Falls: This 4.0-mile segment of the Rogue River Trail begins at the Natural Bridge parking area and heads south to the Woodruff Bridge Picnic Site and the Takelma Gorge segment of the Rogue River Trail. From the parking lot, the southbound trailhead to Knob Falls appears just before the footbridge. Knob Falls, located on a sharp, tight bend in the river at mile 1.5, is not very high but rather scenic. The rest of the route passes no major highlights.

26 Takelma Gorge

A spectacular rock gorge plus views of the Upper Rogue River. Out-and-back option.

Distance: 4.0-mile shuttle
Difficulty: Easy
Elevation loss: Negligible
Best season: Apr–Nov
Maps: USGS Prospect North; Rogue River–Siskiyou National Forest
Trail contacts: High Cascades Ranger district: (541) 560-3400

Parking and trailhead facilities: Northern: A dozen cars can park at the Woodruff Bridge Trailhead, a charming little picnic area and river crossing. Southern: The River Bridge Trailhead accommodates 8 cars and boasts a tiny campground.

Finding the trailhead: Woodruff Bridge (northern): From Medford, take OR 62 north, past Prospect, to milepost 51. Turn left at the Woodruff Bridge / Abbott Camp turnoff on FR 68. Proceed 1.2 miles to a river crossing and picnic area on the left. The southbound trailhead at Woodruff Bridge is well marked. **Trailhead GPS:** N42 51.728' / W122 30.299'

River Bridge Campground (southern): To reach the south trailhead at River Bridge Campground, leave OR 62 past milepost 49, turning left onto FR 6210, following the sign to River Bridge, 0.5 mile away. The northbound trailhead is on the right, just before the river crossing. **Trailhead GPS:** N42 49.339' / W122 29.656'

The Hike

The Native American tribe for which Takelma Gorge is named seems to spell their name Takilma in Josephine County and Takelma in Jackson County. No matter the spelling, a lovely gorge is named in their honor.

The hike is fairly easy and scenic almost the entire 4.0-mile route to the River Bridge Campground. (**Option:** If you only have one car and can't do the shuttle, take a 4.2-mile out-and-back hike to the end of Takelma Gorge from Woodruff Bridge Trailhead.)

From Woodruff Bridge Trailhead, the Upper Rogue Trail (#1034) hugs the river as it wanders through a second-growth forest of Douglas-fir, western hemlock, sugar pine, and ponderosa pine. Watch out for stinging nettles here. (If a finger suddenly swells and begins stinging for no apparent reason, you've probably made contact.)

After a placid initial 1.5 miles, the river enters a narrow, black chasm that is deeper and more impressive than any encountered since the river's origin at Boundary Springs. A sign tacked to a tree announces that you've arrived at Takelma Gorge. The trail surface grows rocky here. Notice the bubbles petrified into the once-boiling and gas-laden lava rock. And watch for a few spots of pahoehoe, also called ropey lava, a sign of fast-moving, highly liquid magma.

Takelma Gorge's far end offers the best views. A little point of land below the trail overlooks the dark defile. Inside, water oozes from between layers of basalt lava

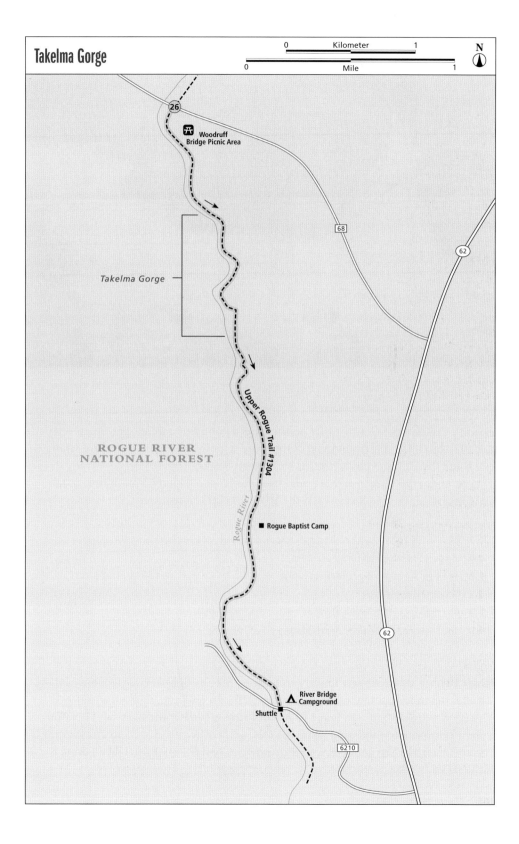

Takelma Gorge

0   Kilometer   1

0   Mile   1

N

26

Woodruff
Bridge Picnic Area

68

62

Takelma Gorge

Upper Rogue Trail #1304

ROGUE RIVER
NATIONAL FOREST

Rogue River

Rogue Baptist Camp

62

River Bridge
Campground

Shuttle

6210

The Rogue River makes a horseshoe-shaped turn before diving into Takelma Gorge. ZACH URNESS

into the whitewater below. This far point makes a good turnaround spot for an out-and-back hike (4.2 miles round-trip). Otherwise, continue downhill past a nice sandy beach and views of the now widened and slowed Rogue.

The rest of the walk to River Bridge, past the Rogue Baptist Camp at mile 3.0, is pleasant and gentle. The hike ends at the River Bridge Campground.

Miles and Directions

0.0 Begin at the Woodruff Bridge Trailhead.

1.5 Arrive at the beginning of Takelma Gorge.

2.1 Takelma Gorge ends.

3.0 The trail passes the Rogue Baptist Camp.

4.0 The hike ends at the River Bridge Trailhead.

Options

River Bridge to Prospect: This is another easy hike past placid river sections, ending after 4.5 miles at a tiny reservoir. For the southern trailhead, turn left at milepost 43, near the Prospect turnoff and a large canal running under the highway. Look for a dirt road to the left (heading north on OR 62). Follow it 0.5 mile to the Pacific Power Recreation Site and reservoir, also known as North Fork Park. The trailhead is at the far end of the picnic area.

27 Golden Stairs

An exhausting low-elevation trail passing spectacular rock formations early on, with panoramas of the High and Western Cascades. The only trail inside the Abbott Creek Research Natural Area.

Distance: 5.0-mile out and back
Difficulty: Moderate (strenuous first mile)
Elevation gain: 1,600 feet
Best season: Apr–June; Oct–Nov
Maps: USGS Abbott Butte; Rogue River–Siskiyou National Forest
Trail contacts: High Cascades Ranger District: (541) 560 3400
Parking and trailhead facilities: The trailhead holds 6 cars, with additional parking and an off-highway-vehicle (OHV) alternate trailhead 0.2 mile down the road.

Special considerations: The Golden Stairs area is a designated OHV area (motorized vehicles and bicycles are not allowed past the wilderness area boundary). The OHV season is July 1 to October 1. This is not such a bad thing, considering that the trail is best explored during spring or late fall because of the extreme midsummer heat. Also, the OHV clubs maintain the entire trail, reinforce the fragile spots, and police usage. Other designated OHV trails do not meet the standards for inclusion in this guide.

Finding the trailhead: From Medford take OR 62 north, past Prospect, to milepost 51. Turn left at the Woodruff Bridge / Abbott Camp turnoff on FR 68. Proceed 5 miles to the junction with Spur 550, which has a prominent Golden Stairs Trail sign. Continue 2 miles up Spur 550 to the trailhead (bearing left at an ambiguous looking junction).
Trailhead GPS: N42 54.561' / W122 29.978'

The Hike

It is unclear whether "Golden Stairs" refers to the trail's horrendous steepness or the sometimes yellowish rock formations it passes, each higher than the last. There are no actual stairs. The path may or may not represent a metaphoric "golden stairway" to a higher spiritual plane. Or the "golden" part of the trail's name might come from a rumored gold mine owned by the Abbott brothers, after whom everything in the area is named. (There were no genuine gold mines in the Cascades, including the Western Cascades.)

The best way to experience the Golden Stairs Trail is just to hike as far as your endurance and interest permit. A nice turnaround and lunch spot is the grassy campground, with wildflowers in spring, at Freddy's Camp, 2.5 miles up the trail. The more adventurous may choose to continue all the way into the Rogue-Umpqua Divide Wilderness.

While the first 2.0 miles are usually snow-free by mid-April or earlier, the route's upper 2.0 miles are often snowed over until May or June.

From the trailhead the path begins inscribing steep switchbacks almost immediately through a forested landscape. At mile 0.4 the trail meets what's labeled the OHV Golden Stairs Loop (from the alternate OHV trailhead) and continues to trek uphill.

The Golden Stairs Trail breaks out into some vistas that stretch across the Southern Cascade Mountains. Zach Urness

Abbot Creek is an undeveloped research natural area (RNA) adjacent to and south of the Rogue-Umpqua Divide Wilderness. The Golden Stairs Trail is its primary hiking access unless you enter cross-country.

The 2,600-acre Abbott Creek Research Natural Area was created in 1947 so that the Oregon State University School of Forestry could study sugar pines. No research has been conducted in the area since the 1950s. It is a beautiful roadless area.

The first open area, where the trail breaks out onto eastward-facing barren rock, is level and easy. Enjoy it while you can. The next breakout is steep and spectacular, with the trail running precipitously along the 2-foot-wide top of a steep, narrow ridge with rock outcrops on either end. At the third, most impressive and final rock area, the path runs just to the west of the narrow crest, which you have to climb 10 feet uphill to reach.

Beyond the rock outcrops, the gradient transitions from "strenuous" to "moderate" and the path largely stays in the woods except for a few small meadows, which include Freddy's Camp at mile 2.5.

Miles and Directions

0.0 Begin hiking at the Golden Stairs Trailhead.

0.4 The trail intersects the OHV loop; go right.

1.2 Pass a series of rock formations.

2.5 Reach Freddy's Camp; return the way you came.

5.0 Arrive back at the trailhead.

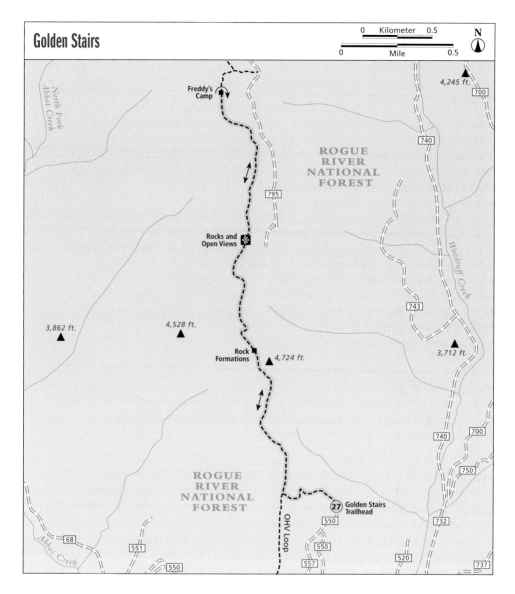

Golden Stairs

Map labels:
- North Fork Abbot Creek
- Freddy's Camp
- ROGUE RIVER NATIONAL FOREST
- 795
- Rocks and Open Views
- 3,862 ft.
- 4,528 ft.
- Rock Formations
- 4,724 ft.
- ROGUE RIVER NATIONAL FOREST
- OHV Loop
- 27 Golden Stairs Trailhead
- 550
- 68
- 551
- 550
- 557
- 520
- 732
- 737
- 750
- 740
- 700
- 4,245 ft.
- 700
- 740
- 743
- Woodruff Creek
- 3,712 ft.
- Abbot Creek

Scale: 0 Kilometer 0.5 / 0 Mile 0.5 · N

Options

Rogue–Umpqua Divide Trail: The last 2.0 miles of the Golden Stairs Trail, above Freddy's Camp, continue to hug the ridgetop, which is still narrow, with views of Abbott Butte and Elephant Head to the northwest.

If you reach the Rogue–Umpqua Divide Wilderness Trail (4.5 miles from the trailhead), turn right to reach Yellowjacket Camp Trailhead in 1.5 miles. If you've brought a good map, go left 1.0 mile to Elephant Head on the Rogue–Umpqua Divide Trail and 3.0 miles to reach the top of Abbott Butte.

28 Cliff Lake / Grasshopper Mountain

An easy hike off the South Umpqua River with interesting geology to a beautiful pair of lakes and then to the top of a mountain.

Distance: 8.4-mile out and back
Difficulty: Moderately strenuous
Elevation gain: 2,092 feet
Best season: May–Nov
Maps: USGS Buckeye Lake; Umpqua National Forest

Trail contacts: Tiller Ranger District: (541) 825-3201
Parking and trailhead facilities: The Skimmerhorn Trailhead accommodates about 20 cars.

Finding the trailhead: From Medford take OR 62 north toward Crater Lake. Turn left at the town of Trail (past milepost 24) onto OR 227 and continue 20 miles to the town of Tiller. At Tiller, turn right up the paved South Umpqua Road 46 and follow it 24 miles, passing South Umpqua Falls (a nice pullout and place to view spawning salmon in fall). Twenty-four miles from Tiller, turn right onto paved FR 2823. From here follow signs for Skimmerhorn Trailhead. Go right at a fork onto FR 2830 as the road turns to gravel. Finally, turn left onto FR 600 for 2 miles to the end of the road. Roads are well marked.
Trailhead GPS: N43 04.668' / W122 32.415'

The Hike

Even without knowing the geology, this is a beautiful area of lakes, dense forests, vertical ridges, and jagged summits. To fully appreciate this short, easy hike from the most popular trailhead in the Rogue-Umpqua Divide Wilderness, one must be aware of a geological event occurring 6,000 years ago. Imagine a 5,500-foot mountain, formed by ancient lava flows, suddenly breaking in half and sending millions of tons of rubble into the valley, 2,500 feet below. Such an event created the escarpment above Cliff Lake and impounded the waters of Buckeye, Cliff, and Fish Lakes.

It's a 1.7-mile hike from the Skimmerhorn Trailhead to Buckeye Lake along the Lakes Trail (#1578). The path is fairly gentle, with slight upgrades in the middle. It's also remarkably wide, as summer use is heavy. Cliff Lake shows up 0.4 mile past Buckeye Lake. The lakes are at a fairly low elevation, and you can often get there as late as mid-December.

Both lakes are nestled amid dense forests at the foot of the cliff described above. Both have excellent, level campsites nearby. Buckeye Lake is larger and reveals more of the escarpment than Cliff Lake. Cliff Lake, as the name implies, hugs the base of the cliff. Both lakes are stocked with brook and rainbow trout.

Just 0.3 mile past Cliff Lake, 2.4 miles from the trailhead, the Grasshopper Trail (#1574) takes off steeply uphill to the right while the Lakes Trail continues to Fish Lake (2.5 miles). A little more than 1.0 mile up the Grasshopper Trail, the Grasshopper

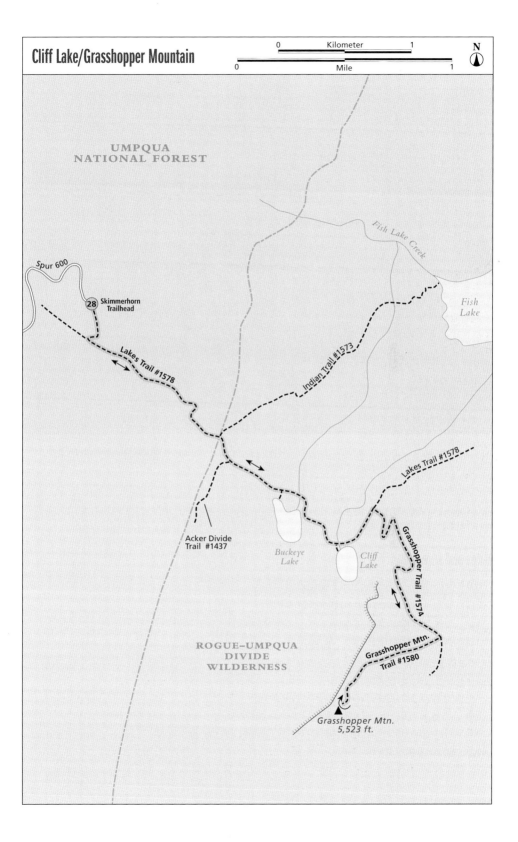

Cliff Lake/Grasshopper Mountain

0   Kilometer   1

0   Mile   1

N

UMPQUA
NATIONAL FOREST

Fish Lake Creek

Fish
Lake

Spur 600

28 Skimmerhorn
Trailhead

Lakes Trail #1578

Indian Trail #1573

Lakes Trail #1578

Acker Divide
Trail #1437

Buckeye
Lake

Cliff
Lake

Grasshopper Trail #157A

ROGUE–UMPQUA
DIVIDE
WILDERNESS

Grasshopper Mtn.
Trail #1580

Grasshopper Mtn.
5,523 ft.

The view from the summit of Grasshopper Mountain looks down upon Buckeye Lake and Cliff Lake in the Rogue-Umpqua Divide Wilderness. ZACH URNESS

Mountain Trail (#1580) breaks off to the right. From here it's 0.7 mile to the lookout site atop Grasshopper Mountain (elevation 5,529 feet), 4.2 miles from the trailhead.

Miles and Directions

0.0 Begin at the Skimmerhorn Trailhead.

0.3 Arrive at the Lakes Trail junction. Turn left.

1.2 Pass the Indian Trail junction.

1.3 Pass the Mosquito Camp Trail junction.

1.7 Arrive at Buckeye Lake.

2.1 Reach Cliff Lake (popular turnaround).

2.4 Arrive at the Grasshopper Trail junction; go right.

3.5 Go right at the Grasshopper Mountain Trail junction.

4.2 Reach the Grasshopper Mountain summit; return the way you came.

8.4 Arrive back at the trailhead.

29 Fish Lake

A large, gorgeous, geologically unusual mountain lake in the Rogue-Umpqua Divide Wilderness. A shorter but steeper optional route.

Distance: 7.6-mile out and back
Difficulty: Moderate
Elevation gain: 1,070 feet
Best season: Apr–Dec
Maps: USGS Buckeye Lake; Umpqua National Forest

Trail contacts: Tiller Ranger District: (541) 825-3201
Parking and trailhead facilities: There are picnic tables, pit toilets, a horse loading ramp, and parking for 20 cars with trailers at the Fish Lake Trailhead.

Finding the trailhead: From Medford take OR 62 north toward Crater Lake. Turn left at the town of Trail (past milepost 24) onto OR 227 and continue 20 miles to the town of Tiller. At Tiller turn right up the paved South Umpqua Road 46 and follow it 24 miles, passing South Umpqua Falls (a nice pullout and place to view spawning salmon in fall). Twenty-four miles from Tiller, turn right onto paved FR 2823. Continue until you reach a fork, and go right onto FR 2830. After 4 miles, fork left onto FR 2840 for 0.5 mile to the Fish Lake Trailhead.
Trailhead GPS: N43 05.294' / W122 33.563'

The Hike

At an elevation of only 3,370 feet, Fish Lake lies well below any other glacial lake in Southern Oregon. This is because Fish Lake was created not by glaciers (although it occupies an ancient glacial valley) but by damming from a tremendous landslide 6,000 years ago off nearby Grasshopper Mountain—the same landslide that created Cliff and Buckeye Lakes. Fish Lake is accessible during any season except the absolute dead of winter. It is the largest and deepest wilderness lake described in this guide.

Two primary trails lead to Fish Lake: the Fish Lake Trail (#1570), described here, and the Beaver Swamp Trail (#1569) (see "Options" below). The Beaver Swamp Trail starts high (4,200 feet) and descends to Fish Lake, while the Fish Lake Trail climbs to the lake, which means the Beaver Swamp Trail's season is shorter.

The main difference between the two paths is that the Fish Lake Trail gets to Fish Lake in 3.8 miles, while the Beaver Swamp Trail gets there in 2.0 miles. The Fish Lake Trail is beautiful throughout; its shorter counterpart descends cross-country, mostly through old clear-cuts.

From the Fish Lake Trailhead, the trail remains nearly level for 1.5 miles as it follows Fish Lake Creek through a beautiful forest with a moss-covered floor and moss-draped trees. The trees are a lot more "Pacific Northwest" than forests at the same elevation in the Rogue River drainage, largely because of the presence of western red cedar (along with Douglas-fir and western hemlock). These three species compose the "Big Three" of low-elevation Northwest forests. Look also for Pacific silver fir,

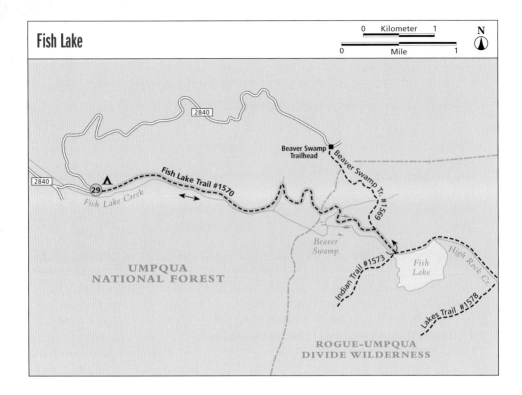

Pacific madrone (also a low-elevation species but extending clear to the lake), bigleaf maple, and vine maple.

There are lots of rhododendron in the first 1.0 mile and tons of salal, trillium, vanilla leaf, and dwarf Oregon grape throughout. These species all love moist, closed-canopy forests and excellent soil.

At mile 1.5 the path swings away from the creek into a side valley, crosses a creek, and climbs steeply to a rocky ledge at the base of vertical cliffs. Rounding a point, the route turns up another side valley, crosses another creek, and starts climbing yet again around another point above the Fish Creek valley floor. There's an excellent vista of the Fish Lake basin, with Highrock Mountain rising behind it.

The third and final side valley is Beaver Swamp, just inside the wilderness boundary. Beaver Swamp occupies a flat, grassy dale that in the spring contains a large, shallow lake. You may see a lodge or other signs of beaver activity.

Just 0.7 mile past Beaver Swamp is the trail junction with Beaver Swamp Trail. Beyond this junction lie a huge waterfall that you can't see very well and, eventually, the narrow gorge of Fish Lake.

The clear, emerald lake covers 90 acres, with dense forest on all sides. Grasshopper Mountain's rocky 5,523-foot flank rises to the southwest (right); craggy Highrock Mountain (6,196 feet) soars abruptly to the southeast (left). The lakeshore is too steep for camping except at the lake's far end, where a delta of silt from various inlet creeks has created a grassy meadow and alder forest.

Fish Lake is among the largest mountain lakes in the Southern Cascades. ZACH URNESS

There's supposed to be a submerged airplane in the middle of the lake, the result of a crash many years ago. Local anglers claim you can see it from a boat, but the forest service insists that this is only a rumor and there is no airplane.

Miles and Directions

0.0 Begin at the Fish Lake Trailhead.

2.7 Arrive at Beaver Swamp.

3.4 Pass the Beaver Swamp Trail junction.

3.8 Reach Fish Lake; return the way you came.

7.6 Arrive back at the trailhead.

Options

Beaver Swamp Trail: This path drops 600 feet from a ridgetop in 1.5 miles and doesn't follow a creek, or pass a Beaver Swamp. It reaches the Fish Lake Trail in 1.5 miles and Fish Lake in 2.0 miles. The trailhead, on the same road as the Fish Lake Trailhead, only 4 miles farther up, accommodates 15 to 20 cars. By using Beaver Swamp and Fish Lake Trailheads, you can make an outstanding shuttle hike that is entirely downhill.

Indian Trail: The Indian Trail (#1573) begins at the outlet of Fish Lake into Fish Lake Creek, where the Fish Lake Trail arrives at the lake. The path breaks off to the right, crosses Fish Lake Creek over the top of a large logjam, parallels the lakeshore briefly, and then climbs 800 feet in 2.5 miles, meeting the Lakes Trail from the Skimmerhorn Trailhead 0.5 mile before Buckeye Lake.

Upper Fish Lake Trail: The Fish Lake Trail parallels the lakeshore for 0.5 mile and then follows Highrock Creek for 3.5 miles to the Rogue-Umpqua Divide Trail, 8.0 miles from the Fish Lake Trailhead and 1.0 mile from the Hershberger Trailhead.

30 Rattlesnake Mountain

A network of trails through a beautiful meadowed valley bounded on both sides by wilderness and high peaks, followed by a steep trek to the summit of the Rogue-Umpqua Divide's second-highest peak.

Distance: 6.0-mile lollipop
Difficulty: Moderately strenuous
Elevation gain: 1,862 feet
Best season: Mid-June–Aug
Maps: USGS Fish Mountain; Umpqua National Forest
Trail contacts: Diamond Lake Ranger District: (541) 498-2531

Parking and trailhead facilities: The trailhead accommodates 3 or 4 cars along the shoulder. The walk from Happy Camp, which has a fire ring and parking for 6 cars, is less than 0.1 mile.
Special considerations: The area is very popular with hunters in autumn. There is no water once you leave the Rogue-Umpqua Divide Trail.

Finding the trailhead: From Medford take OR 62 north past Union Creek. Where OR 62 swings right toward Crater Lake at milepost 57, continue straight on OR 230 toward Diamond Lake. Past milepost 12 on OR 230, opposite the Hamaker Campground turnoff, turn left onto gravel Fish Creek Road (FR 6560). After 4 miles, at the divide, FR 6560 becomes FR 37. Turn left 0.5 mile beyond the divide onto Spur 800, continue 3 miles, past Lonesome Meadow, and turn left again onto Spur 870, the Fish Creek Valley Road.

Continue 4 rough miles up Spur 870 to the trailhead. You'll pass a few other trailheads before reaching a little sign on the right denoting the Rogue-Umpqua Divide Trail (#1470). You can either park on the side of the road or continue a few hundred feet down the road to Happy Camp, which has a parking area on the right.
Trailhead GPS: N43 05.304' / W122 25.354'

The Hike

One of the Cascade Mountains' great secret places lies immediately north of Crater Lake and west of Diamond Lake. Beautiful Fish Creek Valley contains broad floral meadows, dense forests, and an enchanting stream meandering through the middle. Rocky crags and forested ridges rise sharply up the valley's sides.

If you parked at the Happy Camp Trailhead parking area, walk down the road a few hundred feet to a small sign for the Rogue-Umpqua Divide Trail and head off into a gorgeous meadow filled with corn lily, tower delphinium, and myriad other wildflowers. The trail follows Fish Creek, and 6,656-foot Rattlesnake Mountain—your goal—rises directly overhead.

Noble fir, western white pine, mountain hemlock, and lodgepole pine surround the meadow and form picturesque clumps in the meadow.

After an easy 0.9 mile on the Rogue-Umpqua Divide Trail, you'll meet the Whitehorse Meadow Trail (#1477).

The view from the overlook on the Rattlesnake Mountain summit spreads across the Rogue Umpqua Divide Wilderness. ZACH URNESS

Turning left on the Whitehorse Meadow Trail, the path follows a pretty little side creek for 0.2 mile before climbing up to Windy Gap saddle (5,600 feet).

Windy Gap, although there's not much to see, is a crossroads for this hike. The spur to Rattlesnake Mountain's summit heads uphill. After you've finished the summit hike, you'll come back to this point and follow Castle Creek Trail (#1576), also found at Windy Gap, to complete the loop.

The path to the summit follows switchbacks uphill by a stout 1,003 feet in 1.3 miles. Near the top, go left on a side trail toward a meadow where the trail disappears.

Hike across the meadow, toward a grove of trees on the far end, to a patch of rock with unbelievable views straight down into Fish Creek Valley and across to Fish Mountain, Hershberger Mountain, Mount Bailey, the Crater Lake summits, and the Umpqua Valley.

This summit viewpoint makes a nice spot for lunch before heading back downhill to Windy Gap. To finish the loop, simply follow Castle Creek Trail for 0.5 mile to a junction with a sign for Fish Creek Road. Turn left at the junction and hike the easy and wide route a final 0.8 mile to the Happy Camp parking area.

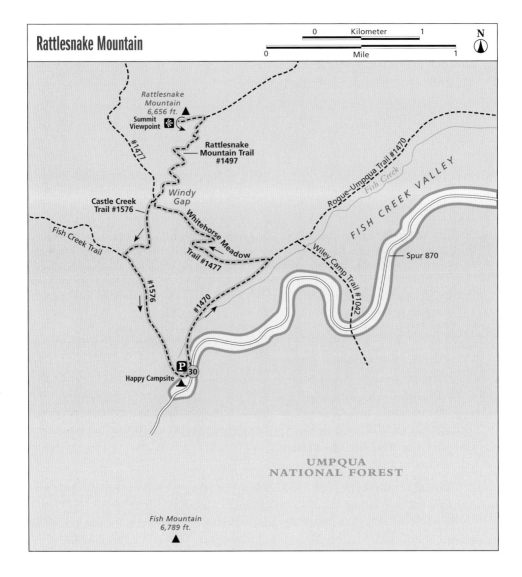

0   Kilometer   1

0   Mile   1

N

Rattlesnake Mountain 6,656 ft.

Summit Viewpoint

Rattlesnake Mountain Trail #1497

#1477

Windy Gap

Castle Creek Trail #1576

Whitehorse Meadow

Trail #1477

Fish Creek Trail

#1576

#1470

Rogue-Umpqua Trail #1470

Fish Creek

FISH CREEK VALLEY

Wiley Camp Trail #1042

Spur 870

P 30

Happy Campsite

UMPQUA NATIONAL FOREST

Fish Mountain 6,789 ft.

Miles and Directions

0.0   Park at the Happy Camp parking area and walk to nearby trailhead.

0.1   Arrive at the Rogue Umpqua-Divide Trailhead. Follow the trail.

0.9   Arrive at the Whitehorse Meadow Trail junction; turn left.

2.1   Reach Windy Gap. Take the Rattlesnake Way Trail, heading uphill.

3.3   Arrive at the trail junction to the summit; go left.

3.5   Reach the Summit Meadow. Explore the summit; then double back to Windy Gap.

4.7   Back at Windy Gap, follow the Castle Creek Trail to the right and downhill.

5.2   Go left on the Fish Creek Trail at a sign for Fish Creek Road.

6.0   Arrive at the Happy Camp parking area.

31 Abbott Butte

A mountaintop lookout tower and an impressive rock formation.

Distance: 7.2-mile out and back with a loop
Difficulty: Moderate
Elevation gain: 1,467 feet
Best season: Late May-Oct
Maps: USGS Abbott Butte; Rogue River–Siskiyou National Forest

Trail contacts: High Cascades Ranger district: (541) 560 3400
Parking and trailhead facilities: The Huckleberry Gap Trailhead accommodates 5 cars.

Finding the trailhead: From Medford take OR 62, past Prospect and milepost 51, to the Woodruff Bridge (Abbott Camp) turnoff (FR 68). Turn left and go 13 miles on FR 68 to the parking pullout of Huckleberry Gap, a small pullout on the left. The eastbound Rogue-Umpqua Divide Trailhead is on the right. **Trailhead GPS:** N42 55.138'/W122 35.051'

The Hike

From the Huckleberry Gap Trailhead, the Rogue-Umpqua Divide Trail (#1470) makes its way gently downhill through dense and gloomy woods on the north face of Quartz Mountain (5,657 feet).

The highlight of the first mile is a huge outcrop of columnar basalt halfway along. Approaching Windy Gap, look for Alaska yellow cedar in the woods, along with Douglas-fir, white fir, noble fir, and western white pine. A brief glimpse of Abbot Butte turns up just before Windy Gap.

At Windy Gap (5,310 feet), the RUD Trail meets the CCC Trail for the first time. The RUD Trail is much more dramatic than the CCC Trail, so go right. This hike will eventually return on the CCC Trail.

The RUD above Windy Gap follows the south side of the ridge, which is very steep and open, with scree slopes and long vistas.

From the RUD side of the ridge, you can see the Crater Lake rim, Mount McLoughlin, and the Abbott Creek drainage. The RUD also offers a close-up view of a towering and impressive lava plug, proof that these are the Western Cascades and not the High Cascades. Much of this portion of the RUD is rocky and outsloped (tilted sideways), with sheer drop-offs.

The RUD Trail touches the CCC Trail 0.5 mile beyond Windy Gap, then again 1.0 mile beyond Windy Gap (2.0 miles from the Huckleberry Gap Trailhead). At this third junction, a sign identical to the one at Windy Gap again informs visitors that horses should use the CCC Trail. If you wish to hike to the Abbott Butte summit, you must follow the old road/CCC Trail from here on.

The 1.0-mile hike on the CCC Trail to the summit is lovely, with long vistas of the meadows on the north side of Abbott Butte and views beyond into the South

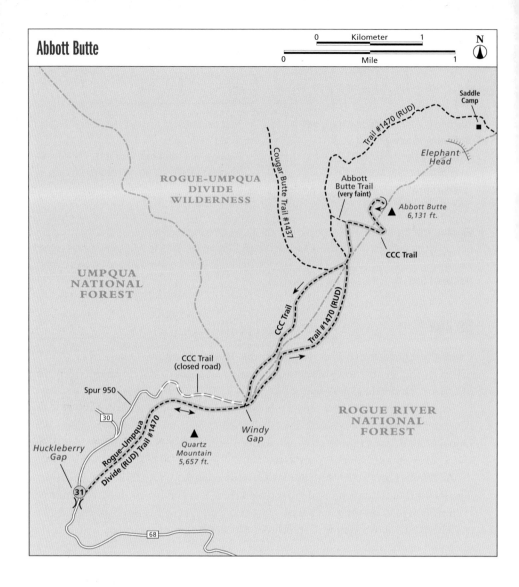

Kilometer

0   1

Mile

0   1

N

Saddle Camp

Trail #1470 (RUD)

Elephant Head

ROGUE-UMPQUA DIVIDE WILDERNESS

Cougar Butte Trail #1437

Abbott Butte Trail (very faint)

Abbott Butte 6,131 ft.

CCC Trail

UMPQUA NATIONAL FOREST

CCC Trail

Trail #1470 (RUD)

CCC Trail (closed road)

Spur 950

30

Huckleberry Gap

Rogue-Umpqua Divide (RUD) Trail #1470

Quartz Mountain 5,657 ft.

Windy Gap

ROGUE RIVER NATIONAL FOREST

31

68

Umpqua drainage. Look for clusters of chokecherry on the way up and, at the top, stands of noble fir and mountain hemlock.

The lookout tower, beautiful from a distance, is quite dilapidated. The ladder is broken, and the structure is condemned.

The best vantage points lie just north and south of the summit. According to the map, it's possible to make your way cross-country from the summit to the top of Elephant Head Rock—a sheer, gray, 500-foot cliff. But there are a couple rock outcrops in between and many opportunities to get lost. From the summit, explore the CCC Trail (a permanently closed road used exclusively as trail) on the way back. It's less scenic but shadier and a little faster, offering some nice wildflowers in early summer.

An old fire lookout marks the summit of Abbott Butte in the Rogue-Umpqua Divide Wilderness. It's not recommended for climbing. ZACH URNESS

The CCC contours down the ridge's north side, which is densely forested with no vistas. It passes a junction with the Cougar Butte Trail (#1437) at the 4.6-mile mark.

Miles and Directions

0.0   Begin at the Huckleberry Gap Trailhead.

1.5   Arrive at the wilderness boundary and the Windy Gap junction. Turn right to follow the RUD Trail, while ignoring the CCC Trail for the moment.

2.7   Arrive at the upper junction with the CCC Trail. Follow the CCC Trail right for Abbot Butte summit.

3.6   Arrive at the Abbott Butte summit; return to the junction of the RUD Trail and the CCC Trail.

4.5   Take the right fork to follow the CCC Trail back down to Windy Gap.

4.6   Pass the junction with the Cougar Butte Trail (#1437).

5.7   Bear right on the RUD and continue back to Huckleberry Gap Trailhead.

7.2   Arrive back at the trailhead.

Options

Elephant Head and the Yellowjacket Camp Trailhead: If you're hiking through to the Yellowjacket Camp Trailhead or the base of Elephant Head, return to the Rogue-Umpqua Divide Trail when done climbing the mountain and then continue east (right) over a vast, grassy flat dotted with rock outcrops.

Crossing the large meadow, the RUD rises to a crest and then drops steeply through the woods for 0.3 mile before leveling off as it approaches Saddle Camp, the closest you come via trail to Elephant Head. This north-slope route retains snow until very late in the season.

From Saddle Camp continue 1.0 mile to the junction with the Golden Stairs Trail (#1092). From there it's a fairly steep 1.0 mile downhill on the RUD Trail to the Yellowjacket Camp Trailhead. One lengthy pitch near the trailhead is especially steep.

32 Viewpoint Mike

A winter and spring hike with lots of wildflowers, leading to a vista point on a barren lava outcrop.

Distance: 5.0-mile out and back
Difficulty: Moderately strenuous
Elevation gain: 1,107 feet
Best season: Oct–May
Maps: USGS McLeod; Rogue River–Siskiyou National Forest
Trail contacts: High Cascades Ranger District: (541) 560-3400

Parking and trailhead facilities: A paved lot across the road from the trailhead has parking for more than 20 cars.
Special considerations: Because of its steepness and low elevation, plus its proximity to Lost Creek Lake, this trail gets very hot and humid in midsummer. It is not recommended if the temperature in Medford is over 90°F. There is no water.

Finding the trailhead: From Medford take OR 62 north to the bridge over the Rogue River, near milepost 29, just past the turnoff to the fish hatchery at Lost Creek Lake. Across the bridge, the first paved side road on the right is Crowfoot Road. Turn right onto Crowfoot Road and follow it a short 0.3 mile to a large and obvious parking area on the right. The Viewpoint Mike Trail begins across the street at a signboard.
Trailhead GPS: N42 39.332'/W122 41.398'

The Hike

This unnumbered path offers an excellent workout and is snow-free nearly all year except after a major winter storm. It's in its glory in spring, when dozens of wildflower species bedazzle the grassy fields and airy woods.

The trail climbs steeply from the outset and rarely lets up as it ascends from an elevation equal to the base of the Lost Creek Dam (1,500 feet) to about 1,000 feet above the top of the dam. Much of the route traverses a grass and Oregon white oak association, indicative of low elevation and extreme summer heat and dryness.

Occasional wooded stands in the first 1.5 miles are open and brushy, with small ponderosa pines, Oregon white oak, California black oak, madrone, whiteleaf manzanita, buckbrush ceanothus (also called wild California lilac), whitethorn ceanothus, birchleaf mountain mahogany, tall Oregon grape, and wild grape.

Many wildflowers flourish along the trail, including cat's ear, wild iris, Indian paintbrush, lupine, Indian pink, ookow, camas, erigonium, lomatium, and the magnificent balsamroot daisy.

Oh, yes, poison oak also flourishes along the trail.

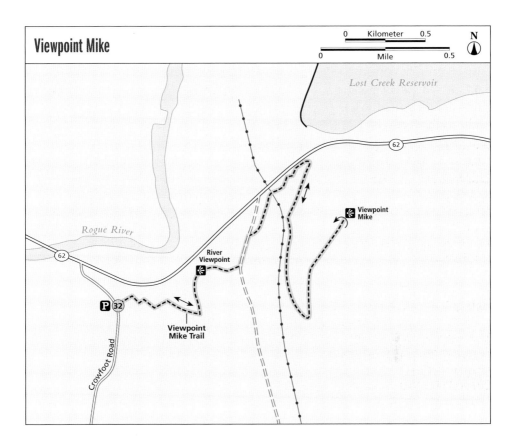

Viewpoint Mike

Lost Creek Reservoir

62

Viewpoint
Mike

Rogue River

River
Viewpoint

62

P 32

Viewpoint
Mike Trail

Crowfoot Road

After 0.7 mile you arrive at a park bench at the top of a deep road cut, with an outstanding view of the dam, the fish hatchery, and the Rogue River. Be careful of poison oak growing out of the wall behind the bench.

After 1.0 mile the path emerges onto a dirt road, which it follows for 0.1 mile (turn left, then right). Past the road, the path continues to climb and continues to parallel OR 62 for another 0.3 mile.

At mile 1.4 the route makes a 90-degree turn to the right, swings away from the highway for good, and ducks behind a large hill. The highway noises fade away and the forest becomes denser and cooler, with larger trees, more Douglas-firs and sugar pines, and fewer ponderosa pines.

The path climbs around rock faces and crosses a ridge, where Lost Creek Lake and OR 62 come back into view, except you're now far above both. The path makes its way across a long, steep lava outcrop to the summit, which has a wooden bench, cliffs, and an outstanding vista. Look for a buzzard roost immediately east. All of Lost Creek Lake is visible from the vista point, along with the dam and Flounce Rock across the lake. On the eastern horizon, Union Peak blends into the Crater Lake rim and Hillman Peak.

Miles and Directions

0.0 Begin at the Viewpoint Mike Trailhead, across the road from the parking lot.

0.7 Arrive at the first viewpoint.

0.9 Reach a dirt road; go left.

1.0 Turn right off the dirt road to continue on the trail.

2.5 Reach the summit; return the way you came.

5.0 Arrive back at the trailhead.

33 Mill Creek Falls

A massive 173-foot waterfall amid boulders the size of houses. An easy, year-round hike.

Distance: 1.0-mile out and back
Difficulty: Easy
Elevation loss: 27 feet
Best season: Year-round
Maps: USGS Cascade Gorge
Trail contacts: None

Parking and trailhead facilities: There are vault toilets and parking for around 40 cars, along with a large signboard with a map on it.
Special considerations: This trail lies entirely on privately owned timberland. Hikers should show the same high level of care and courtesy that they would on any trail.

Finding the trailhead: From Medford take OR 62 north for 41 miles. Turn right at the Prospect Access Road for 0.3 mile and then turn left onto Mill Creek. Drive for 0.6 mile. The parking lot is a large, well-marked area on the right.
Trailhead GPS: N42 44.497' / W122 29.981'

The Avenue of Giant Boulders, near Mill Creek Falls, marks the spot where the Rogue River drops down from the surface of the Mazama lava plateau, into the canyon that the river has cut into the plateau. ZACH URNESS

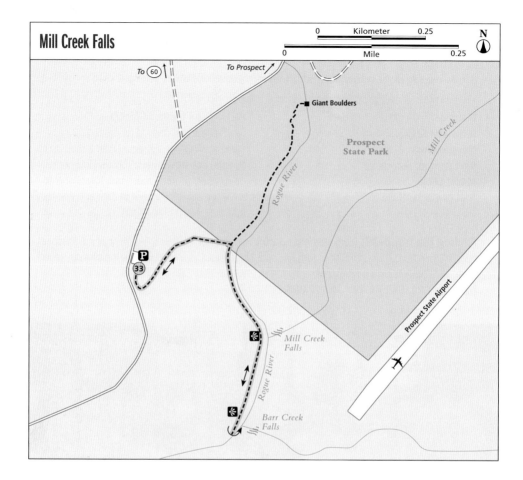

The Hike

The route to Mill Creek Falls is the very definition of easy and spectacular. Open year-round, the falls lure families driving home from Crater Lake National Park and those heading out from Medford for a quick day trip into the small, historic town of Prospect.

The trail begins in a large parking lot and gradually moves downhill on a wide path. At mile 0.4 a signboard points to the Avenue of Giant Boulders to the left and Mill Creek Falls to the right.

There's no wrong answer at this point, but consider checking out the waterfalls first. Heading right, there are multiple viewpoints, first of Mill Creek Falls, then of Barr Creek Falls. Both are vertical plunges on the opposite side of the Rogue River, and both carry a huge amount of water for side creeks. Mill Creek Falls is 173 feet high; Barr Creek Falls is 150 feet high.

Miles and Directions

0.0 Begin at the Mill Creek Falls parking area.

0.4 Arrive at the Giant Boulders-Mill Creek Falls junction. Go straight ahead for the falls, left for the Avenue of Giant Boulders.

0.5 Reach Mill Creek Falls, then Barr Creek Falls; return the way you came.

1.0 Arrive back at the trailhead.

Options

After you've enjoyed the falls, take some time to explore the Avenue of Giant Boulders. As advertised, the rocks here are massive. A popular activity is climbing around on the boulders to find hidden spots between them, or you can try boulder-hopping all the way up to OR 62.

34 Boundary Springs

A beautiful canyon, several magical springs, and the ultimate source of the Rogue River.

Distance: 5.0-mile out and back
Difficulty: Easy
Elevation gain: 328 feet
Best season: June–Oct
Maps: USGS Pumice Desert West; Rogue River–Siskiyou National Forest / Crater Lake National Park

Trail contacts: Prospect Ranger District: (541) 560-4300; Crater Lake National Park: (541) 594-3100
Parking and trailhead facilities: The paved viewpoint parking area holds 30 cars.
Special considerations: Because the trail originates outside Crater Lake National Park, there is no entry fee.

Finding the trailhead: From Medford take OR 62 north to Union Creek. Where OR 62 swings right toward Crater Lake, past milepost 57, continue straight on OR 230 toward Diamond Lake. The main trailhead is located at milepost 19, at the Mount Mazama Viewpoint parking area.

Option: To cut 1 mile off the hike, turn right off OR 230, 2 miles past the viewpoint parking area, onto Spur 760, following signs to Lake West. This is a rough dirt road. A cramped trailhead with limited parking is located 3.2 miles up, where the Rogue passes through a large culvert. Head left (south) on the trail for Boundary Springs.
Trailhead GPS: N43 05.450' / W122 13.295'

The Hike

It's not true that the Rogue rises from a hole in the Crater Lake rim's north side. The water feeding beautiful Boundary Springs, source of the Rogue's main fork, comes instead from runoff and groundwater on Crater Lake's outer slopes.

From the Viewpoint Trailhead the path, which begins as the Upper Rogue Trail (#1034), initially follows a level plateau through a stand of small lodgepole pines. It's 0.7 mile from the parking area to the junction. Turn left (downhill) at a sign for Boundary Springs on the unnumbered trail.

Shortly after the turn, the trail dips into and out of a steep ravine. The bottom may remain snow clogged—and therefore difficult or impossible to cross—until early July, long after the surrounding area clears. Climbing quickly out of the ravine, another level plateau takes you to Spur 760 at mile 1.0.

After crossing the river via Spur 760, the trail rounds a small side creek, then gradually climbs to a bench high above the water and continues south toward the national park boundary. Steep slopes of loose ash border the rushing stream. The volume of water and the immensity of the canyon are surprising considering the nearness of the river's source.

The fully formed Rogue River is seen just a few hundred feet from the source at Boundary Springs. Lynn Bernstein

The trail enters the park 1.8 miles from the trailhead. Beyond, contouring along the hillside, the path hits its high point at mile 2.2. After that, you begin edging closer to the water, where you may be treated to a profusion of monkey flowers and red huckleberry.

As you approach the springs, moss-covered logs span the wide, shallow river.

Beyond the crossing, the path swings away from the river and connects with a closed road leading to the Pacific Crest Trail and the park interior. Follow the road to the left, not to the right. In short order you will arrive at a small hilltop clearing on the left. From the center of the clearing (off the trail), the middle spring may be found through the bushes to the right.

The middle spring is by far the most impressive. From atop a small log, you will see a dry hillside on one side and a full-blown river on the other, with the river gushing out of a rock beneath the log. The newborn stream quickly fans out across a rock face as it begins its journey to the Pacific.

For the two other springs: (1) Follow the small creek you crossed earlier upstream to its source. (2) Bushwhack to a small creek on the far side of the middle spring and follow it to its source.

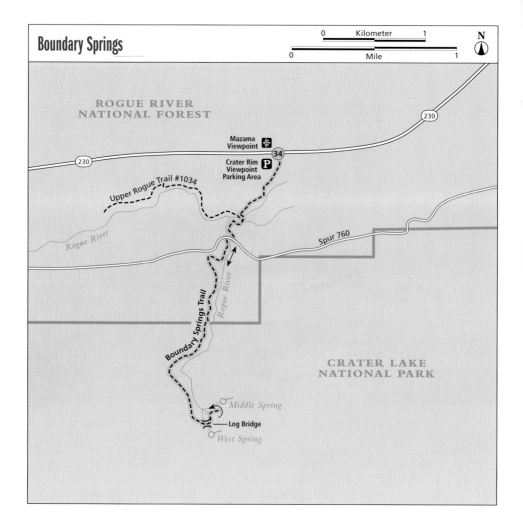

Miles and Directions

0.0 Begin at the Viewpoint Trailhead.

0.7 Arrive at the Upper Rogue Trail junction. Go left (downhill) at a sign for Boundary Springs.

1.0 Reach Spur 760. Cross to the other side of the culvert and continue up the trail.

1.8 Arrive at the national park boundary.

2.5 Reach Boundary Springs; return the way you came.

5.0 Arrive back at the trailhead.

35 Cleetwood Cove

The only access to the shore of Crater Lake. Also the takeoff point for boat rides. Optional (and magnificent) hike on Wizard Island to the top of a large cinder cone.

Distance: 2.2-mile out and back
Difficulty: Moderate (very steep but very short)
Elevation loss: 633 feet
Best season: Mid-June–Oct
Maps: USGS Crater Lake East; Crater Lake National Park
Trail contacts: Crater Lake National Park: (541) 594-3100
Parking and trailhead facilities: The large, paved parking lot can accommodate up to 100 cars, but it's often full on midsummer weekends.
Special considerations: Park entrance fee charged per vehicle. No pets are permitted on trails in Crater Lake National Park. There is no water on this trail, and it can get very hot and humid; however, the hike isn't very long. The trail is almost always crowded, and people on the way up often appear physically stressed.

Finding the trailhead: From the Rim Village at Crater Lake National Park, head north 8 miles on West Rim Drive to the junction with the North Entrance Road. Turn right at the junction, continue 5 miles, and park at Cleetwood Cove.
Trailhead GPS: N42 58.808' / W122 04.940'

The Hike

This is a hike everyone should take and almost everyone who lives in Oregon eventually does. The boat ride around the lake is a great way to experience the most scenic attraction in a very scenic state.

From the trailhead, the path drops relentlessly through several switchbacks and a high-elevation woods of lodgepole pine, western white pine, and mountain hemlock. You'll pass many people on their way up who are red in the face, perspiring, and breathing heavily.

▶ Boat tours leave from Cleetwood Cove every hour from 9 a.m. until 3:30 p.m. Tours last 2 hours; fee required. Tours are canceled if it's windy or raining. Bring water, sunscreen, and a hat. There is a vault toilet at the landing but no opportunities once the boat leaves. Boat rides at midday and on weekends sell out quickly, so you may have to wait a couple hours. You may call ahead (888-774-CRATER [2728]) to reserve tickets.

Two boats a day go to Wizard Island (9:30 a.m. and 12:30 p.m.); a third boat picks up everybody at the end of the day. You will stay on the island a minimum of 3 hours and a maximum of 6 hours. Fee required. Reserve a ticket by calling (888) 774-CRATER (2728).

The only way to get to Cleetwood Cove to take a boat ride is to take this hike.

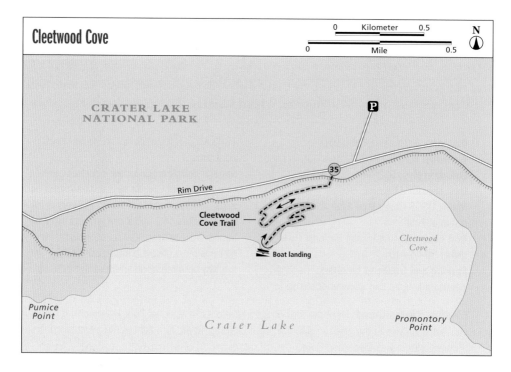

Don't worry, though. The path isn't that difficult, and the trail isn't very long, but it does attract many visitors who aren't used to hiking. There are wooden benches at regular intervals.

After 0.7 mile, forest yields to bare rock, the lakeshore facilities come into view, and the path steepens as it negotiates the last long switchbacks. At the bottom you'll find the boat dock, ticket booth, a ranger hut, and a solar toilet. There's room for a little exploring, but the shore is too steep to permit wandering very far from the dock area. The swimming is wonderful.

Miles and Directions

0.0   Start at the Cleetwood Cove Trailhead.

1.1   Reach the lakeshore and boat dock; return the way you came.

2.2   Arrive back at the trailhead.

Options

Many consider the 0.9-mile Wizard Island Trail to be the most spectacular in Oregon. It is difficult to argue with this. The trail climbs a 755-foot-high volcanic cinder cone to the summit crater, which it then circles. The crater is 500 feet in diameter and 100 feet deep. To while away the hours until the boat returns, there is also a trail around the perimeter of the 315-acre island. Nearby Merriam Cone is twice as high as Wizard Island but is located in a much deeper part of Crater Lake—and the top is 500 feet below the surface.

36 Mount Scott

A splendid panorama of all of Crater Lake and much of Southern Oregon from the highest point in Crater Lake National Park.

Distance: 4.4-mile out and back
Difficulty: Moderate to strenuous
Elevation gain: 1,245 feet
Best season: Mid-July–Oct
Maps: USGS Crater Lake East; Crater Lake National Park
Trail contacts: Crater Lake National Park: (541) 594-3100
Parking and trailhead facilities: Thirty cars can park along the shoulder. A couple of picnic tables offer a place to snack near the trailhead. The nearest camping is at Lost Creek,

7 miles away on the Pinnacles Road, inside the park.
Special considerations: Park entrance fee is charged per vehicle. No pets are permitted on trails in Crater Lake National Park.
This is one of the last roads and trails to open up in the park. Call ahead if coming in early July. There is no water on this trail. It is almost entirely in the open and steep throughout. Sun can be intense because of the high elevation. Bring water and wear sunscreen.

Finding the trailhead: From Medford take OR 62 (Crater Lake Highway) to the south Crater Lake entrance past milepost 73, following signs for the national park. Four miles past the entrance booth, before the Steel Visitor Center, veer right onto East Rim Drive. Follow it for 12 winding miles to a parking pullout and sign on the right.

From the north entrance, turn left onto East Rim Drive and follow it 11 miles, past Cleetwood Cove, to a large switchback just before the Cloudcap turnoff. Look for the well-marked trailhead at the far end of the switchback.
Trailhead GPS: N42 55.141'/W122 01.663'

The Hike

If Crater Lake is the scenic highlight of Oregon, the Mount Scott Trail is the ultimate hike in Crater Lake National Park. If you take your time and persevere, you will experience what is by far the ultimate Crater Lake panorama.

Perhaps 80 percent of the trees on Mount Scott are mountain hemlock, identifiable by their bent or drooping tips. Look also for narrow, spire-like subalpine fir, along with Shasta red fir and lodgepole pine. The stunted little trees hugging the highest ridges are whitebark pines. Most of the trees are concentrated near the lower end of the hike. Above, they are widely scattered. The terrain along most of the trail consists of ash, pumice, and loose gravel.

The trail to the top of "Great Scott," the park's highest point at 8,926 feet, begins to the right of a little hillock. It stays fairly level for the first 0.7 mile as it passes an immense avalanche basin sweeping down from the summit. Reaching the peak's back side, the path attains the summit in a series of switchbacks, each a little shorter

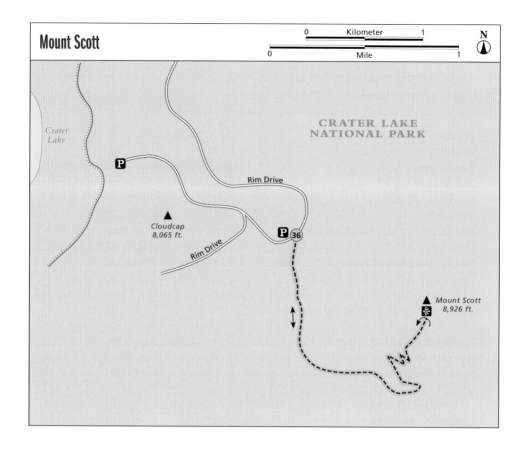

than the last. At the second switchback (mile 1.7), you can peer northward over into the avalanche basin. The view had been of the Sky Lakes, Mount McLoughlin, and Upper Klamath Lake, all to the south.

At mile 2.1 you reach the false summit, the beginning of a narrow, level ridge with the real summit, capped by an old lookout, at mile 2.2. The stairway to the lookout's viewing platform is locked.

Many landmarks may be seen from the Mount Scott summit, including Mount Thielsen, Diamond Lake, Diamond Peak, the South Sister, the Klamath Basin, Mount McLoughlin, and Mount Shasta, but the lake is so overwhelming you will be hard pressed to notice them.

From the summit, the aforementioned avalanche basin—a long, unbroken sweep of ash and loose gravel—shoots straight down almost to the parking area. People occasionally use it as a shortcut down. It's not that difficult, and not much of a short-cut because it only saves you about 5 minutes.

Miles and Directions

0.0 Begin at the Mount Scott Trailhead.

1.7 Arrive at an overlook, the first view north.

2.2 Reach the summit and lookout; return the way you came.

4.4 Arrive back at the trailhead

The view from Mount Scott's summit takes in the entirety of Crater Lake. Mount Scott is the only place where you can see the entire lake at once. NATIONAL PARK SERVICE

37 Garfield Peak

A gorgeous trail beginning at Crater Lake Lodge and climbing a narrow, rocky ridge with cliffs dropping directly to Crater Lake. Outstanding vista from the summit.

Distance: 3.4-mile out and back
Difficulty: Moderate
Elevation gain: 939 feet
Best season: July–Oct
Maps: USGS Crater Lake West and Crater Lake East; Crater Lake National Park
Trail contacts: Crater Lake National Park: (541) 594-3100
Parking and trailhead facilities: The paved lot near the trailhead offers parking for 20 cars; the lodge offers more parking for guests. The lodge has restrooms and a gift shop. You can camp at Mazama Campground, near the south entrance.

Special considerations: Entrance fee per car. There is no water on the trail, but it isn't very long, and there are plenty of shady spots. No pets are permitted on trails in Crater Lake National Park.

Finding the trailhead: From Medford take OR 62 (Crater Lake Highway) to the south Crater Lake entrance past milepost 73. Proceed 6 miles on the South Entrance Road, past Mazama Campground and park headquarters, up the hill to the Rim Village. Continue past the gift shop for 0.3 mile to the far end of the lodge. The trail begins behind the lodge, at the rim above the lake. **Trailhead GPS:** N42 54.577' / W122 08.410'

The Hike

Garfield Peak is not named for a US president or a cartoon cat. It is named for a former secretary of the interior.

As you drive the winding road between Crater Lake's park headquarters and Rim Village, you should catch a glimpse of the Garfield Peak Trail. It is visible clinging to a mass of tortured pink lava above an immense drop-off.

The Garfield Peak Trail is one of the most accessible and spectacular within Oregon's only national park. Although the park's Mount Scott is 900 feet higher, Garfield Peak is part of the actual lake rim, while Mount Scott is set back from the lake. The Garfield Peak Trail is shorter and a little steeper than the Mount Scott Trail. The route is part of a longer trail paralleling the Rim Drive as far as Discovery Point, 3.0 miles from the lodge in the opposite direction from Garfield Peak.

As the path to the Garfield Peak summit heads uphill from the lodge, snaking through enchanted forest pockets and peering over the rim's imposing crags, it passes high-elevation forests of whitebark pine, mountain hemlock, and subalpine fir.

Clean and parklike, with picture-perfect vistas at every turn, the route brings to mind the idealized imagery of a nineteenth-century landscape painting. It is, to quote Walt Whitman, a study in "pure luminous color." The rocks vary from orange to pink to purple to tan to gray to black and are splotched with Day-Glo yellow, red, and

Garfield Peak is a prominent summit on the Crater Lake rim, with the trail beginning behind Crater Lake Lodge. LYNN BERNSTEIN

black lichen. Wildflowers of all hues and descriptions poke from between the rocks and carpet the occasional patches of grass and woods. The lake is a hundredfold bluer than the bluest sky. And the surrounding forests and meadows spread their iridescent greens, yellows, and blue-blacks to the horizon.

At the summit—a roomy flat with a smattering of windswept whitebark pines—cliffs shoot down 1,900 feet to the lake, near the Phantom Ship. Both the Rim Village and park headquarters can be seen far, far below.

This is an ideal spot for orienting yourself to local geography. Aside from old favorites such as Mounts Shasta, McLoughlin, and Thielsen, several other landmarks can be seen. Union Peak's jutting pyramid rises dramatically from the park's southwest corner. To the south and a little farther away, you see Devil's Peak, at the core of the Sky Lakes Wilderness. The Middle Fork of the Rogue flows northward off Devil's Peak, through the spectacular Seven Lakes Basin.

The rugged summits to the northwest belong to the Rogue-Umpqua Divide range and are much older than other mountains in the vicinity. Fish Mountain is the highest peak in that group.

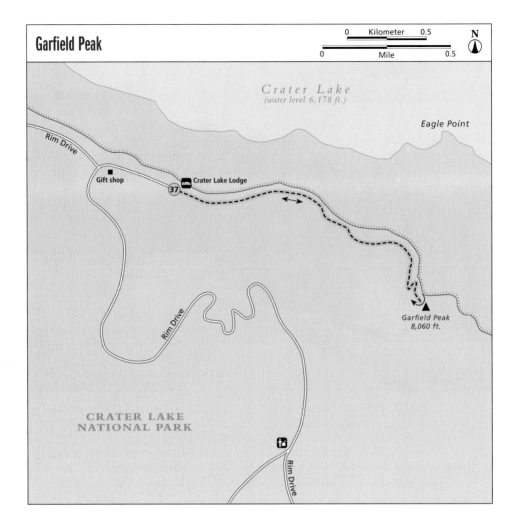

Miles and Directions

0.0   Begin at the Crater Lake Lodge trailhead.

1.7   Reach the summit; return the way you came.

3.4   Arrive back at the lodge trailhead.

38 Annie Creek Loop

A huge, steep-sided ash canyon beginning at Mazama Campground near the Crater Lake National Park South Entrance.

Distance: 1.6-mile loop
Difficulty: Easy to moderate
Elevation loss and gain: 317 feet
Best season: June–Oct
Maps: USGS Crater Lake West; Crater Lake National Park
Trail contacts: Crater Lake National Park: (541) 594-3100
Parking and trailhead facilities: Park at the Mazama Village Store parking lot, since parking at the campground is for paid campers only. In addition to a store, you'll find gas, showers, cabins, and a Laundromat. There are restrooms on each campground loop.

Special considerations: An entrance fee is charged per vehicle. No pets are permitted on trails in Crater Lake National Park.

There is lots of water along this route, most of which comes from a huge spring less than 1 mile away, but don't drink it because of all the people and buildings nearby. The path contains two steep pitches as the loop enters, then leaves, the Annie Creek canyon. The steep, ashy north slopes retain snow in spring much later than the rest of the trail. Attempting to walk across these precarious snowbanks can be dangerous. Mazama Campground is right at the entrance station (which can't be avoided).

Finding the trailhead: From Medford take OR 62 (Crater Lake Highway) to the south Crater Lake entrance past milepost 73. Immediately past the south entrance station, you'll come to the turnoff to Mazama Village, on the right. Park at the store; then continue through the parking lot on foot to the campground road and turn right. It's a 5-minute walk to and through Loop D. The trail runs along the canyon rim at the far end of Loop D (also the far end of Loops C, E, F, and G). The actual trailhead is located at the amphitheater between Loops D and E. Go left at the trailhead for the quickest route into the canyon.
Trailhead GPS: N42 52.058' / W122 10.032'

The Hike

This little orphan of a hike (Get it? Annie?) would be high on the list of magnificent trails at Crater Lake National Park except that there are no views of the lake. Instead the trail explores a spectacular and fascinating ash canyon.

Annie Creek canyon is easy to find. Every loop in the park's Mazama Campground touches it. A popular vista point on OR 62, just east of the south entrance, provides an outstanding view of not only the Annie Creek canyon but of an equally impressive side canyon, Godfrey Glen (see "Options").

The canyon is named for Annie Gaines, who visited Crater Lake in 1865 and reputedly was the first female to do so. The reason for the canyon's flat, parklike bottom is that the soft ash deposit into which the canyon is cut fills an old, much wider, flat-bottomed glacial valley. The present valley bottom is the original, much harder valley floor before it filled up with ash.

Annie Creek Canyon is seen from the rim at Mazama Campground. LYNN BERNSTEIN

Heading left (north) from the trailhead at the amphitheater, the path hugs the rim for 0.2 mile before making a sharp switchback and plunging into the gorge. (Do not try to follow any of the unmarked way trails that also seem to lead into the gorge—they are extremely dangerous.) Views along the rim reveal the steep bluffs and spires of the canyon walls and the grassy meadows of the canyon floor, with Annie Creek running down the middle.

The spires are caused by gas fumaroles that once made their way up through the compacted ash deposits. The minerals in the gas rendered those spots harder and slower to erode than the surrounding ash. The park's best spire formations are seen off the Rim Drive at the Pinnacles.

At the start of the turn into the canyon climb, you can pick up an interpretive booklet for a minimal fee (free if you return the booklet when you're done). The trail reaches the canyon bottom in 0.2 mile and two steep switchbacks. The ashy hillside is

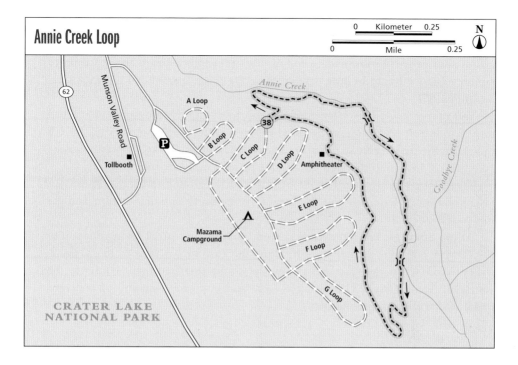

Annie Creek Loop

very steep and loose but not as steep and loose as the hillside on the climb back out, beginning just past the second footbridge (at mile 0.9).

Once at the bottom, the path follows the creek's southwest (campground) side, around the base of some ash slopes, for 0.2 mile. It then crosses a little footbridge (mile 0.5) to the more wooded northeast bank. Look for mountain hemlock, Shasta red fir, subalpine fir, and lodgepole pine. The scene passes a series of small meadows with buttercups, monkey flower, Indian paintbrush, sedge, and horsetails. A highlight is Annie Creek Falls, a 15-foot vertical plunge that's past a slot where the trail crosses a little side creek.

At 0.9 mile the path crosses another footbridge and returns to the southwest bank, arriving back at the rim at mile 1.2 and completing the loop at mile 1.6

Returning to the rim in a series of switchbacks, the Annie Creek Trail contours up a loose, steep, exposed ash slope, emerging at the far end of campground Loop G, 0.3 mile from the trailhead.

Miles and Directions

0.0 Begin at the trailhead, heading left (clockwise) from near the amphitheater.
0.1 Begin the decent into the canyon.
0.5 Cross the first footbridge.
0.9 Cross the second footbridge.
1.2 Arrive back on the rim.
1.6 Arrive at the trailhead at the end of the loop.

Options

Godfrey Glen: At the second footbridge, when the water level is low, an adventurous soul might be inspired to follow the creek downstream for 0.3 mile to Godfrey Glen, a beautiful little flat alongside the creek surrounded on three sides by ash bluffs.

You can view Godfrey Glen from the top by taking the Mazama Valley Road for 0.6 mile past Mazama Campground to the Godfrey Glen Nature Trail. It's 0.3 mile from the parking area to the rim. The trail passes tantalizingly close to Duwee Falls, which flows into the glen but cannot be seen from the trail.

The easiest way to view Duwee Falls is to drive around to the Godfrey Glen vista point on OR 62, just past the turnoff to the south entrance station, and get out your binoculars.

Annie Springs: From the Annie Creek Trailhead, instead of hiking down into the canyon, continue straight (north) along the rim for 0.3 mile to the Mazama Valley Road. Cross the road and follow the continuing trail for 0.1 mile to the source of Annie Creek. The spring is large and impressive but full of concrete, metal, and artificial impoundments.

39 Union Peak

A spectacular panorama from the top of a steep-sided volcanic pyramid.

Distance: 9.6-mile out and back
Difficulty: Easy for 4.3 miles; strenuous for 0.5 mile
Elevation gain: 1,445 feet
Best season: Late June–Oct
Maps: USGS Union Peak; Crater Lake National Park
Trail contacts: Crater Lake National Park: (541) 594-3100
Parking and trailhead facilities: A dirt parking lot at the trailhead accommodates 10 cars. The nearest camping is at Mazama Campground, 1 mile away. To reach the campground, you must pay an entrance fee at the south entrance station in addition to the campground fee.
Special considerations: There is no water on this hike. No pets are permitted on trails in Crater Lake National Park. Although this route lies entirely within Crater Lake National Park, no entrance stations are passed, so no fee is required. The last 0.5 mile to the summit may be impassable well into July.

Finding the trailhead: Drive northeast from Medford on OR 62 (Crater Lake Highway) to the well-marked spot inside Crater Lake National Park where the Pacific Crest Trail (#2000) crosses the highway at milepost 72. The crossing is located 1 mile before (west of) the turnoff to the park's south entrance station.

Look for a well-marked roadside turnout containing an interpretive sign for the PCT on the left (north) side of the highway. This is the trailhead for the PCT northbound to Dutton Creek and Canada. The trailhead for the PCT southbound, to Union Peak and Mexico, is located opposite the interpretive sign on the right (south) side of the highway. An unnumbered 200-foot-long dirt road leads to the southbound trailhead parking area.

Trailhead GPS: N42 52.240' / W122 10.808'

The Hike

Anyone who has approached Crater Lake National Park from the west has seen Union Peak. Just before the park boundary, at milepost 64 on OR 62, an immense black, steep-sided volcanic mountain suddenly looms in front of you. Almost immediately, the highway curves away and the mysterious peak disappears from view. It is never seen again—not from the highway or from any other road.

The hike up Union Peak, the 7,709-foot sentinel of the park's southwest corner, is one of Southern Oregon's more challenging. The peak's 800-foot-high rock pyramid sticks out like a boil amid much more level surroundings. The horrendously steep 0.5-mile final walk up the pyramid is immensely scenic, great fun (if exhausting), and well worth the lengthy trek to the base.

From the trailhead, the first 1.9 miles along the Pacific Crest Trail (#2000) are relatively level and featureless as the path makes its way through a forest of mountain hemlock, Shasta red fir, and lodgepole pine. If you enjoy strolls through the woods, it's lovely; if you don't, the scenery gets much better farther up.

The Union Peak summit lies atop a huge craggy pyramid towering above the trail. VIC HARRIS

After 2.0 miles the path begins a gentle rise out of the Union Creek drainage to the low divide with the Red Blanket Creek drainage. At mile 1.9 the New Union Peak Trail comes in on the left, reaching the summit in 2.9 miles. Be aware that many maps still show only the old route, which starts a mile farther down the PCT.

From the PCT junction, the New Union Peak Trail makes its way up to and along a narrow ridge, with outstanding vistas of Devil's Peak and the Middle Fork Rogue glacial canyon to the south in the Sky Lakes Wilderness. Eventually the Union Peak summit comes dramatically into view.

At mile 4.3—in the middle of a small, open ridgetop area where the closed-off old trail comes in on the left—the path commences the horrendously steep 0.5-mile ascent to the summit. Even if you don't climb to the summit, the close-up view of the pyramid will take your breath away.

The pyramid's main feature is its steepness. At a trail gradient of 1,600 feet per mile, the only steeper path in Southern Oregon is on Mount McLoughlin, whose final trail mile ascends 1,700 feet.

There isn't a more beautiful trail, either. A profusion of wildflowers—penstemon, Indian paintbrush, lupine, and saxifrage—decorate the white, orange, purple, and

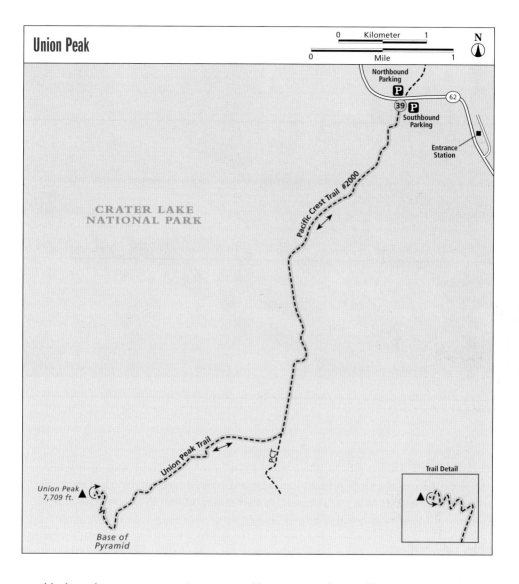

Union Peak

0   Kilometer   1
0   Mile   1

N

CRATER LAKE
NATIONAL PARK

Northbound
Parking
P
39 P
Southbound
Parking

62

Entrance
Station

Pacific Crest Trail #2000

Union Peak Trail

PCT

Union Peak
7,709 ft.

Base of
Pyramid

Trail Detail

black rock outcrops, creating memorable scenery. It's a well-engineered path too, except for the final 100 feet, which scramble up a sharp, cindery rock face. Watch for loose boulders, slippery pitches, and steep drop-offs.

From the summit you can't quite see into Crater Lake, but you can see the cliffs of the far shore, with Mounts Thielsen and Bailey rising behind. To the south, much of the Sky Lakes Wilderness is visible, especially the Red Blanket Creek drainage.

The peak's geology becomes obvious at the summit. The mountain is a volcanic cone of cinder and ash, with much dense, pasty lava in the mix and spatter formations on top. It is not an ancillary cone to Mount Mazama, where Crater Lake is located, but a major summit in its own right.

The beginning of the Union Peak Trail's steep climb up the pyramid is deceptively level. VIC HARRIS

It appears that a south-flowing glacier on Mount Mazama once flowed past Union Peak into Red Blanket Creek. The evidence was later obscured by tons of volcanic ash from the major eruption of Mount Mazama 6,600 years ago, which ultimately formed Crater Lake. Many of the tons of ash burying Union Peak's base no doubt came from Mazama, although a huge amount also spewed from Union Peak itself.

Miles and Directions

0.0 Begin southbound from the PCT trailhead.

1.9 Arrive at the new Union Peak Trail junction; go right.

4.3 Arrive at the base of the pyramid.

4.8 Reach the summit; return the way you came.

9.6 Arrive back at the trailhead.

Options

Union Peak from the Sky Lakes: To reach Union Peak from the Sky Lakes Wilderness, follow the Pacific Crest Trail (#2000) north into Crater Lake National Park. The shortest route would follow the Red Blanket Trail to the Stuart Falls Trail (#1087) to the PCT to the Union Peak Trail, arriving atop Union Peak after 10.5 miles.

40 Plaikni Falls

Wildflowers, a quiet canyon, and a beautiful waterfall on an easy and accessible trail.

Distance: 2.2-mile out and back
Difficulty: Easy
Elevation gain: 100 feet
Best season: Early July–Oct
Maps: USGS Crater Lake East; Crater Lake National Park

Trail contacts: Crater Lake National Park: (541) 594-3100
Parking and trailhead facilities: The parking pullout has room for around 10 to 15 cars.
Special considerations: Pets are not permitted on trails in Crater Lake National Park. The national park has a per-vehicle entrance fee.

Finding the trailhead: From Medford take OR 62 (Crater Lake Highway) to the south Crater Lake entrance past milepost 73. Proceed approximately 3.9 miles on the South Entrance Road, past Mazama Village. Just before the Steel Visitor Center, veer right onto Rim Drive East and follow it 8.5 miles. Just before the Phantom Ship Overlook at Kerr Notch, turn right onto Pinnacles Road. After 1 mile down this paved road, park at a pullout on the left.
Trailhead GPS: N42 54.105' / W122 03.646'

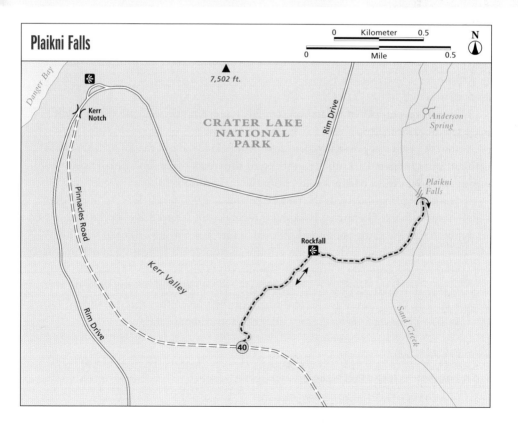

Plaikni Falls

Crater Lake National Park's Plaikni Falls is one of the park's popular hikes that doesn't feature views of the lake, instead opting for a pretty waterfall of about 40 feet. Zach Urness

The Hike

The newest trail at Crater Lake National Park, this quiet and easy path takes visitors away from the crowds of the Rim Drive and into the canyon of an extremely pretty 20-foot waterfall.

The trail was completed in late summer 2011 and, with the exception of a slightly steep section near the trail's end, is wheelchair accessible.

Before the trail was constructed, so few people knew about the falls that it didn't have an official name. Park officials turned to members of the Klamath Tribe, who suggested Plaikni Falls, which means "from the high country."

Indeed, the spring that feeds the falls originates at 7,000 feet before tumbling over a glacier-carved cliff. The spring is fed by snowmelt, not Crater Lake itself.

From the trailhead the path winds through a forest of old-growth mountain hemlock trees and lodgepole pine. At mile 0.5 the canyon's cliffs appear stage left, and at mile 0.8 the route begins winding uphill along Sand Creek.

The waterfall is just beyond, tumbling down a silver cliff with a small viewing area below the falls. Wildflowers are present much of the year in the waterfall's spray, and the hike overall makes a nice and easy side trip from Crater Lake.

Miles and Directions

- **0.0** Begin at the Plaikni Falls Trailhead.
- **1.1** Reach Plaikni Falls; return the way you came.
- **2.2** Arrive back at the trailhead.

41 Middle Fork Rogue River

An easy trek up Southern Oregon's most impressive glacial valley.

Distance: 6.6-mile out and back
Difficulty: Easy
Elevation gain/loss: Negligible
Best season: May–Nov
Maps: USGS Imnaha Creek, Rogue River–Siskiyou National Forest

Trail contacts: High Cascades/Prospect Ranger District: (541) 560-3400
Parking and trailhead facilities: The Middle Fork Trailhead accommodates 10 cars.

Finding the trailhead: Take OR 62 (Crater Lake Highway) north from Medford past milepost 43 to the Prospect turnoff. Turn right, proceed for 1 block, and then turn right again onto Mill Creek Drive. After 0.5 block turn left at the Prospect Hotel onto the Prospect–Butte Falls Road. Continue for 3 miles, then bear left onto FR 37 (paved and gravel). Continue 7.5 miles on FR 37 to FR 3785, then 3 more miles to the trailhead.
Trailhead GPS: N42 43.548' / W122 18.381'

The Hike

The Middle Fork of the Rogue River here flows down an immense glacial valley, the largest and deepest in Oregon, marked by steep, even sides and a flat bottom. Since the river has cut a small canyon into the larger valley, the trail's designers chose to locate the path away from the river, on the more level bench. Hence the scarcity of river approaches on the first portion of the hike.

Between the trailhead and Halifax Junction, there's not a hill, side creek, or clearing, and only three brief glimpses of the river. After 2.0 miles of this, the spot where the trail swings south is a major highlight.

Note: In an earlier edition of this guide, the Middle Fork Trail was part of a lengthy one-way shuttle hike that began at the Seven Lakes Trailhead and involved the King Spruce Trail, the Alta Lake Trail, and the steep upper portion of the Middle Fork Trail. That route is no longer recommended due to an extreme amount of ravel and downed trees from the 2008 Lonesome Complex fire. You'll start running into this as you approach the Halifax junction at mile 2.0. The "official trail" is described to where the route cuts uphill at mile 3.3, but you may not get that far because of the downed trees.

A dominant understory species in the path along the Middle Fork is little princess pine, a member of the wintergreen family. A few years ago, little princess pine officially replaced sassafras as the root of choice in natural root beer. The species is clonal, which means individual plants are connected underground to other plants through root runners. Whatever is harvested (within reason) will grow back within a couple of weeks. *Note:* It's illegal to pick little princess pine without a permit.

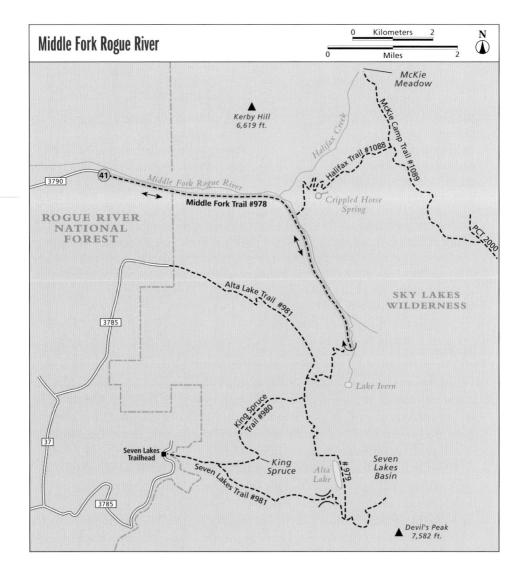

The Halifax Trail (#1088) takes off to the right 2.0 miles from the trailhead. Following it down to the river crossing (via a large log) is recommended. It's only about 0.2 mile to probably the prettiest spot on the Middle Fork Trail.

Above Halifax Junction, the river is much more visible but a fair distance away. The river here is lined with low dirt bluffs, while the trail runs through a very pretty and level wooded area. The recommended turnaround comes at mile 3.3, where the route veers sharply away from the river and eventually starts steeply uphill.

As pretty as the upper portion is, you may not get very far past Halifax Junction because of downed trees and debris. The forest service plans to eventually clear the trail.

Miles and Directions

0.0 Begin at the Middle Fork Trailhead.

2.0 Pass the turnoff to the Halifax Trail.

3.3 The trail leaves the river and starts steeply uphill. This is the recommended turnaround.

6.6 Arrive back at the trailhead.

Options

Halifax Trail: If you can get across the river over the precarious tree-bridge, which you often can't until early August, it's a steep 1.0-mile climb, gaining 1,000 feet in elevation, to Crippled Horse Spring, 3.0 more miles to Solace Camp, and 2.0 more miles (heading north) to McKie Camp. The lower portion of the Halifax Trail is also greatly impacted by forest fire debris.

42 Seven Lakes Basin–West

A popular trail into a magnificent basin, visiting three of the Seven Lakes. This may be Southern Oregon's most scenic hike, especially when combined with the Devil's Peak Trail.

Distance: 9.8-mile out and back
Difficulty: Strenuous
Elevation gain: 2,366 feet
Best season: Late June–Oct
Maps: USGS Imnaha Creek and Devil's Peak; Rogue River–Siskiyou National Forest
Trail contacts: High Cascades Ranger District: (541) 560-3400
Parking and trailhead facilities: The Seven Lakes Trailhead accommodates 20 cars and has a horse-loading ramp. The nearest forest service campground is Big Ben, on FR 37, 2 miles past the FR 3780 turnoff.

Special considerations: The Seven Lakes Trail may contain impassable snow well into July. Also, the mosquito density can be astonishing in the basin in June and July. The situation gets better in August and much better in September. There is adequate water along most routes but also much horse traffic.

Camping within 100 feet of all lakes is prohibited, and equestrians must use designated horse camps. Group size is limited to 12 people unless the group is passing through on a longer trip on the Pacific Crest Trail.

Finding the trailhead: From Medford take OR 62 north to the Prospect turnoff past milepost 43. Follow signs into the town of Prospect. From OR 62 turn right on First Street and right again on Mill Creek Drive. At the Prospect Hotel, turn left onto the Prospect–Butte Falls Road. After 3 miles bear left onto FR 37 and follow it 13 miles to FR 3780. The sign for the Seven Lakes Trailhead at the FR 37– FR 3780 junction can be seen only from the opposite direction. Look for FR 37 to make a right-angle turn right with a wide gravel road talking off left. Proceed 3 miles up FR 3780 to the trailhead.
Trailhead GPS: N42 39.759' / W122 17.134'

The Hike

Few lakes in this guide, or anywhere, can match the stunning beauty of Cliff Lake and the Seven Lakes Basin. Although the trail can be a challenge, the rewards are many.

From the Seven Lakes Trailhead it's a relentless 2.0-mile uphill trek to Frog Lake through a middle-elevation, second-growth forest of white fir, sugar pine, lodgepole pine, and western white pine.

Frog Lake is the forest canopy's first real opening. The charming 2-acre pool signals the start of the real scenery, with impressive lava cliffs just to the east.

Beginning 1.0 mile beyond Frog Lake, the steepening path surmounts a series of switchbacks to Seven Lakes saddle, where the Devil's Peak Trail (#984) takes off to the right. If you have a hankering to climb Devil's Peak and visit the Seven Lakes Basin on the same trip, do Devil's Peak first.

Cliff Lake is the stunning highlight of the Seven Lakes Basin, sitting below Devil's Peak.
ZACH URNESS

Just 0.2 mile beyond the saddle on the Seven Lakes Trail is a junction for Alta Lake. This side trip adds 1.0 mile to your experience, but Alta Lake is the largest, most unusual, and probably the prettiest of the Seven Lakes. (See "Options" for more information.)

After the tantalizing preview from the saddle and a 1.0-mile descent with a 550-foot elevation loss, you reach the basin proper. The descent winds through a forest of Shasta red fir, lodgepole pine, subalpine fir, and mountain hemlock, with several small wildflower meadows breaking the monotony. Much of the terrain is open, offering frequent barren hillsides and long vistas.

The first lake, South Lake, is a clear, steep-sided tarn surrounded by an open lodgepole pine forest. The lake is unstocked, and few campsites are available.

Cliff Lake, 4.9 miles from the trailhead, is among the Sky Lakes' most beautiful. The deep blue pool hugs the base of a tortured, 1,000-foot lava wall that looks like it might have been coughed up from Hell. The cliff is not part of Devil's Peak but belongs to a rocky dome that juts up in the middle of the basin. Although Cliff Lake is the most coveted camping spot because of its beauty and forested shore, there is little level space except near the outlet.

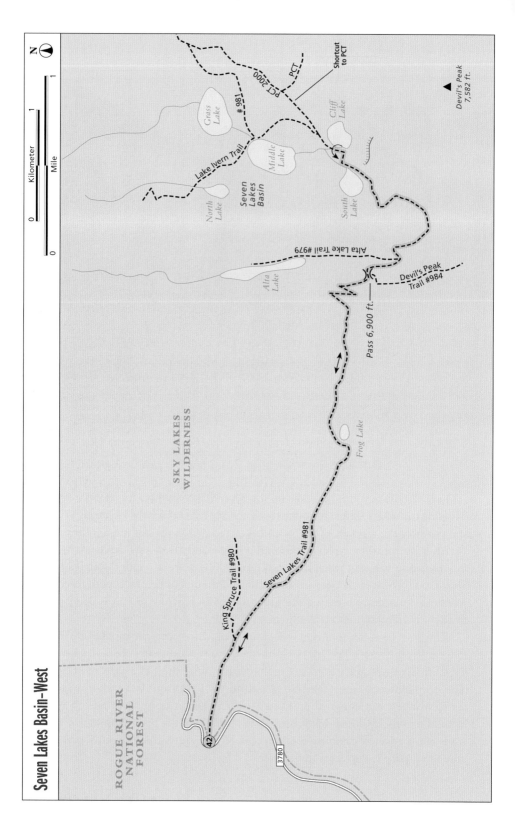

Seven Lakes Basin–West

N

0 — Kilometer — 1

0 — Mile — 1

ROGUE RIVER
NATIONAL
FOREST

SKY LAKES
WILDERNESS

King Spruce Trail #980

Seven Lakes Trail #981

Frog Lake

42

3780

Alta Lake

Alta Lake Trail #979

Pass 6,900 ft.

Devil's Peak
Trail #984

North
Lake

Seven
Lakes
Basin

Middle
Lake

Grass
Lake

#981

Lake Ivern Trail

South
Lake

Cliff
Lake

PCT 2000

PCT

Shortcut
to PCT

Devil's Peak
7,582 ft.

Miles and Directions

0.0   Begin at the Seven Lakes Trailhead.

0.6   Pass the Kings Spruce Trail junction.

2.1   Pass Frog Lake.

3.3   Arrive at the saddle, with the Devil's Peak Trail taking off to the right. Stay on Seven Lakes Trail.

3.5   Pass the Alta Lake Trail junction. (It's 0.5 mile to Alta Lake.)

4.5   Pass South Lake.

4.9   Reach Cliff Lake; return the way you came.

9.8   Arrive back at the trailhead.

Options

Alta Lake Trail: If you count only the lake itself and not the cliffs and mountains around them, Alta Lake is the prettiest of the Seven Lakes group. It's also the largest. The lake's serene beauty is enhanced by mysterious and unusual geology. Unlike every other lake in the region, Alta Lake perches atop a dome-shaped mountain whose summit appears to have been whacked with a giant machete. For the best perspective on Alta Lake's weird setting, hike 1.0 mile up the Devil's Peak Trail from the Seven Lakes summit and look back. The steep-sided lake is 0.5 mile long but only a few hundred feet wide, with a precipitous creek outlet (and a continuation of the trail) leading north to the Middle Fork Trail.

Alta Lake is the result of a "normal fault," a big crack where one side slipped downward, the other side slipped upward, and the up side does not overhang the down side. At Alta Lake, the east side is the down side. Normal faults result from tension, or pulling apart of the land. In the Cascades you're much more likely to find evidence of compression than of tension. The Alta Lake Fault is shown on State of Oregon geological maps.

Alta Lake has lots of fish and far fewer mosquitoes than the six lakes in the basin. To reach Alta Lake, turn at the Alta Lake junction, 3.7 miles from the Seven Lakes Trailhead, and hike 0.5 mile to its shoreline.

43 Seven Lakes Basin–East

Although less popular than the Seven Lakes Trail, this route from the Seven Mile Trailhead, east of the Sky Lakes, is easier and possibly even more scenic. The trail visits two of the Seven Lakes: Grass and Middle, with options to North Lake and Lake Ivern. Cliff and South Lakes aren't too far away either.

Distance: 10.6-mile out and back
Difficulty: Moderate
Elevation gain: 690 feet
Best season: Late June–Oct
Maps: USGS Imnaha Creek and Devil's Peak; Fremont-Winema National Forest
Trail contacts: Klamath Ranger District: (541) 885-3400

Parking and trailhead facilities: There's a small campground with a vault toilet at the Sevenmile Trailhead and parking for 10 cars.
Special considerations: The density of the mosquito population before August can be truly astonishing. Bring industrial-strength insect repellent (all-natural products may not work) or mosquito netting for your hands, face, and neck.

Finding the trailhead: From Medford take OR 62 north 6 miles to White City. Turn right onto OR 140 east and follow it past Lake of the Woods and the Cold Spring turnoff to Westside Road, near milepost 43. Take the paved Westside Road left for 17 miles to where it becomes Sevenmile Road and swings sharply right (east). The gravel FR 3300 takes off here, which you will follow. After 3 miles FR 3300 arrives at a complex junction with a sign directing you to the Sevenmile Trailhead in 6 miles. Follow FR 3334 through old-growth forest to the trailhead and campground.
Trailhead GPS: N42 41.959' / W122 08.294'

The Hike

The popular Sevenmile Trail (#3703) requires a longer hike to enter the Seven Lakes Basin than the Seven Lakes Trail, but it doesn't climb a 6,900-foot saddle to get there. The route offers a far better early-season entry into the area. The trailhead, at a small campground, may be one of the Sky Lakes' prettiest. Although the path follows three different trails, the trajectory is a nearly straight line from northeast to southwest.

From the trailhead the path spends its early portion passing Sevenmile Marsh. The marsh consists mostly of flat, grassy areas alongside a creek, downhill from the gently climbing trail. At 0.8 mile the marsh widens considerably, with the abrupt, forested wall of Klamath Point (7,210 feet) rising on the creek's far side. Then the marsh ends. For the last 1.0 mile to the Pacific Crest Trail (PCT) junction, the path climbs for brief stretches and stays level for long stretches.

At the PCT junction, at 1.8 mile, go left (southwest) for the Seven Lakes Basin, in the Devil's Peak direction. The opposite direction on the PCT (north), takes you to the McKie Camp Trail in 2.0 miles and Crater Lake National Park in 10.5 miles.

Beyond the PCT junction, 2.3 miles from the trailhead amid a gentle, mostly downhill hike, the PCT hits the edge of a rim high above the spectacular Middle

Middle Lake and Grass Lake in the Seven Lakes Basin. VIC HARRIS

Fork Canyon, Oregon's largest glacial valley. The view is partly obscured by trees and not nearly as impressive as the view of the same canyon from Lake Ivern. But it's still pretty impressive. The reddish bulge on the ridgetop to the northeast is Mount Maude (7,184 feet).

Forests along the way alternate between small lodgepole pines on the dusty, ashy areas and mixed middle-elevation forests on the better developed soils. The mixed forests consist of lodgepole and western white pines, subalpine and Shasta red firs, mountain hemlock, and Engelmann spruce. You pass many small, grassy, marshy areas, as well as dryer open areas of red huckleberry, red heather, and pinemat manzanita.

Beyond the rim encounter, the path starts seriously uphill, crossing Honeymoon Creek. The route's highest elevation (6,205 feet) comes shortly after the junction with the Seven Lakes Trail, at mile 4.3, where you will turn right onto the Seven Lakes Trail. Grass Lake is passed at mile 4.9; Middle Lake and the Lake Ivern Trailhead show up at mile 5.3.

Grass Lake is stocked with brook trout. Much of the lake is inaccessible and surrounded by a marshy meadow (hence the name) where horses are not allowed. Camping is permitted at the better defined and more wooded west shore. Several side trails, marked CAMPING AND HORSE CAMP, lead there.

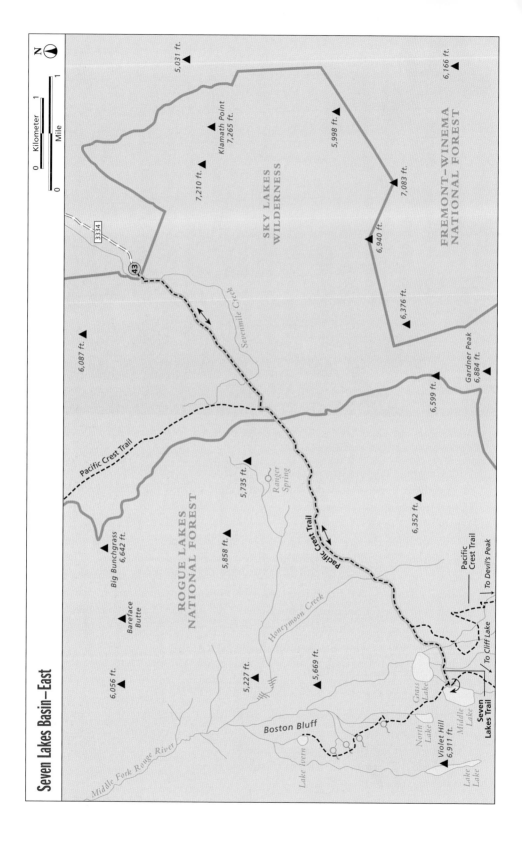

Seven Lakes Basin—East

There is plenty of excellent camping at Middle Lake along the beautiful wooded shore, with Devi's Peak rising just to the south. This is a beautiful spot (once the mosquitoes have slacked off). A maze of side trails near Middle Lake lead to Cliff Lake, Devil's Peak, and Lake Ivern. Middle Lake covers 30 acres and is stocked with brook trout.

Miles and Directions

0.0 Begin at the Sevenmile Trailhead.

1.8 Arrive at the PCT junction; go left.

2.3 Reach a vista of Middle Fork canyon.

4.3 Come to the junction with Seven Lakes Trail; go right.

5.3 Reach Middle Lake and the Lake Ivern Trailhead; return the way you came.

10.6 Arrive back at the parking area and trailhead.

Options

North Lake and Lake Ivern: The 2.2-mile Lake Ivern Trail (#994) from Middle Lake takes you past North Lake to the remote and isolated Lake Ivern, with a spectacular view of the Middle Fork canyon and points north. The route loses 400 feet in elevation from Middle Lake.

The Lake Ivern Trail crosses the Middle Lake outlet and then wanders gently downhill through the woods, passing North Lake after 0.5 mile. There is no trail to North Lake, and it cannot be seen from the Lake Ivern Trail. Look for a small creek crossing with a sign to the right that reads HORSE FEED. Go left there and up the creek for a few hundred feet. The creek soon opens to a large wet meadow with North Lake in the middle and the yellow rock of the Alta Lake ridge directly overhead.

The Lake Ivern Trail's steepest downhill pitch comes shortly beyond North Lake, when the path inscribes a wide switchback through the deep woods. The path crosses several rocky scree slopes and is very pleasant overall. Buckley Spring emerges at the base of a scree slope rock pile at mile 1.3, with a huge flow of water alongside the trail.

At mile 1.8, a side trail takes off downhill to the right, with a sign that says BIG-FOOT SPRING—¼ MILE. The map shows at least two springs in the vicinity. However, the side trail peters out after 0.2 mile without passing any springs. This is not a good place to get lost. ***Note:*** The forest service plans to abandon the Bigfoot Spring Trail.

Eventually the path contours slowly down through the woods to the lake, with the Middle Fork canyon dominating the panorama in the distance. The lake itself isn't much, but it is stocked with brook trout. The trail ends at the lake outlet, where the creek drops straight down over a huge cliff that is part of Boston Bluff.

Even though every lake in the Seven Lakes Basin drains into the Middle Fork canyon, no trail directly connects the two locations. This is partly due to an imposing, waterfall-laden series of cliffs called Boston Bluff. A little off-trail bushwhacking as you approach Lake Ivern will reward you with a close-up view of Boston Bluff.

44 Devil's Peak

From the pass above the Seven Lakes Basin, this hike scales the summit of Devil's Peak. When combined with the Seven Lakes Trail, this is the most scenic route in the Sky Lakes.

Distance: 10.6-mile out and back
Difficulty: Strenuous
Elevation gain: 2,478 feet
Best season: July–Oct
Maps: USGS Devil's Peak; Rogue River–Siskiyou National Forest
Trail contacts: High Cascades Ranger District: (541) 560-3400
Parking and trailhead facilities: The Seven Lakes Trailhead accommodates 20 cars and has a horse-loading ramp. The nearest forest service campground is Big Ben, on FR 37, 2 miles past the FR 3780 turnoff.

Special considerations: The Devil's Peak Trail becomes passable two weeks after the Seven Lakes Trail opens. Unlike the Seven Lakes Trail, there is no water on the Devil's Peak Trail except for melting snowbanks, which can persist into August. Mosquitoes are thick throughout the Seven Lakes Basin until late August.

Finding the trailhead: From Medford take OR 62 north to the Prospect turnoff past milepost 43. Follow signs into the town of Prospect. From OR 62 turn right on First Street and right again on Mill Creek Drive. At the Prospect Hotel, turn left onto the Prospect-Butte Falls Road. After 3 miles bear left onto FR 37 and follow it 13 miles to FR 3780. The sign for the Seven Lakes Trailhead at the FR 37–FR 3780 junction can be seen only from the opposite direction. Look for FR 37 to make a right-angle turn right with a wide gravel road taking off left. Proceed 3 miles up FR 3780 to the trailhead. **Trailhead GPS:** N42 39.759′ / W122 17.134′

The Hike

Devil's Peak offers one of the classic views of the Southern Cascades. From its 7,552-foot summit, the Seven Lakes Basin spreads out below like blue footprints in a valley carved by glaciers ripping through this landscape 7,000 years ago.

The hike is not easy, but it's not killingly difficult, either. Many people combine this hike with a backpacking trek through the Seven Lakes Basin (see "Options" below), but a day hike isn't bad as long as you get an early start.

The journey begins at the Seven Lakes Trailhead and climbs 3.3 rocky miles uphill, passing Frog Lake, to the well-marked junction of Devil's Peak Trail (#984) at a 6,900-foot saddle.

The Devil's Peak Trail is deceptively gentle (at first). The level first half of the 1.3-mile trail, between this summit and the Pacific Crest Trail (#2000), wanders through a beautiful woods and past an exquisite pond before steepening considerably and making its way onto the talus slopes just below the looming cliffs of Mount Lucifer (7,474 feet).

The view from the summit of Devil's Peak looks down upon the Seven Lakes Basin. Seen here are Grass, Middle, and South Lakes. ZACH URNESS

The Mount Lucifer traverse is the route's most impressive, with vistas of Devil's Peak; South, Middle, and Grass Lakes; and an astonishing view of Alta Lake and its strange mountaintop aerie.

The PCT eventually reaches a tree-line saddle offering the hike's first view southward. Stay left on the PCT for Devil's Peak.

Not far beyond the PCT junction, just 0.3 mile, is another saddle with a primitive way trail leading up barren rocky slopes to the left. The PCT plunges downhill to the right (and continues all the way down into the Seven Lakes Basin).

The way trail, which gradually improves, climbs 0.4 mile and 327 feet to the Devil's Peak summit (you'll have to veer left once more at a trail junction near the top). In contrast with the trailhead's dense forests, only a few brave, windswept whitebark pines and mountain hemlocks, along with widely scattered lupine and saxifrage, dot the alpine expanse.

Devil's Peak

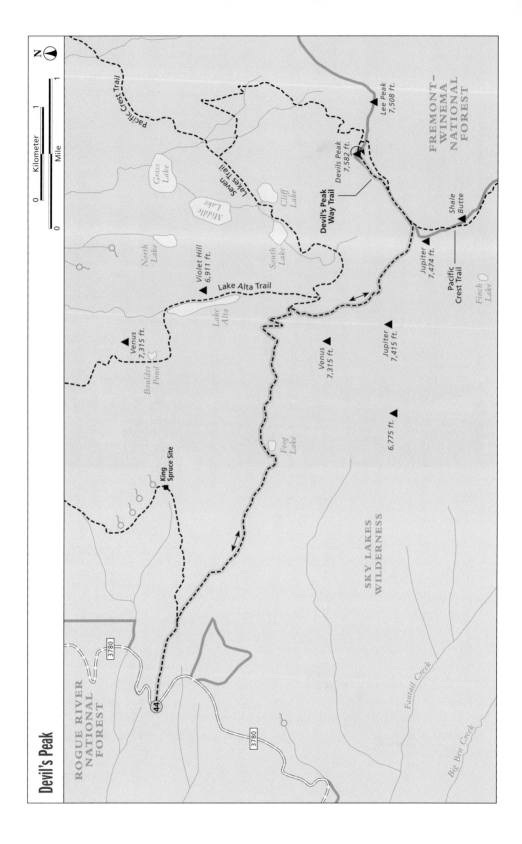

From the little rocky knob atop Devil's Peak, North, Grass, and Middle Lakes are easily visible to the north in the Seven Lakes Basin (Alta and South Lakes have now disappeared). So are Union Peak, Crater Lake's south rim, the Rogue-Umpqua Divide range, and the immense glacial canyon of the Rogue River's Middle Fork. Bear Creek Valley, containing Medford and Ashland, can be seen to the east; the Klamath Basin and Upper Klamath Lake dominate the west.

The view north from Devil's Peak reveals the Seven Lakes Basin as a large, complex glacial cirque. The glacier responsible was a substantial valley glacier. The Middle Fork canyon, leading out of the basin, presents a wide, U-shaped profile typical of the work of that same glacier. The glacier ended where the valley reverts to a V profile, beyond the Middle Fork Trailhead and just before the river crosses FR 37. This means the glacier was about 12 miles long.

Miles and Directions

0.0 Begin at the Seven Lakes Trailhead.

0.6 Pass the Kings Spruce Trail junction.

2.1 Pass Frog Lake.

3.3 Arrive at the saddle, with the Devil's Peak Trail taking off to the right. Go right.

4.7 Arrive at Pacific Crest Trail junction; stay left.

5.0 Go left on the Devil's Peak way trail.

5.3 Reach Devil's Peak summit; return the way you came.

7.3 Arrive back at the beginning of Devil's Peak Trail; turn left onto Seven Lakes Trail.

10.6 Arrive back at Seven Lakes Trailhead.

Options

Loop through Seven Lakes Basin: Backpackers should take the opportunity to spend time in the magnificent Seven Lakes Basin by completing a 14-mile loop incorporating the Seven Lakes Trail, the Devil's Peak Trail, and the PCT.

To complete the 14-mile loop after climbing Devil's Peak, veer left at the little trail junction near the summit and follow the opposite side of the way trail to the PCT. From there the northbound PCT (left) plummets into the Seven Lakes Basin, with the far end of the Seven Lakes Trail showing up in 2.5 miles. From the Seven Lakes–PCT junction in the basin, head left (west) on the Seven Lakes Trail. From this point it's 0.5 mile to Middle Lake, 2.0 miles back to the saddle where the Devil's Peak Trail starts (completing a 7.0-mile loop), and 6.0 miles back to the Seven Lakes Trailhead.

45 Blue Canyon Basin

A beautiful hike visiting numerous lakes and a magnificent trailhead drive. Easy hike to spectacular Blue Lake, with a longer option to Island Lake.

Distance: 4.0-mile out and back
Difficulty: Easy to Blue Lake; more strenuous to Island Lake
Elevation gain/loss: 500-foot loss to Blue Lake; 1,400-foot gain to Island Lake
Best season: June to Oct
Maps: USGS Rustler Peak; Rogue River–Siskiyou National Forest

Trail contacts: High Cascades Ranger District: (541) 560-3400
Parking and trailhead facilities: There is parking for 20 cars at the beautifully landscaped trailhead.
Special considerations: Lots of mosquitoes before mid-July. The uphill section is on the return hike. Plenty of water available.

Finding the trailhead: From Medford take OR 62 north to the Butte Falls turnoff near milepost 16. Turn right and drive 17 miles to the town of Butte Falls. Continue past Butte Falls on the same road for 1 mile to the Prospect turnoff. Cross the bridge and proceed 2 miles to gravel Rancheria Road. Stay on Rancheria, which becomes FR 32, for 15 miles. FR 32 eventually merges with FR 37. After less than 1 mile on FR 37, a red gravel road, FR 3770, takes off right. Follow FR 3770 for 6 miles to the well-developed Blue Canyon Trailhead.

You can also reach the trailhead from Prospect by continuing on FR 37, past the Seven Lakes Trailhead, to FR 3770.

Trailhead GPS: N42 31.783' / W122 17.798'

The Hike

The Blue Canyon area is exciting and accessible. However, many people share that opinion. In summer the route may be crowded, and horses may kick up a lot of dust. September and October are better; there are fewer visitors and mosquitoes, and you can enjoy the fall colors around Butte Falls (though there may be occasional mountain storms).

From the trailhead the Blue Canyon Trail (#982) drops gently but steadily through a forest of Shasta red fir, mountain hemlock, and western white pine. The path skirts around Round Lake after 1.0 mile. At mile 1.5, as you approach Blue Lake, look for a few Engelmann spruce. This mountain dweller is fairly rare in Southern Oregon. It thrives in cold, moist, thick-soil areas. In the central Rockies, Engelmann spruce occupies an entirely different niche, being the region's dominant upland north-slope species, with quaking aspen the dominant upland south-slope species.

Blue Lake, the prettiest (and bluest) lake in the basin, sits exactly 2.0 miles down the trail at the base of a towering cliff headwall. The seasonal Meadow Lake lies near Blue Lake, in a large meadow fringed with subalpine fir, mountain hemlock, and lodgepole pine. Blue Lake is currently unstocked, and its campsites are "resting"

The Judge Waldo Tree is an odd historic marker in the Blue Canyon Basin. The tree, a Shasta red fir, is noteworthy because it was inscribed with the initials of Judge John B. Waldo and his party in 1888, while they were on a horseback journey from Willamette Pass to Mount Shasta —the first group to make that trek. ZACH URNESS

(recovering from the effects of too many campers); however, there are places to camp with a view of the lake located farther back, away from the shoreline. Meadow Lake contains brook and rainbow trout.

Miles and Directions

0.0 Begin at the Blue Canyon Trailhead.

1.0 Pass Round Lake.

2.0 Arrive at Blue Lake and the junction with the South Fork Trail; return the way you came.
(**Option:** Continue straight ahead for Horseshoe and Island Lakes.)

4.0 Arrive back at the trailhead.

Blue Canyon Basin

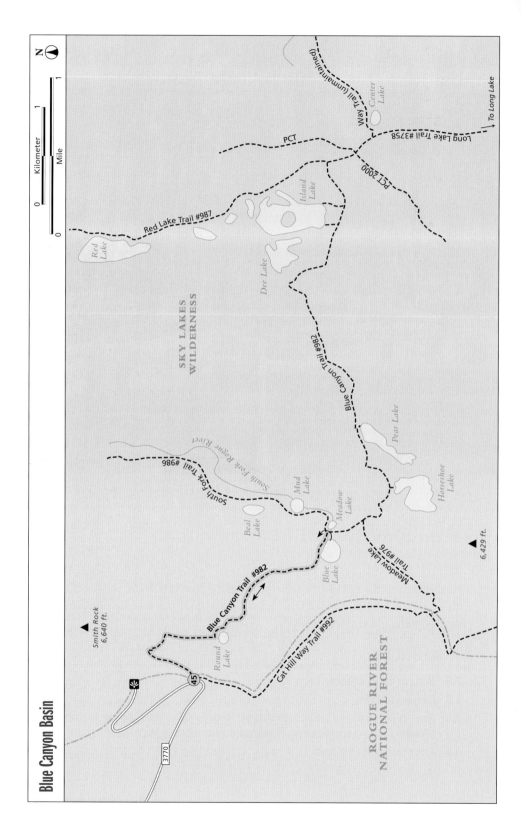

N

Kilometer
0   1
Mile
0   1

Smith Rock
6,640 ft.

Red Lake Trail #987

Red Lake

Dee Lake

Island Lake

PCT

PCT 2000

Way Trail (unmaintained)

Center Lake

Long Lake Trail #3758

To Long Lake

SKY LAKES WILDERNESS

South Fork Rogue River

South Fork Trail #986

Beal Lake

Mud Lake

Meadow Lake

Blue Canyon Trail #982

Pear Lake

Horseshoe Lake

Blue Lake

Meadow Lake Trail #976

6,429 ft.

Blue Canyon Trail #982

Round Lake

45

3770

Cat Hill Way Trail #992

ROGUE RIVER NATIONAL FOREST

Options

Optional points of interest beyond Blue Lake (miles are from Blue Canyon Trailhead):

2.2 Meadow Lake Trail junction

2.4 Cat Hill Way Trail junction

2.8 Horseshoe Lake

3.3 Pear Lake

5.3 Island Lake

Horseshoe and Pear Lakes: Beyond Blue Lake, at mile 2.2 from the Blue Lake Trailhead, you pass the junction with the Meadow Lake Trail (#976) and then the Cat Hill Way Trail (#992) junction at mile 2.4. You reach Horseshoe Lake at mile 2.8 on the main trail, then Pear Lake, 3.3 miles from the trailhead. Both are large and shallow giants, with sinuous shorelines nestled against low headwalls.

In the vicinity of Horseshoe and Pear Lakes, the path crosses areas of jumbled rock, ripped from the mountainside by glaciers and deposited in mounds called moraines. Look on the larger boulders for gouged, smooth-sided facets. The gouges, called striations, result from the glacier passing directly over the rock. Look also for rocks full of tiny bubbles formed when gas escaped from the molten lava as it cooled.

Island Lake: For a more ambitious hike—or a one-night backpacking trip—continue to Island Lake, at 40 acres the largest body of water in the Sky Lakes Wilderness and home to an interesting historical marker. Island Lake is 2.0 miles past Pear Lake (5.3 miles from the trailhead).

From Pear Lake continue through the woods and over glacial moraines for 2.0 miles to the south end of Island Lake. Once Island Lake comes into view, take the second obvious and unmarked trail toward the lake. Not only does the south end provide the best views, it's also home to the Judge Waldo Tree, which has wooden railings around it and is marked with a wooden plaque. The tree, a Shasta red fir, is noteworthy because it was inscribed with the initials of Judge John B. Waldo and his party in 1888 while they were on a horseback journey from Willamette Pass to Mount Shasta—the first group to make that trek. The tree's coordinates are N42 30.972' / W122 14.228'.

Island Lake has very clear water and a large island in the middle. Continue on the same trail for the Red Lake Trail, the north end of Island Lake, and Red Lake.

Island Lake via Lost Creek Trail: Island Lake may also be reached via the unofficial Lost Creek Trail, which involves only 1.5 miles of hiking. The Lost Creek Trail also leads to Long Lake (second-largest in the wilderness) in 2.0 miles.

The Lost Creek Trail is unmaintained, the trailhead is unmarked, and the path is not shown on any current forest service map. According to the forest service, the Lost Creek Trail made it so easy to reach Island, Red, and Long Lakes that overuse became a problem. The trail is unmaintained, and the forest service urges hikers to consider other routes. This is not the only guide that describes the Lost Creek Trail, and it appears on many non–forest service maps.

To find the unsigned Lost Creek Trailhead, follow OR 140 past Lake of the Woods to the Cold Springs turnoff on the left, which is FR 3651. Follow FR 3651 for 8.5 miles to FR 3659, on the left. Continue 1.2 miles to a sharp uphill switchback. Look for a small parking area immediately past the switchback curve. There's parking for four cars at the trailhead turnout plus a few more along the road shoulder.

Red Lake Trail: Beyond Island Lake's south end, it's 0.5 mile to the junction with the Red Lake Trail (#987). Turn left (west) and walk 0.3 mile for a view of Island Lake with Mount McLoughlin rising in the distance.

Past Island Lake, the trail drops down several glacial moraines before meeting the extremely shallow, teardrop-shaped Red Lake, also among the largest in the Sky Lakes. It appears smaller because a goodly portion is filled with marsh grass. There is nothing "red" about Red Lake, and it may simply have been named to go with Blue Lake.

Cat Hill Way Trail: For a loop through the Blue Lake Basin offering close-up views of McLoughlin, try the Cat Hill Way Trail (#992), which branches off from the Blue Canyon Trail in between Blue and Horseshoe Lakes. The trail is steep at first, climbing 617 feet in 1.1 miles to a junction. Then the trail swings north, heading 2.0 miles toward the original Blue Canyon Trailhead. The highlights of this sometimes-faint trail include sweeping views of a wide glacial valley and, through breaks in the trees, outstanding views of Mount McLoughlin. The addition of Cat Hill Way can create a nice 5.0-mile loop that takes in Round and Blue Lakes.

46 Badger Lake

Badger Lake and an impressive view of Mount McLoughlin rising out of Four Mile Lake make for an interesting and fairly easy journey. Option to Long Lake, second largest in the Sky Lakes Wilderness.

Distance: 5.6-mile out and back
Difficulty: Easy
Elevation gain: Negligible
Best season: June–Oct
Maps: USGS Lake of the Woods North; Fremont-Winema National Forest
Trail contacts: Klamath Ranger District: (541) 855-3400
Parking and trailhead facilities: There's room for 15 cars at the Four Mile Lake Trailhead, in the middle of a large campground. There are pit toilets in the campground.
Special considerations: The Badger Lake Trail spends the first 0.5 mile from the Four Mile Lake Trailhead making a wide, confusing loop around the campground. While there are undoubtedly many shortcuts, starting at the designated trailhead is recommended. There is no water except in the lakes.

Finding the trailhead: From Medford take OR 62 north 6 miles to White City. Turn right onto OR 140 east and drive to the Four Mile Lake turnoff (FR 3661), near Lake of the Woods at milepost 37. Proceed 6 miles up the heavily used gravel road to the trailhead parking area in Four Mile Lake Campground. The sign at the trailhead says BADGER LAKE, PCT.
Trailhead GPS: N42 27.329' / W122 15.009'

The Hike

The Badger Lake Trail makes its way for 1.9 miles around a campground and along the driftwood-lined shore of Four Mile Lake before turning inland, offering outstanding vistas of the intensely blue lake and of Mount McLoughlin's overwhelming presence not far away.

At mile 1.9 from the trailhead, the Badger Lake Trail climbs a small rock outcrop and then cuts inland, away from the lake. Soon after, the path climbs steeply up the route's only upgrade, with an elevation gain of a whopping 120 feet. The forest becomes much greener and denser as you move away from the more recent volcanic deposits at the lake, which are predominantly forested with lodgepole pine, a species adapted to poor soils and bare rock. The trail also becomes less dusty and looks like real dirt instead of volcanic ash.

At mile 2.3 you arrive at Woodpecker Lake, a charming green-water pool. Badger Lake makes its first appearance 10 minutes later, and the trail follows the lakeshore for quite a ways, with the designated turnaround at mile 2.8. Badger Lake is one of the lusher and more verdant spots in the Sky Lakes.

Four Mile Lake and Mount McLoughlin as seen from the Badger Lake Trail. Badger Lake is also very nice. LYNN BERNSTEIN

The turnaround is a lovely picnic spot with views of the lake's sinuous shore and a boulder shaped like a chair from which to view the lake. How much better can it get?

Miles and Directions

0.0   Begin at the Four Mile Lake Trailhead.

0.2   Go left at the junction with the Squaw Lake/PCT Trail.

0.4   The trail crosses the campground entrance road.

1.0   The trail crosses Cascade Creek.

1.9   The trail turns inland (east), away from Four Mile Lake.

2.3   Arrive at Woodpecker Lake.

2.8   Arrive at Badger Lake; return the way you came.

5.6   Arrive back at the trailhead.

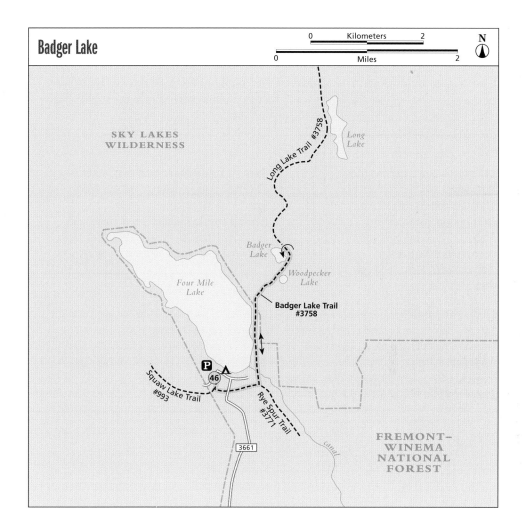

SKY LAKES
WILDERNESS

Long Lake Trail #3758

Long
Lake

Badger
Lake

Woodpecker
Lake

Four Mile
Lake

**Badger Lake Trail
#3758**

P 46

Squaw Lake Trail #993

Rye Spur Trail #3771

3661

canal

FREMONT–
WINEMA
NATIONAL
FOREST

Options

The Badger Lake Trail (#3758) becomes the Long Lake Trail (#3759) beyond Badger Lake and the Red Lake Trail (#987) beyond Long Lake.

Long Lake: Beyond Badger Lake the path winds gradually and uneventfully upward through the woods for 1.7 miles to the aptly but unoriginally named Long Lake—a lovely, elongated blue gem nestled (not surprisingly) in a long, narrow valley. At 37 acres, Long Lake is the second-largest lake in the Sky Lakes Wilderness.

You can also reach Long Lake via the unofficial and unmaintained Lost Creek shortcut. From the Lost Creek parking area, it's 2.0 miles to Long Lake instead of the 4.5 miles from Four Mile Lake.

47 Squaw Lake

Squaw Lake is the closest lake to Mount McLoughlin. What makes this route particularly interesting (the lake itself really isn't that interesting) is that the trail crosses a huge terminal moraine at the base of a giant glacial cirque on McLoughlin. This is the only close-up view of the cirque.

Distance: 4.0-mile out and back
Difficulty: Easy
Elevation gain: Negligible
Best season: June–Oct
Maps: USGS Mount McLoughlin; Fremont-Winema National Forest
Trail contacts: Klamath Ranger District: (541) 855-3400

Parking and trailhead facilities: Fifteen cars fit in the trailhead parking area. The campground has pit toilets.
Special considerations: Lots of creeks and ponds, but most are dried up by August. Mosquitoes are abundant before mid-July.

Finding the trailhead: From Medford take OR 62 north 6 miles to White City. Turn right onto OR 140 and drive to the Four Mile Lake turnoff (FR 3661), near Lake of the Woods at milepost 37. Proceed 6 miles up the heavily used gravel road to the trailhead parking area in Four Mile Lake Campground. The sign at the trailhead says BADGER LAKE, PCT. **Note:** This is also the Badger Lake Trailhead (hike toward the Pacific Crest Trail for Squaw Lake).
Trailhead GPS: N42 27.329' / W122 15.009'

The Hike

From high up on the Mount McLoughlin Summit Trail, the huge, barren lava slopes on the peak's northeast face—extending from near the summit down almost to Four Mile Lake—look for all the world like a crater left by a lateral volcanic blast, with an immense rubble field at the bottom. Only from the Squaw Lake Trail, which crosses the rubble field, does it become clear (from the rounded rocks) that this is a terminal glacial moraine. From Squaw Lake's unique angle, one can see that the barren lava slopes are actually two immense, side-by-side glacial valleys.

From the trailhead at the Four Mile Lake Campground, it's an easy 2.0 miles on the Squaw Lake Trail to Squaw Lake. For Squaw Lake, at the junction 0.2 mile from the trailhead, go straight ahead, where the sign says To PCT.

The route wanders through a lodgepole pine forest and over rolling moraines, with glimpses of Mount McLoughlin. The trail then passes Orris Pond (mile 1.3) and Norris Pond. The former is a small lake surrounded by a small meadow; the latter is a small pool surrounded by an immense meadow. Shortly after Norris Pond, Squaw Lake appears—big, shallow, clear, and surrounded by dense forest. For a knockout view of Mount McLoughlin, make your way around to the lake's eastern shore.

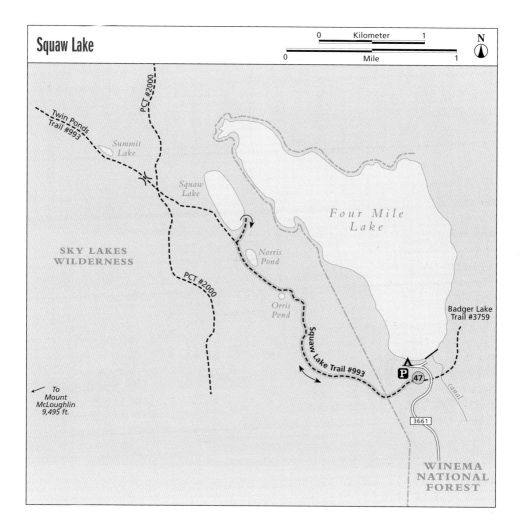

Squaw Lake

Miles and Directions

0.0 Begin at the Four Mile Lake Trailhead.

0.2 Turn right at the Badger Lake/PCT junction.

1.4 Pass Orris Pond.

2.0 Reach Squaw Lake; return the way you came.

4.0 Arrive back at the trailhead.

Options

Twin Ponds Trail: If you continue on the trail past Squaw Lake, it's 0.5 mile up a gentle grade through the woods to a low saddle and the Pacific Crest Trail. If you continue straight and don't turn onto the PCT, the trail passes Twin Ponds, each covering less than an acre, and ends at the Twin Ponds Trailhead, 4.8 miles from Four Mile Lake.

Orris Pond on the way to Squaw Lake from Four Mile Lake LYNN BERNSTEIN

Pacific Crest Trail: A fairly popular 13-mile, two-day loop follows the Squaw Lake Trail from Four Mile Lake to the PCT to the Cat Hill Way Trail to the Meadow Lake Trail into the Blue Canyon Basin. It then follows the Blue Canyon Trail past Island Lake to the Long Lake Trail, which then returns to Four Mile Lake via Badger Lake.

48 Nannie Creek / Puck Lake

A beautiful, out-of-the-way trail to a large, clear lake and some stunning optional hikes.

Distance: 5.2-mile out and back
Difficulty: Easy to moderate
Elevation gain: 940 feet
Best season: June–Oct
Maps: USGS Pelican Butte and Devil's Peak; Fremont-Winema National Forest

Trail contacts: Klamath Ranger District: (541) 883-6714
Parking and trailhead facilities: The trailhead accommodates 10 cars.
Special considerations: Mosquitoes are abundant before mid-July.

Finding the trailhead: From Medford follow OR 62 northeast for 6 miles to OR 140 at White City. Turn right onto OR 140 for 43 miles, past Lake of the Woods to Westside Road, at milepost 43. Turn left onto Westside Road and drive 12 miles to the well-marked Nannie Creek turnoff (FR 3484) on the left. Continue 6 miles up the excellent gravel road to the trailhead.
Trailhead GPS: N42 36.814' / W122 08.864'

The Hike

The Nannie Creek Trail (#3707) and Puck Lake boast two of the most fun names in any wilderness. Puck Lake ranks among the Sky Lakes' most isolated, blue, and serenely beautiful bodies of water. The drive to the trailhead offers majestic panoramas of Upper Klamath Lake (Oregon's largest natural lake), the Upper Klamath National Wildlife Refuge, the flat ranchlands above Upper Klamath Lake, and the high peaks of the Cascades immediately west. Much of the Sky Lakes, the Mountain Lakes basin, and the Crater Lake rim are visible from Westside Road.

The forests along the Nannie Creek Trail are very "east side," with smaller trees and less underbrush than their west-side counterparts due to less precipitation. The reason is that Devil's Peak and Mount McLoughlin form a rain shadow, diminishing weather systems from the west.

Although the trailhead elevation is 6,000 feet, the access road opens about the same time as west-side trailheads 1,000 feet lower. Trees along the access road are mostly lodgepole and ponderosa pine. On the trail, Shasta red fir, western white pine, and mountain hemlock predominate.

From the trailhead the Nannie Creek Trail winds through the woods for 1.0 mile, climbing a moderately steep series of switchbacks to a hilltop. The path then levels off and heads up a long, narrow, shaded creek, meanders up and along a large ridge, drops slightly, and crosses a second creek before reaching the exquisite and surprisingly large lake at mile 2.6.

The lake turnoff is unmarked, but the lake is readily visible from the main trail, so the route is obvious. Though relatively large at 24 acres, Puck Lake is extremely shallow (10 feet deep). At 6,450 feet, it is second only to Alta Lake in elevation in

Puck Lake is a large and shallow lake of remarkable clarity in the Sky Lakes Wilderness.
ZACH URNESS

the Sky Lakes. No major peaks are visible from its shoreline. What makes the lake so gorgeous is the amazing clarity of its water. The biggest drawback is the abundance of mosquitoes before mid-July, when they're the worst, though fishing can be good.

A bit past Puck Lake, on a trail along the north shoreline, is North Puck Lake. It's also very nice and home to some excellent camping spots.

Miles and Directions

0.0   Begin at the Nannie Creek Trailhead.

2.6   Reach Puck Lake; return the way you came.

5.2   Arrive back at the trailhead.

Options

The rest of the Nannie Creek Trail: If you continue on the Nannie Creek Trail past Puck Lake for 1.0 mile, the path emerges at a white rock scree slope with a stunning panorama of the Sky Lakes basin, Mount Luther, and the Cherry Creek canyon.

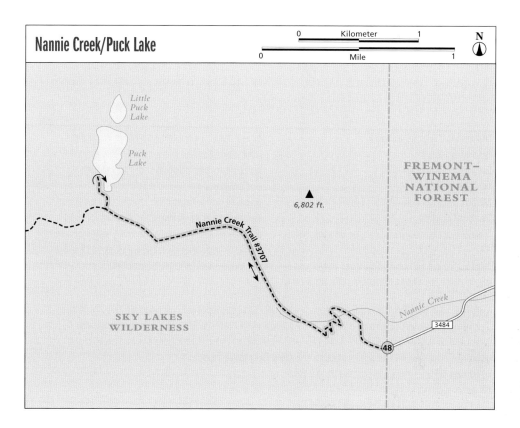

It's 2.0 miles on the Nannie Creek Trail from Puck Lake to the junction with the Snow Lakes Trail. Turning left there, the trail passes the numerous and beautiful Snow Lakes at the base of Mount Luther on its way to Trapper Lake, 6.0 miles from the Nannie Creek Trailhead.

Alternatively, you can continue on the Nannie Creek Trail past the Snow Lakes junction to the Pacific Crest Trail. Go south for a small unnamed lake, among the most beautiful anywhere, and for the pass above Lake Margurette, near the summit of Mount Luther. A side trail at the pass takes you down to Lake Margurette and Trapper Lake, where you can complete a 13-mile loop by returning on the Snow Lake Trail.

49 Lower Sky Lakes

Easy hike to numerous large lakes in the lower and more accessible portion of the Sky Lakes Wilderness's principal basin and namesake.

Distance: 7.7-mile lollipop
Difficulty: Easy
Elevation gain: 857 feet
Best season: June–Oct
Maps: USGS Pelican Butte; Fremont-Winema National Forest
Trail contacts: Klamath Ranger District: (541) 883-6714
Parking and trailhead facilities: There's parking for 20 cars at the popular trailhead, which also boasts a couple of primitive campsites. Cold Spring's water is very cold but probably not safe to drink due to the many horses in the area.

Special considerations: The Sky Lakes basin is famous for its astonishing density of mosquitoes before mid-July. The best water can be found in the lakes but, like all other water in the wilderness, should be purified.

Finding the trailhead: From Medford follow OR 62 northeast for 6 miles to OR 140 at White City. Turn right onto OR 140 and follow it east toward Klamath Falls for 41 miles. At milepost 41, past Lake of the Woods, a gravel road (FR 3651) leads to the left at a COLD SPRING TRAILHEAD sign. Continue 10 miles up the gravel road to the Cold Spring Trailhead.
Trailhead GPS: N42 32.572' / W122 10.848'

The Hike

The Cold Spring Trail (#3710) to Isherwood and Heavenly Twin Lakes may not be quite as scenic as some other trails in the wilderness. On the other hand, many hiking devotees swear by this level, easy, lake-filled pathway into the Sky Lakes basin, for which the wilderness was named. Swimming and picnicking are excellent, although fishing is reputed to be only fair.

While there are many level stretches and little elevation gain or loss, the path rises and falls with surprising frequency. Between miles 1.0 and 2.0, the route skirts the base of Imagination Peak. Farther on, the route crosses numerous glacial moraines (rubble piles bulldozed up by glacial movement).

The smaller lakes in the wide lower basin are mostly tarns. The larger lakes (Isherwood and the Heavenly Twins) are glacial lakes caused by moraine impoundments but without the obvious cliff headwalls that indicate the source of the glacier. In the upper basin, the lakes' glacial origins on Mount Luther are more obvious

The Cold Spring Trail starts off in a forest of mountain hemlock, lodgepole pine, and Shasta red fir. After 0.6 mile, past the wilderness boundary, the South Rock Creek Trail (#3709) enters stage right. Stay on the Cold Spring Trail for now.

Lake Natasha is one of the small but pretty lakes in the Lower Sky Lakes Basin. ZACH URNESS

It is 2.5 miles from the trailhead to the junction with the Deer Lake Trail (#3762) and Sky Lakes Trail (#3739). Follow the Sky Lakes Trail right, then turn left onto the Isherwood Loop Trail at mile 2.8. Almost immediately you'll pass two small but pretty lakes, Natasha and Elizabeth. Soon after, Isherwood Lake pops into view. It's a short, steep scramble downhill to the shore. The trail loops past a couple of ponds near the head of Isherwood Lake, rejoining the Sky Lakes Trail at Big Heavenly Twin Lake, at 25 acres, largest in the Sky Lakes basin.

Hang a right at the Isherwood/Sky Lakes far junction to make a loop that returns to the trailhead. (A left takes you to Trapper and Margurette Lakes after 2.0 miles.)

The southbound Sky Lakes Trail runs alongside the Heavenly Twins, past a skunk cabbage seep. It then swings right, onto the narrow isthmus between Big and Little Heavenly Twin Lakes. From the isthmus, the lake cluster's only panorama can be seen—a fine view of Devil's Peak a few miles north. The isthmus is the lower basin's prettiest spot. Continue past the beginning of the Isherwood Lake Loop, completing the loop, and return to the Cold Spring Trailhead.

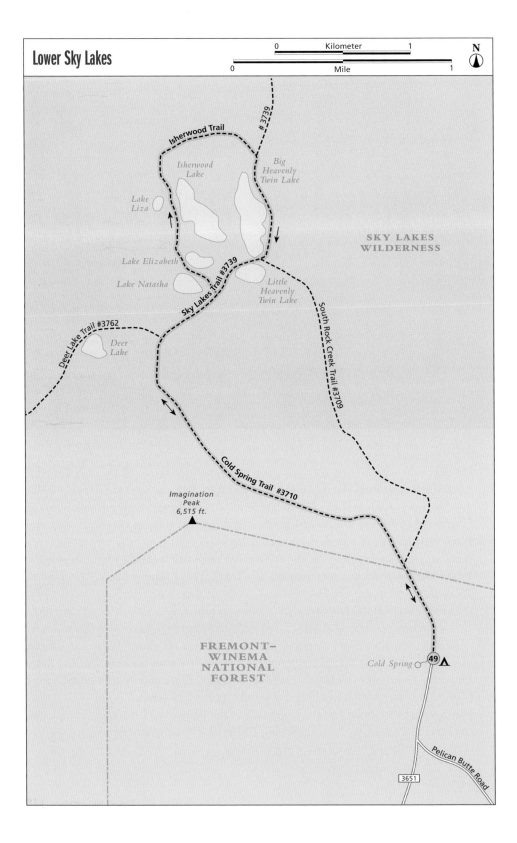

Lower Sky Lakes

0   Kilometer   1

0   Mile   1

N

Isherwood Trail

#3739

Isherwood Lake

Big Heavenly Twin Lake

Lake Liza

SKY LAKES WILDERNESS

Lake Elizabeth

Sky Lakes Trail #3739

Lake Natasha

Little Heavenly Twin Lake

Deer Lake Trail #3762

Deer Lake

South Rock Creek Trail #3709

Cold Spring Trail #3710

Imagination Peak 6,515 ft.

FREMONT– WINEMA NATIONAL FOREST

Cold Spring 49

Pelican Butte Road

3651

Miles and Directions

0.0 Begin at the Cold Spring Trailhead.

0.3 Cross the wilderness boundary.

0.6 Pass the South Rock Creek Trail junction.

2.5 Go right at the Sky Lakes Trail junction.

2.8 Head left at the Isherwood Loop junction.

4.2 Turn right at the Sky Lakes Trail junction.

4.6 Pass the South Rock Creek junction at Little Heavenly Twin Lake.

4.9 Reach the end of the Isherwood Loop. Head left on the Sky Lakes Trail.

7.7 Arrive back at the trailhead.

Options

South Rock Creek Trail: From the South Rock Creek junction at Little Heavenly Twin, you can either return on the same path that brought you or follow South Rock Creek Trail back to the trailhead. South Rock Creek Trail skirts the edge of an old clear-cut before returning to the Cold Spring Trail after 2.0 miles. The path offers a pretty good view of Pelican Butte and is a tiny bit shorter and more level than the Cold Spring Trail. It is also hotter in midsummer.

50 Upper Sky Lakes

Gorgeous big blue lakes and craggy mountains in the upper portion of the Sky Lakes' namesake basin.

Distance: 11.8-mile out and back
Difficulty: Moderately difficult
Elevation gain: 645 feet (1,335 feet from Cold Springs)
Best season: June–Oct
Maps: USGS Pelican Butte; Fremont-Winema National Forest
Trail contacts: Klamath Ranger District: (541) 883-6714

Parking and trailhead facilities: There's parking for 20 cars at the popular Cold Spring Trailhead, which also boasts a couple of primitive campsites. Cold Spring's water is very cold but probably not safe to drink due to the many horses in the area.
Special considerations: Two lakes on this hike are called Mosquito and No-See-Um. What more is there to say? June to mid-July are the worst.

Finding the trailhead: The hike is a continuation of the Lower Sky Lakes basin and also begins at Cold Spring Trailhead, at the 3.4-mile-mark junction of Sky Lakes Trail and Isherwood Loop.

From Medford follow OR 62 northeast for 6 miles to OR 140 at White City. Turn right onto OR 140 and follow it east toward Klamath Falls for 41 miles. At milepost 41, past Lake of the Woods, a gravel road (FR 3651) leads to the left at a COLD SPRING TRAILHEAD sign. Continue 10 miles up the gravel road to the Cold Spring Trailhead.
Trailhead GPS: N42 34.426' / W122 11.741'

The Hike

For the Sky Lakes Basin's most scenic and lake-filled area, continue on the Sky Lakes Trail (#3739) north from Big Heavenly Twin Lake.

The mostly level path winds through a hemlock and lodgepole pine forest before emerging in the stunning heart of the Upper Sky Lakes basin.

Trapper Lake (mile 2.0) is blue and big and clear—easily the basin's prettiest—with lots of level campsites and many side trails nearby. To the north rises Devil's Peak, while the Mount Luther complex swoops abruptly up from the lake's western shore. (Actually, a black cliff headwall rises out of the lake's western shore, with the yellow rock mountain set back above.) To the southeast, Pelican Butte dominates the horizon.

As it turns out, the black cliff and yellow mountain do not rise from Trapper Lake. It's hard to believe, but Lake Margurette lies between Trapper Lake and the cliff. To reach it, head 0.1 mile up the trail past the Cherry Creek Trail junction and turn left at an unmarked junction (Donna Lake Trail). Continue hiking along the topside of Trapper Lake 0.3 miles to unmistakable Margurette Lake.

The best spot for day-hikers (although you can't camp there) is a little rock peninsula sticking out into the lake that makes a heavenly swimming spot. To find it, instead of veering left, stay straight at a junction on the trail as you approach the lake.

Margurette Lake has emerald colored water and sits snugly below cliffs and mountains in the Upper Sky Lakes basin. ZACH URNESS

Lake Margurette is almost as big as Trapper Lake and much deeper. Cliff and mountain rise directly from the western shore of Lake Margurette, which isn't quite as pretty as Trapper Lake (but it's close).

Miles and Directions

0.0   Begin at the Cold Spring Trailhead.

0.3   Cross the wilderness boundary.

0.6   Pass the South Rock Creek Trail junction.

2.5   Go right at the Sky Lakes Trail junction.

2.8   Pass the Isherwood Loop junction.

3.1   Pass the Heavenly Twin Lakes and junction with South Rock Creek Trail. Stay on Sky Lakes Trail, headed north.

3.4   Pass Isherwood Loop junction. Stay on Sky Lakes Trail.

4.2   Pass Land Lake.

5.4   Reach Trapper Lake and Cherry Creek Trail junction.

5.5   Come to Donna Lake Trail junction; turn left.

5.9   Reach Margurette Lake; return the way you came.

9.3   Turn left on Cold Springs Trail.

11.8   Arrive at Cold Springs Trail junction.

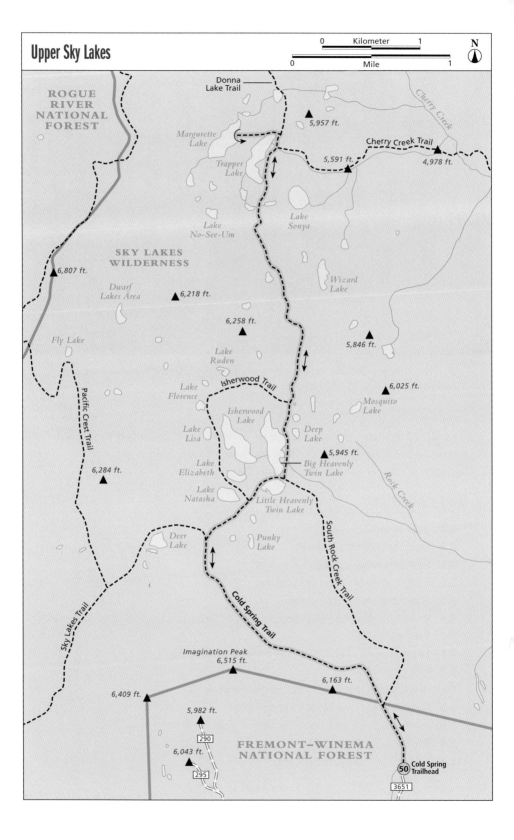

Upper Sky Lakes

0 — Kilometer — 1

0 — Mile — 1

N

ROGUE
RIVER
NATIONAL
FOREST

Donna
Lake Trail

Cherry Creek

▲ 5,957 ft.

Cherry Creek Trail

*Margurette
Lake*

5,591 ft.

4,978 ft. ▲

*Trapper
Lake*

▲

*Lake
No-See-Um*

*Lake
Sonya*

SKY LAKES
WILDERNESS

▲ 6,807 ft.

*Dwarf
Lakes Area*

▲ 6,218 ft.

*Wizard
Lake*

Fly Lake

6,258 ft. ▲

▲ 5,846 ft.

*Lake
Ruden*

Isherwood Trail

▲ 6,025 ft.

Pacific Crest Trail

*Lake
Florence*

*Mosquito
Lake*

*Isherwood
Lake*

*Lake
Lisa*

*Deep
Lake*

Rock Creek

▲ 6,284 ft.

*Lake
Elizabeth*

▲ 5,945 ft.

Big Heavenly
Twin Lake

*Lake
Natasha*

*Little Heavenly
Twin Lake*

South Rock Creek Trail

*Deer
Lake*

*Punky
Lake*

Sky Lakes Trail

Cold Spring Trail

Imagination Peak
6,515 ft.
▲

6,163 ft. ▲

6,409 ft. ▲

5,982 ft.

290

FREMONT–WINEMA
NATIONAL FOREST

6,043 ft. ▲

295

50 Cold Spring
Trailhead

3651

Options

Donna Lake Trail: The Donna Lake Trail is unmarked at Trapper Lake but hard to miss 0.1 mile beyond the junction with the Cherry Creek Trail (where you turned left to reach Marguerette Lake). The route passes Donna and Deep Lakes in 0.5 mile, before joining the Snow Lakes/Sky Lakes (#3739) Trail from Lake Margurette. It is 2.0 easy and scenic miles via the Donna Lake and Snow (or Sky) Lakes Trails, past Martin and Snow Lakes, from Trapper Lake to the junction with the Nannie Creek Trail (#3707). The view of Mount Luther from Donna and Deep Lakes is incredible.

Cherry Creek Trail: The Cherry Creek Trail (#3708) leads from the Cherry Creek Trailhead to Trapper Lake in 4.5 miles, versus 5.5 miles via the Cold Spring and Sky Lakes Trails. The bad news is that the trailhead elevation is 1,600 feet lower than the Cold Spring Trailhead. The path's first 3.5 miles are fairly level and very pretty as the route makes its way along the creek, up a wide, forested canyon carved by the former Cherry Creek Glacier. The last mile rises 1,000 feet. The trail crosses Cherry Creek twice and may be impassable in spring when water is high.

To reach the Cherry Creek Trailhead, follow OR 62 to White City and turn right onto OR 140 toward Klamath Falls. At mile 43, turn left onto Westside Road; continue 10.5 miles to FR 3450, and turn left again. You will reach the Cherry Creek Trailhead in 1.8 miles.

Divide Trail/Mount Luther: Beginning at Lake Margurette, the southbound Divide Trail (#3717) climbs 800 feet in 2.0 miles to the pass immediately south of Mount Luther, where it ends at the Pacific Crest Trail (#2000). From the pass it's a technically easy but very steep off-trail hike (rising 363 feet in 0.2 mile) to the Mount Luther summit.

51 Mount McLoughlin

A magnificent hike to the top of southern Oregon's highest and most beloved volcano.

Distance: 9.8-mile out and back
Difficulty: Extremely strenuous
Elevation gain: 3,777 feet
Best season: Late July–Oct
Maps: USGS Mount McLoughlin; Fremont-Winema National Forest (trailhead); Rogue River–Siskiyou National Forest (summit)
Trail contacts: Klamath Ranger District: (541) 885-3400
Parking and trailhead facilities: There's room for 30 cars at the trailhead.

Special considerations: There is no water or any good place to camp on the trail. Horse travel is not allowed. Forest service descriptions of this trail all begin at the Pacific Crest Trail parking area just off OR 140, which adds 1.5 miles to the route.
  In its fine pamphlet on climbing the mountain, the forest service warns against false trails and recommends following the blazes on rocks and trees as well as the actual trail, especially on the way down. This is VERY good advice.

Finding the trailhead: From Medford follow OR 62 northeast for 6 miles to OR 140 at White City. Turn right onto OR 140 and drive to the Four Mile Lake turnoff (FR 3661), near milepost 37. Turn left and proceed 3 miles to a short side road (FR 3650) on the left. Follow it to a roomy trailhead parking area.
Trailhead GPS: N42 25.332' / W122 15.131'

The Hike

The ascent of southern Oregon's Fujiyama is a major undertaking. The McLoughlin Trail (#3716) rises 3,777 feet in 4.9 miles. Soaring altitude and a final mile that ascends 1,641 feet over arduous terrain make McLoughlin far more difficult even than other nearby volcanoes with a similar gradient and elevation gain.

The trail's first 2.0 miles ascend only about 800 feet, gently exploring a deep woods of white fir, Shasta red fir, white pine, and mountain hemlock. It joins the Pacific Crest Trail (#2000) from the south after 0.9 mile. At the end of the path's only long, level stretch, the PCT peels off northward at mile 1.4. In between, the short Freye Lake Trail takes off to the right. It's 5 minutes to Freye Lake, but few people bother to expend the energy when there's a volcano to climb.

After mile 2.0, increasingly steep and rocky treads with areas of loose gravel begin to show up. The gradient grows serious between miles 2.5 and 3.4. The now tedious pathway slowly leaves the forest behind and enters open, rocky areas dotted with brush and clumps of stunted whitebark pine. Vistas of Klamath Lake, Four Mile Lake, and Lake of the Woods emerge.

If you thought the trail was strenuous up to now, wait until the final mile. Don't feel compelled to make that climb, however.

An overlook at mile 3.4 is worth the trip in itself. At the overlook the trail finally hits the main ridge, unveiling a spectacular vista of the Crater Lake rim and the Sky

A view of Mount McLoughlin, which dominates the skyline above the Rogue Valley like a white knife ZACH URNESS

Lakes to the north. The main summit comes into view for the first time here, as does an immense, barren avalanche basin careening down to Four Mile Lake. Overhead, a giant orange lava plug juts from the sweeping basin's upper end.

The avalanche basin is actually a giant, lakeless, glacial cirque. The rubble pile at the base is a terminal moraine, and the lava plug does not rise from the basin but from a narrow ridge between two glacial cirques.

Snowfields often dot the upper peak even in August. Fortunately, snow melts on the ridge much sooner than on either side of the ridge.

Past the overlook, the route officially becomes a "scramble trail" where you're pretty much on your own. The path holds a level contour for a couple hundred feet, then takes off straight up a seemingly endless rock and ash fall, marked only by paint blazes. When you reach the ridge again, the trail largely disappears. Widely scattered blazes mark the summit route along several interwoven paths.

In following the obvious ridgeline to the summit, you are faced with some choices. A wall of rock extends along much of the ridge. On its south side, hikers must pick their way among large, often cindery, boulders. To the north, the top of the avalanche basin's scree field looks a little more trail-like, but footing is poor in the loose sand and ash. Most hikers end up alternating between the two sides.

It takes three to five hours to reach the summit, depending on your level of conditioning. The peak is topped by a stone wall that used to be the base of a fire lookout. The official summit elevation is 9,495 feet.

The summit view is commanding. To the north, Broken Top, the South Sister, and Diamond Peak cap the horizon. You can also see Mounts Thielsen and Bailey, the summits of the Rogue-Umpqua Divide Wilderness, and the Crater Lake rim, including Mount Scott.

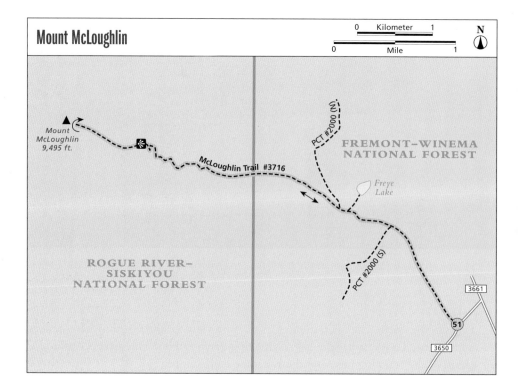

To the east lies Upper Klamath Lake, Yamsay Mountain, Pelican Butte, and the caldera of the Mountain Lakes Wilderness. Southward, Mount Shasta dominates, along with Lake of the Woods, Fish Lake, Howard Prairie Lake, Hyatt Lake, Pilot Rock, and the Marble Mountains.

To the west, the mountains are much farther away. Willow Lake is located easily enough, plus Mount Ashland, Table Rock, the Bear Creek Valley, and the Rogue River canyon between Gold Hill and Grants Pass. Far in the distance, you can make out Eight Dollar Mountain near Selma and Preston Peak south of Cave Junction.

Just below the summit, there's a compelling shortcut back to the overlook that involves sliding down a steep scree slope. The forest service discourages this route because many people get lost each year.

Miles and Directions

0.0 Begin at the McLoughlin Trailhead.

0.9 Arrive at a Pacific Crest Trail junction from the south.

1.4 Reach a PCT junction heading north.

3.4 Arrive at a spectacular overlook of the avalanche basin and points north. Above this point, the route becomes a difficult scramble trail.

4.9 Reach the summit; return the way you came.

9.8 Arrive back at the trailhead.

52 Clover Creek

A beautiful trail up a creek, past a lake, and over ash fields to the rim of a giant caldera with a commanding view of Lake Harriette, largest in the Mountain Lakes Wilderness and one of the most beautiful anywhere. Options to Aspen Butte (highest point in the Wilderness), Lake Harriette, and the Mountain Lakes Loop.

Distance: 9.2-mile out and back
Difficulty: Moderate to difficult
Elevation gain: 1,488 feet
Best season: Late June–Oct
Maps: USGS Aspen Lake; Fremont-Winema National Forest

Trail contacts: Klamath Ranger District: (541) 885-3400
Parking and trailhead facilities: There's a tiny campground at the trailhead and parking for 10 cars.

Finding the trailhead: From Medford follow OR 62 northeast for 6 miles to OR 140 at White City. Turn right onto OR 140 and follow it east toward Klamath Falls. At mile 37, just past the Lake of the Woods turnoff and Great Meadow, turn right onto the paved Dead Indian Memorial Highway (CR 533). Continue 9 miles to the paved Clover Creek Road (CR 603). Turn left and drive 6 miles until you reach the turnoff to FR 3852, on the left. The turnoff to the trailhead is well marked. Proceed 3 miles up FR 3852 to the trailhead.
Trailhead GPS: N42 18.011' / W122 08.182'

The Hike

The Mountain Lakes Wilderness began in 1930 as one of the first three Primitive Areas in the Pacific Northwest set aside by the USDA Forest Service. It is still the only perfectly square wilderness, covering one standard survey township of 6 miles by 6 miles. Inexplicably, the wilderness contains 30 acres more than a standard township.

The area is a collapsed volcanic caldera, much like Crater Lake except considerably older. It's been around long enough for the caldera walls to have been breached (at Varney Creek) so that, unlike Crater Lake, this caldera has a creek outlet. Also, the Crater Lake caldera was formed after the most recent ice age, whereas the Mountain Lakes caldera was formed before the ice age and therefore experienced considerable glaciation.

Cover Creek is a challenging, scenic, and geologically interesting hike up the outside of the caldera to the rim. The first mile or so on the Clover Creek Trail (#3722) crosses a level area of creeks, marsh, and meadows festooned with tower delphinium, buttonweed, corn lily, sedge, grass, and white-topped clover. The path eventually meets Clover Creek and steepens as the trail follows the creek up a little grassy valley with forested slopes on either side.

Look for lodgepole pine, Shasta red fir, western white pine, mountain hemlock, and an occasional Pacific silver fir.

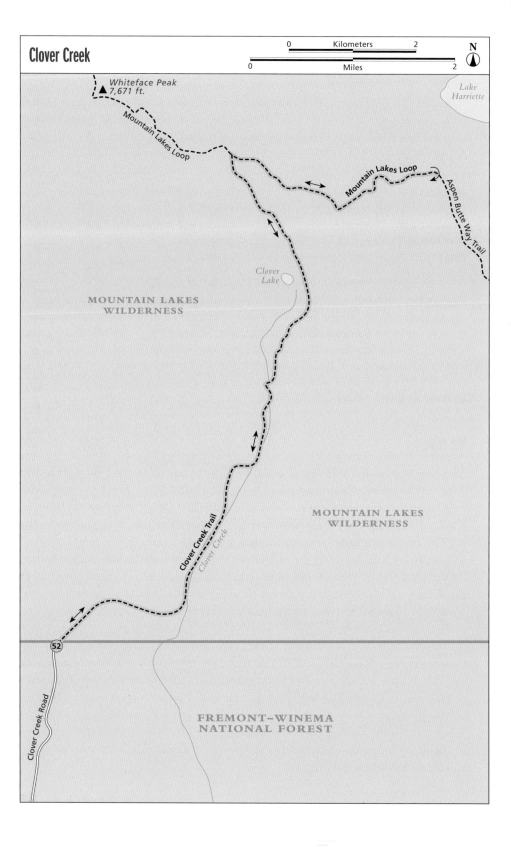

Clover Creek

Kilometers
0   2

Miles
0   2

N

Lake
Harriette

▲ Whiteface Peak
7,671 ft.

Mountain Lakes Loop

Mountain Lakes Loop

Aspen Butte Way Trail

Clover
Lake

MOUNTAIN LAKES
WILDERNESS

MOUNTAIN LAKES
WILDERNESS

Clover Creek Trail

Clover Creek

52

Clover Creek Road

FREMONT–WINEMA
NATIONAL FOREST

At about mile 2.5 the path crosses Clover Creek, swings away from it, and enters a maze of ash hills and open lodgepole pine forests, passing tiny Clover Lake, which is surprisingly pretty considering the bleak surroundings. The fact that the valley has widened considerably is a hint that you are now standing where the Clover Creek Glacier used to be.

The Mountain Lakes Loop Trail shows up at mile 3.3. Go right. The path passes ash bluffs and climbs ash slopes, eventually reaching the crest of an abrupt ridge with forest on one side and a cliff—the top of the caldera rim—on the other. Beyond mile 4.0 you begin to see beautiful Lake Harriette in the distance far below.

The trail crests at mile 4.6 and marks the turnaround spot for this hike.

Miles and Directions

0.0 Begin at the trailhead.

3.3 Arrive at the junction with the Mountain Lakes Loop Trail; go right.

4.6 The trail starts back down. This is the suggested turnaround point.

9.2 Arrive back at the trailhead.

Options

Aspen Butte: Southward and uphill from the trail crest, a very faint way trail follows a distinct ridgeline to the flat summit of Aspen Butte, highest point in the wilderness at 8,208 feet. For a peek at Aspen Butte, follow the trail for another 0.2 mile until Mystic Lake comes into view in a tiny basin far below. Aspen Butte is the top of the immense cliff rising behind Mystic Lake

Mountain Lakes Loop: (Clockwise) Turn left at the junction of the Clover Creek and Mountain Lakes Loop Trails. You'll climb up to the rim, pass the forested end of the Mountain Lakes Trail from Lake of the Woods, and gently drop back down to tiny Eb and Zeb Lakes, near the junction with the Varney Creek Trail. From there it's 2.7 winding and rocky miles to Lake Harriette, passing Lake Como, and 1.2 miles back to the trail crest near Aspen Butte. The entire loop is 8.2 miles.

(Counterclockwise) Continue forward from the trail crest at Aspen Butte steeply downhill for 1.2 miles to Lake Harriette, a brilliant blue 70-acre pool with emerald meadows and a snow-white headwall.

53 Varney Creek

A geologically fascinating trail to one of Oregon's largest and most beautiful alpine lakes.

Distance: 11.8-mile out and back
Difficulty: Difficult (due to length)
Elevation gain: 1,541 feet
Best season: June–Oct
Maps: USGS Aspen Lake and Pelican Bay; Fremont-Winema National Forest

Trail contacts: Klamath Ranger District: (541) 885-3400
Parking and trailhead facilities: The roomy trailhead holds 30 cars. Camping is available at Lake of the Woods and Odessa Creek Campground.
Special considerations: Mosquitoes are horrible before mid-July.

Finding the trailhead: From Medford follow OR 62 northeast for 6 miles to OR 140 at White City. Turn right onto OR 140 and follow it east toward Klamath Falls.

Between mileposts 47 and 48, near the Odessa Creek Campground, a road sign points to the right, up FR 3637, to the Varney Creek Trail. (You want Odessa Creek Road. Do not take FR 3610-Varney Creek Road.) Follow FR 3637 for 2 miles to FR 3664. Turn left onto FR 3664 and follow it 2 more miles to the trailhead, 4 miles from OR 140.
Trailhead GPS: N42 23.987' / W122 06.047'

The Hike

Even though it's 5.9 miles to Lake Harriette, this most popular of all routes into the Mountain Lakes Wilderness goes by quickly. Each of the first 4.0 miles on the Varney Creek Trail is different from the last, and they're all interesting.

The first mile follows the east side of Varney Creek and ends at the creek crossing. The second mile follows the steep slope on the west side of Varney Creek, through more open country, with Mount Harriman (7,979 feet) rising opposite. In the third mile, you reach the glaciated area, the valley widens out, and the trail starts crossing glacial moraines. The fourth mile, while somewhat similar to the third, is a little steeper, and during this segment the barren scree slopes of the high peaks come into view. During the last 0.5 mile before the junction with the Mountain Lakes Loop Trail (4.5 miles from the trailhead), the path crosses a low summit and descends into the forested basin.

Technically you entered the Mountain Lakes caldera (a collapsed volcano much like Crater Lake only older and more glaciated) in the second mile, when you passed Mount Harriman. Varney Creek, however, has eroded well into the formation so that the present basin, or what's left of it, is quite small and marked only by the barely noticeable divide at the head of Varney Creek. In fact, the glacier that formed Lakes Como and Harriette ate clear through the massive ridge between Mount Harriman

Mount Harriman from the Varney Creek Trail into the Mountain Lakes Wilderness, a volcanic caldera similar to Crater Lake but older. VIC HARRIS

and Mount Carmine so that Como and Harriette now drain into the Klamath Basin via Moss Creek.

From the trailhead it's 1.0 mile through the woods on the Varney Creek Trail (#3718) to the wilderness boundary just before the creek crossing. It used to be 0.2 mile, but the trailhead was relocated in 1982. During this initial mile, the view from the heavily wooded path evolves from the Klamath Basin and Mount McLoughlin to the opposite side of Varney Creek, far below.

There's an interesting vegetation transition as you hike up Varney Creek, from a land of middle-elevation Douglas-fir and sugar pines to upper-elevation Shasta red fir, mountain hemlock, and western white pine, with millions of lodgepole pines at all elevations. Look for a few Engelmann spruce near the Varney Creek crossing.

The fireweed along miles 2.0 and 3.0 and the delphinium (larkspur) at the end of mile 3.0 are noteworthy. Fireweed grows in extremely hot and open but fairly

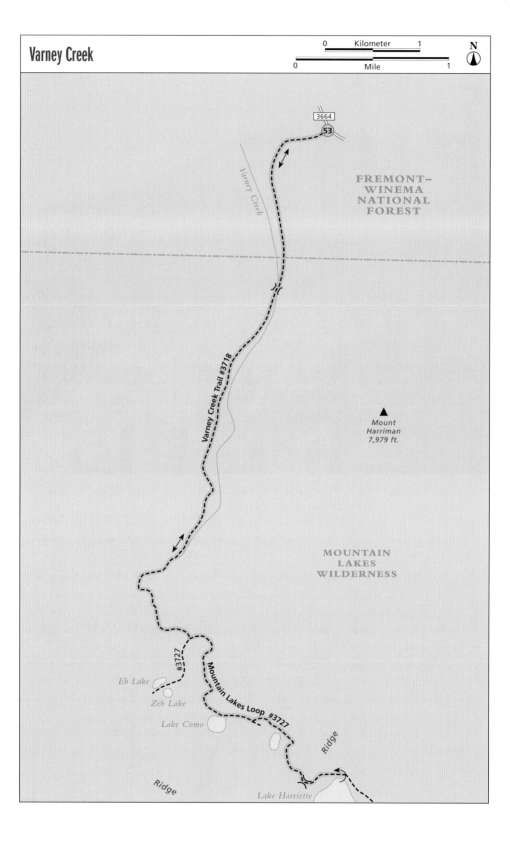

Varney Creek

0   Kilometer   1

0   Mile   1

N

3664

53

FREMONT–
WINEMA
NATIONAL
FOREST

Varney Creek

Varney Creek Trail #3718

▲
Mount
Harriman
7,979 ft.

MOUNTAIN
LAKES
WILDERNESS

#3727

Eb Lake

Zeb Lake

Mountain Lakes Loop #3727

Lake Como

Ridge

Ridge

Lake Harriette

moist areas that have burned within the past 10 or 20 years. The high, purple (tower) delphinium grows in moist seeps and no doubt denotes the elusive springs shown on the wilderness map.

The Varney Creek Trail ends 0.2 mile beyond the trail crest, at the junction with the Mountain Lakes Loop Trail (#3727). Head left on the Mountain Lakes Loop Trail for Lakes Como (in 0.4 mile) and Harriette (in 1.9 miles).

Past the junction, in the Lake Como direction, the trail enters an enchanted land of lakes, cliffs, yellow scree slopes, lingering snowfields, and subalpine forests. Beautiful, shallow Lake Como is nestled at the foot of a low headwall. Past Lake Como, the trail begins a steep rise through a jumble of boulder fields and ridges, passing a lovely unnamed lake almost as large as Lake Como but set in a wider, more open basin.

Near the second lake, the path bumps into a wall. To surmount it, the trail takes a steep, if blessedly short, uphill pitch with outstanding views of the basin and a small, lakeless glacial cirque.

Soon after, the path emerges at a narrow, rocky saddle atop a 150-foot headwall above Lake Harriette, the Mountain Lakes' largest and most beautiful body of water. Lake Harriette is the largest glacial lake described in this guide and the second-largest lake that's also a hiking destination (after 90-acre Fish Lake, in the Rogue-Umpqua Divide Wilderness). A vertical white cliff rises up from the 6,850-foot saddle crossed by the trail just before Lake Harriette and wraps around the south half of the lake.

From the saddle, the view southwest peers across the South Pass basin, revealing part of Aspen Butte. At 8,208 feet, Aspen Butte is the highest peak in the wilderness, a blocky wedding cake with sheer cliffs on at least two sides. The actual summit lies just to the right of the blocky part.

Lake Harriette, 5.9 miles from the trailhead, is not only the prettiest of the Mountain Lakes but also the prettiest lake in Southern Oregon and perhaps all of Oregon. At 70 acres, it is quite large for an alpine glacial lake. Opposite the white bluffs, a beautiful little flat with an open forest stand and green grass underneath lines the northwest shore. To the east, the lake is held in place by a large glacial moraine that drops off into the immense Moss Creek glacial valley.

Miles and Directions

0.0 Begin at the trailhead parking area.

1.4 The trail dips down to Varney Creek, crosses a footbridge, and climbs back up.

4.5 Varney Creek Trail ends. Go left on the Mountain Lakes Loop Trail for Lake Harriette.

4.9 Arrive at Lake Como.

5.9 Arrive at Lake Harriette; return the way you came.

11.8 Arrive back at trailhead.

54　Lower Table Rock

A fairly steep hike up a spectacular flat-topped mesa with rare plants and outstanding views.

Distance: 5.2-mile out and back
Difficulty: Moderate
Elevation gain: 846 feet
Best season: Year-round
Maps: USGS Sam's Valley; BLM Medford District
Trail contacts: BLM Medford District Office: (541) 618-2200
Parking and trailhead facilities: The trailhead parking area accommodates 20 cars and has a vault toilet.

Special considerations: While rated "moderate" in difficulty, the trail contains some extremely steep pitches. In summer, because the route is at a low elevation, exposed, and humid until the top, it can be excruciatingly hot and uncomfortable. In winter the path becomes extremely muddy. Late winter and spring are best for viewing rare wildflowers around the seasonal ponds. No pets. Parking is free.

Finding the trailhead: From I-5 north of Medford, take exit 33 for Central Point. Turn left onto Biddle Road for about 1.6 miles and then turn left onto Table Rock Road. Follow Table Rock Road for 7.7 miles, past Tou Velle State Park, to milepost 10 (the road makes a big left and right curve). Turn left onto Wheeler Road and continue 0.8 mile to a large and obvious trailhead.
Trailhead GPS: N42 28.123' / W122 56.732'

The Hike

This immense formation with the look of a flat-topped desert mesa is one of the prominent landmarks along the middle section of the Rogue River. Lower and Upper Table Rocks are fascinating in their geology, botany, and history. The trail makes a pleasant afternoon jaunt in winter or spring. March and June are best for wildflowers. Beautiful golden fields of flowers (including a species called goldfield) blanket the top in March, while myriad wildflowers bloom in June. The trailhead area was built by The Nature Conservancy, which also maintains the trail and owns a piece of the rock. They've done a commendable job.

The unnumbered path begins in an open, low-elevation woods of Oregon white oak, madrone, and ponderosa pine. Poison oak abounds, along with several ceanothus species. This part of the trail cooks in summer, as confirmed by dry-site vegetation such as white oak, so bring water. After passing the Oak Savanna Loop junction (a quick 0.5-mile loop), the route begins its uphill climb of 838 feet in 1.4 miles. Many people on this popular trail seem unprepared for this fairly steep climb up a talus slope, but if you take your time, it's not too bad.

The good news is that once you reach the top, it's easy going on the flat-as-a-pancake surface. Great views can be had immediately by heading left about 0.3 mile. But to reach the best viewpoints, follow the main route across an abandoned airstrip for 1.0 mile to the mesa's southern tip.

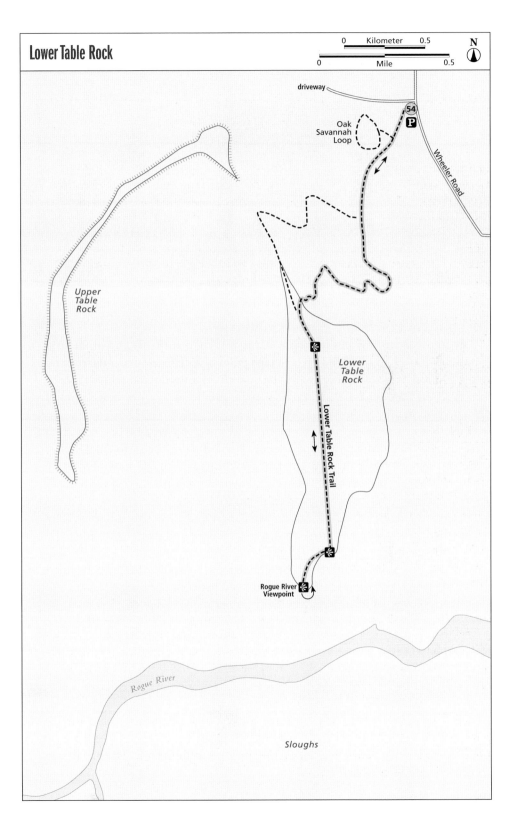

Lower Table Rock

0   Kilometer   0.5

0   Mile   0.5

N

driveway

54

Oak
Savannah
Loop

Wheeler Road

Upper
Table
Rock

Lower
Table
Rock

Lower Table Rock Trail

Rogue River
Viewpoint

Rogue River

Sloughs

One of the viewpoints atop Lower Table Rock looks out over the Rogue River below. ZACH URNESS

For an excellent view of the Rogue River, veer right at the far end of the strip to a clump of trees. You will end up on a high point of rock overlooking the river far below. You may scare off ten or twenty buzzards from a nearby roost. Don't worry; they don't eat live humans. Rattlesnakes may be another worry. You hear stories of them up here, but the authors have never seen any.

Table Rock is supposedly the farthest outrider of a still-eroding lava flow from ancient Crater Lake (Mount Mazama). It rises 800 feet above the surrounding valley. Once on top, look for "patterned ground," gravel mounds unique to level volcanic surfaces and largely unexplained. The species of wildflowers growing on the mounds are different from those growing between them.

Formerly (and briefly) the Takelma Indian Reservation, the site boasts several rare wildflowers. Look for Brewer's rock cress, scarlet fritillary, and three-bract onion.

Nearly the entire earthly range of a plant called dwarf meadowfoam is confined to the tops of Upper and Lower Table Rock around the vernal pools that form in winter and spring (and the Agate Desert near White City, between Kirtland, Antelope, and Table Rock Roads, which also has patterned ground and vernal pools). The pools are also home to several species of waterfowl, mostly mallards.

Miles and Directions

0.0 Begin at the Lower Table Rock Trailhead.

0.1 Pass the Oak Savanna Loop junction.

1.4 Arrive at the Lower Table Rock rim.

2.3 Reach the overlook near the southern tip of Lower Table Rock.

2.6 Arrive at the best Rogue Valley vista at the tip of the little point; return the way you came.

5.2 Arrive back at the trailhead.

55 Upper Table Rock

A steep hike up a spectacular flat-topped mesa with rare plant species and an impressive view. The cliffs aren't as high as those at Lower Table Rock, but the surface is larger and there's much more trail on top.

Distance: 3.6-mile out and back
Difficulty: Moderate
Elevation gain: 780 feet
Best season: Year-round
Maps: USGS Sams Valley; BLM Medford District
Trail contacts: BLM Medford District Office: (541) 618-2200

Parking and trailhead facilities: The trailhead parking area accommodates 20 cars and has a vault toilet.
Special considerations: The trail starts a little higher than at Lower Table Rock and isn't quite as steep—or as hot in summer. Winter and spring are best for viewing the rare wildflowers around the seasonal ponds. Parking is free; no pets are allowed.

Finding the trailhead: From I-5 north of Medford, take exit 33 for Central Point. Turn left onto Biddle Road for about 1.6 miles and then turn left onto Table Rock Road. Follow Table Rock Road for 5.2 miles, past Tou Velle State Park. Turn right onto Modoc Road and follow it 1.5 miles to a large and signed trailhead parking area on the left.
Trailhead GPS: N42 27.974' / W122 52.909'

The Hike

Upper Table Rock is a fascinating afternoon diversion for those who have conquered Lower Table Rock but have not had their fill of flat-top rocks. The trail is shorter and less steep than its lower counterpart and a little more open, with better views. The low elevations are not quite as hot in midsummer.

The Upper Table Rock Trail switches back and forth across grass, patches of ceanothus and manzanita, and clumps of oak and madrone. Like its sister (or brother) trail, the rim is visible from the trailhead but not from most of the trail until near the top.

At mile 0.5, after climbing a couple of switchbacks beyond a house-size boulder, you come to a little wooden bench. Intended for sitting and contemplating the view of the Bear Creek Valley, the bench is used extensively as a boot scraper. The path can get pretty muddy in winter.

After 1.4 miles, past another bench and a talus slope, the trail gently meets the top of the mesa. The upper rock has more flat surface than its counterpart and forms a tighter horseshoe. The center of the Upper Table Rock horseshoe is a pretty little rock gorge (see "Options").

Following the trail at the top, you'll quickly come to a trail junction that leads to two viewpoints. Go straight 0.1 mile for views of Lower Table Rock and the Siskiyou

The view from Upper Table Rock ZACH URNESS

Mountains in the distance. After you've had your fill here, head back to the junction and head left for 0.2 mile to an even grander view.

The view from the southern tip is similar to that from Lower Table Rock, with a panorama of the Rogue Valley, Medford, the Siskiyous, and the Cascades. The seasonal wetlands on Upper Table Rock dry up in summer to form shallow, flower-filled depressions. Dwarf meadowfoam, found only atop the Table Rocks (and at the Agate Desert near White City, between Kirtland, Table Rock, and Antelope Roads), grows at the edges of the seasonal pools. In winter, collected water is extensive enough to attract hundreds of ducks. If you scare them off, the sky becomes black with waterfowl.

Spring is the best time to visit, as the rock is home to many rare, and some not-so-rare, wildflowers. Still, even at Christmas, one can find tiny yellow flowers scattered among the mosses and weeds.

Miles and Directions

0.0 Begin at the parking area at the Upper Table Rock Trailhead.
0.5 Pass the Table Rock viewpoint.
1.3 Arrive at the rim.
1.4 Come to a trail junction; go left.
1.5 Arrive at the first viewpoint. Return to the junction.
1.8 Reach the overlook above the Rogue River valley. Return the way you came.
3.6 Arrive back at the trailhead.

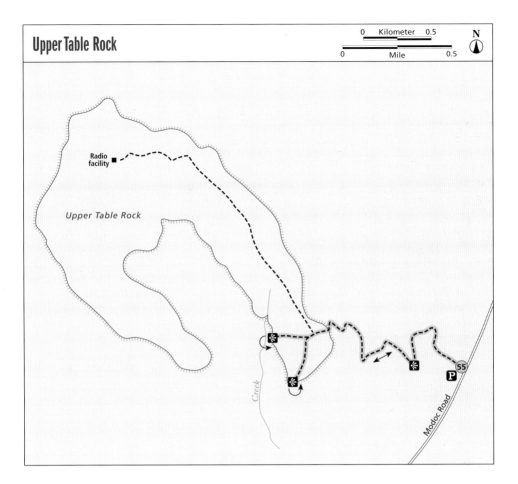

Upper Table Rock

Radio facility

Upper Table Rock

Creek

Modoc Road

55

Options

A trail that bears exploring takes off right (northward) 0.1 mile onto the rim. From the junction, it looks like the path leads to a small monument a few minutes away. The monument is actually a radar installation 2.0 miles away and three stories high. The route visits both the head of the canyon forming the middle of the horseshoe and the mesa's north rim.

56 Rogue River Greenway

Paved bike path along the Rogue River between the city of Rogue River bridge and the Program Area at Valley of the Rogue State Park.

Distance: 2.5-mile shuttle
Difficulty: Easy
Elevation gain: Negligible
Best season: Year-round
Maps: USGS Rogue River
Trail contacts: Rogue River Greenway Foundation: (541) 582-4488
Parking and trailhead facilities: Rogue River has plumbed toilets and parking for 20 cars.

Valley of the Rogue State Park has plumbed toilets at the rest area. There's parking for 30 cars at the Program Area.
Special considerations: Trail surface is black asphalt. No water. Pets must be on-leash. Lots of dog walkers, joggers, and cyclists—all friendly. No entrance fee at Valley of the Rogue State Park.

Finding the trailhead: West (Rogue River): Leave I-5 at the city of Rogue River (exit 48) and cross the bridge. There's a small park (Fleming Memorial Park) and boat ramp immediately to the right of the bridge. Park, take the stairs back to the bridge, and walk across.
Trailhead GPS: N42 25.848' / W123 10.294'
East (Valley of the Rogue State Park): Leave I-5 at exit 45B, Valley of the Rogue State Park Rest Area. Follow the signs that say CAMPING. Once inside the campground, follow signs that say PROGRAM AREA. Park at the Program Area. The shuttle for hikers from the city of Rogue River arrives from the right.
Trailhead GPS: N42 24.514' / W123 08.729'

The Hike

The 31-mile Rogue River Greenway and the 20-mile Bear Creek Greenway boast many outstanding sections and plenty of trailheads. In the opinion of the authors, the 2.5-mile segment from the city of Rogue River bridge to Valley of the Rogue State Park is the best.

The route begins at Fleming Memorial Park, where a short stairway leads up to the bridge's pedestrian walk. Immediately across the bridge, on the left, is the Greenway trailhead, which loops through a pretty little rock garden and under the bridge.

You'll pass a wooden marker indicating Mile 0 near the trailhead (for the total distance hiked, add 0.2 mile from the parking area). There are similar wooden markers every 0.25 mile until Mile 1.25, where they mysteriously end.

From the mile 0.0 to mile 1.0 marker (passing mile markers 0.25, 0.5, and 0.75), there is little variation and not that many good views of the river. It's a pleasant and mostly shaded hike, though. Look for ponderosa pine, Douglas-fir, incense cedar, and Pacific madrone, along with riparian hardwoods such as Oregon ash, western cottonwood, and red alder.

The west trailhead for the Rogue River Greenway begins at a bridge over the Rogue River at Fleming Memorial Park. LYNN BERNSTEIN

Himalayan blackberry, an invasive species, abounds, although the state park is attempting to eradicate it.

Just past the mile 1.0 marker, the trail breaks out of the woods and enters a lengthy area with four fenced pastures on the left and riparian woods on the right, also with occasional views of the river. One of the four pastures contains a settling pond, and one is an overflow area for the campground. The overflow is a frequent base camp for large-scale forest fire–fighting operations. One of the pastures usually contains cows in summer.

The pasture area can get extremely hot and humid in the afternoon in summer. Bring water for yourself and especially for your dogs.

The pastures end at mile 2.2, at a vault toilet, an interpretive sign, a gravel side road into the campground, and a small footbridge.

The hike ends at the Program Area. Look for a small hill on the left, a power line across the trail, and the path swinging sharply to the left. The parking lot should come into view immediately after.

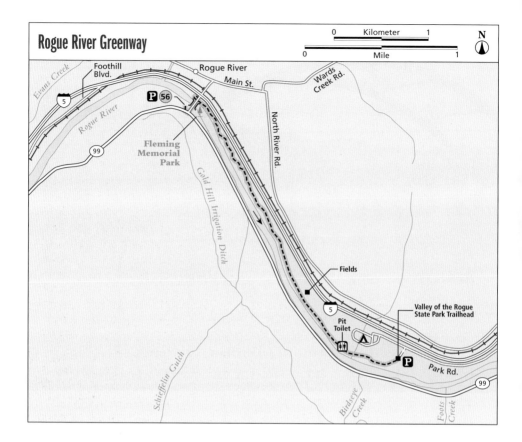

Rogue River Greenway

Miles and Directions

0.0 Begin at the west parking area at Coyote Evans Wayside and walk across the bridge.

0.2 The actual greenway trailhead is immediately over the bridge, on the right.

1.2 Break out of the woods at the beginning of the fenced fields.

2.5 Arrive at the Program Area.

Options

A very nice dirt side trail parallels the river more closely in Valley of the Rogue State Park, beginning at the far end of the fields, with many access points and continuing to the rest area. If you decide to end the hike at the rest area, add 0.7 mile to the distance, but be aware that some of the greenway path runs along the road shoulder.

When completed, the Rogue River Greenway will extend for 31 miles—from Grants Pass to Central Point—with a footbridge over the Rogue just past Gold Hill city park. The greenway path will eventually tie into the 20-mile Bear Creek Greenway (at I-5 exit 35/Three Oaks), connecting Central Point, Medford, and Ashland.

57 Pilot Rock

A winding trail to a famous pioneer landmark, featuring stunning views and a thrilling climb.

Distance: 3.6-mile out and back
Difficulty: Moderate to base; strenuous and dangerous to summit
Elevation gain: 1,036 feet
Best season: May–Nov
Maps: USGS Siskiyou Pass; BLM Medford District
Trail contacts: BLM Medford District Office: (541) 618-2200 (Don't let them divert you to their regional office in Seattle.)

Parking and trailhead facilities: There's room for 20 cars at the trailhead.
Special considerations: The climb to the summit has many vertical drop-offs and should be attempted with utmost caution. People have been killed falling off Pilot Rock. Avoid this hike in wet weather or if there's snow on the peak. The trail up Pilot Rock has been rerouted a few times. The route described here is very new and expected to open to the public in August 2014.

Finding the trailhead: From Ashland take I-5 south to exit 6 for Mount Ashland (22 miles south of Medford). After leaving the freeway, head uphill on Mount Ashland Road (marked Old Highway 99) along I-5 for 0.5 mile. Continue straight, past the turnoff to Mount Ashland Ski Area and below the freeway, a total of 2 miles from the freeway exit until a dirt road on the left bears a BLM sign denoting Pilot Rock Road. Proceed up this very bumpy road for 2 miles, bypassing a Pacific Crest Trail marker, and turn right into a large gravel pit parking area and the trailhead. There are several side roads, but you should meet your objective simply by heading toward Pilot Rock, which you can see occasionally along the road. The road used to go farther but has been barricaded by the creation of the Soda Mountain Wilderness and now serves as part of the trail.
Trailhead GPS: N42 02.188' / W122 34.235'

The Hike

The sentinel guarding Oregon's border against invaders from the south has long been a landmark to pioneers. Visible for miles from the south and east, it is the second Oregon landmark—after Mount McLoughlin—that people notice as they head up I-5 from California.

The rock is an immense volcanic plug—a cylindrical tower of lava—the innermost remnant of an old volcano. There are other such plugs in Southern Oregon (Rabbit Ears in the Rogue-Umpqua Divide comes to mind). All lie within a fragmented mountain system called the Western Cascades. Much older than the more extensive High Cascades, the Western Cascades have experienced several million more years of erosion.

Pilot Rock measures 500 feet in diameter and 400 feet high. From a distance its sides appear nearly perpendicular and the structure seems uniformly round and insurmountable, which is not actually the case.

The hike itself should be viewed as two different experiences. There's a forested, pretty, and semi-steep hike to the base of Pilot Rock. This is a fine vantage point and a

The scramble climb up to the summit of Pilot Rock is not for those faint of heart. ZACH URNESS

nice place to spend the afternoon or eat lunch. The more difficult experience involves following a scramble route to the actual summit of Pilot Rock. The scramble route requires you to hoist yourself up and over rocks on a very steep climb that doesn't require ropes but could easily prove fatal if you fell.

The trail heading up to this historic and beautiful spot has gone through a few different iterations over the years. The trail described here is scheduled to open to the public in August of 2014. Even if you arrive before then, the route should be easy to follow.

The hike begins at a gravel pit, where an old road has been barricaded. That old road serves as the first 0.7 mile of the hike. It winds through a pleasant forest environment and climbs an easy 225 feet.

Soon the old trailhead and the Pacific Crest Trail (#2000) come into view on the left. Follow the PCT for a very short 0.2 mile to a sign where Pilot Rock Trail breaks off on the right.

The next 0.8 mile to the northern base of Pilot Rock is new and scheduled to be completed in August 2014. It replaces a very steep and ragged older trail the BLM plans to decommission.

Following switchbacks gradually uphill, the trail swings hikers around to the rock's northern face overhead. At mile 1.7, the trail ends at a steep talus slope that emerges from a little canyon, forming a natural entry into the fortress. Here, choose to hike around Pilot Rock and enjoy the view below, or prepare for the scramble route to the top.

This is where the scramble climb to the top really begins.

If you're up for it, the first move comes at a tiny notch where you'll need to pull yourself up over the top of a narrow overhang. If you're fairly agile, this should pose no barrier.

Above the overhang, the route emerges into a tiny basin, like a slice in the rock. From there simply pick your way to the top. The climbing isn't exactly tough, but the steepness and exposure can be nerve-racking. You'll likely find yourself using hands and feet to make your way up.

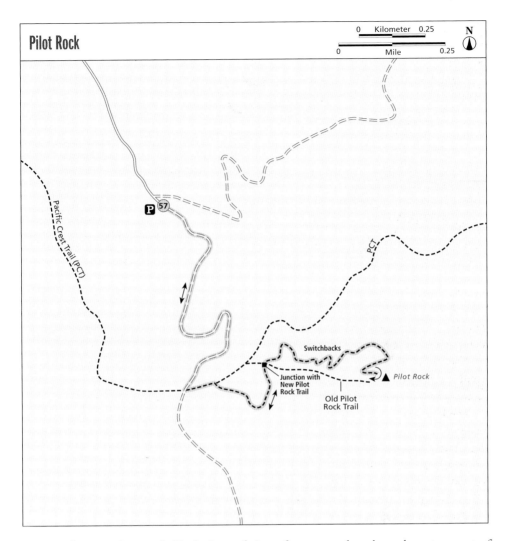

The summit, remarkable for its profusion of survey markers, has a decent amount of room for soaking in the views, including a view of the Shasta Valley and Mount Shasta.

The scramble is probably rated Class 3 or 4 on the Yosemite Decimal System, meaning a fall might well be fatal. A successful climb to the top, though, is exhilarating.

Miles and Directions

0.0 Begin at the Pilot Rock Trailhead.

0.7 Arrive at the Old Pilot Rock Trailhead and PCT; go left.

0.9 Come to the Pilot Rock Trail junction; turn right.

1.7 Arrive at the base of Pilot Rock and begin scramble route.

1.8 Reach the summit of Pilot Rock; return the way you came.

3.6 Arrive back at the trailhead.

58 Hobart Bluff / Pacific Crest Trail

An easy path into the Western Cascades geological region and the undeveloped Cascade–Siskiyou National Monument, not far from Ashland. Terrific vistas.

Distance: 2.6-mile out and back
Difficulty: Mostly easy with a difficult segment
Elevation gain: 220 feet
Best season: May–Nov, or when snow-free
Maps: USGS Soda Mountain; Cascade-Siskiyou National Monument; BLM Medford District
Trail contacts: BLM Medford District Office: (541) 618-2200 (Don't let them divert you to their regional office in Seattle.)

Parking and trailhead facilities: There's room for 10 cars along the shoulder near the PCT emblem.
Special considerations: Portions of the trail are semidesert and can get very hot on a summer afternoon. Be sure to carry water, especially if you have a pet with you.

Finding the trailhead: Take I-5 to the second Ashland exit (exit 14) and follow OR 66 toward Klamath Falls. Proceed 15 miles, past Emigrant Lake, to Soda Mountain Road, just before Green Springs Summit. Take Soda Mountain Road right for 3.5 miles to the second power line crossing at a grassy meadow, which is also the PCT crossing. Look for a PCT marker. The described hike goes left (east).
Trailhead GPS: N42 05.122′ / W122 28.917′

The Hike

Cascade–Siskiyou National Monument was established in 2000 in the waning days of the Clinton administration, without congressional approval (not required in the creation of a national monument). The unique geological feature is the only mountainous link between the volcanic Cascade Mountains and the Klamath-Siskiyou Mountains, an immense, essentially granitic rock mass. Mount Ashland is in the Siskiyous, Soda Mountain is in the Western Cascades, and Siskiyou Summit is the actual land link.

A natural inclination upon reaching the PCT crossing on Soda Mountain Road is to hike in the opposite direction on the PCT—away from Hobart Bluff, south toward Soda Mountain's 6,200-foot summit. While not a bad hike for a while, the route misses the summit and ends up following old jeep roads. Besides, 0.2 mile farther up the road from the trailhead, a side road scales Soda Mountain in 1.5 miles. The top is festooned with antennas, satellite dishes, and other equipment.

The trek eastward toward Hobart Bluff is not only far easier and less snowbound but also impressive in its own right. The route may be more scenic than the Soda Mountain direction.

After crossing a little grassy flat, the PCT heading east toward Hobart Bluff winds through alternating wooded patches of white and Douglas-firs and grassy openings

A portion of the Western Cascades lava cliffs that form Hobart Bluff. Mount McLoughlin is seen rising to the northeast. JUSTIN ROHDE

dotted with scrub white oak, mountain mahogany, and elderberry. All are drought-loving species, especially scrub white oak. Look also for rabbitbrush, a high-desert shrub related to sagebrush (both are in the Sunflower family). Forested stands tend to be sparse, especially on south-facing slopes.

After 0.5 mile Hobart Bluff's stone precipice briefly appears in the distance, then quickly vanishes as the trail cuts behind it to the right. Exactly 1.0 mile from the trailhead, a well-marked (but unnumbered) side path takes off uphill to the left, attaining the level bluff top at mile 1.3.

On the side path, the scenery changes dramatically, with elegant stone outcrops and windswept junipers decorating the landscape. The route soon attains an impressive, rocky summit. That, however, is not the end of the trail. The actual overlook lies a precarious few hundred feet away, at the tip of a narrow, rocky finger protruding west from the main formation with vertical drop-offs on three sides. It's 300 feet to the bottom.

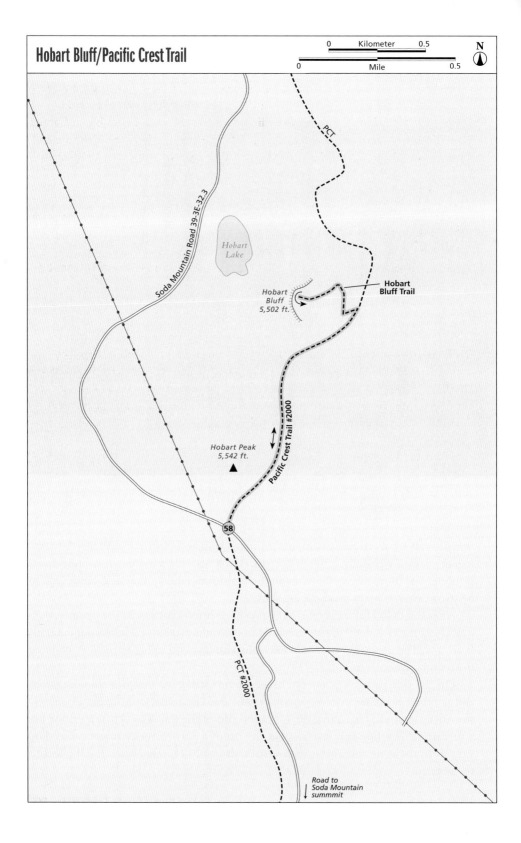

As you hike out on the finger, look for tilted rock strata. A primary indicator that you're in the Western Cascades and not the High Cascades is that all the bedded rock formations are tipped 18 degrees, with the low end to the southeast and the high end to the northwest. In the High Cascades, bedded lava flows are horizontal. The High Cascades, including Crater Lake and all the big volcanoes, are younger and farther east than the Western Cascades, which feature more rolling hills dotted with occasional rocky cores of former volcanoes, now eroded away. Pilot Rock is an excellent example.

Miles and Directions

0.0 Begin at the PCT trailhead.

1.0 Arrive at the junction with the Hobart Bluff Trail. Go left.

1.3 Reach the end of the trail near the summit, at the end of a jutting rock overlook; return the way you came.

2.6 Arrive back at the trailhead.

Options

PCT to Green Springs Summit: Soda Mountain Road begins at Green Springs Summit, where the PCT crosses OR 140. It's possible to make Hobart Bluff a shuttle hike by parking one car at the upper trailhead (described above) and another car at the Greens Springs Trailhead. The hike would be 3.5 miles one-way. The best scenery lies in the mile leading up to Hobart Bluff, but it's all terrific.

59 Grizzly Peak

Multiple panoramic views of the valley surrounding Ashland on a fairly level loop trail.

Distance: 5.2-mile lollipop
Difficulty: Moderate
Elevation gain: 980 feet
Best season: May–Nov
Maps: USGS Grizzly Peak; BLM Medford District
Trail contacts: BLM Medford District Office: (541) 618-2200 (Don't let them divert you to their regional office in Seattle.)

Parking and trailhead facilities: The trailhead at the end of the road holds 10 cars.
Special considerations: This is a popular trail only 11 miles from downtown Ashland. It can get very hot in summer, and there is no water. A 2002 wildfire burned the western side of the peak, creating a lack of shade.

Finding the trailhead: From Ashland take Siskiyou Boulevard east to Dead Indian Memorial Highway, just past the city limits. (From I-5 take exit 14 onto Siskiyou Boulevard and turn left for 0.7 mile.) Turn left onto Dead Indian Memorial Highway and follow it out of town. Between mileposts 6 and 7, turn left onto Shale City Road (paved) and proceed 3.1 miles to the Grizzly Peak Trail sign (BLM 38-2E-9.2). Turn left at the sign and follow the gravel road 0.7 mile to a complex intersection. Take the uphill road on the center left 1.7 more miles to the trailhead. (**Note:** The name "Dead Indian" sounds racist and is an embarrassment to many Ashlanders. In fact, the Dead Indian Plateau was named for two deceased Native Americans encountered by some pioneers, who sincerely intended the naming to honor these unfortunate gentlemen.)
Trailhead GPS: N42 16.323' / W122 36.386'

The Hike

Grizzly Peak was named in honor of a famous bear named Old Reelfoot, the last known Southern Oregon (or California) grizzly, who roamed the region for fifty years before being shot by a 17-year-old hunter in 1890. The nickname had to do with the animal, at some point, losing several toes in a leg-hold trap. The beast's stuffed body resided in a local museum for many years but has long since disappeared. Grizzly Peak and the Ashland High School nickname, the Grizzlies, honor Old Reelfoot.

From the trailhead, Grizzly Peak Trail immediately enters a dense forest and climbs 1.1 miles and 577 feet to a trail junction that begins the loop. Head right and after just 0.2 mile reach a junction to the peak's summit. As far as summits go, this one is quite disappointing—there are zero views.

Don't despair, though, because at mile 1.9 the trail reaches the western edge and the views remain plentiful for the next 1.5 miles, showcasing just about every major peak in the Siskiyous and Southern Cascades, along with the city of Ashland, 3,000 feet below.

The only downside is that the summit and ledge area features little shade and can become very hot in the middle of summer. Also, there are rough, rocky stretches of the trail that can become a bit tricky.

Grizzly Peak

After affording views of Emigrant Lake, Mount Ashland, Mount Shasta, and Pilot Rock, the trail eventually winds around and back into the unburned forest. The final stretch before ending the loop traverses grassland full of wildflowers such as fawn lily, trillium, waterleaf, and larkspur and then returns through the forest to the trailhead.

Miles and Directions

0.0 Begin at the Grizzly Peak Trailhead.

1.1 Arrive at the begging of the loop trail; head right.

1.3 Pass the summit marker.

3.9 The loop segment ends. Bear right to return to the trailhead.

5.2 Arrive back at the trailhead.

60 Mount Ashland Meadows / Pacific Crest Trail

An easy, magnificent, and popular segment of the Pacific Crest Trail, traversing a large basin just west of the Mount Ashland summit through open meadows, seasonal runoff creeks, dwarf aspen groves, and upper elevation forest.

Distance: 1.8-mile shuttle
Difficulty: Easy
Elevation loss: 160 feet
Best season: Mid-June–Oct
Maps: USGS Mount Ashland; Rogue River–Siskiyou National Forest
Trail contacts: Ashland / Siskiyou Ranger District: (541) 552-2900

Parking and trailhead facilities: The upper trailhead area accommodates at least 10 cars. There is room at the lower trailhead for 2 or 3 cars on the shoulder and a couple more on the opposite shoulder.
Special considerations: There is no water on this very popular trail. The downhill direction is recommended simply because it is the downhill direction.

Finding the trailhead: From Ashland take I-5 south to exit 6. Proceed less than 1 mile to the Mount Ashland turnoff. Turn right and proceed to the Mount Ashland Ski Area. Continue past the ski area to the farthest end of the farthest parking lot to an open gate and the beginning of a narrow gravel forest road (FR 20).

Upper trailhead: Approximately 0.3 mile past the gate, there will be a turnoff to the left. Take note of the spot, but continue on FR 20 for another approximately 2.4 miles, past the Mount Ashland summit road on the right to a large open flat where FR 20 starts uphill and another side road takes off left. The Pacific Crest Trail crosses the road here. Head downhill on the PCT, in the direction of Mount Ashland.
Trailhead GPS: N42 04.462' / W122 43.019'

Lower trailhead: Approximately 0.3 mile from the gate on FR 20, a gravel side road veers to the left. Follow this for approximately 0.3 mile to the PCT crossing.
Trailhead GPS: N42 04.897' / W122 44.369'

The Hike

For an easy hike close to town, nothing beats this magnificent segment of the PCT. In fact, the entire 40 miles of FR 20 is amazingly scenic (if uncomfortably narrow in spots), following the Siskiyou crest from Mount Ashland past Dutchman Peak to the Applegate Valley, with southward views into the Red Buttes, Marble Mountains, and Mount Shasta. The tiny highlighted segment of the PCT gets you out of the car and presents the entire experience in microcosm.

The trail is mostly downhill and feels like it drops considerably more than 160 feet.

From the trailhead, in an open area of grass, brush, and wildflowers, the path heads slightly downhill, then slightly uphill, then slightly downhill—always with

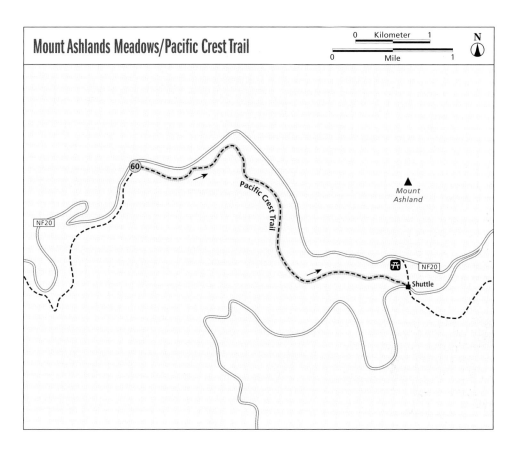

Mount Ashlands Meadows/Pacific Crest Trail

0   Kilometer   1

0   Mile   1

N

a view of Mount Ashland directly ahead. You'll pass scattered groves of Shasta red fir and mountain hemlock.

As the trail gradually curves from west to the south, it winds through an enchanted area of stunted aspen groves. They are spectacular in fall, especially from FR 20 but also from the trail. Be aware that all the trees in each grove or cluster of aspens have interconnected roots. The individual trees are all clones of the original tree.

Eventually the trail leaves the meadow area and enters a more substantial forest, still with occasional highly scenic grassy openings. There are a couple of uphill tracks here, followed by a long downhill to the lower trailhead.

Miles and Directions

0.0   Begin at the upper trailhead.

1.8   Arrive at the lower trailhead.

Options

Immediately before the lower trailhead, a side trail leads up a small picnic area on FR 20 with a pit toilet and a lot more parking. The trail is 0.2 mile long and quite steep. Many day-hikers park at the picnic area and do this hike as a 4.0-mile out-and-back.

The PCT will eventually take you north to Canada or south to Mexico. The segment heading immediately south parallels the Mount Ashland Road and eventually turns north. The PCT segment heading immediately north journeys into the Red Buttes, eventually turning south.

If you have a good high-clearance vehicle, don't miss the Mount Ashland summit drive.

61 Tunnel Ridge / Sterling Mine Trail

An unusual, low-elevation hike following a historic mining ditch. Magnificent spring wildflowers and vistas of the Applegate Valley. Options for a longer loop hike.

Distance: 2.0-mile out and back
Difficulty: Easy
Elevation gain: 521 feet
Best season: Year-round
Maps: USGS Sterling Creek
Trail contacts: Star Ranger Station: (541) 899-3800

Parking and trailhead facilities: A turnout opposite the trailhead can accommodate 8 cars.
Special considerations: Many hiking options and alternate trailheads. Very little water. Poison oak abounds.

Finding the trailhead: From Grants Pass take OR 238 south for 25.5 miles to the small town of Ruch (or north 8 miles from Jacksonville). From Ruch follow the Applegate River Road (CR 859) south for 3 miles to Little Applegate Road. Turn left onto Little Applegate Road and proceed east 10 miles, past the Bear Gulch Trailhead, to the Tunnel Ridge Trailhead.
Trailhead GPS: N42 09.503' / W122 54.199'

The Hike

This easy and lovely hike through the brushy foothills of the Little Applegate is ideal for a sunny afternoon in any season, with a picnic basket and all the kids you can round up. Wildflowers abound in spring.

The described route, the Tunnel Ridge Trail, is a connecting link to the Sterling Mine Trail, a 17-mile path popular with equestrians and mountain bikers along an old mining ditch. From the 1870s to the 1930s, the ditch channeled water to the gold mines on Sterling Creek. The highlight of the 26-mile engineering feat is the 100-foot tunnel through Tunnel Ridge.

At the trailhead, be sure to walk down to the creek before heading up the path. It's particularly pretty. On the trail it's an easy (slightly uphill) 1.0-mile walk up a sheltered draw to the ditch and tunnel. Most of the route runs through a forest of young white oak and ponderosa pine, a typical low-elevation, south-slope forest. The last 0.2 mile becomes a bit steep as the route loops up an open, grassy area with excellent views of the Little Applegate canyon and 7,140-foot Wagner Butte. Look for scarlet fritillary (listed as threatened but common within its small range), Oregon shooting star, and many other wildflowers in spring.

The trail reaches the tunnel—which you can actually crawl inside—at the junction with Sterling Mine Trail. The grassy lawn above, surrounded by oaks, makes a fine picnic site. From the tunnel, the Sterling Mine Trail can be followed in either direction. It's 2 miles west to the turnoff to the Bear Gulch connecting trail and 5 miles east to the Sterling Mine Trailhead (see "Options").

What remains of the 100-foot tunnel through Tunnel Ridge on the Sterling Mine Trail. From the 1870s to the 1930s, the ditch channeled water to the gold mines on Sterling Creek.
Zach Urness

Miles and Directions

0.0 Begin at the Tunnel Ridge Trailhead.

1.0 Reach the tunnel; return the way you came. (See "Options" for loop.)

2.0 Arrive back at the trailhead.

Options

Bear Gulch Trail: To complete a loop with the Bear Gulch Trail, follow the ditch trail (Sterling Mine Trail) left for 2.0 miles, and then turn left where the Bear Gulch Trail joins in. Continue 1.0 mile on the Bear Gulch Trail back down to the road and then 0.7 mile along the road back to the Tunnel Ridge Trailhead. The Bear Gulch Trail is a little less scenic than the Tunnel Ridge Trail but also less steep. There's an outstanding view of the Little Applegate canyon and Wagner Butte where the Bear Gulch Trail meets the ditch trail.

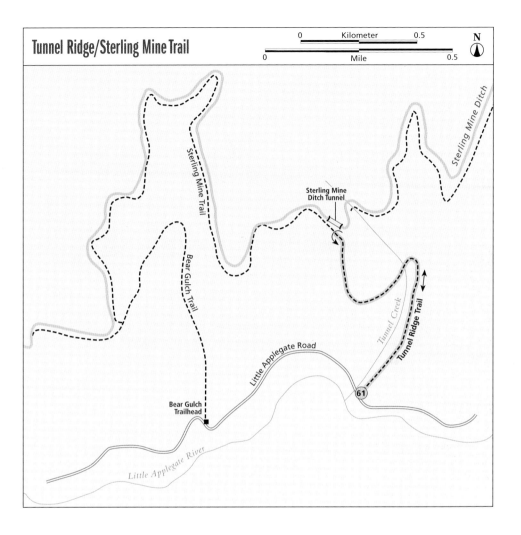

Sterling Mine Trailhead: A third trailhead, 1.7 miles past the Tunnel Ridge Trailhead on Little Applegate Road, also connects to the Sterling Mine Ditch Trail after 1.0 mile. Continue 5.0 miles from that trailhead to the tunnel, partly over private land. The Bureau of Land Management plans to relocate this part of the route away from the private inholding. This third connecting trail, at the Little Applegate Recreation Site, is steeper than the other two.

62 Wagner Butte

The highest hikeable mountain overlooking Bear Creek Valley.

Distance: 10-mile out and back
Difficulty: Strenuous
Elevation gain: 2,630 feet
Best season: June–Oct
Maps: USGS Siskiyou Peak; Rogue River–Siskiyou National Forest

Trail contacts: Ashland / Siskiyou Ranger District: (541) 552-2900
Parking and trailhead facilities: There is space for 15 cars at the parking area.

Finding the trailhead: From Medford drive south on I-5 to exit 21 in Talent. Turn right onto West Valley Road / Siskiyou View, cross over OR 99, and continue into downtown Talent. Turn left onto Talent Avenue and almost immediately right onto East Wagner Street. Stay on Wagner Street through town, heading south as it becomes Wagner Creek Road.

The road is narrow, steep, and winding beyond the end of the pavement. Be alert for oncoming log trucks. At the top of the hill—after 6.9 miles—bear left onto gravel FR 22 (ignore a paved road, FR 2250, that takes off to the right). Follow the gravel exactly 2 miles, past the cattleguard at Wagner Gap, to the trailhead. Look for a large parking area on the right and a trailhead sign on the left. **Trailhead GPS:** N42 06.867' / W122 48.029'

The Hike

Wagner Butte towers directly above the Bear Creek Valley immediately west of Medford and Ashland. At 7,140 feet, it's only 200 feet lower than Mount Ashland, the Siskiyous' highest peak. If you ever wished there was a wilderness trail to the top of Mount Ashland instead of a network of roads, consider tackling Wagner Butte.

From the trailhead the path (#1011) snakes through the woods for 0.1 mile and then hits a trail junction and a closed-off logging road. Follow the logging road to the right, up some horribly steep and badly eroded pitches, to a little meadow 0.5 mile from the trailhead. The meadow offers good views of the Red Mountain area west of Mount Ashland. Note the meadow's misplaced sagebrush. Note also the arrow at the far end indicating the trail route.

After 1.2 miles the trail enters a large grassy area, referred to on an interpretative sign as the Sheep Creek Slide. On May 28, 1983, a debris avalanche exploded from near the top of Wagner Butte; 400,000 tons of material thundered down the hillside and eventually landed in the Little Applegate River. The slide was one of the largest ever recorded in the Pacific Northwest.

Beyond the slide, the path skirts a small marsh as it reenters the woods, alternating between woods, grassy areas, and stands of Douglas-fir, white fir, ponderosa pine, and a little Shasta red fir. Corral Creek, at mile 1.6, is icy cold and extremely welcome on the way down (don't drink without filtering or purifying, though).

The summit of Wagner Butte is an old lookout base, with views of Mount Ashland, Mount McLoughlin, Soda Mountain, the Marble Mountains, Ashland, and Medford. ZACH URNESS

At mile 2.3 the route breaks into the open, takes off sharply uphill for 0.8 mile, and climbs 466 feet to Wagner Glade Gap junction. Head sharply left (north), following the trail up the mountain's crest.

The route here is fairly level for a while, with stunning vistas everywhere. This area is mostly brush, broken by picturesque tree clumps. Look for mountain mahogany, sagebrush, and some lovely aspen groves. At Cold Spring (mile 4.4), a long, wet seep (possibly with grazing cattle), you will find muddy spots, willow brush, abundant wildflowers, and an icy pipe spring (from which people will be drinking, although we know not to do that).

Beyond Cold Spring the trail begins a steep ascent up a boulder-strewn, wildflower-covered hillside to the ridgetop. It ends at the base of a large rock outcrop that constitutes the ultimate summit. It's a 5-minute climb up the rocks to an old lookout base with views of Mount Ashland, Mount McLoughlin, Soda Mountain, the Marble Mountains, Ashland, and Medford.

Wagner Butte

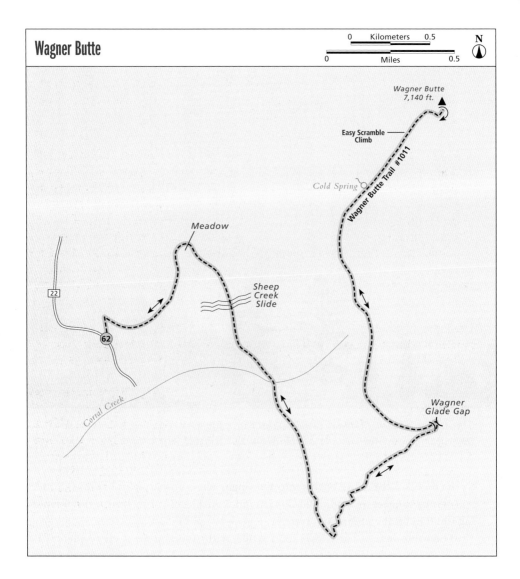

Miles and Directions

0.0   Begin at the Wagner Butte Trailhead.

1.2   Pass the Sheep Creek Slide.

1.6   Pass Corral Creek.

3.2   Arrive at Wagner Glade Gap.

4.4   Arrive at Cold Spring.

5.0   Reach the Wagner Butte summit; return the way you came.

10.0   Arrive back at the trailhead.

63 Tanner Lakes

Two small and beautiful glacial cirque lakes sitting on the Oregon–California border. Reaching the trailhead involves an adventurous drive through some of the prettiest country in the Oregon Siskiyous high country.

Distance: 2.4-mile out and back
Difficulty: Easy
Elevation gain: 474 feet
Best season: Mid-June–Oct
Maps: USGS Oregon Caves; Rogue River–Siskiyou National Forest
Trail contacts: Star Ranger Station: (541) 899 3800
Parking and trailhead facilities: There is parking for 10 cars along the road and at the barricade. As of summer 2012, there was no message board or official notice that this is the trailhead. The hike begins a few hundred feet back up the road at a twisty little uphill trail.
Special considerations: On just about every map and sign, the lakes are referred to as "Tannen" due to a longtime spelling mistake. The Oregon Geographical Names Board changed the official name to "Tanner" in 2002, but many maps and signs still bear the mistake.

Finding the trailhead: From Grants Pass take US 199 south a total of 35 miles, passing Cave Junction to milepost 35. Turn left onto Waldo Road and drive 5 miles to an intersection. Continue straight onto Happy Camp Road / Grayback Road at a sign for Bolan Lake and follow it for 13 winding miles to a mountain pass.

At a sign for Bolan Lake Campground, turn left onto FR 4812. The road is poorly marked, so pay close attention.

Follow FR 4812 for 1.8 miles (a couple of roads branch off, but stay on the main route). When you reach the 1.8-mile mark, bear right at the fork and follow the road that heads slightly downhill. Drive another 2.4 miles until you reach an intersection with a sign pointing to Bolan and Tannen Lakes.

Continue straight, following the TANNEN LAKE sign, for 3 miles to another intersection at King's Saddle, an open clear-cut area. Go left (downhill) at the saddle on Road 041 and follow it 1.5 miles to its end, where the road has been barricaded. The unmarked trail begins back up the road a few hundred feet.

Trailhead GPS: N42 00.750' / W123 24.882'

The Hike

The lakes and mountain described in this chapter have always been known as "Tannen." However, in 2002 it was discovered that they were originally named for an Illinois Valley miner, Ezra Sherman Tanner, who lived at the base of the mountain in the mid 1800s.

Thanks to the hard work of Ezra Tanner's great-granddaughter, Hazel Gendron, the mistake was brought to light and corrected (though many maps still carry the old name).

No matter what you call them, both alpine lakes and indeed the entire area are remote and scenic.

Tanner Lake sits in a pretty glacial basin on the border of Oregon and California. ZACH URNESS

From the barricaded road where you parked, hike back up the road a few hundred feet to a trail that switchbacks uphill through the woods. You'll pass a broken signboard that used to inform hikers that this was the correct route. Hopefully the forest service will fix it soon.

The Tanner Lake Trail is short, easy, and interesting, and it's only 0.4 mile to the lake. Look for a profusion of wildflowers, rhododendron, and shrub called Sadler oak. Sadler oak resembles a rhododendron except that its large evergreen leaves, in a whorled arrangement, have saw-toothed edges. Being an oak, the plant also has acorns. Sadler oak grows only in moist, high-elevation areas of the Siskiyou and Marble Mountains. Though considered threatened, it is abundant within its narrow range.

The trail reaches sparkling Tanner Lake at a small campsite. The lake occupies a small high-walled cirque with a creek outlet at one end. It has a steep, willow-choked shore with little access other than the campsite near the outlet.

Swimming is difficult because the bottom is covered with mushy silt that when stepped on gives way to a maze of submerged logs. The lake is stocked periodically, and fishing can be good (though not spectacular).

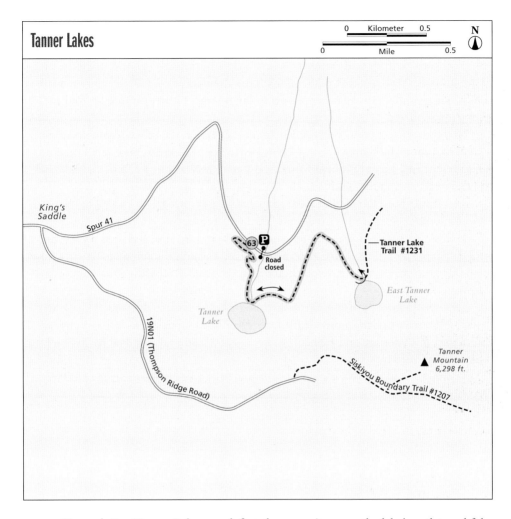

Tanner Lakes

King's Saddle

Spur 41

63 P
Road closed

Tanner Lake

Tanner Lake Trail #1231

East Tanner Lake

19N01 (Thompson Ridge Road)

Tanner Mountain 6,298 ft.

Siskiyou Boundary Trail #1207

To reach East Tanner Lake, turn left at the campsite, cross the lake's outlet, and follow the trail east. The trail wanders through the forest, passes a wonderful mountain view at mile 1.0, and reaches East Tanner after a total of 1.2 miles from the trailhead.

The brushy lake is smaller and sits at the base of Tanner Mountain. Fishing is good there too.

Miles and Directions

0.0 From the parking area, hike back up the road a few hundred feet to a trail that switchbacks uphill through the woods.

0.1 Reach the Tanner Lake Trailhead.

0.4 Arrive at Tanner Lake.

1.2 Reach East Tanner Lake; return the way you came.

2.4 Arrive back at the trailhead.

Options

Tanner Mountain: To climb Tanner Mountain via the Siskiyou Boundary Trail (#1207), turn right instead of left at King's Saddle during the drive. You will be on Thompson Ridge Road (FR 570). Look for the Boundary Trail 2.0 miles up the road on the left, possibly marked by a square post but no sign. There's parking for four cars along the shoulder.

From the trailhead the path ascends through a dense forest of western white pine, white fir, mountain hemlock, and incense cedar. For the expert, both Shasta red fir and the virtually identical noble fir may be found. This is unusual, because the two species interbreed in the Siskiyous.

At 0.5 mile from the trailhead, the route comes out on a grassy knoll. The Tanner summit can be seen 0.2 mile away from the knoll, on the left, rising above the grass. Since there's no trail to the summit, simply walk toward the peak and follow the ridgeline up. The hike is a little precarious toward the end, climbing up and around some steep rock outcrops, but you should end up perched atop the gray outcrop in less than 20 minutes.

From the summit, boasting a cozy little nest-like depression, the view is awesome. You can see most of the north half of the Marble Mountains, as well as much of the Siskiyou Wilderness and Klamath Canyon. The California state line lies 0.2 mile south of Tanner Mountain.

Thompson Ridge Road is a long, fascinating drive that ends at the Klamath River Road just east of the town of Happy Camp.

64 Frog Pond

A charming, somewhat steep hike into the Red Buttes Wilderness. Opens up earlier in the season than other mountain trails. Historical and botanical interest.

Distance: 5.6-mile out and back
Difficulty: Moderately difficult
Elevation gain: 1,600 feet
Best season: May–Nov
Maps: USGS Kangaroo Mountain; Rogue River–Siskiyou National Forest
Trail contacts: Star Ranger Station: (541) 899-3800

Parking and trailhead facilities: Ten cars can park along the shoulder.
Special considerations: Although this has been hiked as a loop in the past, the downhill segment past Cameron Meadows was brutal as of summer 2012 and was never a great connection to begin with. The main route leads past Frog Pond to Cameron Meadows; the loop is offered as an option.

Finding the trailhead: From Grants Pass take OR 238 south for 25.5 miles to the small town of Ruch (or north 8 miles from Jacksonville). From Ruch follow the Applegate River Road (CR 859) south for 15 miles, passing Applegate Lake and driving to its upper end. At a paved T junction, turn left to stay on Applegate Road for 1.5 more miles to a gravel junction.

Swing a sharp right onto gravel FR 1040 and drop down in the area of the Upper Applegate River. Follow this somewhat rough road along the river for 5 miles. At an intersection, turn left to follow FR 1040 (ignore FR 1035) across a bridge and begin climbing uphill. The trailhead you're looking for is 6 miles up FR 1040 on the left and is labeled Frog Pond Trailhead. You'll know you're almost there when the road crosses a small washout ditch.
Trailhead GPS: N41 59.703' / W123 15.208'

The Hike

This pretty path with floral meadows, looming cliffs, botanical oddities, and a few excellent views of the Red Buttes boasts all the trappings of a nearly perfect day hike.

From the described trailhead (labeled Frog Pond), the path ascends up a wooded ridgetop hillside, initially through a forest of Douglas-fir and white fir. Farther up, western white pine, Shasta red fir, and the rare and elegant Brewer spruce shade the route.

At mile 1.5 the landscape opens out to the expanse of Frog Pond Meadow. The large, lily pad–choked pond with its convoluted shoreline provides an exquisite centerpiece to the meadow, the upper end of which is guarded by the soaring cliffs of Mount Emily. There may be black bears in the meadow, so exercise caution. The path winds along the meadow's periphery and then disappears into a sea of wildflowers. Look for, among others, tiger lilies, spirea, corn lilies, Indian paintbrush, daisies, monkshood, penstemon, and cinquefoil.

Although the trail vanishes for 100 feet or so here, the route is obvious. Near the top of the meadow, look for an "X" sign on a tree and other markers showing the trail veering back into the woods.

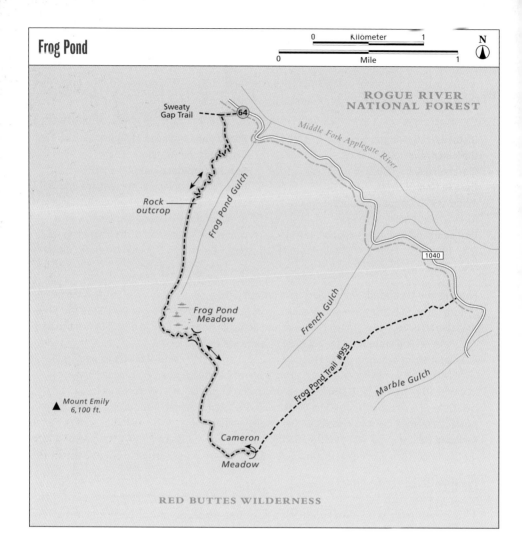

As the path leaves the Frog Pond area, it passes a smaller meadow at the base of an immense rock outcrop. The droopy-looking trees there are an extremely rare stand of Alaska cedar. Common in the Northern Cascades, the species is confined in the Siskiyou Mountains to six or seven tiny, stunted, widely scattered clumps.

Beyond the Alaska cedars, the trail climbs through a rugged and somewhat overgrown area as it shoots uphill almost 400 feet in 0.5 mile to a boulder-strewn ridgetop.

The next 1.0 mile features open views of the region's heights. Look for Whiskey Peak (opposite), Pyramid Peak (to the rear), and immense, orange, double-humped Red Butte (dead ahead).

The path eventually drops into the Cameron Meadow basin at mile 2.8. Higher and less lush but no less impressive than the Frog Pond Meadow basin, the surrounding

Frog Pond sits in a pretty little glacial valley in the Red Buttes Wilderness. ZACH URNESS

rock faces are broken by patches of wildflowers, grass, and picturesque conifer clusters. Spend your time exploring, or perhaps scaling the ridgetop, instead of trying to sleuth out the continuing trail, which disappears at the meadow's edge. Return the way you came.

Miles and Directions

- **0.0** Begin at the Frog Pond Trailhead.
- **0.1** Pass the junction with the Middle Fork Trail (of the Applegate River).
- **1.5** Arrive at Frog Pond Meadow.
- **2.8** Reach Cameron Meadow; return the way you came.
- **5.6** Arrive back at the trailhead.

Options

To complete the full loop, locate the continuing path on the edge of Cameron Meadows and head downhill 2.5 miles to FR 1040. The trail beyond Cameron Meadow is difficult to follow, badly overgrown, and totally lacking in scenery. The forest service has plans to improve this trail. Upon hitting FR 1040, turn left and complete the loop by hiking 2.0 miles up the road and across the large creek to the upper trailhead.

65 Azalea Lake

The most spectacular trail in the Red Buttes Wilderness (which contains several spectacular trails) to a lake surrounded by wildflowers.

Distance: 11.4-mile out and back
Difficulty: Strenuous
Elevation gain: 2,189 feet
Best season: June–Oct
Maps: USGS Grayback Mountain and Figurehead Mountain; Rogue River–Siskiyou National Forest

Trail contacts: Star Ranger Station (541) 899 3800
Parking and trailhead facilities: There is room for 10 cars at the trailhead.
Special considerations: The trail is very thick with brush in some sections; be sure to wear long pants.

Finding the trailhead: The roads to the trailhead are not well marked, so follow the directions carefully; use a GPS device if you have one. From Grants Pass drive south on OR 238 for 18 miles to the green bridge at the town of Applegate. (From Medford drive to Jacksonville and then follow OR 238 to Applegate.) Just before the green bridge over the Applegate River, turn south onto Thompson Creek Road and proceed 12 miles to a gravel hilltop amid a maze of side roads.

Continue straight, ignoring the two roads on the right, through the intersection for 2.8 miles on gravel Carberry Creek Road (CR 777). Turn right across a bridge onto FR 1030, following a ragged Fir Glade marker (that may have come down). Follow FR 1030 for 5 miles along a creek; turn left onto Spur 400 and proceed for another 5 miles. Eventually the road crests and becomes FR 1040. Just beyond the gap, turn right onto the rugged Spur 800 for 0.6 mile and fork left into a small parking lot. It's actually not that hard to find.

Trailhead GPS: N42 00.332' / W123 17.414'

The Hike

The Fir Glade/Azalea Lake Trail (#955) may be the most scenic pathway into the Red Buttes Wilderness. Although fairly lengthy at 5.7 miles and traversing extremely steep terrain, the miles disappear quickly on this surprisingly level path.

The Red Buttes Wilderness was impacted by the Goff Fire in late summer 2012. Initial reports indicate that the trails were not badly damaged, but downed trees may become an issue in the next few years. However, because the far end of the Fir Glade / Azalea Lake route crosses a fair amount of open country, fire damage may not be too noticeable.

From the trailhead it's an easy 1.3-mile walk to Fir Glade, a vast meadow with the remains of a cabin and a profusion of wildflowers. The trail heads sharply left and downhill just before the meadow.

The 3.0 miles past Fir Glade are surprisingly level, holding a contour high above Phantom Meadow. The path crosses patches of dense forest, areas of more open woods and shrubs, and countless meadows and small springs.

Azalea Lake sits in a large valley with the reddish orange peaks of the Red Buttes — for which the wilderness is named — in the distance. ZACH URNESS

Wildflowers (Indian paintbrush, penstemon, monkshood, and others) abound. The black, craggy face of Buck Mountain is the most visible landmark, rising to the south on the other side of Phantom Meadow and the Middle Fork Canyon. The Steve's Fork Trail enters stage right at mile 2.6 (see "Options"). A closed way trail leads down to Phantom Meadow just past the Steve's Fork turnoff.

As of 2012, the Azalea Lake Trail was badly in need of maintenance, with brush encroaching on either side, making it uncomfortable to hike in short pants. The Siskiyou Mountain Club of Ashland is planning to work on the area between 2013 and 2014. *Note:* Tent only in marked campsites outside the loop around Azalea Lake.

The route steepens considerably at the Thompson Creek Divide at mile 3.8, a pass between the Middle Fork Applegate and Thompson Creek, a tributary of the Klamath River. Look for views of Whiskey Peak back toward the trailhead and towering Preston Peak in the distance to the west. Brewer spruce adorns the pass, along with some of the Siskiyous' highest-elevation knobcone and sugar pines.

After another 0.9 open, rocky mile, the trail reaches a second, higher pass and then descends sharply for 1.0 additional mile to the lake, at mile 5.7. Coming into view at the second pass, the lake nestles inside a small glacial cirque near Figurehead Mountain's sheer cliffs. The view down the Butte Fork to the aptly named Red Buttes is memorable.

Surrounded by lodgepole pine, the lake itself is small but beautiful, and the area around it is botanically interesting. True to its name, azalea bushes line its banks.

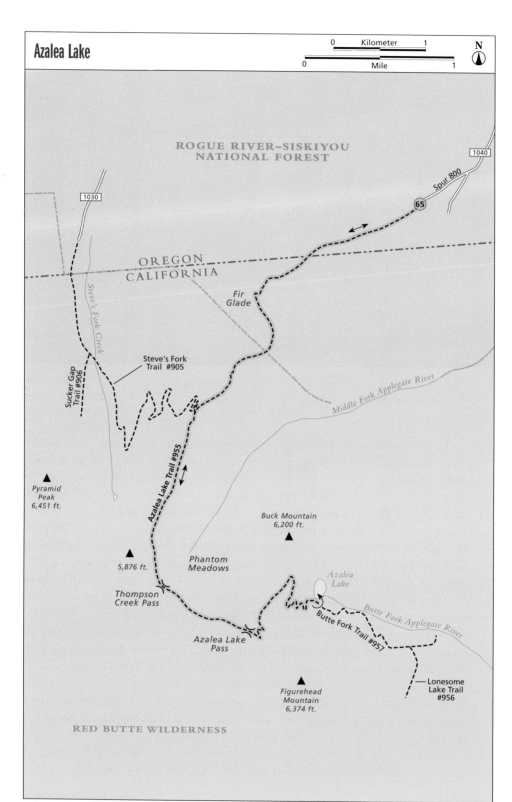

0   Kilometer   1

0   Mile   1

N

ROGUE RIVER–SISKIYOU
NATIONAL FOREST

1040

Spur 800

65

1030

OREGON
CALIFORNIA

Steve's Fork Creek

Fir
Glade

Steve's Fork
Trail #905

Sucker Gap
Trail #906

Middle Fork Applegate River

Azalea Lake Trail #955

▲
Pyramid
Peak
6,451 ft.

▲
5,876 ft.

Buck Mountain
6,200 ft.
▲

Phantom
Meadows

Azalea
Lake

Thompson
Creek Pass

Butte Fork Applegate River

Azalea Lake
Pass

Butte Fork Trail #957

▲
Figurehead
Mountain
6,374 ft.

Lonesome
Lake Trail
#956

RED BUTTE WILDERNESS

The lake boasts a firm gravel bottom (which becomes a little silty in the center) and clear, shallow, warm water. Swimming is excellent, but fishing is reportedly only so-so. The lake becomes less attractive and more overgrown later in the season; it's at its best in late June and July.

Miles and Directions

0.0 Begin at the Fir Glade Trailhead.

0.5 Pass a small pond.

0.9 Pass the state line (unmarked).

1.3 Arrive at Fir Glade and follow the trail left.

2.6 Pass the Steve's Fork Trail junction.

3.8 Arrive at the wilderness boundary and Thompson Creek Pass.

4.7 Come to Azalea Lake Pass.

5.7 Reach Azalea Lake; return the way you came.

11.4 Arrive back at the trailhead.

Options

Lonesome Lake: For Lonesome Lake, continue past Azalea Lake for 0.6 mile on the Butte Fork Trail. Turn right onto the Fort Goff Trail (#956) and continue for 1.1 miles. Eventually the trail reaches a junction where you turn right. The lake is small but deeper than expected in a rocky basin surrounded by azaleas and stupendous, soaring peaks. A large rock on the far side invites you to excellent swimming.

Steve's Fork Trail: The Steve's Fork Trail (#905) to Azalea Lake is extremely scenic and about the same length as the route from the Azalea Lake Trailhead. However, it begins at an elevation 900 feet lower than the Azalea Lake Trail. To find the Steve's Fork Trailhead, instead of turning up Spur 800 for the Azalea Lake Trailhead, continue on FR 1030 (Steve's Fork Road) to its end (milepost 10.5).

From the trailhead (0.2 mile before the state line), the path winds through the woods above the creek for 0.7 mile, hits a junction (go left), and crosses Steve's Fork Creek immediately after. After another 0.7 mile, the trail begins a series of moderately steep switchbacks through a forest of Douglas-fir, mountain hemlock, white fir, Shasta red fir, sugar pine, and Brewer spruce. The path joins the Azalea Lake Trail after 4.0 miles at a junction 2.6 miles from the Azalea Lake Trailhead.

The Steve's Fork Trail features outstanding views of the looming rock face of Pyramid Peak across a small cirque basin. At certain times of the year, a creek runs down the entire face of the mountain, summit to base. The vista compensates for the route's steepness compared with the Azalea Lake Trail.

Note: The Steve's Fork Trailhead is not in quite the same place that it was ten years ago, when the state line ran right through it. Much of the lower trail system has been rerouted in the past few years.

66 Red Buttes / Pacific Crest Trail

Close-up exploration of the beautiful namesake peak of the Red Buttes Wilderness, plus two exquisite little lakes.

Distance: 9.6-mile out and back
Difficulty: Moderately difficult
Elevation gain: 1,880 feet
Best season: May–Nov
Maps: USGS Kangaroo Mountain; Rogue River–Siskiyou National Forest; Klamath National Forest
Trail contacts: Star Ranger Station: (541) 899-3800
Parking and trailhead facilities: There is parking for 15 cars at Cook and Green Pass.
Special considerations: The Red Buttes Wilderness was impacted by the Goff Fire in late summer 2012, which burned around 23,000 acres. You'll see burn marks about halfway down this trail, but the damage doesn't appear to be severe. Snags and downed trees could become an issue in coming years.

The total distance given presumes that you hike on the Pacific Crest Trail (PCT) from Cook and Green Pass. You can shorten the hike 2.3 miles each way by driving up an extremely low-quality road from the pass to the base of Red Buttes, but it is recommended only for people with four-wheel-drive, high-clearance vehicles and excellent driving skills.

Finding the trailhead: From Grants Pass take OR 238 south for 25.5 miles to the small town of Ruch (or north from Jacksonville 8 miles). From Ruch follow the Applegate River Road (CR 859) south for 15 miles, passing Applegate Lake and driving to its upper end. At a T junction, turn left to stay on Applegate Road for 1.5 miles to a gravel junction with roads going in multiple directions. Continue straight at the junction onto FR 1050 for 1 mile and turn right onto FR 1055. Follow this somewhat rough gravel road 10 miles to the ridgetop junction of Cook and Green Pass. You'll see signs for the PCT.
Trailhead GPS: N41 56.512' / W123 08.716'

The Hike

The Red Buttes pop up now and then on many Southern Oregon back roads, usually just for a second. Their double-humped camelback outline is an instant giveaway. Also, they are red (orange actually).

Trails converge everywhere at Cook and Green Pass. To hike the Red Buttes, choose the PCT direction heading west, uphill through the forest, on the right side of the road you drove in on. (The PCT segment heading east leads to Copper Butte; see "Options.")

A rugged, bumpy jeep road leads in the same direction as the trail, and while still open, it is in poor condition and misses a couple of the trail's best views.

From the trailhead you'll hike uphill through a forested setting for 0.9 mile to where the trail opens up to excellent views of Mount Shasta to the south. Just beyond, the mighty Red Buttes make their first appearance.

Robyn Orr looks up at Red Butte, the namesake peak of the Red Buttes Wilderness. ZACH URNESS

Continue 2.5 miles to the Echo Lake overlook. Echo Lake is a small (3 acres) pool set a few hundred feet below in a narrow glacial cirque. The overlook is impressive, and it's worth following a rugged path 0.5 mile downhill to the lakeshore. However, this adds a difficult extra mile to the hike.

At mile 3.0 you descend to the upper end of the jeep road on a meadowed flat at the base of the Red Buttes. This is as close to Red Buttes' massive orange summit as the trail gets.

Just before Lily Pad Lake, there's a scenic little rocky gap. If you have a hankering to climb Red Butte, this is the place to start—the route follows a ridge, and there are no cliffs.

Lily Pad Lake, at mile 4.0, occupies a large meadow, covers 1 acre, and is filled with pond lilies. The PCT here runs between the meadow above the lake and some large rock outcrops. Soon after, the trail crosses over a pass with tremendous views of the Seiad Creek valley and Devil's Peak.

The route enters the magnificent cirque of Kangaroo Spring at mile 4.8. The sheer, brilliant orange cirque walls are made even more stunning by a band of white

Red Buttes/Pacific Crest Trail

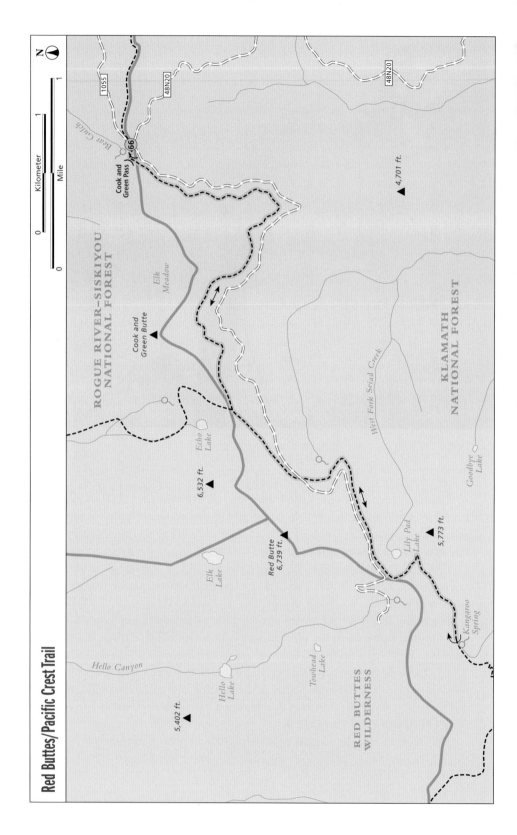

marble that runs through the formation. There is no obvious spring or lake, but lots of clear water runs through the basin's green meadows.

Miles and Directions

0.0 Begin hiking west (right) on the PCT from Cook and Green Pass.

2.5 Arrive at the Echo Lake overlook and trail junction.

3.1 Cross the upper road.

4.0 Pass Lily Pad Lake.

4.8 Reach Kangaroo Spring; return the way you came.

9.6 Arrive back at the trailhead.

Options

East on the Pacific Crest Trail: Heading east from Cook and Green Pass, away from the Red Buttes, the PCT stays in the woods for 1.5 miles and then crosses the rocky summit of Copper Butte (elevation 6,194 feet). Continue 6.0 miles over two more summits, including 7,112-foot Condrey Mountain (the trail doesn't quite hit the Condrey Mountain summit), to a trailhead on an incredibly long, winding road up from the village of Klamath River in California.

67 Taylor Creek

A pleasant hike along a beautiful creek, beginning at Lone Tree Pass and ending at English Flat Trailhead, with many access points along the way.

Distance: 7.2-mile shuttle
Difficulty: Moderate
Elevation loss: 1,126 feet
Best season: Year-round
Maps: USGS Onion Mountain, Chrome Ridge, and Galice; Rogue River–Siskiyou National Forest
Trail contacts: Wild Rivers Ranger District: (541) 471-6500
Parking and trailhead facilities: There's parking for 6 cars at Lone Tree Pass, 10 cars at China Creek, 3 cars at Minnow Creek and Burned Timber Roads, 5 cars at Tin Can Camp-ground, and 4 cars at English Flat. There's a pit toilet at Tin Can Campground.

Special considerations: The description assumes a one-way hike in the downhill direction, beginning at Lone Tree Pass. If you have only one car and don't feel comfortable hitch-hiking, do the route as an out-and-back hike. Since the path has numerous access points, it can also be hiked piecemeal. There is plenty of water, but it should be purified.

If you hike the trail in winter when the water is high, be wary. There are two creek crossings that could be difficult at high water.

Finding the trailhead: From I-5 north of Grants Pass, take exit 61 to Merlin. Continue straight on Merlin-Galice Road 3.2 miles into Merlin and then another 8.5 miles toward Galice. Turn left onto paved FR 25 (Briggs Valley Road) toward Big Pine Campground. Along the way you'll pass several well-marked trailheads for the Taylor Creek Trail.

The first and most obvious trailhead is English Flat at mile 3, just beyond the Taylor Gorge Overlook (a small parking area on the left). There are also trailheads at Burned Timber Road (Spur 035, mile 4.5), Tin Can Campground (mile 5.3), Minnow Creek Road (Spur 052, mile 6.7), China Creek Trail (large parking pullout on left, mile 7.3), and Lone Tree Pass (FR 2509, mile 10). Lone Trees Pass is the highest trailhead, with trails going both directions and a small parking area. The final trailhead is at Sam Brown Campground, on the left at mile 13.

Trailhead GPS: Lone Trees Pass: N42 28.908' / W123 39.989'; English Flat: N42 31.503' / W123 35.810'

The Hike

The Taylor Creek Trail actually extends 10 miles from Sam Brown Campground to English Flat. Of these, the 7.2 miles from Lone Tree Pass to English Flat are the most interesting.

While the trail parallels FR 25 with uncomfortable proximity, the designers attempted to keep it as far from the pavement as possible. They came up with a beautiful, easy, well-constructed route visiting some magnificent pools, rock outcrops, waterfalls, and other scenic features.

Since the trail hits FR 25 every mile or so, options are myriad. The shortest segment is the 0.3 mile from Burned Timber Road to Tin Can Campground. Other

Taylor Creek Trail drops steeply downhill from Lone Tree Pass. The trail is sometimes populated by mountain bikers. ZACH URNESS

segments run 1.0 to 2.0 miles between trailheads. This is a wonderful route to explore piecemeal with children, one segment at a time.

For the most part the trail is gouged into an extremely steep, densely forested goat slope hillside. An abundance of canyon live oak, which loves steep, shallow-soiled, and shady low-elevation slopes, tells you much about the area's ecology. Canyon live oak has the hardest wood of any North American tree species.

The trail's initial 1.0 mile down from Lone Tree Pass hugs the creek well away from the road. This is the trail's steepest segment, especially the first 0.5 mile, which drops down from the pass in a long north-slope switchback.

After crossing the West Fork—which can be difficult during high water—the trail reaches the large China Creek Trailhead at mile 2.7 and continues on the opposite side. The next important point is Minnow Creek Road (Road 052) at mile 3.4. Crossing Minnow Creek may require walking over downed logs. The bridge was washed out as of winter 2012, but it may have been replaced.

The trail's bypassing of Tin Can Campground, at mile 5.1, is an especially nice design feature. Located high above the creek, the path is held in place by retaining walls. The initial construction of these walls was unsuccessful—they collapsed during a storm in 1993 and had to be rebuilt. Below Tin Can Campground, the route alternates between dense woods, rocky outcrops, and grassy meadows. Above, it's mostly dense woods.

The trail passes Road 035 and reaches a beautiful waterfall at mile 5.5, then crosses a junction with Burned Timber Trail—a short nature trail loop of 0.7 mile. The final stretch heads down into a meadow (English Flat), crosses a bridge, and climbs switchbacks up a steep bank to the lower trailhead.

Miles and Directions

0.0 Begin at Lone Tree Pass Trailhead and hike downhill.

2.6 Cross the West Fork Creek (difficult in winter) to China Creek Trailhead. Continue through the parking area to the trail's outlet on the other side (a good turnaround point).

3.4 Cross Minnow Creek on logs and then cross Road 052.

5.0 Pass the Minnow Creek Trail junction.

5.1 Pass Tin Can Campground, which can be seen on the opposite side of Taylor Creek.

5.4 Cross Road 034.

5.5 Come to a view of Burned Timber Creek Falls.

5.9 Pass a junction with the Burned Timber Trail.

7.2 Arrive at English Flat (the first trailhead on the Taylor Creek Trail system).

Options

Minnow Creek Trail: For excellent panoramas of the Taylor Creek basin, follow the Minnow Creek Trail, which meets the Taylor Creek Trail 500 feet west of Tin Can Campground. This new section of the Minnow Creek Trail makes a couple of wide, steep switchbacks uphill and through the brush and hardwood to a forested ridgetop, linking up with the old Minnow Creek Trail after 0.5 mile.

Reach the old Minnow Creek Trailhead by driving up Minnow Creek Road, the next left off FR 25 after Tin Can Campground. Follow the main road through two left turns to a well-marked trailhead.

The 0.2-mile path linking the old trailhead to the new path up from Tin Can Campground is among the steepest in these parts. It's so steep that it's actually more stressful going down than up (downhill stresses the knees and feet; uphill stresses the heart and lungs).

The bulk of the Minnow Creek Trail follows a dry, densely wooded ridgetop, with panoramas in two directions. The second-growth stand offers an excellent lesson in natural succession. The forest consists of large hardwoods (black oak, live oak, tanoak, and madrone) that invaded after logging thirty or forty years ago. The scattered larger conifers are either pines, which also invaded after logging, or defective residuals left as seed trees. In between these larger trees, thousands of young Douglas-firs are slowly

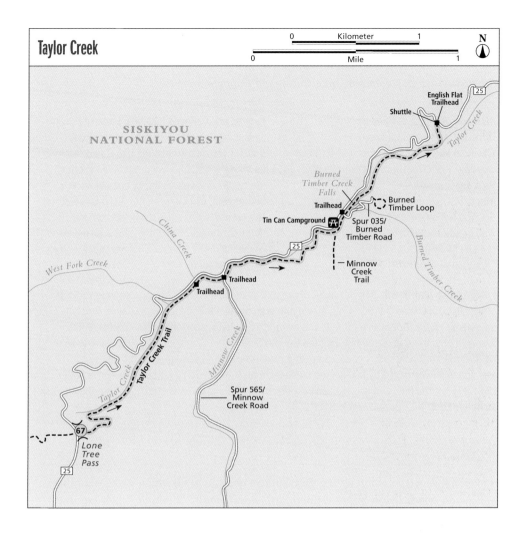

Taylor Creek

working their way from the understory, up through the hardwood and pine foliage, on their way to eventual dominance.

In a couple places the path emerges at grassy openings that offer excellent views in both directions, particularly of the Taylor Creek drainage, with Mount McLoughlin on the eastern horizon. After 3.0 miles the Minnow Creek Trail connects to a road spur in the vicinity of Onion Mountain.

68 Briggs Creek

A pleasant and easy creekside hike among old mines and big trees.

Distance: 8.4-mile out and back
Difficulty: Easy to moderate
Elevation loss/gain: 190-foot loss to Briggs crossing; 1,500-foot gain to Onion Creek
Best season: Any
Maps: USGS Chrome Ridge; Rogue River–Siskiyou National Forest
Trail contacts: Wild Rivers Ranger District: (541) 471-6500

Parking and trailhead facilities: Fifteen cars can park at the Sam Brown Campground trailhead.
Special considerations: The trail is accessible for hiking year-round, but in winter and spring the creek crossings, including one across a beaver dam, can be tricky. The 2010 Oak Flat Fire burned some areas along the trail and at the trailhead—making the area a bit more confusing than in the past but not significantly altering the route.

Finding the trailhead: From I-5 north of Grants Pass, take exit 61 to Merlin. Continue straight on Merlin-Galice Road 3.2 miles into Merlin and then another 8.5 miles toward Galice. Turn left onto paved FR 25 (Briggs Valley Road) and follow it 13.4 miles, passing Big Pine Campground. Turn right onto Road 2512 briefly and then left into Sam Brown Campground. Follow the entrance road all the way back, past a horse camp, to a picnic shelter and parking area. The trail sign was apparently damaged by the fire and unreadable as of winter 2012 (although this may have changed), but the trailhead was marked by a stack of rocks and obvious from the picnic shelter. **Trailhead GPS:** N42 26.442'/W123 41.254'

The Hike

There's no shortage of interesting spots on this quixotic trail, which passes old mines and roads, winds below massive ponderosa pines, requires multiple creek crossings, and above all follows gorgeous Briggs Creek.

For the semi–adventurous hiker, the trail is open year-round but requires three tricky creek crossings. More leisurely hikers will enjoy the trail best in summer, when the shade of the canyon and cool water helps beat the heat, or autumn, when the vine maple, bigleaf maple, and dogwood change color.

Although the trail is easy enough to follow if you're paying attention, the mixture of old mining roads and damage from the Oak Flat Fire can make it slightly confusing. Make sure to look for and follow signposts along the way.

This area rich in mining history offers two distinct goals: the Briggs Creek crossing, 2.7 miles down the trail, or Onion Creek, 4.2 miles. The challenges are described below.

The trail begins at Sam Brown Campground, one of the more famous spots in Josephine County. From the parking area and picnic shelter, the trail heads toward Briggs Creek and turns right (with several paths leading to the banks) to the crossing of Dutchy Creek. In winter and early spring, this requires crossing atop a beaver dam.

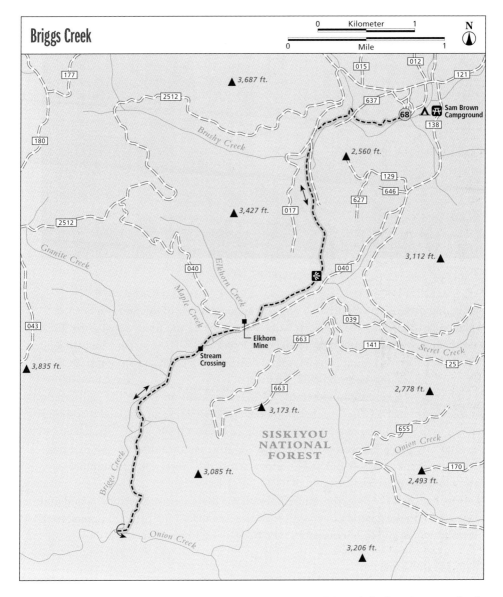

Kilometer

Mile

N

3,687 ft.

Sam Brown
Campground

2,560 ft.

3,427 ft.

3,112 ft.

Granite Creek

Elkhorn
Mine

Stream
Crossing

3,835 ft.

Secret Creek

3,173 ft.

2,778 ft.

SISKIYOU
NATIONAL
FOREST

Onion Creek

3,085 ft.

2,493 ft.

Briggs Creek

Onion Creek

3,206 ft.

FR 017 interrupts the trail at mile 0.8. Follow it left briefly before dropping back into the woods and coming to the Brushy Creek crossing (another one that's tricky in winter and spring).

Immediately after, the trail passes an old hydraulic gold mining area. The site's steep banks, with overhanging tops, are characteristic of hydraulic mining. Soil was washed from the hillsides with a giant nozzle. It was then run through a sluice to extract gold and returned, laden with much silt, to the creek.

The 1.0 mile beyond the creek crossing is gorgeous as the path winds 50 to 100 feet above the stream through a majestic old-growth stand. The creek becomes rockier,

A beautiful view of Briggs Creek from the trail ZACH URNESS

wider, and more enchanting as you progress, although some of this area was burned.

At mile 2.3 comes the Elkhorn Mine. According to the forest service, the 1933 enterprise was a major employer during the Depression. All that remains are hydraulic mining scars, gravel tailings, bits of rapidly deteriorating litter, and an outhouse. Several more mines dot the path below Elkhorn.

The trail is a bit confusing because an old forest road interrupts the path briefly, so follow trail markers and stay left along the creek (avoiding an old road that shoots uphill) until you finally reach a wide crossing of Briggs Creek.

The easiest way to cross is to bushwhack a short distance downstream to a huge tree that makes a narrow but stable bridge across the creek. On hot summer days, enjoy fording the creek.

On the opposite side, the trail climbs above the creek and features wonderful views for 1.5 miles, passing open groves of tree-size manzanita before dropping back down to where an old mining cabin used to sit along Onion Creek.

Miles and Directions

0.0 Begin near the picnic shelters at the Sam Brown Campground trailhead.

0.4 Pass the junction with the Dutchy Creek Trail; then cross Dutchy Creek itself (tricky in winter and early spring).

0.8 Arrive at FR 017 and follow it briefly before dropping back into the woods.

0.9 Cross Brushy Creek.

2.3 Pass Elkhorn Mine.

2.4 Reach the FR 040 junction; stay left along the creek.

2.7 Arrive at the Briggs Creek crossing. Cross on a log over the creek or turnaround here.

4.2 Reach Onion Creek; return the way you came.

8.4 Arrive back at the trailhead.

69 Kerby Peak

Very steep, very scenic trail to the top of one of Josephine County's predominant peaks.

Distance: 6.4-mile out and back
Difficulty: Strenuous
Elevation gain: 2,676 feet
Best season: May–Nov
Maps: USGS Kerby Peak
Trail contacts: Wild Rivers Ranger District: (541) 592-4000

Parking and trailhead facilities: A large flat on the left side of the road can accommodate 10 cars.
Special considerations: There is no water on the trail, and it is very steep.

Finding the trailhead: From Grants Pass take US 199 south for 20 miles to the town of Selma. In Selma turn left onto Deer Creek Road (CR 5070). Proceed 8 miles on this paved road that eventually becomes one lane; veer right across a bridge onto White Creek Road (Road 38-6-18). Drive another 0.5 mile and turn left onto East Fork White Creek Road (the second left). Continue 3 miles to the trailhead, which is obvious and well marked.
Trailhead GPS: N42 14.775' / W123 27.394'

The Hike

Years ago, if you wanted to climb Kerby Peak, it was an easy 1.0-mile trek from the end of Rabbit Lake Road. Those days are long gone, because the end of Rabbit Lake Road is rapidly returning to nature. Too bad, because in the 1970s it was one of Josephine County's prettier drives.

Not to worry! Even with the new trail longer and starting 2,000 feet lower, Kerby Peak is a great hike. The 5,545-foot mountain, one of Josephine County's most prominent summits, towers above Lake Selmac, south of US 199 near Selma.

When the new Kerby Peak Trail above White Creek was constructed by the Young Adult Conservation Corps in 1978, the project drew lots of attention. But the trail attracted little use because the old Rabbit Lake route was so much easier. Over twenty years the trailhead sign fell over, brush grew up around the trailhead, and the last 0.5 mile of trail became completely obscured. The path's first 0.2 mile was so steep and slippery, you couldn't walk on it in wet weather.

The White Creek–Kerby Peak Trail's Sleeping Beauty era ended in 1998. The most noticeable improvement was rerouting the initial 0.2 mile, which now makes a long, reasonable switchback instead of charging up a slick, compacted slope suited more to mountain goats than humans.

The path's initial mile is uniformly steep as it inscribes dozens of switchbacks through a middle-elevation forest of Douglas-fir, white fir, incense cedar, and sugar pine, with the usual black oak and madrone hardwood cohorts. It's not an old-growth forest but a beautiful, closed-canopy second-growth forest.

The Kerby Peak Trail winds through open vistas and odd rock formations en route to the summit. ZACH URNESS

The rock overlook at mile 1.0 offers an excellent hiking destination any time of year. The west-facing perch provides a fine panorama of the Deer Creek Valley and the trail's first view of Kerby Peak.

Beyond the overlook, the path steepens slightly as it continues its relentless upward march through the woods. Approaching mile 1.4, the route breaks out of the woods onto a large rock outcrop. Soon after, the trail hits a pass, with a rocky knob just to the left. Beyond, the path swings along the ridgetop, levels off for a while, and cuts around to the south face.

On the dry and fire-prone south face, the vegetation changes dramatically from forest to a bramble of low, dense brush. The main species are pinemat manzanita, green manzanita, and squaw carpet ceanothus. The path makes its way up through the steep, brushy slopes in a series of switchbacks before finally attaining the summit at mile 3.2.

The summit is gorgeous, with green meadows, brown rock outcrops, a tremendous panorama of Lake Selmac, and a sheer cliff dropping off to the northwest. Look for the rare and beautiful Brewer spruce growing just over the cliffs.

Kerby Peak

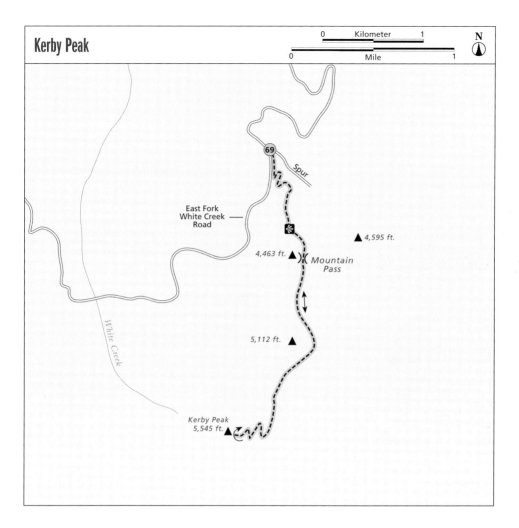

Miles and Directions

0.0 Begin at White Creek Trailhead.

1.0 Arrive at an overlook of Deer Creek Valley (optional turnaround).

1.4 Reach the mountain pass.

3.2 Reach the Kerby Peak summit; return the way you came.

6.4 Arrive back at the trailhead.

70 Dollar Mountain

The trailhead is located within the Grants Pass city limits. The hike, to the top of a small mountain, is short, very steep, and an excellent example of a lowland ecosystem.

Distance: 2.2-mile out and back
Difficulty: Moderate to difficult, but short
Elevation gain: 744 feet
Best season: Year-round
Maps: USGS Grants Pass; BLM Medford District
Trail contacts: BLM Medford District: (541) 618-2200
Parking and trailhead facilities: There is parking for 8 cars on a wide spot on the road shoulder opposite the trailhead. There are no trailhead facilities.

Special considerations: This is the only trailhead in this guide located within a city (Grants Pass, population 35,000). Although all the trailhead signs were put up by the city, most of the trail is on BLM land. The BLM is responsible for maintaining the trail, and their rules apply. (Open 24 hours; pets must be on-leash or under voice command; mountain bikes are OK but no motorized vehicles.) The trailhead is in a residential neighborhood, so be respectful. Also be cautious; homeless people may be camping nearby. No water. After hiking in spring and summer, check yourself and your pet for ticks.

Finding the trailhead: Leave I-5 at exit 55 and head into Grants Pass. You will be on Sixth Street. Continue south to "A" Street and turn right (at City Hall). Take "A" Street to Dimmick (by the old hospital) and jog left for 1 block to "B" Street, where you will start seeing Trail signs. Go right on "B" Street and follow the main road through a number of sharp curves to the trailhead. (Technically the trailhead is on Crescent Drive, but you're still on the same street.) Park across the street on the shoulder.
Trailhead GPS: N42 26.905' / W123 20.592'

The Hike

This is a favorite local hike through a low-elevation woodland consisting mostly of Pacific madrone (with the orange peeling bark); California black oak; and large, almost tree-size, whiteleaf manzanita. There are also a fair number of small ponderosa pines and a few Douglas-firs and incense cedars.

Beginning in April, the trail becomes a wildflower paradise, with several waves of flowers coming in and out of bloom as the season wears on. The most spectacular and abundant spring flower is the western shooting star. In spring also look for a beautiful red, bell-shaped flower called scarlet fritillary. The tiny low-elevation woodland species is considered threatened but holds its own within a very narrow range.

Madrone is a deciduous hardwood with a difference. Unlike other deciduous trees, the thick, shiny leaves fall off in late spring, just as the new leaves are emerging. The carpet of crunchy red madrone leaves on the ground brightens any hike.

Wildflowers are common along Dollar Mountain Trail during spring. LYNN BERNSTEIN

From the trailhead the path heads immediately and relentlessly uphill. It levels off slightly at one point but becomes even steeper toward the end. As noted, the trail is not very long, so there's no need to hurry.

About one-third of the way up, you will come to a fork followed by an extremely steep pitch. If you go right, the route is leveled out slightly by a long switchback. (**Suggestion:** Take the switchback up and the straight pitch down.)

The summit is a fenced-off area full of small buildings and electronic equipment, including a cell tower (a locked, gated road on the other side of the mountain allows vehicle access).

Vistas of Grants Pass, the Rogue Valley, the Siskiyous, and, on the eastern horizon, the major volcanoes of the High Cascades entertain hikers throughout the journey.

Miles and Directions

0.0 Begin at the trailhead on Crescent Drive.

1.1 Reach the Dollar Mountain summit; return the way you came.

2.2 Arrive back at the trailhead.

Options

If you continue on the trail past the summit, there is an alternate, slightly longer and slightly less steep route back down. But it does not come out at a marked trailhead, and much of the route parallels a road.

71 Limpy Creek Botanical Loop

A short, botanically diverse and very pretty loop along a creek, passing forest, rock outcrops, dry grassy areas, and an exquisite (if small) waterfall.

Distance: 1.0-mile loop
Difficulty: Easy
Elevation gain: 170 feet
Best season: Year-round
Maps: USGS Wilderville and Onion Mountain; Rogue River–Siskiyou National Forest
Trail contacts: Wild Rivers (Grants Pass) Ranger District: (541) 471-6500
Parking and trailhead facilities: There's room for 10 cars in the gravel lot; vault toilet.

Special considerations: One online resource inexplicably rates this trail as "moderate to strenuous." Actually it's a great place to introduce small children to hiking. Dogs are OK, but no bikes. Watch out for poison oak. This is one of Grants Pass Parks and Recreation's favorite places to send families who seek a short, scenic, child-friendly hike that's close to town.

Finding the trailhead: From Grants Pass take US 199 south for 7 miles. Immediately after crossing the Applegate River bridge, turn right onto Riverbanks Road. After 4.5 miles you will come to Limpy Creek Road, on the left. Follow the narrow blacktop 2 miles to the trailhead.
Trailhead GPS: N42 25.642'/W123 32.654'

The Hike

This lovely little loop is easy, pleasant, and informative—and doesn't take too long. There are numerous benches and interpretive signs along the way. Because of the diversity of botanical ecosystems, there are supposedly 250 different plant species to be seen along the trail (although they don't all bloom at the same time). Part of the site contains serpentine soil (derived from ultra-basic igneous rock), on which many common species won't grow and which tends to contain many threatened and endangered species.

Standouts include Jeffrey pine, which looks similar to ponderosa pine except that in Southern Oregon, Jeffrey pine grows only on serpentine soil. The trail has ponderosa and Jeffrey pine. There are several ways to tell them apart, but the most fun identifier is that Jeffrey pine bark smells like pineapple.

California coffeeberry, scrub white oak (Brewer's oak), rock cress, and western azalea are all serpentine-adapted species. Port Orford cedar (with the drooping tips) also does well on serpentine. Red alder, vine maple, bigleaf maple, and willow grow along the creek, while Douglas-fir and ponderosa pine grow everywhere but on the serpentine soil. Incense cedar is a common forest species that will grow on serpentine soil and just about anywhere else. Cat's ear, camas lily, and calypso orchid are also standouts.

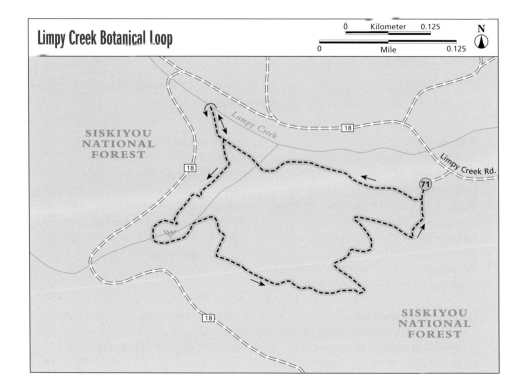

Taking the right-hand side of the loop from the trailhead, the path follows alongside the creek, with a couple of short side trails to explore the creek further. Approaching the 0.5-mile mark, the path climbs to the top of a beautiful waterfall (about 30 feet high) that cascades steeply over some green, moss-covered rocks (at mile 0.6).

Then it's back down to the lowlands, across a dry grassy meadow, and back to the trailhead.

Miles and Directions

0.0 Begin at the trailhead, following the right-hand (counterclockwise) side of the loop.

0.6 Arrive at the top of the waterfall.

1.0 Arrive back at the trailhead at the far end of the loop.

72 Grayback Mountain

A beautiful meadow, old cabins, and an adventurous climb to the highest point in Josephine County. Options for a difficult or easy hike.

Distance: 5.4-mile out and back
Difficulty: Strenuous to summit
Elevation gain: 2,586 feet to summit
Best season: June–Oct
Maps: USGS Grayback Mountain; Rogue River–Siskiyou National Forest.
Trail contacts: Star Ranger Station: (541) 899-3800

Parking and trailhead facilities: There is parking for 6 cars at the trailhead. There is no room for a trailer turnaround and barely room for an auto turnaround.
Special considerations: There is water on the trail near the former site of Crouse Cabin and sometimes at Cold Spring.

Finding the trailhead: From Grants Pass drive south on OR 238 to the green bridge in the town of Applegate (from Medford, drive to Jacksonville and then follow OR 238 to Applegate). Just before the green bridge over the river, turn south onto Thompson Creek Road and proceed 12 miles to a gravel hilltop junction amid a maze of side roads.

Turn sharply right at the hilltop junction onto O'Brien Creek Road (FR 1005), clearly marked on the right. Follow O'Brien Creek Road a total of 4 miles to the end. At mile 2 you'll pass a lower trailhead. Equestrians or those with low-clearance cars should consider stopping here and following the pleasant trail about 1 mile to the upper trailhead. The final 2 miles of road to the upper trailhead is very steep, rocky, and narrow.
Trailhead GPS: N42 06.642' / W123 17.245'

The Hike

At 7,055 feet, mighty Grayback Mountain is the highest summit in Josephine County. It is one of five Siskiyou peaks over 7,000 feet. While Grayback is no Shasta, Grants Pass residents feel a certain fondness for the old gray mound, so aptly named and looking like a beached whale. A trip up Grayback won't guarantee membership in the Explorers Club, but it does require some route finding, provides a workout, and offers pleasant scenery.

The trail (#900) begins at the road's end. It starts out by winding through the woods for 1.0 mile, mostly uphill but not killingly so, to a trail junction.

At this point it's time to make a choice. To explore a wildflower-filled meadow with a very cool cabin—the Grayback Snow Survey Cabin—turn left and hike 0.3 mile into the meadow. To climb to the summit, go right, following the pointers to the Boundary Trail.

If you elect to explore the meadows, you'll pass the cabin first, which during summer is a funky bunkhouse with an iron stove where many people have spent the night in the past and left an assortment of Christmas lights, canned goods, even a wooden flute.

The meadow beyond is open, green, full of wildflowers, and quite overgrown. A cabin belonging to the Crouse family—a prominent logging family in the Illinois

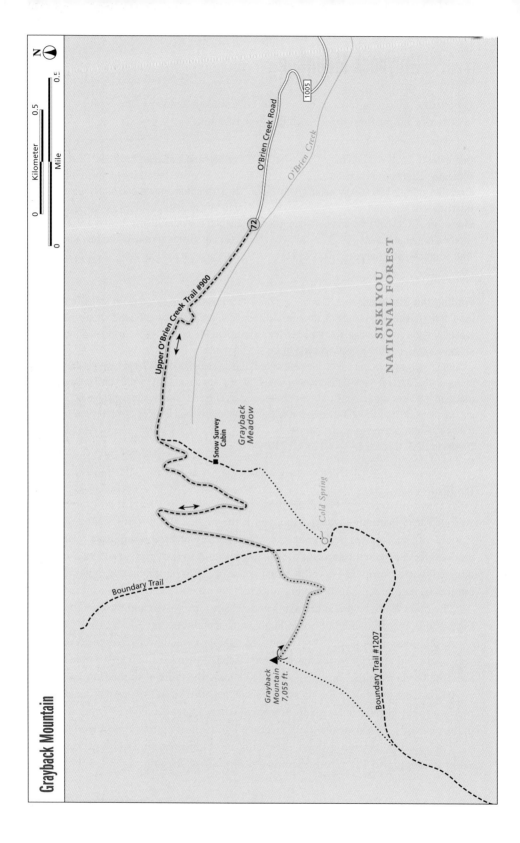

Grayback Mountain

The summit of Grayback Mountain offers views that stretch all the way to the Pacific Ocean on clear days. ZACH URNESS

Valley—used to stand in these meadows, but in 2001 three teenagers from Medford accidentally burned it down. The only evidence of the cabin today is an old iron stove sticking out of the meadow like a black thumb.

The route to Grayback summit used to lead through the meadows, but in recent years it has become so overgrown that it's difficult to bushwhack through the brush. To climb the mountain, head back to the trail junction at the 0.9-mile mark and head uphill on the trail.

From the junction the trail switchbacks 1.2 miles to the junction with the Boundary Trail. From the signpost at the junction, follow the trail left 133 feet and head off-trail to the right, climbing southwest through a grassy meadow toward a silver-gray peak rising 342 feet above. The off-trail route is obvious. Once you reach the silver-gray peak, follow a faint trail through a wooded ridgeline and climb the final 559 feet and 0.8 mile to the summit.

The off-trail section climbs 901 feet in 1.0 mile and is not easy (the colony of blackflies that call the summit home don't help). From the summit the view extends to the Pacific Ocean and includes the Red Buttes, the Siskiyou Wilderness, and Mount Shasta, to name just a few highlights.

Miles and Directions

0.0 Begin at Upper O'Brien Creek Trailhead.

0.9 Arrive at the Grayback Meadows Trail junction. To head to the summit, go right. (For a short hike to the meadows, go left.)

2.1 Arrive at the Boundary Trail junction and go left (but only briefly). Step off-trail on the right, heading straight/left (southwest) toward the ridgetop above.

2.3 Arrive at the ridgetop and swing right (northwest) to climb to the summit.

2.7 Reach the Grayback summit; return the way you came.

5.4 Arrive back at the trailhead.

73 Rainie Falls

A beautiful and popular hike through the wild Rogue River canyon on the opposite side of the river from the Rogue River Trail. This hike affords the best view of Rainie Falls; in autumn, leaping salmon are a common sight.

Distance: 4.0-mile out and back
Difficulty: Easy to moderate
Elevation gain: 110 feet
Best season: Year-round
Maps: USGS Mount Reuben; Rogue River–Siskiyou National Forest
Trail contacts: Grants Pass Interagency Office: (541) 471-6500; Smullin Visitor Center: (541) 479-3735

Parking and trailhead facilities: Parking is along the road shoulder just before the bridge over the Rogue. There's close-in parking for 10 or 15 cars. On a summer weekend you may have to park a couple hundred feet away from the trailhead.
Special considerations: Rock surfaces on the trail and at the falls can be very slippery, so be very careful. Two people have died after falling into the river during the past ten years, making caution important.

Finding the trailhead: From I-5 north of Grants Pass, take exit 61 to Merlin. Continue straight on Merlin-Galice Road for 3.2 miles into Merlin and then another 8.5 miles toward Galice, a popular rustic store, restaurant (with outdoor seating), and rafting stop on the river. From Galice continue another 6 miles. Just before a bridge crosses over the river, park along the side of the road. The trail begins on the left side of the river and follows it downstream.
Trailhead GPS: N42 38.924' / W123 35.133'

The Hike

The Rogue River Trail is among the most famous pathways in Oregon, following the world-famous whitewater canyon through the splendor of the Oregon Siskiyous. Problem is, that trail is 40 miles long.

The Rainie Falls Trail, located on the opposite side of the river, is popular because it provides a sample of the Rogue canyon's charms—cliffs, rapids, birds soaring overhead, and salmon leaping upstream—on an accessible 4.0-mile hike.

The spelling isn't a mistake. The falls are named for an old man named Rainie who lived in a cabin near the falls and made a living snatching salmon that attempted to jump up the falls to reach upstream spawning grounds. (This is now illegal; anglers must fish 100 feet downstream of the falls.)

Near the trailhead, just past the Grave Creek boat landing on the opposite shore, look for the rumble and crash of Grave Creek Rapids and the narrow chute of Grave Creek Falls (both Class III).

At mile 0.5 the trail passes a viewpoint that looks deep into the canyon downstream and will keep photographers busy. In the next 1.5 miles, the trail drops downhill

Rainie Falls

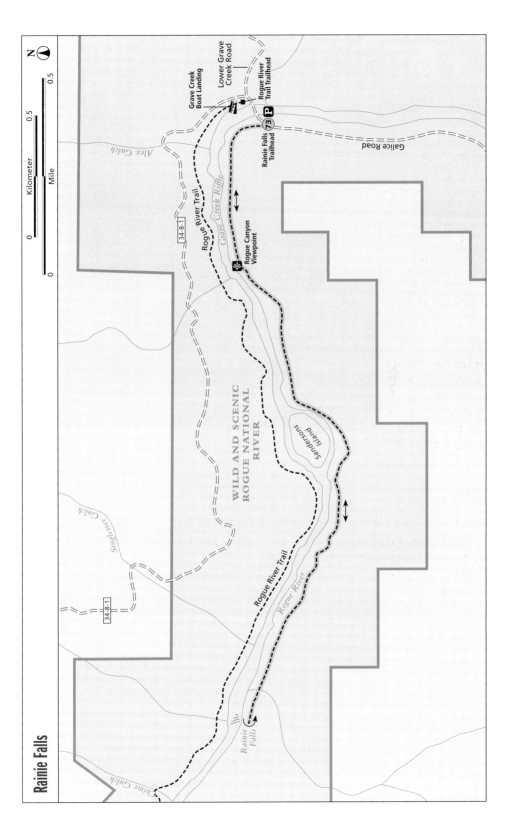

N

Kilometer
0   0.5
Mile
0   0.5

Alex Gulch

Grave Creek Boat Landing

Lower Grave Creek Road

Rogue River Trail Trailhead

Rainie Falls Trailhead

73 P

Galice Road

34-8-1

Rogue River Trail

Grave Creek Riffle

Rogue Canyon Viewpoint

WILD AND SCENIC ROGUE NATIONAL RIVER

Sandersons Island

Singletree Gulch

34-8-1

Rogue River Trail

Rogue River

Chime Gulch

Rainie Falls

The views of the Rogue River canyon on the Rainie Falls Trail are outstanding. ZACH URNESS

and veers away from the river at times before finally reaching the collection of rocks that overlook the thundering power of Rainie Falls.

One of the first things people notice about the falls is that it's not much of a falls at all. The water drops only about 6 feet. Still, it's an impressive sight, and if you're lucky you'll get to watch a boater attempt to run the Class V rapid's powerful middle chute (most boaters go around the falls via a dynamited fish ladder passage on the river's north side).

The best time to see salmon jumping upstream here is late August and September.

Miles and Directions

- **0.0** Begin at the Rainie Falls Trailhead.
- **0.5** Arrive at a Rogue River canyon viewpoint.
- **2.0** Reach Rainie Falls; return the way you came.
- **4.0** Arrive back at the trailhead.

74 Rogue River Trail–Grave Creek to Foster Bar

This is the longest and best hike in the Oregon Siskiyous. The path follows the world-famous whitewater gorge of the Wild and Scenic Rogue River as it cuts through the Siskiyou Mountains and Coast Ranges to the Pacific.

Distance: 39.5-mile shuttle
Difficulty: Moderate but very long
Elevation gain: Generally flat, with some incline
Best season: Year-round
Maps: USGS Mount Reuben and Marial;
BLM Medford District; Rogue River–Siskiyou
National Forest
Trail contacts: Grants Pass Interagency Office:
(541) 471-6500; Smullin Visitor Center: (541)
479-3735

Parking and trailhead facilities: There are porta-potties and parking for 25 cars at the Grave Creek boat launch, but overnight parking is not allowed. The best place to park at Grave Creek is on the sides of the road above the boat launch. At the trail's far end, there is a pit toilet and parking for 8 cars at the trailhead just before Foster Bar. There is parking for 100 cars at the actual Foster Bar boat launch site.

Finding the trailhead: Grave Creek: From I-5 north of Grants Pass, take exit 61 to Merlin. Continue straight on Merlin-Galice Road 3.2 miles into Merlin and then another 8.5 miles toward Galice, a small Rogue River outpost. From Galice continue another 6 miles. Just across a bridge over the Rogue River, a road shoots steeply downhill to Grave Creek boat launch. The trail begins here, on the north side of the river.
Grave Creek Trailhead GPS: N42 39.054' / W123 35.187'
Foster Bar / Big Bend Trailhead (from Rogue Valley; open during summer only):
From I-5 north of Grants Pass, take exit 61 to Merlin and continue on Merlin-Galice Road. At mile 15 on Merlin-Galice Road, just before Galice, turn left onto FR 23, the road to Gold Beach. Continue 37 magnificent blacktopped miles, over a 5,000-foot pass, to FR 33, the road along the Lower Rogue River from Gold Beach, on the coast, to Agness and Powers. Turn right onto FR 33 and proceed 2 miles, over the bridge, to the Foster Bar turnoff on the right. It's 3.4 more miles to the Foster Bar spur road and 3.6 miles to the Rogue River Trail spur road, both on the right. The trailhead is located 0.2 mile up the dirt spur road.
Foster Bar / Big Bend Trailhead (from Gold Beach; open year-round): Just before the bridge over the Rogue River in Gold Beach, turn right onto Jerry's Flat Road (FR 33) and continue 21 miles. Turn right onto Agness Illahe Road for 3 miles to Foster Bar on the right.
Foster Bar / Big Bend Trailhead GPS: N42 38.317' / W124 03.338'

The Hike

It would certainly be possible to write an entire book about the history and glory of the Rogue River Trail, originally constructed more than a century ago for pack mules supplying miners in this wild canyon. Alas, we don't have that type of space. What follows instead is a look at some of the trail's highlights and options for enjoying it.

Flora Dell Falls is a waterfall and chilly swimming hole along the Rogue River Trail. ZACH URNESS

The trail can be used in multiple ways from Grave Creek boat ramp and trailhead. It's well marked and mostly level and mixes wide-open canyon scenery with beautiful forested side canyons where clear streams jump down toward the Rogue.

(*Options:* For a quick day hike consider Rainie Falls [3.4 miles round-trip] or Whiskey Creek Cabin [6.2], a National Historic Landmark museum. Or consider a one-night backpacking trip to Tyee [9.8 miles round-trip] or Russian Creek [11.4 miles round-trip].)

Backpacking the entire stretch, while requiring plenty of planning, is one of the West Coast's great trips. (For options on staying at lodges or taking a raft-supported trip from outfitters, see "Special considerations.")

From Grave Creek, the first 9.0 miles are filled with wonderful campsites where green water pools below oak trees and in spring a profusion of wildflowers are found.

Beyond Bunker Creek (8.9), the trail becomes a bit steeper and there are fewer campsites. A trail to a landing across from Black Bar Lodge, built in 1932, intersects at mile 9.3.

At Horseshoe Bend, mile 11.1, the river makes a huge curve and a trail leads down to campsites very popular with rafters.

At mile 16.6 you come to Battle Bar, visible on the opposite side of the river. Battle Bar is the site of skirmishes between the US Army and the Takelma Indians in 1855 and 1856. The cabin at Battle Bar was built in 1947. Tragically, the owner, Bob Fox, died before he could finish it. For hikers, camping at Battle Bar is on the north side of the river, at Ditch Creek.

Two more historic places can be explored next, beginning with Winkle Bar and Zane Grey's cabin at mile 17.3. Grey was the most commercially successful writer of the 1920s. He wrote rollicking Western tales of brave men and violent times—but also penned a story about the river titled "Rogue River Feud."

ROGUE RIVER TRAIL

1) The description here is cursory and for trip planning only. The BLM publishes a detailed, 36-page pamphlet on the Rogue River Trail that is indispensable. Supplemental maps are also essential and can usually be found at the Grave Creek Trailhead.

2) The trail is usually snow-free all year. In winter it is cold and rainy, side creeks are high, and campsites may be soggy. In midsummer—July and August—the canyon can be boiling hot.

3) Depending on the time of year, campfires may be banned. Call ahead. Campfires within 400 feet of the river must be confined to a fire pan.

4) Black bears are common, especially in the lower third segment, between Paradise Bar Lodge and Tacoma Camp area. Always hang food 10 feet high and 5 feet out. Many campsites have bear-proof facilities.

5) From May to mid-October, backpackers can stay at rustic lodges along the way that serve dinner and breakfast and pack hikers a lunch. They are expensive. Call in advance for reservations at Black Bar (mile 9.3; 541-479-6507), Marial Lodge (mile 23.9; 541-474-2057), Paradise Bar Lodge (mile 27.4; 541-842-2822), and Clay Hill Lodge (mile 33.2; 503-859-3772).

6) Raft-supported hiking tours offered by local outfitters have become a popular option for those willing to shell out $900 to $1,200 per person. Guides take hikers' gear downstream in rafts (and allow them to ride when tired), set up lunches, serve craft wines and beer, and make reservations at lodges. Trips are offered May, June, September, and October at Rogue Wilderness Adventures (541-479-9554), Orange Torpedo Trips (541-479-5061), and Rogue River Journeys (866-213-7754).

7) Setting up a shuttle can be a huge hassle. Outfitters will shuttle your car from Merlin to Foster Bar, depending on the season, for $100 to $150. Call Rogue Wilderness Adventures (541-479-9554) or Orange Torpedo Trips (541-479-5061).

8) There's a chance you'll come away from this hike smitten by the whitewater bug. Should that occur, check at the Smullin Visitor Center to find out about permit requirements and when and where it's OK to go on the river. Stop by or call any of the numerous raft rental services in Merlin or Galice.

9) There is a single access road halfway down the trail, at Marial, that allows the option to do this hike in two separate segments—Grave Creek to Marial and Marial to Foster Bar.

More history arrives at mile 22.7 with the emergence of the Rogue River Ranch, which has been turned from an old homestead into a museum administered by the BLM. The oldest known human habitation site in Oregon is an archaeological dig located near Rogue River Ranch.

At the ranch's far end, the trail emerges onto Marial Road, the only access point on the trail. Numerous signs point hikers along the road, which passes Marial Lodge at mile 23.9 and Marial Trailhead at mile 24.4.

The second half of the trail begins with the trail's most spectacular 3.0 miles—the Rogue River Trail segment from Marial to Paradise Bar Lodge, which features Mule Creek canyon, Blossom Bar, and Paradise Bar Lodge (the eating, drinking, and sleeping type).

Mule Creek canyon, a very narrow defile, empties into a whirlpool called the Coffeepot. Take a minute to watch as rafters are bounced through this area. Beyond the Coffeepot, the river calms down as it passes the two-tiered Stair Creek Falls, seen from the trail at Inspiration Point. The canyon widens slightly as Blossom Bar Rapids come into view in the distance. Here, massive stones clog the river, creating Class IV rapids. A spur trail on the left after Blossom Bar Creek offers a closer look at the rapids. This is popular spot for watching more rafters negotiate the rapids, so sit for a spell.

Beyond Blossom Bar continue to Paradise Creek and a great swimming hole to the left of the trail. Arrive at the spur that leads to the Paradise Bar Lodge. The bar itself smells of aged wood and smoke. Photos of river guides and past US presidents cover the walls—in this area, the former is more important than the latter. Paradise Bar Lodge can only be reached by foot or by float. Call ahead (see the Rogue River Trail sidebar) to have lunch ready when you arrive. Otherwise, snacks and lemonade are available. The price to spend the night at Paradise Bar Lodge is high, and reservations must be made well in advance.

Beyond Paradise, at mile 30.2, you come to the large Brushy Bar Campground, which boasts a forest service guard station, toilets, and running water. How uptown can you get?

Another stretch of outstanding campsites begins with Solitude Bar, at mile 31.2. Deep canyon scenery, sandy beaches, pools of green, and fishing holes can be found scattered between Solitude and Tacoma Camp (mile 32.7), generally ending at Clay Hill Lodge (mile 33.2). Bears are common in this area, so be sure to hang food or use the bear-proof boxes, electric fences, and hoists provided.

Tate Creek, at mile 32.5, is notable for a 25-foot waterfall that you cross on a footbridge. Flora Dell Falls, mile 35, drops into an emerald pool alongside the trail and constitutes what's certainly among Oregon's great swimming holes.

The final 5.0 miles are the least interesting of the entire trail. Beyond Flora Dell Falls, the trail eventually moves away from the river and climbs up and down a series of hills, which is fairly torturous for those trying to finish 40 miles.

Finally the trail rejoins the river, then crosses Billings Creek and a road to Illahe Lodge, and finishes up in a large cow pasture that makes an odd ending to a trail that stayed almost entirely in the canyon throughout.

Rogue River Trail—Grave Creek to Foster Bar

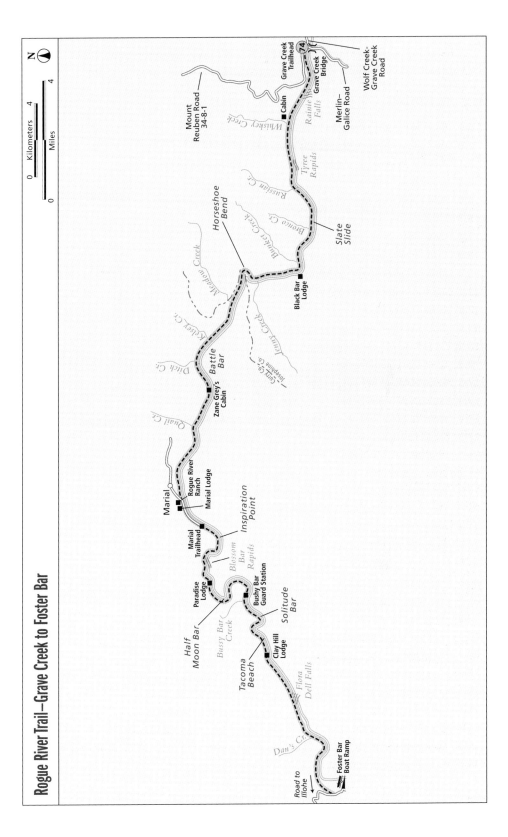

After crossing the pasture, a gate, and two sets of stile steps, the trail ends at mile 39.5 at the Big Bend Trailhead, a mile shy of the Foster Bar boat launch site.

Miles and Directions

0.0 Begin at the Grave Creek Trailhead.

1.8 Pass junction down to Rainie Falls (camp).

3.1 Arrive at Whiskey Creek cabin (camp; popular turnaround spot for day hikes).

3.8 Arrive at Big Slide (camp).

4.9 Pass Tyee Rapids (camp).

5.7 Cross Russian Creek (camp).

7.1 Cross Slate Creek (camp).

8.9 Cross Bunker Creek (camp).

9.3 Arrive at junction to Black Bar Lodge (across the river).

11.4 Arrive at junction to Horseshoe Bend (camp).

12.3 Cross Copsey Creek.

13.6 Cross Meadow Creek (camp).

15.4 Cross Kelsey Creek (camp).

16.3 Cross Ditch Creek (camp).

17.3 Arrive at Winkle Bar and junction to Zane Grey's cabin.

19.4 Cross Quail Creek (camp).

22.7 Arrive at Rogue River Ranch/Museum. The trail moves onto a well-signed gravel road.

23.9 Arrive at Marial Lodge.

24.4 Arrive at Marial Trailhead.

25.2 Arrive at Inspiration Point.

26.5 Pass unmarked trail leading to view of Blossom Bar Rapids (camp).

26.9 Pass North and South Gleason Bars (camp).

27.4 Arrive at Paradise Bar Lodge.

28.0 Pass Half Moon Bar (camp).

30.2 Pass Brushy Bar Guard Station.

30.5 Pass Brushy Bar (camp).

31.2 Pass junction to Solitude Bar (camp).

32.5 Cross Tate Creek (camp).

32.7 Pass junction to Camp Tacoma (camp).

33.2 Pass Clay Hill Lodge and rapids.

35.0 Pass Flora Dell Falls (camp).

35.7 Cross Hicks Creek.

36.8 Cross Dan's Creek.

38.9 Cross Billings Creek.

39.0 Cross road that leads to Illahe Lodge.

39.5 Arrive at Big Bend Trailhead.

75 Rogue River Trail—Marial to Paradise Bar Lodge

The most spectacular 3-mile segment of the 40-mile Rogue River Trail. The Marial access road is unpaved, narrow, very steep, and very curvy—not for everyone.

Distance: 6.6-mile out and back
Difficulty: Easy
Elevation gain: 309 feet
Best season: Apr–Nov (In winter the upper portion of the Marial access road is often covered with snow. Regardless, it opens fairly early in the season.)
Maps: USGS Marial; Rogue River–Siskiyou National Forest
Trail contacts: Smullin Visitor Center, Rand: (541) 479-3735; Gold Beach Ranger District:

(541) 247-3600; Grants Pass Interagency Office: (541) 471-6500
Parking and trailhead facilities: There is parking for 6 cars at the trailhead. Accommodations are available at Marial Lodge (541-474-2057).
Special considerations: The canyon can be extremely hot in summer. If you phone ahead, you can have lunch waiting for you at Paradise Bar Lodge (541-842-2822).

Finding the trailhead: From I-5 north of Grants Pass, take exit 61 to Merlin. Continue straight on Merlin–Galice Road 3.2 miles into Merlin and then another 8.5 miles toward Galice, a small Rogue River outpost. From Galice continue another 6 miles, just across the Grave Creek bridge and a boat landing.

Turn left immediately over the bridge and head up the mountain on gravel Road 34-8-1 for 15 miles. The road is very narrow and winding for the 3 miles between Whiskey Creek Road and Sawmill Gap. At mile 15.1 the road merges with the upper end of Whisky Creek Road and becomes Road 32-7-19.3. At mile 15.6, you pick up Road 32-8-31, a one-lane blacktop road from Glendale. Turn left, toward Powers, and go another 5 miles to Marial Road (Road 32-9-14.2) on the left. The gravel Marial Road is 15 miles long, very steep, very winding, and very pretty. It's suggested that you put your car in a lower gear or you won't have any breaks left by the bottom. Four-wheel drive also won't hurt. Proceed past Tucker Flat Campground and Rogue River Ranch, through Marial, to the small trailhead parking area at the road's end, 2 miles past Rogue River Ranch. The last mile is quite rough.
Trailhead GPS: N42 42.317' / W123 53.726'

The Hike

The best 3.0 miles of the Rogue River Trail—the most delicious morsel of a five-star meal—requires driving a long and winding road to the remote outpost of Marial, nestled snug in the wild Rogue River canyon.

Before heading out on the trail, stop by the Rogue River Ranch (well signed just past Tucker Flat Campground) and the BLM museum there, with its neatly tended grounds. The museum sits on the canyon's only level spot. The area boasts much history—of pioneers, gold miners, and Native Americans. A nearby archaeological site has uncovered the oldest evidence of human habitation in Oregon, from 9,000 years ago.

From Inspiration Point on the Rogue River Trail, Stair Creek Falls drops into Mule Creek Canyon on the Rogue River. ZACH URNESS

From the trailhead you'll enter a ledge above the river and look out on one of Oregon's most spectacular vistas. For 2.0 miles the path is gouged into sheer rock up the side of the gray-green canyon.

Soon the path meets the river and you enter Mule Creek canyon. The extremely narrow defile, appropriately dubbed the Narrows, empties into a circular, whirlpool-filled hole known to river runners as the Coffeepot (mile 0.5). Look for boats careening from one wall to the other or spinning helplessly. The Coffeepot can be fun if you're in an inflated raft, but the tendency to crash into the wall is hard on drift boats.

Beyond the Coffeepot, at mile 0.7, the river calms down as it passes the two-tiered Stair Creek Falls on the river's opposite bank, seen from the trail at a place called Inspiration Point. The aptly named falls crash down the narrow gorge of Stair Creek, with a small pool between the two tiers.

The canyon widens slightly as Blossom Bar Rapids come into view in the distance (mile 2.1). Identifiable by the massive stones that clog the river, the Class IV rapids are the most notorious on the Rogue River and in the state. The most obvious rock is called the "Volkswagen Rock." Seven people lost their lives at Blossom Bar

Rogue River Trail—Marial to Paradise Bar Lodge

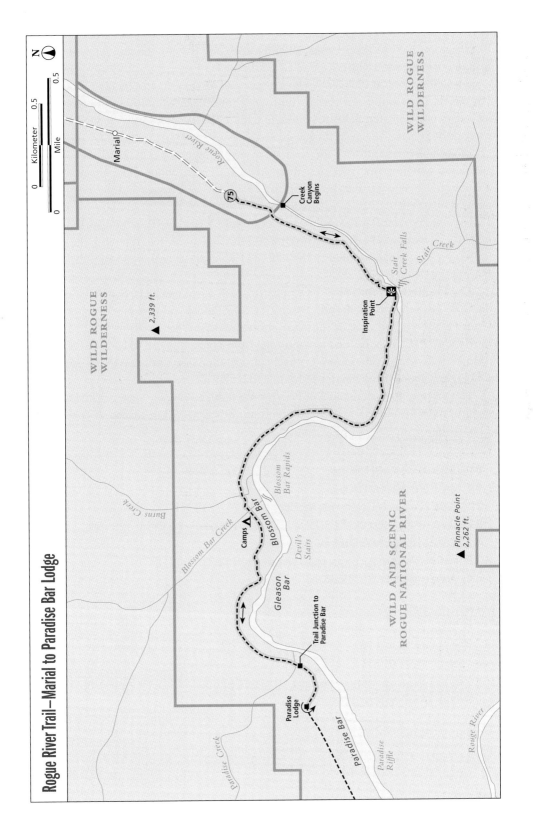

Rapids from 2007 to 2013—even while wearing life jackets—because of a sinister feature boaters must navigate around called the Picket Fence.

For a closer look at the rapids, follow a spur trail on the left after crossing Blossom Bar Creek. The section of river was impassable until Glen Wooldridge, the Rogue's legendary guide, blasted a channel through in the 1920s. Wooldridge is credited as the first person to run the Lower Rogue.

Blossom Bar is a favorite spectator spot, so find a good perch above the rapids and enjoy watching the rafters test their skill. Every rock, chute, and formation has a name, and bystanders will be happy to explain the best routes and the technical prowess involved.

Beyond Blossom Bar the trail continues to mile 3.1, where Paradise Creek drops in. There's a wonderful swimming hole just off the trail on the left. You reach the spur to Paradise Bar Lodge at mile 3.3. You'll have to walk a little farther to reach Paradise Bar itself.

The bar inside the lodge has the wonderful smell of old rustic places with wooden interiors. Its walls are filled with pictures of river guides and past presidents of the United States. (In this area, the former is more important than the latter.)

Paradise Bar Lodge has that romantic appeal of a place you can only reach by foot or by float. If you call ahead (see "Special considerations") it's possible to have lunch ready when you arrive. Otherwise, snacks and lemonade are available.

The price to spend the night at Paradise Bar Lodge is high—$160 per hiker, per night, as of this printing—and reservations must be made well in advance.

Miles and Directions

0.0 Begin at the Marial Trailhead.

0.7 Arrive at Inspiration Point.

2.1 Arrive at a view of Blossom Bar Rapids.

2.2 Reach Blossom Bar Creek and the spur to a view of Blossom Bar Rapids on the left.

3.1 Come to the Paradise Creek swimming hole.

3.3 Arrive at Paradise Bar Lodge; return the way you came.

6.6 Arrive back at the Marial Trailhead.

76 Bear Camp Prairie

A short, mostly easy and pleasant hike through coastal forest and a large prairie, beginning at the summit of Bear Camp Road.

Distance: 1.4-mile out and back
Difficulty: Easy
Elevation gain: 295 feet
Best season: May–Nov
Maps: USGS Brandy Peak; Rogue River–Siskiyou National Forest
Trail contacts: Wild Rivers Ranger District: (541) 471-6500
Parking and trailhead facilities: There's parking for 6 cars across the highway from the trailhead. The Bear Camp picnic site and vista point, with vault toilets, is 0.5 mile down the road. Be careful, though; the picnic site is sometimes overrun with immense blackflies.
Special considerations: There is no water on the trail. There are several endangered wildflower species in the prairie; do not pick or touch them. Bear Camp Road is heavily used by river outfitters as a shuttle route. Watch out for them. The usual opening date for Bear Camp Road is May 31.

Finding the trailhead: Take I-5 to Merlin (exit 61) and follow Merlin-Galice Road through Merlin, past Hellgate Canyon, over Hellgate Bridge, and past Taylor Creek/Briggs Valley Road to Galice Creek Road, just before the Galice store. The sign at the turnoff sign says To Coast. The road eventually becomes FR 23. Park at mile 20, where the road crests and Burnt Ridge Road (FR 2308) takes off to the left.
Trailhead GPS: N42 37.587' / W123 50.144'

The Hike

Bear Camp summit is a popular and highly scenic spot on the 37-mile Bear Camp Road from Galice to Agness. It's even nicer since they built the trail. The short hike up to the prairie and back is a well spent 45 minutes.

From the trailhead the path crosses a little flat, then winds rather sharply uphill for some distance. The forest is typical middle to high elevation, with Douglas-fir, noble fir (or possibly Shasta red fir), grand fir, and a few western hemlocks.

What makes this forest stand out is the Pacific silver fir. The species is fairly common in middle-elevation forests from the Umpqua River drainage northward but is extremely rare to nonexistent in the Rogue River drainage and southward. (It's not the only off-site relic species in the area, either.)

Pacific silver fir can be identified by its needles, which cover only the upper half of the twigs. Even more revealing is that some of the needles on the twig's upper midline point straight forward rather than straight out. That is unique to the species.

After maybe 0.4 mile, the path emerges from the woods onto Bear Camp Prairie. A "prairie," in local parlance, describes a dry, upland meadow, usually at or near a ridgetop and surrounded by woods. There are lots of them in the area, and they are almost all extremely pretty (soils are usually very thin).

Sadler oak is a small shrub that always grows near rhododedron. The species is found only in the Klamath-Siskiyou Mountains at upper-middle elevations, including Bear Camp Summit.
LYNN BERNSTEIN

Bear Camp Prairie is home to a couple of endangered wildflower species. The forest service used to mark them with flagging but eventually concluded that the practice did more harm than good.

From the prairie you can see the peaks around Shasta Costa Creek to the north and Indigo Creek to the south. To the west, not far away, rises the black, rocky pyramid of Brandy Peak, at 5,298 feet the highest point in Curry County (where Brookings and Gold Beach are located).

A good turnaround spot is the far end of the prairie. Beyond that point, the trail heads back into the woods for another 0.5 mile, coming out at Burnt Ridge Road, 1.0 mile from the trailhead, near Spur 016. The trail supposedly continues on the other side of Spur 016.

Miles and Directions

- **0.0** Begin at the Bear Camp Trailhead.
- **0.4** Arrive at Bear Camp Pasture.
- **0.7** Reach the far end of the prairie; retrace your steps.
- **1.4** Arrive back at the trailhead

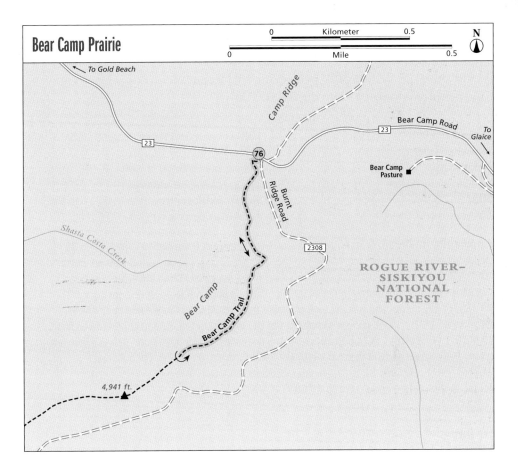

Bear Camp Prairie

To Gold Beach

Camp Ridge

Bear Camp Road

23

23

To Glaice

76

Bear Camp Pasture

Burnt Ridge Road

Shasta Costa Creek

2308

ROGUE RIVER–
SISKIYOU
NATIONAL
FOREST

Bear Camp

Bear Camp Trail

4,941 ft.

Options

The Bear Camp Trail supposedly continues for another 11 miles, past Brandy Peak to Squirrel Peak. It does not climb Brandy Peak. A large portion of this trail is on or very near Burnt Ridge Road.

Brandy Peak is a steep but relatively easy bushwhack up a gravelly ridgeline. There is no trail, but the route is obvious and fairly direct from Burnt Ridge Road. The summit is predictably spectacular, particularly when the canyons below are filled with fog.

Spur 016 merits a few minutes of your time. Drive down the steep incline to where the road levels off and makes a "U" around a small meadow. This is one of the area's few glacial cirques. In the middle of the meadow is a small cluster of somewhat dwarfed Alaska yellow cedar. The tree is common at middle to upper elevations from the central Oregon Cascades northward. In Southern Oregon, it is limited to a half dozen remote spots exactly like this one.

77 Mount Bolivar

A short, steep hike to the highest point in the Wild Rogue Wilderness, with a stupendous view down Mule Creek to the Rogue Canyon.

Distance: 2.8-mile out and back
Difficulty: Moderate
Elevation gain: 1,167 feet
Best season: May–Nov
Maps: USGS Mount Bolivar; Rogue River–Siskiyou National Forest

Trail contacts: Gold Beach Ranger District: (541) 247-3600
Parking and trailhead facilities: There is parking for 6 cars at the trailhead.
Special considerations: There is no water, and the trail can become very hot.

Finding the trailhead: From I-5 north of Grants Pass, take exit 61 to Merlin. Continue straight on Merlin-Galice Road 3.2 miles into Merlin and then another 8.5 miles toward Galice, a small Rogue River outpost. From Galice continue another 6 miles to the bridge and Grave Creek boat landing.

Turn left just over the bridge and head up the mountain on gravel Road 34-8-1 for 15 miles. The road is very narrow and winding for the 3 miles between Whiskey Creek Road and Sawmill Gap. At mile 15.1 the road merges with the upper end of Whiskey Creek Road and becomes Road 32-7-19.3. At mile 15.6 pick up Road 32-8-31, a one-lane blacktop road from Glendale. Turn left, toward Powers, and go 13.8 miles to the Mount Bolivar turnout, on the left. The trailhead is just off the road. Eventually Road 32-8-31 becomes FR 3348.
Trailhead GPS: N42 47.384' / W123 49.600'

The Hike

The hike to the top of this highest point in the Wild Rogue Wilderness isn't particularly long, but driving to the trailhead takes forever. The trail offers perhaps the best single view of the deepest part of the Rogue River canyon. If you have the time, throw in the nearby Hanging Rock Trail.

From the Mount Bolivar Trailhead, the path is quite steep with lots of switchbacks. But it's short, so just take your time. It begins in a forest of Douglas- and white firs, with lots of rhododendron decorating the understory. The open, rocky areas are overgrown mostly with manzanita and scrub chinquapin.

The summit looks down Mule Creek to Marial and the Rogue River. Directly opposite, across the canyon, Bobs Garden Mountain can be seen with far more clarity than it can from Bear Camp Road, which runs right past it. Look for the rugged Saddle Peaks radiating southwest from Bolivar.

The foundation of an old fire lookout adorns the Bolivar summit. There is also a small monument with a bronze plaque. The plaque was presented to the people of Oregon from the people of Venezuela in 1984 to recognize that the peak was named for Simon Bolivar, the legendary South American general responsible for the

Mount Bolivar

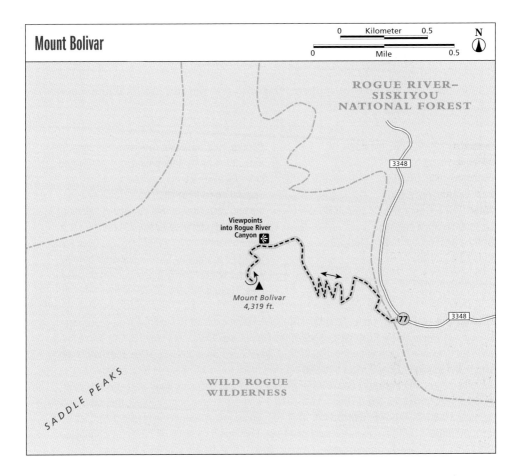

independence of many countries, including Venezuela. It's an interesting tribute to self-determination in the middle of a vast and beautiful wilderness.

Note: The mountain was actually named for a pioneer named Simon Bolivar Cathcart, but why quibble?

Miles and Directions

0.0 Begin at the Mount Bolivar Trailhead.

1.4 Reach the summit of Mount Bolivar; return the way you came.

2.8 Arrive back at the trailhead.

78 Hanging Rock Trail

A short hike to a magnificent and terrifying rock outcrop and overlook in the peaks above the Wild Rogue Wilderness.

Distance: 1.8-mile out and back
Difficulty: Easy
Elevation gain: 160 feet
Best season: Apr–Dec
Maps: USGS Mount Bolivar; Rogue River–Siskiyou National Forest
Trail contacts: Gold Beach Ranger District: (541) 247-3600

Parking and trailhead facilities: Six cars can park at the pretty little trailhead, in a forested grove by a creek.
Special considerations: There is no water, and the end of the trail is very dangerous (overhanging drop-off with a steep slope leading up to it and no handholds or guardrails). The Buck Point Trailhead to Hanging Rock is a shorter drive by 4 miles, but the trail is longer and much steeper (see "Options").

Finding the trailhead: From I-5 north of Grants Pass, take exit 61 to Merlin and proceed west 23 miles on Merlin-Galice Road past Galice to the Grave Creek bridge and boat landing. Turn left just over the bridge and head up the mountain on gravel Road 34-8-1 for 15 miles. The road is very narrow and winding for the 3 miles between Whiskey Creek Road and Sawmill Gap. At mile 15.1 the road merges with the upper end of Whisky Creek Road and becomes Road 32-7-19.3. At mile 15.6 turn left, toward Powers, on Road 32-8-31, a one-lane blacktop from Glendale that eventually becomes FR 3348. At Barker Creek, 24.4 miles from where you picked up the blacktop, turn left onto FR 5520 where a sign says, Panther Ridge Trail—1 mile. Continue 5 miles up FR 5520 (which makes a very hard right at mile 1.5), then 1 mile (right) up Spur 140 to the Hanging Rock Trailhead. **Trailhead GPS:** N42 44.623' / W123 56.389'

The Hike

A segment of the 12.5-mile Panther Ridge Trail (#1253), this short, fairly easy route leads to one of Southern Oregon's least-visited and most impressive landmarks. Hanging Rock is the source of Blossom Bar Creek, a principal destination among Lower Rogue rafters.

The 75-mile drive to the trailhead from Grants Pass takes forever. Much of it is unpaved, one-lane, winding—and exceptionally scenic. It takes three hours to reach the closer of the two trailheads that access Hanging Rock.

The two trailheads are the Hanging Rock Trailhead, described here, and the Buck Point Trailhead, described under "Options." Both routes are gorgeous, and neither is very far off the main road. They wind through verdant old-growth stands of Douglas-fir and western hemlock. The understory's main component is rhododendron, along with salal, Sadler oak, and chinquapin. In May and June the route is resplendent with wildflowers.

From the Hanging Rock Trailhead, the path winds through the woods, meeting the Panther Ridge Trail after 0.3 mile. It then traverses through more woods and crosses a meadow, a beautiful flat-rock surface, and a creek before reentering the forest and climbing slightly.

After 0.6 mile you arrive at the Hanging Rock Trail, on the right. If you continue straight, you will end up at the Buck Point Trailhead after 1.5 miles.

The Hanging Rock Trail dead-ends at Hanging Rock after 0.3 mile. Hanging Rock is a large smooth rock outcrop with an overhanging, 200-foot plunge. Mount Bolivar and the craggy Saddle Peaks are easily visible to the northeast; Bear Camp Summit and Bobs Garden Mountain rise to the southeast, across the canyon. A small stretch of the Rogue can be seen, probably in the vicinity of Winkle Bar. Mule Mountain blocks the view of Marial and Blossom Bar.

Reaching the top of Hanging Rock, 100 feet away from and 30 feet higher than the trail's end, requires crossing a 3-foot-wide wasp-waist rock outcrop with sheer drop-offs on either side, then scaling a steep, slick-sided dome. The short

Hanging Rock is one of the prettiest and least visited spots in spots in Southern Oregon. This is not a safe place for children or dogs because of the many high cliffs. LYNN BERNSTEIN

scramble to the actual top of Hanging Rock is not for the faint of heart and definitely not recommended. The worst case outcome of a slight misstep is too terrible to contemplate.

The rim near the trail's end, adjacent to the rock, is also an overhanging, 200-foot cliff. It is safer than the summit because the edge is squared rather than dome shaped.

Hanging Rock lives up to its billing as a local scenic wonder. Be exceedingly careful, however. Safety ropes might not be a bad idea if you tackle the summit or if you have small children along. Better yet, leave small children at home.

Miles and Directions

0.0 Begin at the Hanging Rock Trailhead.

0.3 Arrive at the Panther Ridge Trail junction; go left.

0.6 Come to the Hanging Rock Trail junction; go right.

0.9 Reach Hanging Rock; return the way you came.

1.8 Arrive back at the trailhead

Options

Buck Point Trail: Via the Buck Point Trailhead, the trek to Hanging Rock is 1.5 miles long with an elevation rise of 1,200 feet. That is quite steep. As it turns out, Buck Point itself is nothing more than a high spot on a densely wooded trail. The route boasts no glorious mountaintops or panoramas. So unless your agenda includes a stiff workout,

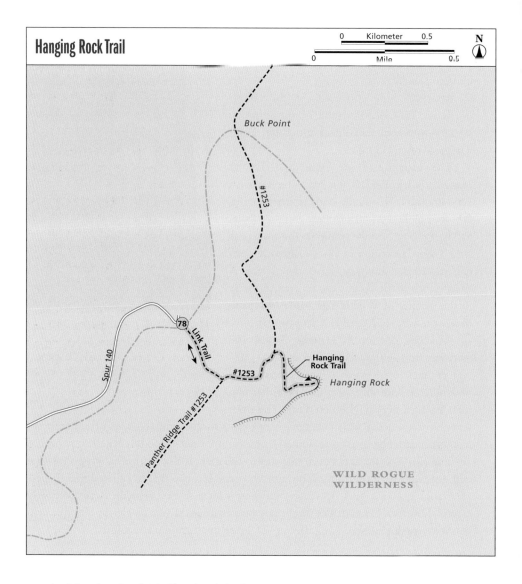

use the Hanging Rock Trailhead. While the drive to the latter is 4.5 miles longer, the path from the Hanging Rock Trailhead is shorter and rises only 160 feet.

To reach the Buck Point Trailhead, go 1.5 miles up FR 5520. Where the road swings sharply right and crosses the creek, bear left on Spur 230 for 0.3 mile to the trailhead. Take the Panther Ridge Trail right, not left. The Hanging Rock Trail intersects on the left after 1.3 miles.

Panther Ridge Trail: The 12.5-mile Panther Ridge Trail begins at Bald Knob, 7.0 miles west of Hanging Rock, and follows the ridge above the Rogue River canyon, at the north edge of the wilderness. The 2.3-mile segment around Hanging Rock is the best part. East of the Buck Point Trailhead, the Panther Ridge Trail winds through the woods for 4.0 miles but doesn't really go anywhere.

79 Illinois River–East

A fairly easy path though one of America's most beautiful Wild and Scenic River canyons. Much botanical interest.

Distance: 12-mile out and back
Difficulty: Easy to York Creek; moderately strenuous to Pine Flat
Best season: Year-round
Elevation gain: 1,353 feet
Maps: USGS Agness, Horse Sign Butte, and York Butte; Rogue River–Siskiyou National Forest
Trail contacts: Wild Rivers Ranger District, Cave Junction: (541) 592-4000

Parking and trailhead facilities: There are picnic tables, a pit toilet, and parking for 10 cars at the trailhead.
Special considerations: Both the eastern and western (this one) trailheads for the Illinois River Trail are at places called Oak Flat. This trailhead is sometimes referred to as Briggs Creek Trailhead as well (which makes more sense, since it crosses Briggs Creek).

Finding the trailhead: From Grants Pass follow US 199 south for 20 miles to the town of Selma. At a blinking yellow light, turn right onto Illinois River Road. Follow the winding road for 11 miles of pavement and another 8 miles of very rough, bumpy road to its end at the Briggs Creek picnic site. The last few miles are very rough on passenger cars and can become muddy in winter and spring.
Trailhead GPS: N42 22.681'/W123 48.262'

The Hike

Among its many attractions, the Illinois River Trail is the shortest path from which to view the rare kalmiopsis plant, for which the Kalmiopsis Wilderness Area is named. The tiny, pink/purple azalea-like flowers bloom from May through August. Add in one of the country's great river canyons, remote and mysterious coastal mountains, and other botanical rarities and you have one of the Pacific Northwest's great hikes.

The path begins by crossing Briggs Creek via footbridge and heading out into an open meadow. This area was torched by the 2002 Biscuit Fire, and the blackened trees and open spaces throughout this hike are a stark reminder. Still, more than ten years on, grass and wildflowers are starting to reclaim the land with a colorful carpet of green below the burned trees. The fire also damaged the bridge, but it is safe to walk on.

At mile 1.2 the trail slips into the most stunning section of the route. The next 1.5 miles feature sheer cliffs and rockfalls overlooking the rapids of the Illinois. On the other side of the river rise the orange, weathered serpentinite slopes of Nome Peak and Granite Butte, with side canyons and waterfalls crashing down into the water.

At mile 2.4 the trail crosses the steep, rocky West Fork of York Creek (0.5 mile past the larger but less interesting East Fork). Stop here to enjoy some of the most interesting biology in the world.

The Illinois River flows hundreds of feet below the Illinois River Trail, on the east side outside Selma. ZACH URNESS

The first stop on the amazing plant tour comes when you first see the West Fork of York Creek in the distance on the trail. At that spot begins a 60-foot circle of kalmiopsis plants. Looking like a dwarf rhododendron or azalea, and very much like a species called kalmia, all four plants are members of the Heath family. The species forms a prostrate mat only a few inches high with purple, bell-shaped flowers. In the entire world, there are perhaps fifteen such mats, almost all within the Kalmiopsis Wilderness.

The plant cluster was apparently damaged in the 2002 Biscuit Fire and was not looking too good in 2010. But it appears to be recovering.

Once you reach West York Creek, follow a faint trail upstream (right) about 20 feet to a large grove of carnivorous cobra lilies, or *Darlingtonia;* also called pitcher plants. These carnivorous plants trap unsuspecting flies and spiders with nectar and then force them downward with a combination of slippery wax and pointed hairs. Eventually the victims are entombed and digested.

Below the trail, along the creek, look for some unusual lady's slipper orchids. Normally lady's slippers are extremely rare and elusive. They seldom grow over a few inches high and rarely produce more than a half dozen of their exquisite white

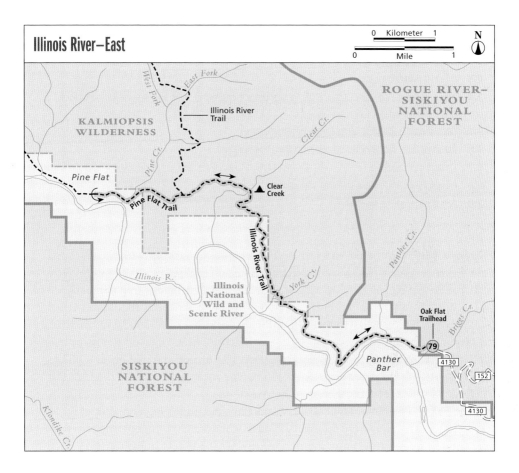

flowers. Something in the Biscuit Fire was extremely beneficial to these plants, and many of them are now 2 to 3 feet high with seventy to one hundred flowers per plant.

York Creek makes a good turnaround spot for a 4.8-mile hike. Not a bad day, but you'd be missing out on a beautiful spot yet to come.

Beyond York Creek the trail moves inland. For the next 2.0 miles, views of the river are infrequent as the path winds through forests of pine and Douglas-fir interspersed with low-elevation black oak and madrone.

Finally the route forks at the top of a hill. To the right lies the trail to Bald Mountain and the other Oak Flat, near Agness. To the left is the steep, 0.5-mile side trail that descends to Pine Flat. Go left.

Pine Flat is perfectly named. It is quiet and out of the way, with good water, excellent campsites, steelhead fishing opportunities, and an outstanding river view.

After hiking downhill, you cross Pine Creek at mile 5.7 (which can be tricky at high water), pass through a marshy area, and head into wide-open Pine Flat. There are numerous camping spots, with the best at the far end below trees and next to the clear green pools of the Illinois River.

Miles and Directions

0.0 Begin at the Briggs Creek/Oak Flat Trailhead, crossing a footbridge over Briggs Creek.

0.5 Cross Panther Creek.

2.4 Arrive at West Fork York Creek. (This is a popular turnaround spot and a good place to look for rare plants.)

4.1 Pass Clear Creek and Clear Creek primitive camp.

4.9 Arrive at Pine Flat junction; go left on the Pine Flat Trail.

5.7 Cross Pine Creek.

6.0 Reach Pine Flat; return the way you came.

12.0 Arrive back at the trailhead.

Options

Florence Way: On the far end of Pine Flat, you'll join back up with the river and cross Florence Creek. Just over the creek is a sign and trailhead for the Florence Way Trail (#1219A). This incredibly rugged, difficult, and treacherous trail climbs 2,300 feet in just 1.5 miles through burnt forest. Eventually it intersects the Illinois River Trail near the top of Bald Mountain. **Trailhead GPS:** N42 24.173'/W123 52.812'

Hiking through: Back at the Pine Flat junction, head right on the main trail (N42 23.953'/W123 51.108'). Beyond the Pine Flat turnoff the trail heads uphill to Bald Mountain in 2.1 miles and then continues for another 17 miles to the Oak Flat Trailhead near the town of Agness on the coastal side.

The trail is difficult and wild. Bald Mountain is the route's highest point at 3,811 feet and swings far away from the river. If you're wondering why the trail goes to such great lengths to avoid the river, the Illinois here lies 2,500 feet straight down in one of the most treacherous whitewater canyons anywhere. In the winter of 1997–98, the canyon made national news when several rafters drowned in the river's Green Wall Rapids during the worst storm since 1964.

The famed insect-eating pitcher plants, or cobra lilies, grow near York Creek on the Illinois River Trail. Zach Urness

80 Little Falls Loop

A short but scenic loop down to a cute little waterfall and beach on the Illinois River.

Distance: 0.8-mile lollipop
Difficulty: Easy to moderate
Elevation loss/gain: 142 feet
Best season: Year-round
Maps: USGS Eight Dollar Mountain; Rogue River-Siskiyou National Forest

Trail contacts: Wild Rivers Ranger District, Cave Junction: (541) 592-4000
Parking and trailhead facilities: The trailhead area contains parking for 20 cars, a vault toilet, and a small campground.
Special considerations: There is no water. The trail is fairly hot in midsummer.

Finding the trailhead: Head south on US 199 from Grants Pass for 20 miles to the town of Selma. Past Selma, go 3.4 more miles to Eight Dollar Road (FR 4201). Turn right and go about 3 miles, past the Boardwalk Nature Trail (which you will want to see), to the Little Falls Trailhead area. **Trailhead GPS:** N42 14.431'/W123 40.584'

The Hike

There's something about the Illinois River area that is inherently unique. The area even seems to have its own color scheme (a kind of sparse yellowish-green foliage with red-brown tree trunks, jumbled gray rocks, brilliant emerald green water in the river, and lots of sunlight). Throw in orange mountains and several strange plant species adapted to serpentine soil and things start to get amazing pretty fast.

Rapids on the Illinois River above Little Falls, from the Little Falls Loop LYNN BERNSTEIN

Illinois River below some rapids and just above Little Falls, from the Little Falls Loop
LYNN BERNSTEIN

The Little Falls Trail offers an excellent opportunity to observe these features close-up. Be aware that Eight Dollar Mountain, the nondescript forested dome that rises up from the other side of FR 4201, is considered one of the most botanically diverse locations in Oregon and a treasure trove of rare and endangered species.

The forest alongside the loop trail is scraggly and open due to the underlying serpentine soils. Most of the trees are Jeffrey pine (which look similar to ponderosa pines except the bark smells like pineapple and the prickers on the cone scales are curved under), incense cedar, western white pine, and a few stunted and unhappy looking Douglas-firs.

From the campground trailhead, walk down the trail for 500 feet, past the far end of the loop on the left. You shortly come to a side trail leading to a small *Darlingtonia* bog. *Darlingtonia* (cobra lily, or California pitcher plant) is a carnivorous species that traps and digests insects. Associated species usually include coffeeberry, azalea, and tiger lily. If the area were slightly less marshy, you might also find the extremely rare and beautiful Waldo gentian and a tiny, rosette-shaped plant with sticky leaves called butterwort, which also traps and absorbs insects.

Back on the main trail, the route levels off upon reaching the river and the falls appear soon after, at mile 0.5. The falls aren't very high, 5 feet maybe, but they are very pretty. The rocky canyon is spectacular, and the water is beyond clear. Shortly after the falls, the path arrives at a large sandy beach (that apparently receives a fair amount of use).

Little Falls Loop

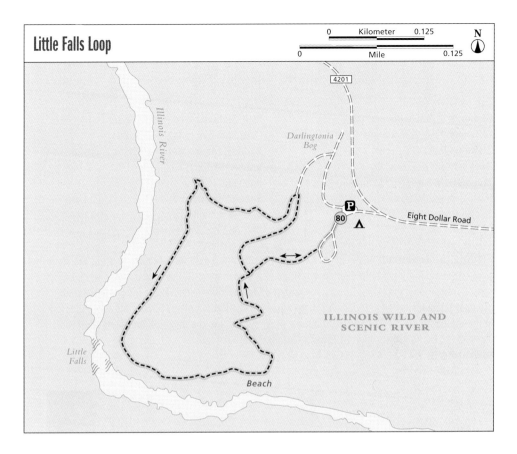

After that, the path shoots a straight uphill for 0.2 mile, levels off, and hits the end of the loop (go right). Continue 500 feet back to the trailhead.

Miles and Directions

0.0 Begin at the Little Falls Trailhead. The loop starts in 500 feet; go straight (counterclockwise) at the loop junction.

0.5 Pass Little Falls.

0.6 Pass a beach.

0.8 Arrive at the top of the loop; turn right and continue 500 feet to the trailhead.

Options

Boardwalk Nature Trail: This must-see is located 1.0 mile up Eight Dollar Road from the US 199 turnoff. Walk up the uphill side road across the highway for several hundred feet to the beginning of the boardwalk. The boardwalk isn't very long, but it traverses a very large *Darlingtonia* bog. Back at the parking area, a 1.0-mile loop trail leads to a vista point above the Illinois River. The boardwalk is on BLM land; Little Falls is on USDA Forest Service land.

81 Babyfoot Lake

One of the few glacial-cirque lakes in the Kalmiopsis Wilderness. A popular local hike.

Distance: 2.4-mile out and back
Difficulty: Easy to moderate
Elevation loss: 460 feet
Best season: May–Nov
Maps: USGS Josephine Mountain; Rogue River–Siskiyou National Forest; Gold Beach Ranger District

Trail contacts: Wild Rivers Ranger District, Cave Junction: (541) 592-4000
Parking and trailhead facilities: There is a vault toilet and parking for 15 cars at the trailhead.
Special considerations: The Babyfoot Lake basin was badly damaged by the 2002 Biscuit Fire, and the entire area is burned out.

Finding the trailhead: From Grants Pass drive south on US 199 for 24 miles, passing the small town of Selma. Turn right onto Eight Dollar Road at a sign marked KALMIOPSIS WILDERNESS AREA—17 MILES. Continue on Eight Dollar Road 3 miles to a bridge over the Illinois River, then veer right as the road becomes gravel and drive 12 more miles uphill. At about mile 15, veer left at a major fork in the road onto Spur 140 to arrive at a large parking area and the trailhead on the right. (If you veer right at the fork onto Spur 142, you'll end up at the Kalmiopsis Rim Trailhead.)
Trailhead GPS: N42 13.475' / W123 47.570'

Babyfoot Lake is a pretty little lake in the Kalmiopsis Wilderness that was burned out during the 2002 Biscuit Fire. ZACH URNESS

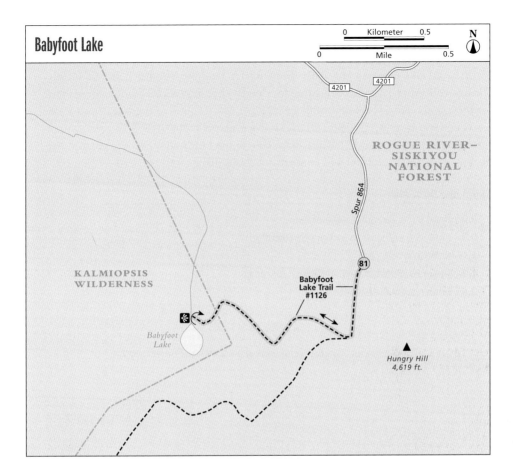

The Hike

Few areas were more impacted than Babyfoot Lake by the 2002 Biscuit Fire that torched almost 500,000 acres in the Siskiyou Mountains. It completely changed the landscape, and the recovery process is fascinating to observe. You can now see the huge rock head-wall and the glacial cirque basin containing Babyfoot Lake from the trailhead (you can't see the lake, though).

The Forest Service Botanical Area surrounding Babyfoot Lake was created decades ago primarily to preserve the rare and elegant Brewer spruce (the trees with the long, angling, whiplike branches) growing near the lake. Botanists later discovered that the species wasn't nearly as rare as they originally thought. There are other threatened species there as well, however.

The Babyfoot Lake Trail, an extremely popular local hike, was almost totally burned out in 2002. For years this made for difficult hiking because of ravel and fall-down from dead trees. Today the trail is open due to the hard work of groups such as the Siskiyou Mountain Club in Ashland and local volunteers.

From the trailhead the hike heads downhill through a forested setting to a junction at mile 0.3. Stay right for Babyfoot Lake.

Beyond the junction the path drops into a densely wooded basin of mostly Douglas-fir. After 1.1 miles you come to a lovely vista spot with a commanding view of the Chetco River basin. From there it's just a few minutes to the lake.

The lake, at mile 1.2, sits in a little wooded glacial cirque, maybe 3 acres, with a cliff headwall on one side. The area at the base of the headwall is flat. The green water is stocked with brook trout and contains much deadfall.

Miles and Directions

0.0   Begin at the Babyfoot Lake Trailhead.

0.3   Arrive at a trail junction and go right (downhill).

1.1   Come to a vista point.

1.2   Reach Babyfoot Lake; return the way you came.

2.4   Arrive back at the trailhead.

82 Magic Canyon

A route into the remote upper canyon of the Wild and Scenic Chetco River's emerald waters. A challenging and adventurous trip to a wilderness gem.

Distance: 20.6-mile out and back
Difficulty: Strenuous
Elevation loss/gain: 2,975 feet
Best season: May–Nov
Maps: USGS Josephine Mountain; Rogue River–Siskiyou National Forest; Gold Beach Ranger District
Trail contacts: Wild Rivers Ranger District, Cave Junction: (541) 592-4000; Siskiyou Mountain Club: siskiyoumountainclub.org

Parking and trailhead facilities: There is a vault toilet and parking for 15 cars at the trailhead.
Special considerations: This collection of trails is part of the proposed Trans-Kalmiopsis Route through the heart of the wilderness. Although the damage from the 2002 Biscuit Fire causes dead trees to fall across the trail each year, the Siskiyou Mountain Club has committed to yearly trail maintenance to keep the route open. There is very little shade or water until you reach Carter Creek.

Finding the trailhead: From Grants Pass drive south on US 199 for 24 miles, passing the small town of Selma. Turn right onto Eight Dollar Road at a sign marked KALMIOPSIS WILDERNESS AREA—17 MILES. Continue on Eight Dollar Road 3 miles, and cross the bridge over the Illinois River, then veer right as the road becomes gravel and drive 12 more miles uphill. At about mile 15, veer left at a major fork in the road onto Spur 140 to arrive at a large parking area and the Babyfoot Lake Trailhead on the right. (If you veer right at the fork onto Spur 142, you'll end up at the Kalmiopsis Rim Trailhead.)
Trailhead GPS: N42 13.475'/W123 47.570'

The Hike

This long and strenuous route that drops almost 3,000 feet to the upper gorge of the Chetco River—known as Magic Canyon—is one of Southern Oregon's great adventures.

It's a place where locals travel to find solitude, swim, and fish among emerald green pools and silver-orange walls. Hearty kayakers sometimes carry boats down this route to begin one of the West Coast's wildest river trips.

The hike is difficult, traversing a virtual desert of serpentinite rock and rare flowers. It should not be undertaken lightly. A good map, compass, or handheld GPS device is essential on this combination of trails through an area torched by the 2002 Biscuit Fire. Dead trees that have fallen across the trail are sometimes an issue.

Luckily the route is part of the Siskiyou Mountain Club's proposed Tran-Kalmiopsis Route, which eventually will traverse the entire wilderness. The Ashland nonprofit group has committed to the challenging task of keeping the trail open and doing maintenance each year. Consider making a donation (siskiyoumountainclub.org).

The upper Chetco River begins to appear along the Bailey Cabin / Bailey Mountain Trail.
JUSTIN ROHDE

Start at the Babyfoot Lake Trailhead and follow the trail 0.3 mile. At the first junction, go left, veering uphill (the trail downhill on the right goes to Babyfoot Lake). After following the rim above Babyfoot Lake—with views that extend across the wilderness—you'll reach an old road called the Kalmiopsis Rim Trail at mile 1.7. Follow it left, heading southwest.

The old road continues past mile 3.2, where the trail officially becomes the Emily Cabin Trail (#1129); stay right, all the way to an open saddle and junction at mile 4.9. This is an important junction.

Turn off the old road and onto Bailey Cabin Trail on the right going west (this is also an old road but is narrower). Avoid the privately owned Emily Cabin Trail, which veers left (south), steeply downhill.

The trail continues dropping, passing the old Bailey Cabin site at mile 6.9. Nothing of note remains except a spring, which on a hot day might seem heaven-sent. Beyond this point, the trail shoots downhill with a vengeance, dropping almost 2,000 feet in 2 miles (not much fun for the hike back up) as the Chetco River begins to emerge below.

Bailey Cabin / Mountain Trail arrives at Carter Creek at mile 8.9 at a nice, small campsite. The trail continues along the shimmering, emerald Chetco River, above the gorgeous walls of Magic Canyon, a total of 10.3 miles to Blake's Bar.

Magic Canyon

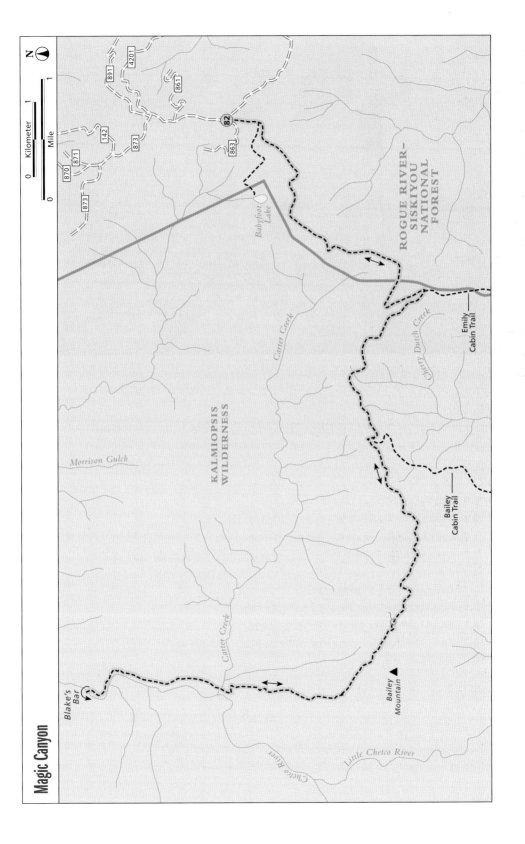

The rare wildflower, Kalmiopsis leacheana, *found only in a few places in the world, can be found along the route to the upper Checto River in the Kalmiopsis Wilderness.* JUSTIN ROHDE

The featured trail stops at Blake's Bar, a beautiful spot with a campsite, swimming hole, and nice places to explore this gorgeous patch of the upper Chetco.

Miles and Directions

0.0   Begin at the Babyfoot Lake Trailhead.

0.3   Arrive at the Babyfoot Lake junction. Go left (uphill).

1.7   Intersect the Kalmiopsis Rim Trail, an old road; go left.

3.2   Come to the Emily Cabin Trail; continue following the old road to the right.

4.9   Arrive at an open saddle and the Emily Cabin / Bailey Cabin junction. Turn right onto the Bailey Cabin Trail, heading west.

6.9   Pass the Bailey Cabin site and a spring for water.

8.9   Reach Carter Creek camp and cross the creek.

10.3   Arrive at Blake's Bar on the edge of Chetco River; return the way you came.

20.6   Arrive back at the trailhead.

Options

Although the trail comes to a river crossing at Blake's Bar, it's possible to ford the river and continue onward along the Chetco River 5 or 6 miles to Taggarts Bar. It's hoped that the proposed Trans-Kalmiopsis Route will run all the way to Vulcan Lake, a total of 28 miles when completed.

83 Eagle Mountain

A beautiful hike along the rugged Siskiyou crest, high above the Illinois River canyon along the edge of the Kalmiopsis Wilderness.

Distance: 5.6-mile out and back
Difficulty: Easy, then strenuous
Elevation gain: 1,700 feet to Eagle Mountain
Best season: May–Nov
Maps: USGS Josephine Mountain and Pearsoll Peak; Rogue River-Siskiyou National Forest
Trail contacts: Wild Rivers Ranger District, Cave Junction: (541) 592-4000

Parking and trailhead facilities: There's a vault toilet and parking for 10 cars in the flat around the trailhead.
Special considerations: This area was badly impacted by the 2002 Biscuit Fire. Downed trees, dead branches, and ravel from burned trees still are an issue at times, but through the hard work of local volunteers, the route remains in reasonably good shape to Eagle Mountain. Beyond Eagle Mountain is another matter.

Finding the trailhead: From Grants Pass drive south on US 199 for 24 miles, passing the small town of Selma. Turn right onto Eight Dollar Road at a sign marked KALMIOPSIS WILDERNESS AREA—17 MILES. Continue 3 miles to a bridge across the Illinois River, then veer right as the road becomes gravel. Continue uphill on Eight Dollar Road for 12 more miles until you come to a fork. Veer right onto Spur 142 for the Kalmiopsis Rim Trailhead, which you can see soon after turning at the fork. (The left fork, Spur 140, leads to the Babyfoot Lake Trailhead.)
Trailhead GPS: N42 14.401' / W123 48.026'

The Hike

This exhilarating pathway follows the heights of the Kalmiopsis region along the divide between the Chetco and Illinois Rivers. While the Eagle Mountain summit is fairly strenuous, it ranks among Josephine County's most beautiful hikes, and many of the highlights lie within 1.0 mile of the trailhead.

From the parking area the trail climbs gently for 0.3 mile through a burned forest of Douglas-fir, white pine, and Brewer spruce, with rhododendron and Sadler oak in the understory. The path then breaks out into an open area of serpentine soil and rock with spectacular vistas. Serpentine is a type of parent rock related to granite but with a very high percentage of ultra-basic minerals.

The sheer brown rock face of Whetstone Butte dominates the scene here. Approaching it, you can see the Chetco headwaters (west), the Illinois River canyon (east), and the towering orange mass of Pearsoll Peak (north). A careful observer might also note Vulcan Peak and the Big Craggies far to the northwest. The often-snowcapped summits of the high Cascades, including Mount McLoughlin and the Crater Lake rim, decorate the eastern horizon.

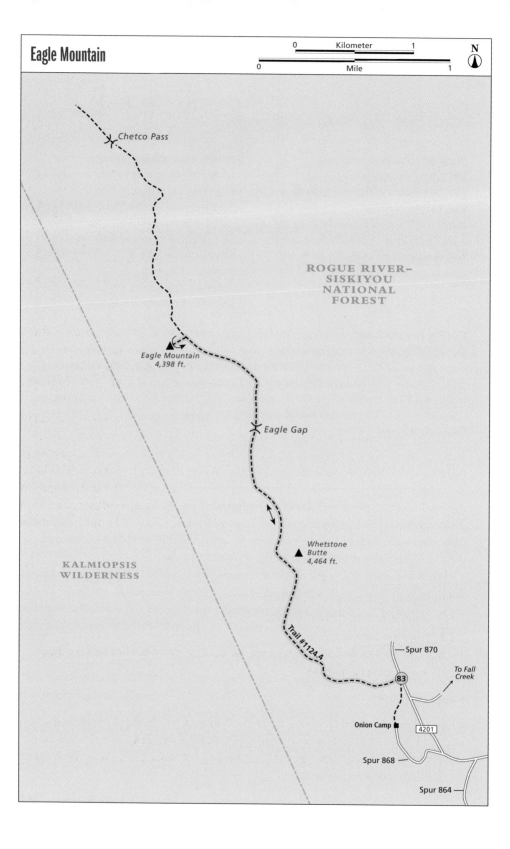

0   Kilometer   1

0   Mile   1

N

Chetco Pass

ROGUE RIVER–
SISKIYOU
NATIONAL
FOREST

Eagle Mountain
4,398 ft.

Eagle Gap

Whetstone
Butte
4,464 ft.

KALMIOPSIS
WILDERNESS

Trail #1124.4

Spur 870

83

To Fall
Creek

Onion Camp

4201

Spur 868

Spur 864

The Kalmiopsis Rim Trail offers wide-open views of the surrounding mountains and Whetstone Butte. ZACH URNESS

Whetstone Butte presents a rewarding 1.1-mile destination. Beyond Whetstone Butte, the trail begins to drop as it reenters the woods and a burned area where fallen debris can make the trail difficult (although locals have been working hard to keep it clear).

Over the next 0.8 mile, to mile 1.9, the trail loses 500 feet before emerging at Eagle Gap.

The segment between Eagle Gap and the top of Eagle Mountain is the hike's most difficult, climbing about 690 feet in 0.8 mile (to mile 2.7). The difficulty is offset by spectacular scenery. After trudging up slopes of rock and loose scree amid stunted, windswept pines, the path emerges at the lip of a cliff that sweeps dramatically down to the Illinois.

Where the trail levels out on the top of the mountain, look for a short spur to the left leading to the actual summit. The summit's stacked-rock marker is easily seen from the trail (although many people are so distracted by the view in the opposite direction that they fail to notice it).

Miles and Directions

0.0 Begin at the Kalmiopsis Rim Trailhead.

1.1 Arrive at the base of Whetstone Butte.

1.9 Cross over Eagle Gap.

2.8 Reach the Eagle Mountain summit, just to the left off the main trail; return the way you came.

5.6 Arrive back at the trailhead.

Options

Chetco Pass: The trail continues another 1.5 miles along an old road to Chetco Pass with an 800-foot drop. This is another area where fire-related fall-down becomes a major problem. While there are excellent views of Pearsoll Peak, the route is pretty much impassable as of this writing.

84 Big Tree Loop

A pleasant hike featuring woods, marble outcrops, an excellent vista of the Illinois Valley, and a big tree. Option to an alpine lake.

Distance: 3.5-mile loop
Difficulty: Moderate
Elevation gain: 1,168 feet
Best season: May–Nov
Maps: USGS Oregon Caves; Oregon Caves National Monument
Trail contacts: Oregon Caves National Monument Visitor Center: (541) 592-2100

Parking and trailhead facilities: Monument facilities include plumbed restrooms, a gift shop, and parking for 200 cars. The restaurant, coffee shop, and lodge are open from mid-June to early September.
Special considerations: There is no water on the trail, but there is plenty of water at the national monument facilities. Parking is free, but there is a charge for cave tours.

Finding the trailhead: From Grants Pass take US 199 south to Cave Junction. At the far end of Cave Junction, proceed up Caves Highway (OR 46) 19 miles to Oregon Caves National Monument. The trailhead is located through the gift shop arch, to the left of the cave entrance.
Trailhead GPS: N42 05.879' / W123 24.397'

The Hike

The loop trail around Oregon Caves National Monument is among the most frequently trodden paths in Southern Oregon. Hikers from all over the country return with glowing enthusiasm. The trail is pleasant enough and greatly enhanced by returning via the monument's short but spectacular Cliff Nature Trail.

The Big Tree Loop Trail begins under the arch between the ticket window and gift shop. The described hike starts in the left-hand (clockwise) direction, following the sign reading BIG TREE—1.3 MILES. You can also take the loop in the other direction. The path is moderately steep as it winds through middle-elevation woods of Douglas-, white-, and grand firs and Port Orford cedar.

Big Tree, at mile 1.3, is an immense Douglas-fir with a broken top and an extremely thick trunk. It's what foresters call a "wolf tree," very poor in form and towering above the other trees. Most trees in the vicinity are its offspring.

At mile 1.8 the trail crosses a wet meadow of wildflowers, Douglas maple, and the showy corn lily. Then it's back into the woods.

At mile 2.0 a side trail leads to Mount Elijah. The Mount Elijah Trail (see "Options") explores several of the Siskiyous' high peaks, none of which are visible from the cave area. It also leads to Bigelow Lakes (see "Options"), a pretty little alpine lake tucked below Mount Elijah.

At mile 3.3 the path merges with the Monument's Cliff Nature Trail. This route adds 0.5 mile to the journey but is highly recommended. (If you go right, you'll be

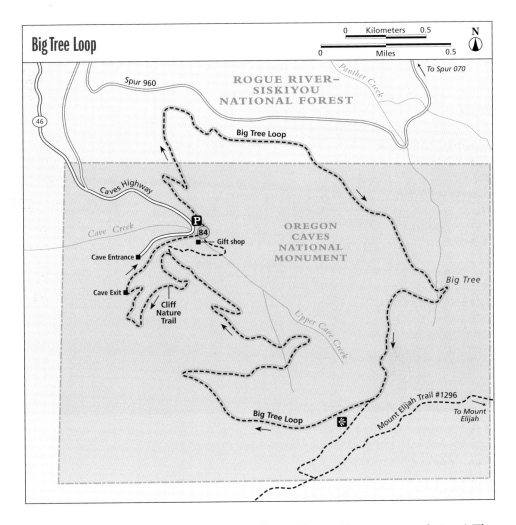

Big Tree Loop

Spur 960

Spur 070

Panther Creek

ROGUE RIVER–
SISKIYOU
NATIONAL FOREST

Big Tree Loop

Caves Highway

Cave Creek

P

84

Gift shop

Cave Entrance

OREGON
CAVES
NATIONAL
MONUMENT

Big Tree

Cave Exit

Cliff
Nature
Trail

Upper Cave Creek

Big Tree Loop

Mount Elijah Trail #1296

To Mount
Elijah

back at the trailhead in 0.2 mile but will miss the marble outcrops and vistas.) The trail left goes over the top of the marble formation in which the cave is located. There's a terrific vista point there, with a view down Sucker Creek into the Illinois Valley. After that, the trail winds down to the base of the marble, passes the cave exit, and returns to the entrance.

Miles and Directions

0.0 Begin at the Big Tree Trailhead; turn left (clockwise).

0.2 Arrive at Old Growth Trail junction.

1.3 Arrive at Big Tree.

1.7 Reach the Mount Elijah/Bigelow Lake junction (see "Options").

3.2 Reach the Cliff Nature Trail junction; go left.

3.5 Arrive back at the trailhead, ending the loop.

A view of Bigelow Lake from the shoreline. Located just off-trail on this optional hike, Bigelow Lake is a hotspot for rare plants near the Oregon Caves National Monument. Zach Urness

Options

Cave Tour: Escorted cave tours are available from the end of March to the beginning of October. Tours take about 45 minutes. Although this isn't Carlsbad, there are lots of flowstone formations, an underground river, and one huge chamber. There are some low ceilings and very steep ladders in the 0.7-mile tour. If you arrive midday during summer, expect a wait of 30 minutes to an hour for cave tours. For the more adventurous, consider the guided off-trail Introduction to Caving Tour (requires advance sign-up).

Bigelow Lake and Mount Elijah: Bigelow Lake is a lovely little pond-lily lake in an exquisite glacial cirque basin beside a large meadow at the foot of Mount Elijah. From the junction on Big Tree Loop, follow signs 2.0 miles to the summit of Mount Elijah, home to fantastic views of the Siskiyous from a rocky summit.

From the summit simply head downhill for 1.5 miles to Bigelow Lake. Go left at the grassy trail junction at the saddle just below the summit and follow the switchbacks down. The lake is somewhat off-trail but hard to miss. (There is also a Lower Bigelow Lake, but it is very difficult to find and has no trail access.)

85 Vulcan Lake

A beautiful alpine lake in the Kalmiopsis Wilderness, at the base of Vulcan Peak. A serpentinite area of geological and botanical interest.

Distance: 2.8-mile out and back
Difficulty: Easy to moderate
Elevation gain: 794 feet
Best season: May–Nov
Maps: USGS Chetco Peak; Rogue River–Siskiyou National Forest
Trail contacts: Gold Beach Ranger District: (541) 247-3600

Parking and trailhead facilities: The trailhead has room for 6 to 8 cars.
Special considerations: The road is extremely bumpy and rough. You can get there with a low-clearance passenger car, but drive slowly to ensure your vehicle doesn't fall apart. The final few miles follow the edge of a steep, exposed road cut with no guardrails.

Finding the trailhead: From Brookings take the North Bank Chetco River Road (which becomes FR 1376) for 15 miles. Just across a bridge over the South Fork Chetco River, turn right onto FR 1909, which takes off up the mountain. Continue 12 increasingly rough miles on FR 1909 to the trailhead (stay right at any questionable junctions). Near the top you'll come to a split in the road with signs pointing to Vulcan Lake (left) and Vulcan Peak (right). Go left, but consider hitting Vulcan Peak on the way out (see "Options").
Trailhead GPS: N42 11.758' / W123 59.555'

The Hike

The drive past the Vulcan Peak Trail out to the Vulcan Lake Trail, and the first part of the hike, were all heavily impacted by the 2002 Biscuit Fire that burned 500,000 acres in and around the Kalmiopsis Wilderness. This won't affect the hike, aside from making the first 1.5 miles a little more open, with more vista opportunities. Watching the forest slowly recover on this already harsh site can be interesting.

The weathered, buff-orange bedrock in which beautiful Vulcan Lake nestles, with Vulcan Peak rising abruptly behind it, contains such a high percentage of serpentine rock that some of the area is a virtual desert. The few trees and shrubs are stunted and bizarre.

Of the many alpine glacial lakes in Southern Oregon and Northern California, this is the only one reached from the coast. The drive up from Brookings, through vast Douglas-fir forests broken by grassy openings called "prairies," affords views of the ocean, the Chetco River valley, and surrounding peaks such as the Big Craggies. Even if you skip the trail, it's a beautiful drive to the trailhead.

The path is only 1.4 miles long. It begins life on an old mining road but after a few hundred feet veers off to the right at a marker. The Vulcan Lake Trail climbs 1.0 mile and rises 503 feet over a rocky ridge from which you can see clear across the Kalmiopsis Wilderness to Pearsoll Peak, highest in the wilderness. There are steep spots, but the walk isn't difficult.

Vulcan Lake sits in a bright orange basin of serpentine rock in the Kalmiopsis Wilderness. Yes, the water really is that color. ZACH URNESS

The trail descends sharply to the lake. Look for serpentine-adapted plants such as Sadler oak, manzanita, Jeffrey pine, western white pine, and azalea. This is a great place for amateur botanists, so bring a plant guide to help identify the many rare shrubs and flowers.

Fishing in Vulcan Lake's brilliant emerald waters can be frustrating; swimming is probably more fun. The lake sits on a rocky orange ledge with a steep drop-off to the east and the orange summit of Vulcan Peak rising immediately to the northwest. One-acre Lisa Lake (unstocked) is 0.2 mile away via trail, down the hill.

Miles and Directions

0.0 Begin at the Vulcan Lake/Johnson Butte Trailhead on an old road.

0.1 Arrive at the Vulcan Lake junction; go right, leaving the old road.

1.0 Cross over a pass into Vulcan Lake's basin.

1.4 Reach Vulcan Lake; return the way you came.

2.8 Arrive back at the trailhead.

Options

Vulcan Peak Trail: The Vulcan Peak Trail (#1120) is a steep, 1.0-mile trek over brush and rock to an old lookout site (elevation 4,655 feet) offering a panorama of the Kalmiopsis and the coast. On the drive to Vulcan Lake, 1.0 mile before the Vulcan Lake Trailhead, follow the pointer off Spur 260 toward Vulcan Peak.

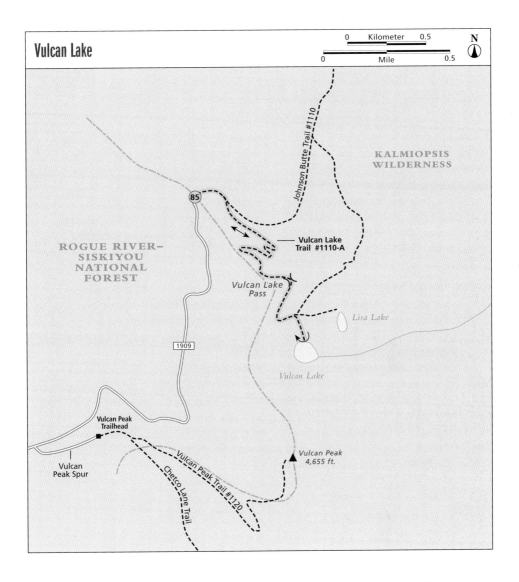

Vulcan Lake

KALMIOPSIS WILDERNESS

Johnson Butte Trail #1110

85

ROGUE RIVER-
SISKIYOU
NATIONAL
FOREST

Vulcan Lake
Trail #1110-A

Vulcan Lake
Pass

Lisa Lake

1909

Vulcan Lake

Vulcan Peak
Trailhead

Vulcan Peak
4,655 ft.

Vulcan
Peak Spur

Vulcan Peak Trail #1120

Chetco Lane Trail

The Chetco Divide Trail (#1210) takes off from the same trailhead as the Vulcan Peak Trail. One and a half miles down the Chetco Divide Trail, side trails (#1105 and #1105-A) lead to the Navy Monument and Cottonwood Camp. The Navy Monument Trail, actually an old cat track, drops 2,200 feet in 2.5 miles. It ends near the South Fork of the Chetco at the wreckage of a World War II Navy transport plane that crashed in 1944. The monument stands nearby.

Johnson Butte Trail: This very long route begins at the Vulcan Lake Trailhead. Go left instead of right at the junction with the Vulcan Lake Trail. The path follows a wide former road for 4.0 miles to Salamander Lake. After about 10 miles it ties in with the Tincup Trail near Mislatnah Peak.

This trail visits the beautiful, steep, and rocky lower Illinois River canyon, near the confluence with the Rogue River. Highlights include two stunning creeks.

Distance: 9.4-mile out and back
Difficulty: Moderate to strenuous
Elevation gain: 2,087 feet to Indigo Creek
Best season: Year-round. If coming from Grants Pass, be aware that Bear Camp Road is typically closed mid-Nov to Memorial Day (check because this changes). During closure, approach from Gold Beach.

Maps: USGS Agness, Brandy Peak, and Silver Peak; Rogue River–Siskiyou National Forest; Gold Beach Ranger District
Trail contacts: Gold Beach Ranger District: (541) 247-3600
Parking and trailhead facilities: There is a small picnic area and parking for 15 cars.

Finding the trailhead: From Gold Beach (open year-round): Follow US 101 to the south end of the bridge across the Rogue River and turn onto Jerry's Flat Road. Follow this paved road along the Rogue River, which becomes FR 33, for a total of 27 miles. Immediately after crossing a major bridge, where the Rogue and Illinois Rivers come together, turn right onto Oak Flat Road and follow it 3.2 miles to a sign pointing to the trailhead on the left.

From Rogue Valley (open in summer after Memorial Day): Leave I-5 at exit 61 for Merlin. Proceed west on the Merlin-Galice Road, through Merlin, for 15 miles. At mile 15, just before Galice, turn left onto FR 23, the road to Gold Beach. Follow the pavement 37 miles over a 5,000-foot pass at Bear Camp to FR 33, the road along the Lower Rogue River from Gold Beach. Turn left onto FR 33 and go south 2 miles to Oak Flat Road, just before the bridge over the mouth of the Illinois River. Turn left and follow Oak Flat Road for 3.2 miles to a sign pointing to the trailhead on the left.
Trailhead GPS: N42 31.151' / W124 02.536'

The Hike

In many ways, the west side of the Illinois River Trail is very similar to the east side. The Illinois canyon is spectacular, the terrain is rugged, and wildflowers abound.

The main differences on the west side are a pair of truly stunning creeks—Indigo and Silver—with scenic bridges that cross them. Indigo Creek makes a good day–hike goal (9.4 miles round-trip) and offers rocky beaches and possible swimming holes at Indian Flat.

Silver Creek is a much more difficult backpack hike of almost 18 miles round-trip (see "Options").

The path's initial 0.3 mile offers excellent views of the river and the canyon. The route then works its way inland, crossing Nancy Creek in a myrtlewood grove, climbing above the river, and crossing Ethel's Creek at mile 1.9.

Buzzard's Roost, at mile 2.9, is a rocky promontory offering a panorama of the river from a high vantage point. The spot was well known to Native Americans and

A scenic footbridge crosses Indigo Creek on the Illinois River Trail from the west. ZACH URNESS

is now an archaeological preserve. A scramble trail leads up Buzzard's Roost, and it is possible to climb to the top. ***Caution:*** There is a vertical drop-off here; a fall would not end well.

Beyond Buzzard's Roost the path swings around an open slope and heads toward Indigo Creek.

At mile 4.5 the trail reaches a fork. Go left for 0.3 mile and reach Indian Flat's grassy bench along Indigo Creek, where turquoise pools form along rock beaches in a deep canyon. This makes a good lunch spot or place to tent for the night.

Continuing another 0.2 mile down the main trail, you'll reach an almost unbelievably beautiful bridge spanning the narrow rock chasm of Indigo Creek. This stunning bridge is your turnaround point.

Miles and Directions

0.0   Begin at the Oak Flat Trailhead.

2.9   Arrive at Buzzard's Roost.

4.5   Come to unmarked Indian Flat junction. Go left to visit Indian Flat.

4.7   Cross the bridge over Indigo Creek; return the way you came.

9.4   Arrive back at the trailhead.

Options

Silver Creek: From Indigo Creek the trail climbs over a ridge, passes a creekside camping spot at Frantz Ranch, and continues along a ridgeline for 3.0 miles to yet another dramatic footbridge, this one spanning Silver Creek.

Silver Creek runs through one of the most spectacular canyons in Oregon. It is extremely narrow and lined with vertical rock walls and fern grottoes. The clarity of

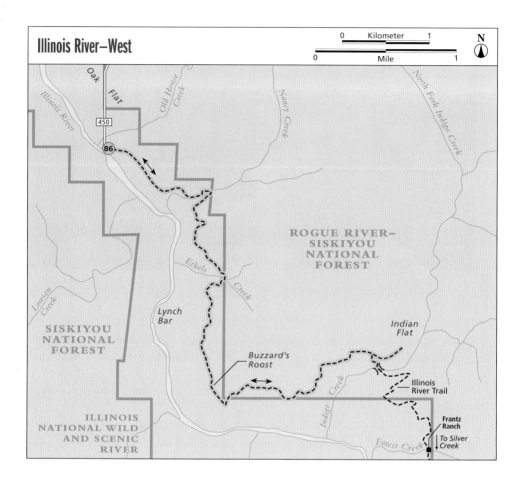

0   Kilometer   1

0   Mile   1

N

its water is remarkable. You can stand in a pool up to your neck and your feet don't even look blue.

Miles and Directions beyond Indigo Creek:

5.9   Pass Frantz Ranch.

8.7   Arrive at the bridge over Silver Creek; return the way you came.

17.4   Arrive back at the trailhead.

Hiking through: Beyond Silver Creek the Illinois River Trail climbs 2,000 feet in 2.5 miles as it ascends to the summit of Bald Ridge and South Bend Mountain. The route eventually drops back down and becomes the far end of the trail from Oak Flat and Pine Flat on the Illinois Valley side.

87 Windy Valley

A beautiful hike with many vistas, leading to a secluded valley with a grassy meadow by a creek. Much botanical interest.

Distance: 3.8-mile out and back
Difficulty: Easy
Elevation loss: 776 feet
Best season: May–Nov
Maps: USGS Collier Butte; Rogue River–Siskiyou National Forest
Trail contacts: Gold Beach Ranger District: (541) 247-3600

Parking and trailhead facilities: The trailhead has a vault toilet, a picnic table, and an outstanding view of the Big Craggies. There is a small parking area and additional room along the wide shoulder.
Special considerations: Windy Creek, which you must cross to reach the meadow, may not be passable due to water volume early or late in the season. The log bridges get very slippery in wet weather, and the water can be fast and cold.

Finding the trailhead: From Brookings follow the North Bank Chetco Road (which becomes Road 1376) for 15 miles to a bridge across the South Fork Chetco River. Bear left to stay on Road 1376 and follow it another 10 miles up a long, steep hill and past High Prairie, a nice picnic area on the right. The trailhead is 3 miles past High Prairie, on the left, just past Spur 220. Look for a vault toilet and an open metal gate on a road that leads down to a small parking lot.
Trailhead GPS: N42 18.705' / W124 08.241'

The Hike

Before visiting this remote, easy trail amid some of the most bizarre country anywhere, you should first check out a few things by car. The road between High Prairie and Snow Camp Mountain is a must. Coming up from the Chetco River, just past High Prairie, the dense, almost rain forest of Douglas-fir suddenly opens into a vast expanse of orange peridotite and serpentinite rock, sparsely covered with manzanita and stunted Jeffrey, western white, and knobcone pines.

The Windy Valley–Snow Camp Trail (#1103) is charming and not too difficult. After passing the collapsed shelter at Cedar Camp, the route winds behind the huge, unnamed rock outcrop seen from the trailhead. It's a short, steep, but rewarding scramble to the top of the rock. From there the Pacific Ocean can be seen through the mouth of the Pistol River.

Just past the rock, a vista unfolds to the left amid this open country's stunted, scraggly, serpentine-adapted vegetation. The trail contours around a steep hillside and crosses several creeks and springs, a myrtlewood grove or two, two patches of insect-eating *Darlingtonia*, and endless bear grass and azaleas. Watch for views of Snow Camp Lookout.

Windy Valley is an open grassy meadow surrounded by Windy Creek. Zach Urness

During the second mile the way steepens and the forest, now mostly Douglas-fir and Port Orford cedar, grows much denser as the trail approaches the valley. Windy Creek soon comes into view, signaling that you're almost there.

The trail's most important point comes at mile 1.6. The trail splits, and while there's a post, the sign apparently had vanished as of summer 2012. Turn right to reach Windy Valley (avoiding the path that goes left/straight across the creek toward Snow Camp).

Eventually the trail arrives at Windy Creek at mile 1.8, where several downed trees offer a dry route across the wide creek into the valley itself.

Across the creek, the open field is sunny and inviting, if a little swampy in the center. At the far end, in the trees along the creek, you'll find the ruins of an old homestead, a campsite, and a couple of fine swimming holes. The spot offers fair fishing and is quite popular in summer.

Miles and Directions

0.0   Begin at the Windy Valley Trailhead.

0.4   Arrive at a rock outcrop with an excellent view on the top.

1.6   Come to a possibly unmarked Snow Camp Trail junction; go right.

1.8   Cross Windy Creek on a log.

1.9   Reach Windy Valley; return the way you came.

3.8   Arrive back at the trailhead.

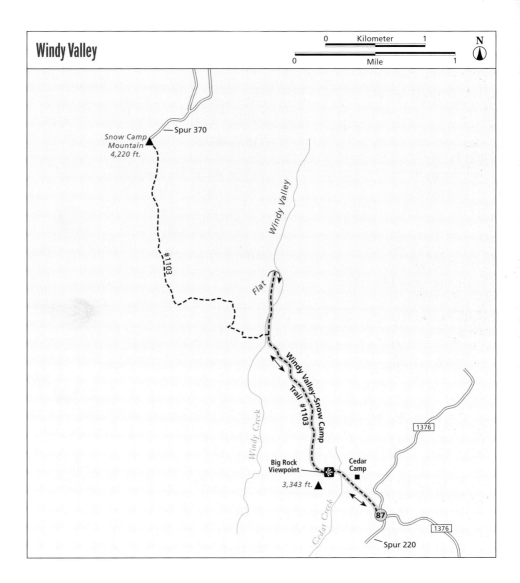

Options

Snow Camp Lookout: Be sure to drive the rest of the way up FR 1376 to Snow Camp Lookout, the actual terminus of the Windy Valley Trail. The lookout (elevation 4,220 feet) offers views of Windy Valley, every peak within 100 miles, and the ocean.

To reach the lookout by car, follow FR 1376 for 4.5 miles beyond the Windy Valley Trailhead to where the road becomes narrow and takes off sharply uphill. Look for a gated road on the left (Spur 550). Park and walk 1.5 miles to the lookout.

Note: If you hike to the lookout from Windy Valley, it's 1.5 miles from the junction at Windy Creek, with a 1,400-foot elevation gain. The short walk up the road is much easier.

88 Loeb State Park / Redwood Nature Loop

This route combines the emerald Chetco River and the northernmost grove of Oregon redwoods.

Distance: 2.6-mile lollipop
Difficulty: Easy
Elevation gain: 527 feet
Best season: Year-round
Maps: USGS Mount Emily; Rogue River-Siskiyou National Forest; Gold Beach Ranger District

Trail contacts: Gold Beach Ranger District: (541) 247-3600
Parking and trailhead facilities: Loeb State Park is a highlight in itself, with rental cabins, campsites, and fishing opportunities. The park has parking for at least 20 cars; another 10 to 15 cars can fit at Redwood Nature Loop (which is part of the featured trail).

Finding the trailhead: In Brookings turn off US 101 onto North Bank Chetco River Road (following signs for Loeb State Park) for 7 miles to a large sign for Loeb State Park. Park next to a trailhead sign designating Riverview Trail.
Trailhead GPS: N42 06.766'/W124 11.225'

The Hike

With the northernmost grove of old-growth redwoods and a stretch along the emerald Chetco River, it's no wonder this route from Loeb State Park is among the South Coast's most famous hikes.

The hike is actually two different trails—each with its own trailhead—separated by North Bank Road. Both stretches are so pretty and easy that it wouldn't make sense to hike one and not the other.

Start at Loeb State Park's Riverview Trailhead—just across from an old-growth myrtlewood grove—and follow the trail through thick, mossy forest along the river.

After 0.7 mile you'll cross North Bank Road to the Redwood Nature Loop Trailhead, which has its own parking lot. An interpretative brochure can be obtained here, which is helpful during the 1.1-mile clockwise loop that traverses a forest cut by a small creek and a collection of the world's tallest species of tree, *Sequoia sempervirens*.

The largest tree can be found about halfway through the loop. According to the brochure it is 296 feet tall, 34 inches in diameter, and around 800 years old. The tree supposedly contains enough wood to construct eight two-bedroom houses! The current tallest coastal redwood is 379 feet.

Once you've finished the loop, cross back over the road and follow the Riverview Trail back to your car at Loeb State Park.

Loeb State Park / Redwood Nature Loop

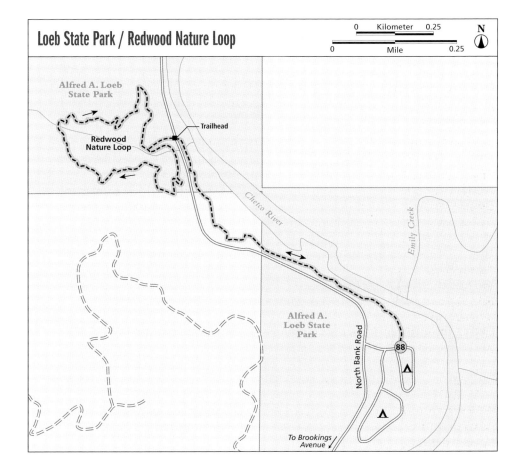

Miles and Directions

0.0 Begin at Riverview Trailhead at Loeb State Park.

0.6 Cross North Bank Road and begin hiking clockwise on the Redwood Nature Loop.

1.9 Reach the end of the Redwood Nature Loop and cross North Bank Road back onto the Riverview Trail.

2.6 Arrive back at the Riverview Trailhead.

89 Coquille Falls

This short but extremely steep trail drops 450 feet through the dense coastal forest of the Coquille River Falls Research Natural Area to one of the most beautiful waterfalls anywhere.

Distance: 1.4-mile out and back
Difficulty: Strenuous (especially toward the bottom)
Elevation loss/gain: 450 feet
Best season: Year-round except when it snows at low elevations
Maps: USGS Illahe; Rogue River–Siskiyou National Forest
Trail contacts: Powers Ranger District, Rogue River–Siskiyou National Forest: (541) 439-6200

Parking and trailhead facilities: There's parking on the shoulder for about 6 cars.
Special considerations: This is an extremely steep trail, with the uphill portion on the return trip. The elevation at the base of the falls is less than 1,300 feet, so it's theoretically possible to visit year-round (except when it has recently snowed at a low elevation). The flow varies greatly from season to season, but every season has its own beauty.

Finding the trailhead: The best way to reach the trailhead is via the Coos Bay Road (OR 42) from Winston (I-5 exit 119), 7 miles south of Roseburg. Forty-seven miles west of Winston, you'll come to the Powers turnoff (CR 542). Go left and proceed 18 miles to Powers. Continue through Powers (the road becomes CR 219 and then FR 33) for 16 miles to the junction with FR 3348. Bear left on FR 3348 (the sign says To Glendale). Continue about 1.5 miles to the trailhead on the left. It's also possible to reach the trailhead from Grants Pass via Bear Camp Road and Agness, as well as the road from Galice to Marial, via Eden Valley Road. Both routes are extremely long and slow.
Trailhead GPS: N42 42.802' / W124 01.377'

The Hike

This short, very steep hike is beautiful throughout and culminates with one of Oregon's best waterfalls.

From the trailhead the path descends relentlessly downhill. As you hike, try not to think about the fact that this is the easy part. You can stay occupied by admiring the dense coastal forest of western hemlock, Port Orford cedar, and Douglas-fir (plus bigleaf maple and red alder), with an understory of fern (including maidenhair), Sadler oak, and sorrel. (If you turn over the shamrock–like sorrel leaves, you will see that the undersides are green. In the redwoods, their undersides are purple.)

Crossing the little footbridge is a sign that the falls are about to come into view. It is also a sign that the trail is about to become much steeper. The final approach to the falls is a series of very short, very steep switchbacks that tend to be very slippery due to frequent rain and mist from the falls. Be very careful.

You will soon find yourself out of the woods, on the boulder-strewn banks of the South Fork Coquille River looking up in awe and amazement.

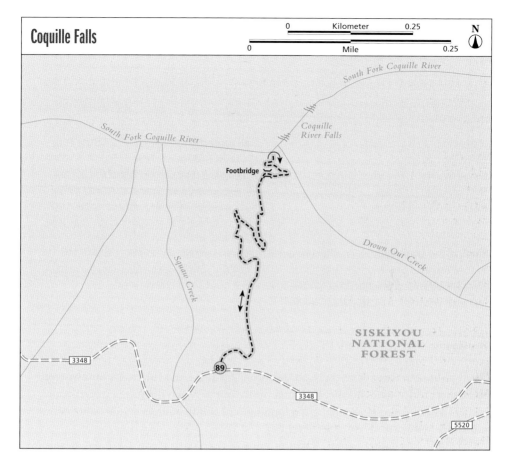

The double-tiered falls begin with a 45-foot vertical plunge. Below that is an exquisite "horsetail" (a waterfall that fans out over a rock face), with a 65-foot drop. In summer two distinct horsetails fall over the rock face. In winter the two merge as the flow rate hugely increases. The total height of the falls is 110 feet.

Miles and Directions

0.0 Begin at the trailhead.

0.7 Arrive at the base of the falls; return the way you came.

1.4 Arrive back at the trailhead.

Options

If you come via Eden Valley Road from Grants Pass, you will pass the trailheads for Mount Bolivar and Hanging Rock. If you come via Bear Camp Road from Grants Pass, you will pass the Bear Camp Trailhead. There are numerous trailheads off FR 33 in the vicinity of Coquille Falls: the Panther Ridge Trail, the Barklow Mountain Trail, the Rock Creek Trail, and the Azalea Lake Trail—not to mention the Rogue River Trail from Foster Bar.

90 Humbug Mountain

A massive headland rising above the Pacific Ocean, featuring a lush old-growth forest and an interesting history.

Distance: 5.2-mile lollipop
Difficulty: Strenuous
Elevation gain: 1,757 feet
Best season: Year-round
Maps: USGS Port Orford

Trail contacts: Humbug Mountain State Park: (541) 332-6774
Parking and trailhead facilities: There is parking for around 25 to 30 cars, along with numerous campsites, water, and other amenities just across the road at Humbug Mountain State Park.

Finding the trailhead: Humbug Mountain Trailhead sits along US 101 at milepost 307, just north of the state park entrance. A signboard for the trailhead can be seen easily from the road. The trailhead is 22.5 miles north of Gold Beach and 5.6 miles south of Port Orford.
Trailhead GPS: N42 41.248' / W124 26.367'

The Hike

The old-growth forest is so thick on this headland above the Pacific Ocean that you half expect to see dinosaurs peeking their heads out between the myrtlewood, maple, and Douglas-fir trees that highlight a looping trail culminating in a 1,761-foot summit. (The trail starts nearly at sea level.)

Oddly, while Humbug Mountain dominates the South Coast for miles around, the trail offers few views of the Pacific.

Not that it matters. With easy access, a well-maintained trail, and a strenuous but not overwhelming amount of elevation gain, the trail makes an excellent day outing.

To get started, park at the large trailhead and hike along a pretty little creek that splashes down through a forest that celebrates every possible shade of green. (If you're staying at the state park campground, a trail leads under the highway to the trailhead.)

After 0.9 mile and 600 feet of climb, the trail reaches a junction for the beginning of the loop. The west loop (right) reaches the summit a bit quicker, so head right, passing one of the best ocean views at the 1.4-mile mark and passing a trail junction that leads to the summit meadows at mile 2.3. The summit features a bench sitting in a grassy meadow and a view of the ocean.

Back on the loop, the trail continues through an old-growth ecosystem that is home to more than eight species of trees, twelve species of plants, and wildlife that include chickadees, Douglas squirrels, black-tailed deer, and numerous slugs.

The thickness of the forest helps provide a reference for the history behind the mountain's odd name. Originally called Sugarloaf Mountain, the more cynical moniker was applied after an ill-fated expedition through these same woods.

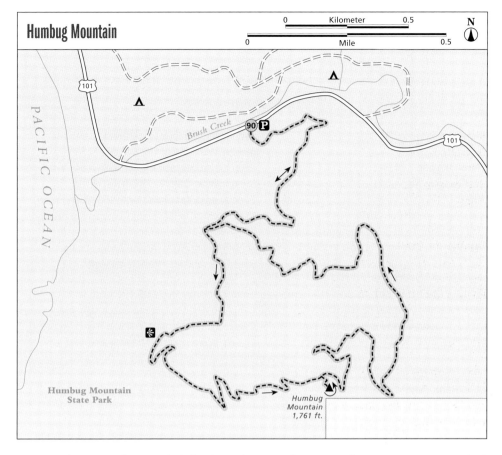

Humbug Mountain

The story changes slightly depending on the source, but in 1851 Port Orford founder Captain William Tichenor sent several men on foot to explore the mountain and look for a route through the Coast Ranges.

The search went badly awry, with the men apparently getting lost in deep ravines and thick forest and never finding anything resembling a route to the interior. In honor of the failure, they renamed the peak Tichenor's Humbug.

The trail winds its way 1.8 miles back down the mountain, passing another ocean view and a small waterfall before reaching the loop junction and heading back to the trailhead.

Miles and Directions

0.0 Begin at the Humbug Mountain Trailhead.

0.9 Come to the beginning of the loop; go right.

2.3 Reach a junction that leads to the summit; go right.

2.4 Arrive at the summit. Hike back to the junction and continue on the loop.

4.3 Reach the end of the loop; go right.

5.2 Arrive back at the trailhead.

91 Boardman Scenic Corridor–Indian Sands

A gorgeous and multifaceted stretch of Oregon Coast scenic area showcasing dunes, coastline, and the state's tallest bridge.

Distance: 3.0-mile shuttle
Difficulty: Easy
Elevation gain: 844 feet
Best season: Year-round
Maps: USGS Cape Ferrelo; Samuel H. Boardman State Scenic Corridor
Trail contacts: Gold Beach Ranger District: (541) 247-3600

Parking and trailhead facilities: The small dirt parking area has room for 6 to 8 cars. Farther down the access road is a picnic area and vault toilet. Thomas Creek has room for 30 cars.
Special considerations: Samuel H. Boardman State Scenic Corridor features multiple short hikes along the South Coast. Visitors should consider stopping at Natural Bridge, Thunder Rock Cove, and Arch Rock to the north.

Finding the trailhead: Whaleshead Picnic Area: From Brookings follow US 101 north for 8 miles (or south 20 miles from Gold Beach). After passing the first Whaleshead Beach sign, continue a bit farther and turn left at the next sign, for Whaleshead Picnic Area. Follow a paved access road a few hundred feet and almost immediately turn right into a small dirt parking area next to Rough Road and Slide Ahead signs. The trail begins at the Coastal Trail post in the parking area.
Trailhead GPS: N42 08.819' / W124 21.325'
Thomas Creek: From Whaleshead Picnic Area continue up US 101 for 1.3 miles to a large parking lot on the left at Thomas Creek Bridge.
Trailhead GPS: N42 09.855' / W124 21.528'

The Hike

Samuel H. Boardman State Scenic Corridor might well be the most spectacular stretch of coast in the entire state of Oregon—it's certainly a strong contender.

The problem is there are so many pullouts, picnic areas, and very short trails that it's difficult to decide where to spend your time. Further, the area's proximity to US 101 can lessen the experience.

With all those factors in mind, one of the best continuous stretches of trail is between the Whaleshead Picnic Area and Thomas Creek Bridge. The trail passes a multitude of ocean overlooks, crosses the eerie dunes of Indian Sands, and winds past wildflowers and a small waterfall before ending at Oregon's tallest bridge.

There is a very short stretch along US 101, but that's the cost of doing businesses at Boardman. The trail can be hiked as a 3.0-mile shuttle or a 6.0-mile round-trip.

The route begins at a post for the Coastal Trail near the entrance to Whaleshead Picnic Area. The first 0.7 mile features two outstanding views—the first off Cape Ferrelo to the south and the next a cove to the north. Then the trail hits US 101, following the guardrail briefly before heading up a dirt road and going back into the forest.

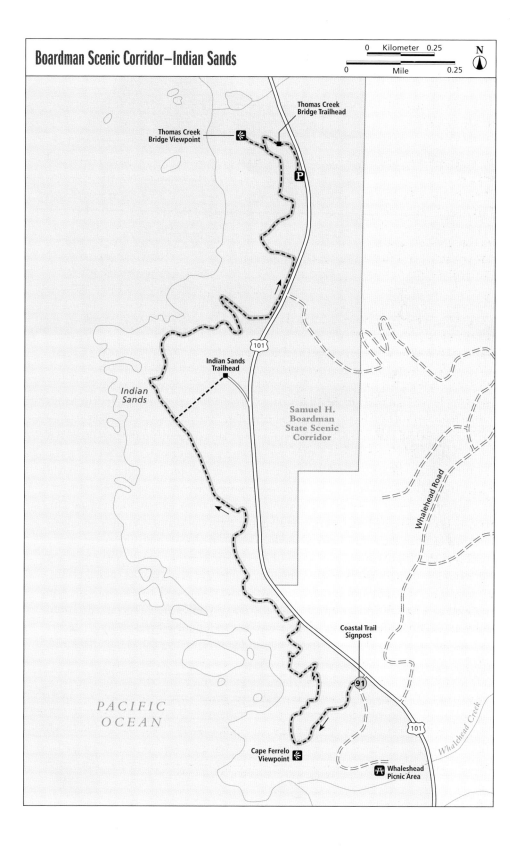

Boardman Scenic Corridor–Indian Sands

0   Kilometer   0.25
0   Mile   0.25
N

Thomas Creek
Bridge Trailhead

Thomas Creek
Bridge Viewpoint

P

101

Indian Sands
Trailhead

Indian
Sands

Samuel H.
Boardman
State Scenic
Corridor

Whalehead Road

Coastal Trail
Signpost

91

PACIFIC
OCEAN

101

Whalehead Creek

Cape Ferrelo
Viewpoint

Whalehead
Picnic Area

The Indian Sands are a strange patch of dunes sitting high above the Pacific Ocean. Zach Urness

At mile 1.5 the trail reaches the strange, undulating dunes of the Indian Sands sitting above the ocean. The trail becomes faint here, but walking north while exploring the nooks and crannies of this sweeping sandy landscape isn't difficult. (There is a parking area and a very steep 0.2-mile trail down to Indian Sands off US 101.)

What makes Indian Sands bizarre is that they are not on the beach but perched atop a rocky cliff. Apparently the sand comes from a sandstone seam in the rock strata that has devolved back into sand. The coolest spot is a deep, narrow rock chasm with surging ocean at the bottom and the sand going right up to and over the cliff edges.

On the far side of the dunes, the edge drops off sharply into the ocean and a small trail tightropes along a cliff above the ocean. Numerous small wildflowers can be found here in spring, along with tunnels cut into the dense mat of coastal plants.

The next 0.5 mile includes nonstop views of the craggy cove below while the trail heads uphill. The trail winds along the highway one last time before dropping back into the forest and heading 0.7 mile to the viewpoint of Thomas Creek Bridge—at 345 feet, the tallest in Oregon. A spur that climbs to the parking area marks the route's end.

Miles and Directions

0.0   Begin hiking the Coastal Trail from Whaleshead Picnic Area Trailhead.

0.7   Arrive alongside US 101.

0.8   Follow a dirt road to continue the trail.

1.5   Reach the Indian Sands; continue along the ocean.

3.0   Arrive at the Thomas Creek Bridge view and parking area.

92 Boardman Scenic Corridor–Cape Ferrelo

An open, wildflower-covered cape with ocean views in every direction famous for sunset views. Options for a longer hike.

Distance: 1.0-mile lollipop
Difficulty: Easy
Elevation gain: 166 feet
Best season: Year-round
Maps: USGS Cape Ferrelo; Samuel H. Boardman State Scenic Corridor

Trail contacts: Gold Beach Ranger District: (541) 247-3600
Parking and trailhead facilities: There's parking at the trailhead for 5 to 10 cars.

Finding the trailhead: From Brookings follow US 101 north for 5.1 miles (or south from Gold Beach for 23 miles). After passing a Lone Ranch Beach sign, continue just a bit farther and turn left at the sign for Cape Ferrelo Viewpoint. An access road leads to a small parking lot. **Trailhead GPS:** N42 06.405' / W124 20.784'

The Hike

Home to wide-open ocean views and a multitude of wildflowers, Cape Ferrelo has just about everything a person could hope for in an extremely easy coastal hike.

Trails leading in different directions begin at the small circular parking lot. For the featured loop across the cape, go left. The right-hand path is discussed in "Options" below.

After passing through a stand of trees, the trail splits at mile 0.2 on a small hillside to begin the loop. Choose the trail on the right, which heads uphill. You will immediately be rewarded by an ocean panorama and will pass a Coastal Trail marker.

Continue hiking toward the point of the cape, which during spring is covered in wildflowers and is well known to photographers for its sunset views.

To the south are Twin Rocks and Lone Ranch Beaches, a sandy picnic area bisected by Lone Ranch Creek. Northward are the coastline and House Rock and Whaleshead Island.

Follow the trail, which at times becomes overgrown, in a loop around the point and head back toward the trail junction and your car. The end of the cape is a preferred whale watching spot in winter and spring.

Miles and Directions

0.0 Begin at the small Cape Ferrelo Viewpoint parking area.
0.2 Arrive at a small unmarked split in the trail. Go right (uphill) on the loop.
0.5 Pass the tip of Cape Ferrelo.
0.8 Reach the end of the loop; turn right.
1.0 Arrive back at the trailhead.

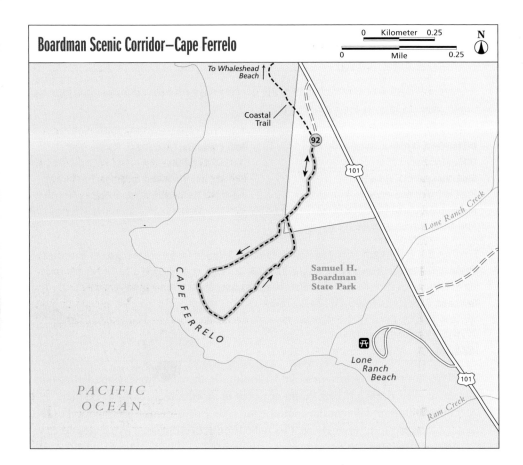

Boardman Scenic Corridor–Cape Ferrelo

To Whaleshead Beach

Coastal Trail

92

101

Lone Ranch Creek

Samuel H. Boardman State Park

Lone Ranch Beach

101

Ram Creek

CAPE FERRELO

PACIFIC OCEAN

0 Kilometer 0.25

0 Mile 0.25

N

Options

House Rock and Whaleshead Beach: If the hike to Cape Ferrelo isn't enough for you, hike north (right) from the parking area. This stretch of Coastal Trail heads north along the bluff 1.5 miles to House Rock Viewpoint and will take you to Whaleshead Beach after a total of 4.0 miles.

The highway approaches the trail at a few points, but the trail's mix of forest and ocean views more than compensates. There are multiple spur trails to sandy beaches, including one, accessed about 1.0 mile beyond House Rock Viewpoint, that stretches a full 1.0 mile to Whaleshead Beach.

93 Oregon Redwoods

The largest concentration of old-growth redwood groves in Oregon.

Distance: 1.8-mile lollipop
Difficulty: Easy
Elevation gain: 350 feet
Best season: Year-round
Maps: USGS Mount Emily; Rogue River–Siskiyou National Forest
Trail contacts: Gold Beach Ranger district, (541) 247-3600

Parking and trailhead facilities: Vault toilets and room for 20 cars
Special considerations: The Oregon Redwoods Trail has two options—a longer and a shorter loop—but the short loop (1.0 mile) misses the grandest grove.

Finding the trailhead: From Brookings drive south on US 101 for 5 miles (or north of Crescent City, California, 20.6 miles). Turn left (east) onto Winchuck Road at an Oregon Redwoods Trail sign and follow it 1.5 miles. Turn right across a bridge over the Winchuck River onto Peavine Ridge Road and follow it over 4 miles of bumpy gravel to the trailhead. The route has many signs pointing people in the correct direction.
Trailhead GPS: N42 00.516' / W124 08.826'

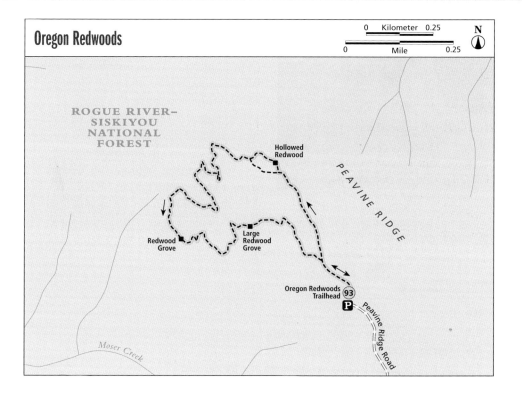

The Hike

In the beginning, this hike doesn't feel much different from the few thousand other trails populating Oregon's coastal forest.

There's a bumpy logging road, trailhead signs, the smell of ocean air, and a path

Just past the first grove of redwoods is a hollowed-out redwood you can walk into, just off the trail. Zach Urness

into the lush twilight of a Douglas-fir and sword fern forest immediately familiar to anyone from the Beaver State.

But something is lurking 0.5 mile down this particular trail that makes it special—that makes your heart skip a beat when the sight of giant redwoods twist almost 300 feet into the sky.

The Oregon Redwoods Trail is one of only a few places to view the world's tallest trees on Oregon soil. And while California's redwoods are deservedly more famous, there's something special about walking along the northern boundary of these ancient giants.

The trail starts out in a typical coastal Douglas-fir forest and is fairly unimpressive until you reach the first of three old-growth groves at a trail junction at mile 0.4. Go right; just beyond is a hollowed-out redwood you can walk inside.

At mile 0.5 turn right at a second junction and follow the trail into a forested canyon across a few small creeks.

After a stretch without big trees, a second large grove appears at mile 1.3. The largest grove turns up at mile 1.5. Take a moment to sit among these giants before looping back to the original trail and your car.

Miles and Directions

0.0 Begin at the Oregon Redwoods Trailhead.

0.1 Come to the beginning of the loop; go right.

0.5 Reach a second junction; go right.

1.7 Come to the end of the loop; go right to return to the trailhead.

1.8 Arrive back at the trailhead.

94 Black Butte

This hike to Young's Valley encompasses high-mountain scenery, panoramas, glacial canyons, forest, meadows, and serpentine ecology. Options for a shorter hike and access to the East Fork Illinois River Trail.

Distance: 9.4-mile out and back
Difficulty: Moderate
Elevation gain: 1,112 feet
Best season: June–Oct
Maps: USGS Polar Bear Mountain; Klamath National Forest; Siskiyou Wilderness

Trail contacts: Gasquet Ranger Station: (707) 457-3131
Parking and trailhead facilities: The trailhead is on a pretty little open flat with room for 10 cars and excellent views of the rocky south face of Black Butte and the formerly glaciated canyon of the East Fork of the Illinois River.

Finding the trailhead: From Grants Pass take US 199 south 28 miles to Cave Junction; continue toward the end of town. Turn left up Caves Highway (OR 46) for 2 miles, and then turn right onto Holland Loop. In 2 miles turn right onto Bridgeview-Takilma Road (CR 5820). Proceed on Takilma Road 4 miles past the Happy Camp turnoff (Grayback/Waldo Road), then continue 3.7 miles through Takilma village.

When the pavement ends, bear left onto FR 4904 and continue 1.8 miles. Turn right on a bridge over Dunn Creek onto FR 4906 (there is a sign in the opposite direction only), which becomes Spur 053. Proceed 10 miles from the bridge, following the best-looking route at questionable junctions, to the trailhead on the right.
Trailhead GPS: N41 55.820'/W123 36.387'

The Hike

This trail penetrates the snowcapped crags that pop into view on the skyline as you enter the Illinois Valley from Grants Pass on US 199. The group of summits rises above the head of the East Fork Illinois River, just over the California line.

Note: The trailhead and trail are entirely in California, but the route is most easily reached via Oregon's Illinois Valley. To make a one-way shuttle hike or backpacking trip, combine this route with either the East Fork Illinois River Trail or Young's Valley/Raspberry Lake.

Approaching the trailhead, there is no mistaking Black Butte—a narrow, rocky projection towering above the area. The first part of the route circles around Black Butte's mysterious rocky crest and across a serpentine-soil area in an open, parklike forest of Jeffrey and western white pines. The view of the East Fork Illinois, far below, is spectacular.

After 1.6 miles you come to a forked junction marked by a sign. For the described hike, go right, following the pointer for Young's Valley. Continuing straight (along the Polar Bear Trail) will take you to Polar Bear Gap and, if you're feeling adventurous, Twin Valley (see "Options").

Black Butte Trail eventually ends at the cliff-walled paradise of Young's Valley, home to many wildflowers in early summer. ZACH URNESS

Despite a few steep ups and downs, Black Butte Trail is surprisingly level. This is a beautiful area of meadow, forest, creek, and an occasional Port Orford cedar stand.

At mile 4.1 you will find yourself stepping across a shallow, 4-foot-wide stream surrounded by dense brush. This is the headwaters of the Illinois River's East Fork and the upper trailhead of the East Fork Illinois River Trail. (The actual trail begins at a small unmarked camping spot just off the trail on the right near the river.)

After crossing the Illinois East Fork, the trail in summer becomes overgrown in a meadow filled with wildflowers. At mile 4.5, just beyond a small saddle, you reach the trail into Young's Valley. The wildflower-filled valley, to the left on the trail, is surrounded by craggy mountains, and an excellent place to camp. The trail from Young's Valley continues to Raspberry Lake. In the opposite direction, the trail leads to the Young's Valley Trailhead.

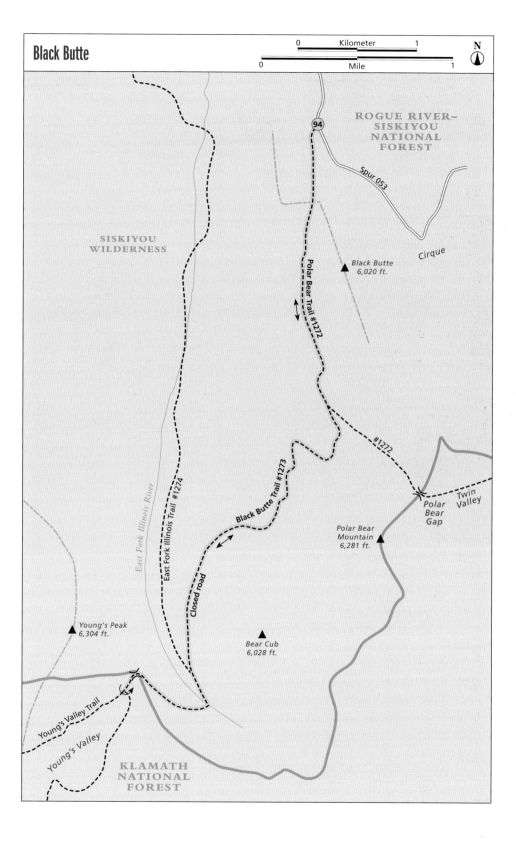

Black Butte

0 | Kilometer | 1
0 | Mile | 1

N

ROGUE RIVER–
SISKIYOU
NATIONAL
FOREST

94

Spur 053

Cirque

SISKIYOU
WILDERNESS

▲ Black Butte
6,020 ft.

Polar Bear Trail #1272

#1272

Twin
Valley

Polar
Bear
Gap

Black Butte Trail #1273

East Fork Illinois Trail #1274

East Fork Illinois River

Closed road

Polar Bear
Mountain
6,281 ft. ▲

▲ Young's Peak
6,304 ft.

▲ Bear Cub
6,028 ft.

Young's Valley Trail

Young's Valley

KLAMATH
NATIONAL
FOREST

Miles and Directions

0.0 Begin at the Black Butte Trailhead.

1.6 Reach the Polar Bear Gap junction; go right at signs pointing toward Young's Valley.

2.9 Arrive at an old mine and a pass. Stay right (do not take old road uphill).

4.1 Pass the East Fork Illinois River Trailhead and cross over the river.

4.7 Arrive at Young's Valley Trail; explore the valley; return the way you came.

7.8 Reach the Polar Bear Gap Trailhead; turn left.

9.4 Arrive back at the trailhead.

Options

Polar Bear Gap / Twin Valley: From the junction with the Black Butte Trail—at the 1.6-mile mark described above—continue straight (instead of turning right) for 1.0 mile to the wide-open saddle of Polar Bear Gap, stuck snugly between Lookout and Polar Bear Mountains. If you turn around here, the entire hike is just 5.0 miles.

Beyond Polar Bear saddle the trail drops steeply downhill and can become confusing. Near the bottom, follow stacked-rock cairns across a rocky field of downed trees into Twin Valley, which has a lower and an upper meadow. These wet, floral meadows have some nice campsites and views of Polar Bear and Lookout Mountains.

95 East Fork Illinois River

A glacier-carved river canyon surrounded by high mountains and lined with old-growth forest featuring a wilderness route and an option for an easy day hike.

Distance: 14-mile shuttle
Difficulty: Moderately strenuous
Elevation loss: 3,637 feet
Best season: June–Nov
Maps: USGS Polar Bear Mountain; Klamath National Forest; Rogue River–Siskiyou National Forest; Siskiyou Wilderness
Trail contacts: Gasquet Ranger Station: (707) 457-3131; Wild Rivers Ranger District, (541) 592-4000
Parking and trailhead facilities: There's parking for 1 car at the Osgood Ditch Trailhead. (The area is quite steep, so set your emergency brake and block your tires.) An additional 2 cars can park on the shoulder 100 feet up the road. At the Black Butte Trailhead there's parking for 12 cars along the road's shoulders.

Special considerations: The described hikes feature sections on the 9.9 miles of East Fork Illinois River Trail between the Osgood Ditch Trailhead (lower) and the (upper) junction with the Black Butte Trail in the Siskiyou Wilderness. The upper trailhead can only be reached by hiking in via Black Butte Trail or the Young's Valley / Raspberry Lake Trail.

The described hike does not use the official East Fork Illinois Trailhead (which you'll pass driving to the Osgood Ditch Trailhead). The trail from the East Fork Illinois Trailhead is a confusing disaster of ATV tracks, bunny trails, and old mining roads. The Osgood Ditch Trail, not far away, is much easier to follow and a better hike.

Finding the trailhead: Lower/northern (Osgood Ditch) trailhead: Leave a shuttle car here. From Grants Pass take US 199 south 28 miles to Cave Junction; continue toward the end of town. Turn left up Caves Highway (OR 46) for 2 miles and turn right onto Holland Loop. In 2 more miles turn right onto Bridgeview-Takilma Road (CR 5820). Proceed on Takilma Road 4 miles past the Happy Camp turnoff (Grayback / Waldo Road), then continue 3.7 miles through Takilma Village.

Where the pavement ends on Takilma Road, follow the pavement downhill and right onto Spur 011. Proceed 0.5 mile to the green bridge over the East Fork, where the blacktop ends. Turn immediately left and go 1.9 miles, passing the official East Fork Illinois Trailhead, to the Osgood Ditch Trailhead sign on the left, where the road makes a sharp switchback north.
Trailhead GPS: N41 59.448' / W123 38.091'

Upper / southern (Black Butte) trailhead: Continue straight when the pavement ends on Takilma Road and follow FR 4904 for 1.8 miles. Turn right on a bridge over Dunn Creek onto FR 4906 (there is a sign in the opposite direction only), which eventually becomes Spur 053. Proceed 10 miles from the bridge, following the most used looking route at questionable junctions to the Black Butte Trailhead on the right.
Trailhead GPS: N41 55.820' / W123 36.387'

The Hike

The East Fork Illinois River Trail is a wild, beautiful, and sometimes confusing trail through some of the most remote country in Southern Oregon and Northern California.

Because of the 3,657-foot elevation loss, it makes more sense to start high and work your way down. To get to the high end, follow the Black Butte Trail from the Black Butte Trailhead. Four miles into the hike, on the right side of the trail, you'll see a small campsite and sign on a tree that says YOUNG'S VALLEY.

This imperfect spot is the upper trailhead for the East Fork Illinois River Trail—you'll know it's the spot, because the river itself is just a few feet away. Do not cross the river. The trail junction shows up just before the main trail crosses the river.

Walk across the campsite clearing and the trail is easy enough to find, even without being marked (coordinates: N41 53.185'/W123 37.015'). The trail heads downhill away from the river, dropping 900 feet in 2.0 miles, along a ridgeline with views of the massive, flat-bottomed glacial canyon into which you are hiking.

At mile 2.2 you'll finally rejoin the river and cross it for the first time. Clear water trickles through a beach of medium-size boulders. Now deep in the glacial valley, the trail levels off amid forest, flowers, and a peaceful breeze.

At mile 3.3 the trail becomes fairly overgrown and brushy as it heads toward the second crossing on another shallow rock beach. The second crossing offers a nice riverside camping spot, though an even better one is just 0.7 mile beyond.

Past the idyllic camping spot, the trail climbs 270 feet in 1.0 mile up a ridgeline as the river thunders into Sanger Canyon. After the climb, the relentless trek downhill continues, losing 1,204 feet in 2.0 miles. At mile 7.1 you will arrive at a beach and swimming hole that is the third river crossing.

The final stretch is easy and pleasant, hitting the Osgood Ditch Trail junction at mile 8.3 (go left) and the Osgood Ditch Trailhead at mile 9.9.

Miles and Directions

0.0 Begin at the Black Butte Trailhead.

1.6 Reach the Polar Bear Gap junction; go right at signs pointing toward Young's Valley.

2.9 Arrive at an old mine and a pass. Stay right (do not take old road uphill).

4.1 Arrive at East Fork Illinois River Trailhead. The trailhead is a small campsite clearing on the north side of the river, near a sign on a tree that says YOUNG'S VALLEY. **Coordinates:** N41 53.185'/W123 37.015'

6.3 Cross the East Fork Illinois River for the first time.

7.4 Cross the East Fork Illinois River a second time, and pass a small campsite.

8.1 Pass a riverside camping spot.

11.2 Cross the East Fork Illinois River a third time at a nice swimming hole and rock beach.

12.4 Reach the Osgood Ditch junction; go left.

14.0 Arrive at the Osgood Ditch Trailhead.

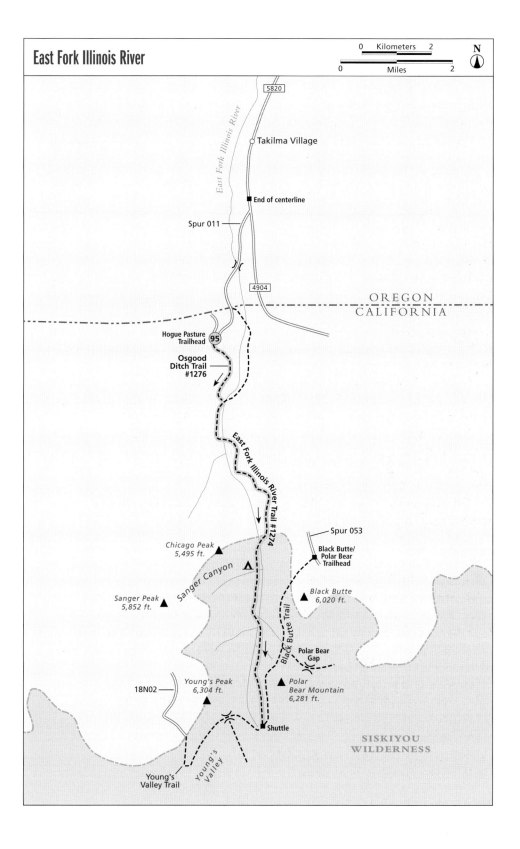

East Fork Illinois River

Kilometers 0 — 2

Miles 0 — 2

N

5820

East Fork Illinois River

Takilma Village

End of centerline

Spur 011

4904

OREGON
CALIFORNIA

Hogue Pasture
Trailhead

95

Osgood
Ditch Trail
#1276

East Fork Illinois River Trail #1274

Spur 053

Chicago Peak
5,495 ft.

Black Butte/
Polar Bear
Trailhead

Sanger Canyon

Black Butte
6,020 ft.

Sanger Peak
5,852 ft.

Black Butte Trail

Polar Bear
Gap

18N02

Young's Peak
6,304 ft.

Polar
Bear Mountain
6,281 ft.

Shuttle

SISKIYOU
WILDERNESS

Young's
Valley Trail

Young's Valley

The East Fork Illinois River Trail crosses the river for a fourth and final time near the junction with the Osgood Ditch Trail. ART BERNSTEIN

Options

Out-and-back day hike from Osgood Ditch: The day hike begins at the Osgood Ditch Trailhead, which is typically open year-round. This easy route runs for 1.6 miles along the old ditch before joining the East Fork Trail. Turn right (or go left for a lovely little river crossing). Look for excellent panoramas of the canyon and Siskiyou Wilderness. At mile 2.6 the trail reaches a rock beach and swimming hole of crystal water, small waterfalls, and massive silver boulders. This day hike is a nice one.

Longwood Gulch Fire: Very much in evidence throughout the hike is the Longwood Gulch Fire of 1987, which destroyed 50,000 acres of forest. Note the mosaic pattern of the burn, with some areas devastated and other areas completely bypassed. Along most of the trail, you will see only an occasional charred tree. In such areas the burn was fairly "cold," taking out hardwood and underbrush and charring tree trunks but killing only a few conifers. The Osgood Ditch Trail was more severely burned but is also recovering nicely.

Osgood Ditch Origin: The Osgood Ditch Trail follows an old canal used at the turn of the twentieth century to channel water from the East Fork to various gold mines. Because the ditch tends to trap water, vegetation is lush despite the surrounding forest-fire destruction.

96 Raspberry Lake

An emerald lake surrounded by white azaleas, filled with brook trout, and located just below the Siskiyou Wilderness's highest peak (see "Options" to climb it).

Distance: 13.6-mile out and back
Difficulty: Strenuous
Elevation gain: 2,693 feet
Best season: June–Nov
Maps: USGS Polar Bear Mountain; Six Rivers National Forest; Siskiyou Wilderness
Trail contacts: Gasquet Ranger Station: (707) 457-3131

Parking and trailhead facilities: There's room for 10 cars at the trailhead.
Special considerations: Permits are required from the Gasquet Ranger Station for campfires or camp stoves. The area is home to a plentiful amount of black bears, so make sure to hang your food.

Finding the trailhead: From Grants Pass head southwest on US 199 a total of 47 miles, past Cave Junction and across the California border toward Crescent City, California. After passing through the Collier Tunnel, continue 3.5 miles and turn left onto Knopki Creek Road (Road 18N07). Follow this gravel road 14 miles—staying right at any questionable junctions—to the T junction with FR 4803. Turn right onto FR 4803 and follow the increasingly rough road 1 mile to a parking area.
Trailhead GPS: N41 53.388' / W123 39.283'

The Hike

A sparkling emerald paradise nestled deep in the Siskiyou Wilderness, Raspberry Lake is a popular spot in this remote glacial basin.

A group or two can be found camping here most weekends from mid-June to August, but it's not uncommon to find this Shangri-La empty midweek or after Labor Day.

Although not as visually stunning as its neighbor to the north, Devil's Punchbowl, Raspberry Lake has better campsites, swimming, and fishing (brook and rainbow trout) and offers the chance to climb Preston Peak, a striking black monolith that's the highest point in the wilderness (see "Options").

The hike isn't bad either—featuring views of the major Siskiyou peaks while winding past Young's Valley—although it does follow an old road most of the way.

From the Young's Valley Trailhead, follow the closed road for 0.8 mile to the old trailhead at the wilderness boundary. Here the trail, still a closed road, begins to drop very steeply. At mile 3.0 you pass the Black Butte Trail junction.

Young's Valley, at mile 3.4, is a flat green meadow full of wildflowers in late June and July and surrounded by Young's Peak and El Capitan. It has numerous campsites and serves as the wilderness's Grand Central Station, with paths branching off down the Clear Creek, Black Butte, and Twin Valley Trails.

Raspberry Lake shimmers bright green in a tight valley in the Siskiyou Wilderness. ZACH URNESS

The trails are marked—not well, but well enough—and a small sign points you toward Raspberry Lake on the far side of Young's Valley. If you get confused, just remember to stay on the old road.

The next 2.0 miles make up for elevation lost earlier by climbing past Bell Echo Campground, with views of Devil's Punchbowl in the distance.

At mile 5.9 you'll reach the scattered remains of the Chrome Mine and the end of the old mining road. (Before the wilderness was created, you could drive to the Chrome Mine.) A narrow trail continues from the road's end, and the hiking becomes much tougher, scrambling 1.1 miles across two passes before dropping into the basin that's home to Raspberry Lake.

Across the first pass you'll come face to face with Preston Peak rising 7,313 feet into the sky. After the second, you'll begin to see Raspberry Lake shimmering below, an inviting green pool in the dry landscape. To reach the lake, you have to descend a series of switchbacks.

The best campsite is to the left, on the lake's eastern shore above a wonderful rock outcrop that invites swimming and fishing. Brook and rainbow trout can be caught here throughout June and early July.

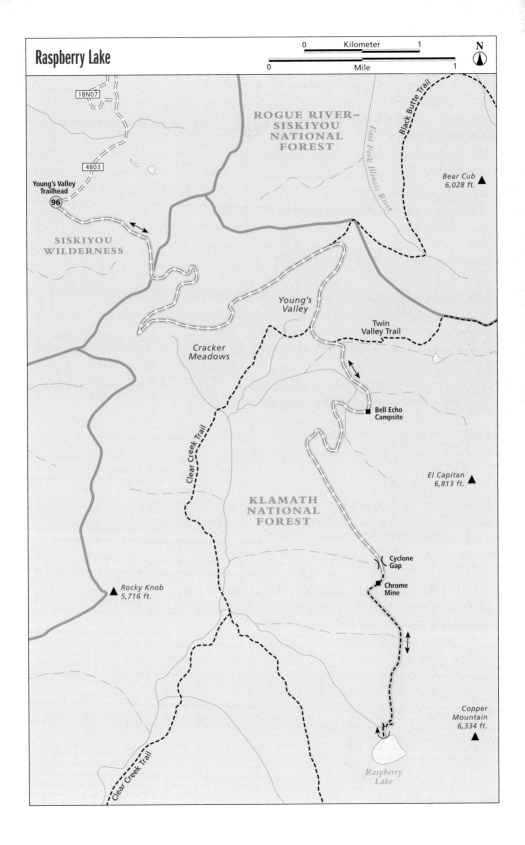

Raspberry Lake

0 Kilometer 1

0 Mile 1

N

18N07

4803

Young's Valley
Trailhead

96

SISKIYOU
WILDERNESS

ROGUE RIVER–
SISKIYOU
NATIONAL
FOREST

East Fork Illinois River

Black Butte Trail

Bear Cub
6,028 ft.

Young's
Valley

Twin
Valley Trail

Cracker
Meadows

Clear Creek Trail

Bell Echo
Campsite

El Capitan
6,813 ft.

KLAMATH
NATIONAL
FOREST

Cyclone
Gap

Chrome
Mine

Rocky Knob
5,716 ft.

Copper
Mountain
6,334 ft.

Clear Creek Trail

Raspberry
Lake

Miles and Directions

0.0 Begin at the Young's Valley Trailhead on a closed road.

0.8 Pass the wilderness boundary.

3.0 Pass the Black Butte Trail junction on the left.

3.4 Arrive at Young's Valley.

3.5 Pass the Clear Creek Trail junction.

3.7 Pass the Twin Valley Trail junction.

4.2 Pass the Bell Echo Campsite.

5.9 Arrive at the Chrome Mine, the end of the old road, and continue onto a narrow, rough trail.

6.8 Reach Raspberry Lake; return the way you came.

13.6 Arrive back at the Young's Valley Trailhead.

Options

Preston Peak: Although it's the second-tallest peak in the Siskiyou Range—Mount Ashland is tops at 7,531 feet—Preston Peak's 7,313 feet are far more impressive, rising above everything around it like a black beacon above the wilderness. To climb it, Raspberry Lake makes a perfect base camp. The climb is tough, rising 2,313 feet in just 2.0 miles, and although it's a nontechnical ascent (ropes aren't required), there is some steep exposure where a fall could mean trouble.

The route is simple. From the northwest shoreline of Raspberry Lake (follow the trail right from where you arrive), scramble up a steep rockfall to the ridgeline and follow the ridgeline left toward the unnamed peak directly above the lake. Behind the peak you come face to face with Preston Peak and can see the steep, ramp-like route to the top.

The ascent up Preston Peak, although it requires an occasional scramble, is best characterized as a grueling trudge up a black staircase. From the summit the view includes the Pacific Ocean, along with every major mountain and valley in Southern Oregon and Northern California.

Clear Creek. From Young's Valley, Clear Creek Trail takes off to the south-southeast, following the clear stream. It reaches Trout Camp in about 5.0 miles near a junction with the Doe Flat Trail and the route to Devil's Punchbowl. In about 8.0 miles it reaches Wilderness Falls, a small waterfall, and continues all the way to a trailhead on Road 15N32, which comes out of the Happy Camp, California, area along the Klamath River.

97 Devil's Punchbowl

A spectacular stone cathedral surrounding a pair of small lakes in the Siskiyou Wilderness. A difficult but beautiful trek.

Distance: 9.6-mile out and back
Difficulty: Strenuous
Elevation gain: 2,367 feet
Best season: June–Nov
Maps: USGS Preston Peak; Six Rivers National Forest
Trail contacts: Gasquet Ranger Station: (707) 457-3131

Parking and trailhead facilities: There's parking for 15 to 20 cars, plus a vault toilet.
Special considerations: Permits are required from the Gasquet Ranger Station for campfires or camp stoves. The little lake basin is almost devoid of trees due to the serpentine rock, so very little firewood is available. The area is home to a plentiful amount of black bears, so make sure to hang your food.

Finding the trailhead: From Grants Pass head southwest on US 199 a total of 53 miles, past Cave Junction and across the California border toward Crescent City, California. After passing through the Collier Tunnel, continue 9 miles and turn left onto Little Jones Creek Road (FR 17N05). Follow this paved road 10 miles. Turn left onto gravel road FR 16N02 at signs for Doe Flat and continue 3 miles to the road's end and scenic parking area.
Trailhead GPS: N41 48.845' / W123 42.411'

The Hike

This spectacular cathedral of silver-gray stone surrounds a small emerald lake high in the Siskiyou Wilderness in an eerie, phantasmal landscape polished almost bare by glaciers.

Devil's Punchbowl is one of the most unusual destinations in this guide—or anywhere—but the hike does require some effort. At 9.6 miles and a little more than 2,300 feet of elevation gain, the route isn't a killer overall. The problem is, the elevation gain comes all at once, in a brutal climb that leads into the barren landscape where the trail all but disappears in favor of stacked-rock cairns.

The hike used to be tougher, around 14 miles with an even steeper climb. The current, rerouted trail is fairly new and has increased the number of people who visit the punchbowl.

The route begins at a scenic trailhead and follows an old road, passing views of the Pacific Ocean after 0.1 mile before continuing to mile 0.6, where the old road becomes a proper trail.

The next 3.0 miles aren't extraordinary or particularly difficult. At mile 1.6 you'll pass a junction for Buck Lake—a pleasant, shallow pool full of green water and surrounded by forest. Continue 0.2 mile to the lake.

Devil's Punchbowl is a cliff-walled cathedral of stone polished almost bare by glaciers in the Siskiyou Wilderness. ZACH URNESS

At mile 3.1 views of Preston Peak, the wilderness's highest point, appear on the left. Just beyond, at mile 3.4, comes the turnoff to Devil's Punchbowl. The junction is marked by a small sign that points to the right and is easy to miss.

The trail shoots brutally uphill from the junction, climbing 600 feet on ill-built switchbacks, before reaching a creek crossing. Beyond the crossing, the trail mostly gives out in the barren glacial valley where stacked-rock cairns mark the route.

At mile 4.3 a beautiful, pear-shaped lake appears that's scenic enough to fool many into believing it's the punchbowl. Not so. Continue around the left edge of the lake and up the opposite side, following a creek that passes through a narrow rock gateway and eventually opens up into the jaw-dropping basin of Devil's Punchbowl proper. The cliffs seem to scrape the sky, and few trees populate the serpentine rock basin.

A number of campsites can be found in the basin, but they fill up quickly on summer weekends. The basin's increasing popularity may bring additional regulations in the future.

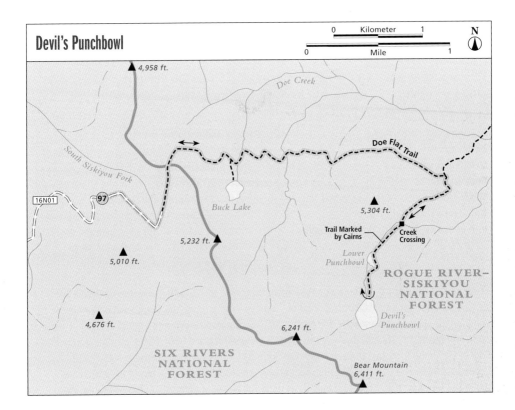

Miles and Directions

0.0 Begin at the Doe Flat Trailhead.

0.6 The old road becomes a proper trail.

1.6 Pass Buck Lake junction. The lake is located just 0.2 mile down the spur.

3.4 Arrive at Devil's Punchbowl junction, marked by a small sign on the right. Turn right and begin a steep uphill climb.

4.0 Cross over a creek and begin a section where the trail is marked primarily by stacked-rock cairns.

4.3 Reach the Lower Punchbowl; follow the trail around the left shoreline.

4.8 Arrive at Devil's Punchbowl; return the way you came.

6.2 Return to the junction with the Doe Flat Trail; turn left.

9.6 Arrive back at the trailhead.

Options

Clear Creek: If you continue beyond the turnoff to Devil's Punchbowl, the trail soon reaches Trout Camp along Clear Creek. On the Clear Creek Trail, it's about 5.0 miles (left) to Young's Valley.

98 Stout Grove

The most famous grove of old-growth redwoods in Jedediah Smith Redwoods State Park. A very short, easy, and popular loop along with a world-class drive. Many options.

Distance: 0.7-mile lollipop
Difficulty: Very easy
Elevation loss: 68 feet
Best season: Year-round
Maps: USGS Crescent City; Redwood National and State Park system
Trail contacts: Jedediah Smith Redwoods State Park: (707) 458-3018

Parking and trailhead facilities: There is parking for about 15 cars. Additional parking can be found on pullouts alongside Howland Hills Road.
Special considerations: The parking lot sometimes fills up on spring and summer weekends. Pets are not allowed on any national park trail in California. To assure compliance, they are also not allowed on trails in the three state parks embedded within Redwood National Park.

Finding the trailhead: From Grants Pass head southwest on US 199 across the California border toward Crescent City, California, a total of 70 miles. After passing the small town of Gasquet, continue 10 miles; just before the bridge across Myrtle Creek, turn left onto South Fork Road. You'll immediately cross a bridge over the Smith River and then a second bridge over the South Fork of the Smith River to a three-way junction. Turn right at the junction, following signs for Stout Grove, and follow the paved road 1.5 miles through a residential area. The paved road becomes the gravel Howland Hills Road as it enters the park. Follow this winding, stunningly beautiful road 0.8 mile to a parking area and well-marked trailhead on the right.
Trailhead GPS: N41 47.385' / W124 05.092'

The Hike

The Redwood National and State Park system stretches up the Northern California coast in a patchwork of semi-connected properties protecting what remains of the old-growth groves of *Sequoia sempervirens,* the tallest trees on Earth. The tallest tree on Earth, at the moment, is Hyperion, a 379-foot coastal redwood at an undisclosed location (the tallest tree ever recorded was a 392 foot Oregon Douglas-fir).

Before logging began in 1850, redwood forests covered roughly 2 million acres of land. Today less than 5 percent of that original unlogged forest remains. Redwoods are fairly hardy and fast-growing, but the ancient old-growth stands have a definite aura that tends to inspire people.

Jedediah Smith Redwoods State Park, home to some of the largest and most impressive trees, is located in the extreme northwest corner of California and is easily reached via Oregon. It has been rumored that the Ewoks scenes from the movie *Star Wars: Return of the Jedi* were filmed at Stout Grove. Not so, but they were filmed at Jedediah Smith Redwoods State Park.

Deborah Achor steps below some of the massive redwoods in Stout Grove, in Jedediah Smith Redwoods State Park. ZACH URNESS

Jed Smith, as it's commonly known, is a favorite among redwood lovers because its dense, lush, massive, and remote forest feels almost primeval, as though you've time-traveled back to the Jurassic.

The park is bisected by Howland Hills Road, a rough gravel route that twists below the ancient druid giants for almost 10 miles between Hiouchi and Crescent City.

The first and most popular stop on Howland Hills Road is Stout Grove, with an easy loop trail beneath immense redwoods. The loop connects to many of the park's trails.

The route begins at the trailhead parking area as a paved, closed road that heads downhill to the beginning of the loop. Head right along a wide path and savor every step. The largest (and stoutest) redwood, Stout Tree, is no longer marked to protect it from people tromping around it, but it sticks out in the middle of the forest. Stout Tree is 340 feet tall and 16 feet in diameter.

Just up the path, a trail veers off to the right. If you're up for a short detour, follow the spur through more large redwoods to Cedar Creek and back. (The trail continues to Little Bald Hill Trail; see "Options.") The short out-and-back detour is less than 0.3 mile and worth your time.

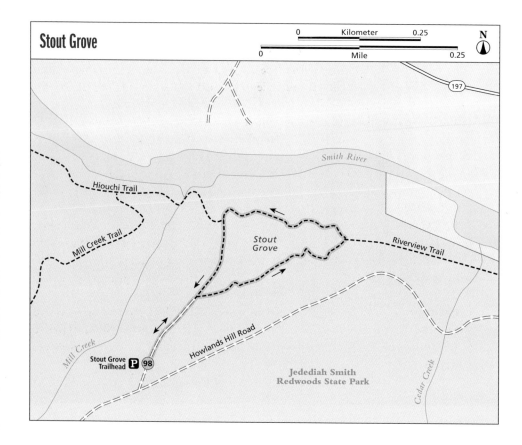

The loop eventually turns left—the turquoise waters of the Smith River glow through the trees just a few hundred feet away—and at the 0.5-mile mark passes a junction that accesses Mill Creek Trail, Hiouchi Trail, and a summer bridge that crosses the Smith River to Jed Smith Campground (see "Options").

The short loop ends too soon, back at the main parking area.

Miles and Directions

0.0 Begin at the Stout Grove Trailhead.

0.1 Reach the beginning of the loop; go right.

0.3 Pass the junction with the Riverview Trail.

0.5 Pass the Hiouchi / Mill Creek Trail junction.

0.6 Reach the end of the loop; go right.

0.7 Arrive back at the trailhead.

Options

Riverview Trail: From Stout Grove continue east from the first trail junction along the Smith River past Cedar Creek, a total of 0.5 mile, to a parking area on Howland Hills Road. Highlights include occasional views of spawning salmon and the Smith River.

Little Bald Hills Trailhead (mountain bikes and horses): The trailhead can be found up a short access road on the left off Howland Hills Road (marked by a sign) before you reach Stout Grove. Probably best known because mountain biking and horseback riding are allowed—both are prohibited on all other Jed Smith Trails—the trail runs through redwoods for 3.3 miles to a primitive campsite, 4.8 miles to the park's boundary, and a total of 10 miles to South Fork Road.

Mill Creek Trail: From the second trail junction at Stout Grove, follow pointers and cross a footbridge (in summer) or ford the river (in spring and winter) to access this 7.4-mile one-way trail through redwood groves and more open maple trees. The trail crosses Howland Hill Road a few times in the middle (another possible starting point) and ends near the Boy Scout Tree Trailhead.

Campground/Hiouchi Trail: From the second trail junction at Stout Grove, follow the Hiouchi Trail to a summer plank bridge that crosses the Smith River to the Jed Smith Campground area. In summer, many people cross the plank bridge to explore Stout Grove.

99 Boy Scout Tree Trail

A longer and more remote hike into the old-growth groves of Jedediah Smith Redwoods State Park that ends at a small waterfall.

Distance: 5.6-mile out and back
Difficulty: Moderate
Elevation gain: 922 feet
Best season: Year-round
Maps: USGS Crescent City; Redwood National and State Parks system
Trail contacts: Jedediah Smith Redwoods State Park: (707) 458-3018

Parking and trailhead facilities: The small parking pullout at the trailhead has room for about 6 cars. Many cars park at pullouts along the road.
Special considerations: The trail is sometimes busy on spring and summer weekends. Consider coming in winter or midweek.

Finding the trailhead: From Grants Pass head southwest on US 199 across the California border toward Crescent City, California, a total of 70 miles. After passing the small town of Gasquet, continue 10 miles; just before the bridge across Myrtle Creek, turn left onto South Fork Road.

You'll immediately cross a bridge over the Smith River and then a second bridge over the South Fork Smith River to a three-way junction. Turn right, following signs for Stout Grove, through a residential area for 1.5 miles. The paved road becomes gravel Howland Hill Road where it enters the park. Follow this winding, beautiful road a total of 3.2 miles, past Stout Grove, to a trailhead on the right.
Trailhead GPS: N41 46.116' / W124 06.614'

The Hike

Although Stout Grove is the most popular trail in Jedediah Smith Redwoods State Park, most would consider Boy Scout Tree the best overall hike.

The old-growth trees are so dense it occasionally feels as though you're walking indoors, through a wood cathedral with a sword fern floor and canopy ceiling.

The only downside is the occasional weekend crowds during summer. Luckily the trail is long enough that crowds don't get as bunched up as at Stout Grove.

From the trailhead the path immediately heads into the trail's largest and most impressive redwood grove. The massive trunks soar high into the mist on rainy days; on clear afternoons, pencil-thin rays of sunlight stream through the canopy.

The trail crosses a number of footbridges and after 1.0 mile heads slightly uphill into a more open area where the trees are smaller.

The old-growth redwoods are uniformly massive on the Boy Scout Tree Trail in Jedediah Smith Redwoods State Park. ZACH URNESS

At mile 2.4 a side trail leads to Boy Scout Tree, a redwood where two trees have joined in one massive 40-foot-diameter trunk. The tree splits off as it rises, as though giving the two-finger Boy Scout salute.

Beyond, the trail heads through a bramble of blackberries along Jordan Creek to the grotto of Fern Falls, a small cascade that slides down a rock face.

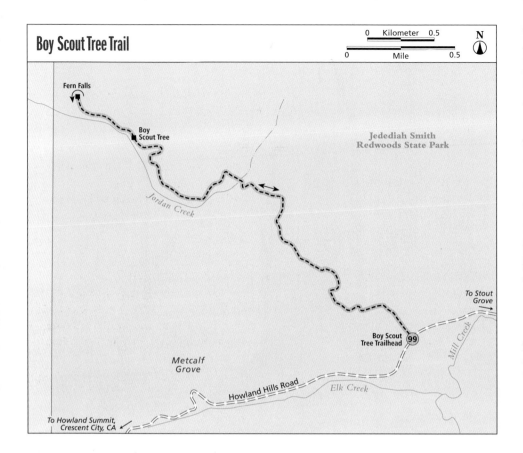

Boy Scout Tree Trail

Fern Falls

Boy Scout Tree

Jordan Creek

Jedediah Smith
Redwoods State Park

To Stout
Grove

Boy Scout
Tree Trailhead 99

Mill Creek

Metcalf
Grove

Howland Hills Road

Elk Creek

To Howland Summit,
Crescent City, CA

0   Kilometer   0.5
0   Mile   0.5

N

Miles and Directions

0.0 Begin at the Boy Scout Tree Trailhead.

2.4 Come to a junction for the Boy Scout Tree.

2.8 Reach Fern Falls; return the way you came.

5.6 Arrive back at the trailhead.

100 Hatton Trail

A redwood hike on the north side of Jedediah Smith Redwoods State Park to an enchanting grove. See "Options" for a stretch along the Smith River and access to Stout Grove and campground.

Distance: 4.2-mile out and back
Difficulty: Easy to moderate
Elevation gain: 730 feet
Best season: Year-round
Maps: USGS Crescent City; Redwood National and State Parks system

Trail contacts: Jedediah Smith Redwoods State Park: (707) 458-3018
Parking and trailhead facilities: The small pullout along US 199 has room for 3 cars.

Finding the trailhead: From Grants Pass head southwest on US 199 across the California border toward Crescent City, California, a total of 73.6 miles. Just past the town of Hiouchi, US 199 crosses the Smith River in Jedediah Smith Redwoods State Park. Continue for another 2 miles to a sign that says Ruth Perry Hatton Grove on the left (south) side of the highway. The trailhead is opposite the developed interpretive area with a vault toilet. Park at a pullout on the right side of the highway and cross the highway to the trailhead.
Trailhead GPS: N41 48.660' / W124 06.389'

The Hike

Although not quite as impressive as Stout Grove or Boy Scout Tree, the Hatton Trail features easier access, a good length, interesting options, and huge redwoods.

The featured route works its way around old-growth trees along the south side of US 199 to a wonderful hidden grove. (**Note:** The proximity to US 199 creates easy access but also, occasionally, a little too much noise on the trail.) An optional extension continues along the crystal-clear waters of the Smith River all the way to Stout Grove.

From the Ruth Perry Hatton Grove sign, you'll start with the short and beautiful Hatton Loop. Take the time to hike this 0.3-mile loop before continuing on the main Hatton Trail.

The redwoods at the beginning are the most impressive, rising above sword fern and smaller trees (mostly western hemlock, smaller redwoods, and tanoak) in massive grayish-white and dark brown columns.

The trail climbs a moderately steep ridge away from the highway at first, then heads back toward the highway. In general the forest is thick enough to muffle the sounds of cars passing, but some noise does slip through.

At mile 1.8, after a stretch that feels fairly close to the highway, keep your eyes peeled for the trail junction that points to Lohse Grove on the right. From the junction continue 0.4 mile to Lohse Grove on a trail that sees little use and is a bit ragged. The grove itself is not quite what you'd expect—basically five very large trees

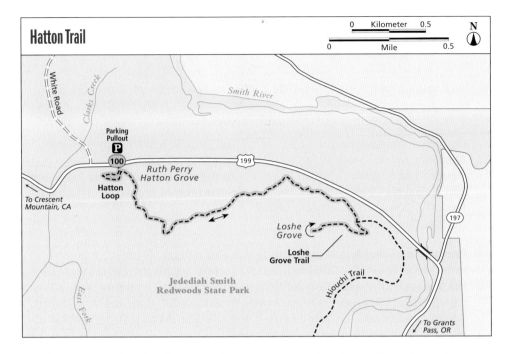

Hatton Trail

standing in a small circle. If you stand between them, there's a feeling of entering a very narrow room, almost a circular tube, with the trees rising high above. The trail's end is marked by a dedication sign for Lohse Grove.

Miles and Directions

0.0 From the parking area, cross over US 199 to a sign that says Ruth Perry Hatton Grove.

0.1 Begin hiking the Hatton Loop.

0.3 Finish the Hatton Loop and continue down the Hatton Trail.

1.8 Arrive at the Lohse Grove / Hiouchi Trail junction; go right.

2.1 Reach Lohse Grove; retrace your steps to the trail junction.

2.6 Back at the Lohse Grove / Hiouchi Trail junction, turn left, back the way you came.

4.2 Arrive back at the trailhead.

Options

Hiouchi Trail: Beyond the Lohse Grove junction, the Hatton Trail continues for another 0.3 mile to a junction with the Hiouchi Trail. Although it doesn't feature many redwoods, there are excellent views and beach access along the Smith River, which on a sunny day shimmers a bright, aqua blue color that testifies to the water's clarity. The path runs 1.8 miles to a summer footbridge that accesses Jedediah Smith Campground and another summer footbridge that crosses Mill Creek to Stout Grove. The total distance from the Hatton Trailhead to Stout Grove is 4.0 miles one-way (assuming you don't take the Lohse Grove spur).

APPENDIX A: HIKER'S CHECKLIST

Always make and check your own checklist!

If you've ever hiked into the backcountry and discovered that you've forgotten an essential, you know why it's a good idea to make a checklist and check the items off as you pack so that you won't forget the things you want and need. Here are some ideas:

Clothing

❑ Dependable rain parka
❑ Rain pants
❑ Windbreaker
❑ Thermal underwear
❑ Shorts
❑ Long pants or sweatpants
❑ Wool cap or balaclava
❑ Hat
❑ Wool shirt or sweater
❑ Jacket or parka
❑ Extra socks
❑ Underwear
❑ Lightweight shirts
❑ T-shirts
❑ Bandanna(s)
❑ Mittens or gloves
❑ Belt

Footwear

❑ Sturdy, comfortable boots
❑ Lightweight camp shoes

Bedding

❑ Sleeping bag
❑ Foam pad or air mattress
❑ Ground sheet (plastic or nylon)
❑ Dependable tent

Hauling

❑ Backpack and/or day pack

Cooking

❑ 1-quart container (plastic)
❑ 1-gallon water container for camp use (collapsible)
❑ Backpack stove and extra fuel
❑ Funnel
❑ Aluminum foil
❑ Cooking pots
❑ Bowls/plates
❑ Utensils (spoons, forks, small spatula, knife)
❑ Pot scrubber
❑ Matches in waterproof container

Food and Drink

❑ Cereal
❑ Bread
❑ Crackers
❑ Cheese
❑ Trail mix
❑ Margarine
❑ Powdered soups
❑ Salt/pepper
❑ Main-course meals
❑ Snacks
❑ Hot chocolate
❑ Tea
❑ Powdered milk
❑ Drink mixes

Photography

❑ Camera and memory cards (or film)
❑ Filters
❑ Lens brush/paper

Miscellaneous

- ❑ Sunglasses
- ❑ Map and compass and/or GPS device
- ❑ Toilet paper
- ❑ Pocketknife
- ❑ Sunscreen
- ❑ Good insect repellent
- ❑ Lip balm
- ❑ Flashlight with good batteries and a spare bulb
- ❑ Candle(s)
- ❑ First-aid kit
- ❑ Your FalconGuide
- ❑ Survival kit
- ❑ Small garden trowel or shovel
- ❑ Water filter or purification tablets
- ❑ Plastic bags (for trash)
- ❑ Soap
- ❑ Towel
- ❑ Toothbrush
- ❑ Fishing license
- ❑ Fishing rod, reel, lures, flies, etc.
- ❑ Binoculars
- ❑ Waterproof covering for pack
- ❑ Watch
- ❑ Sewing kit

APPENDIX B: REFERENCES

There are any number of wildflower, bird, and tree guides in print, all of them excellent. We like to use the nature guides listed below. The list includes all sources from which information was drawn for this book.

Bernstein, A. *90 Best Day-Hikes, Southern Oregon and Far Northern California.* Grants Pass, OR: Cloudcap Books, 1994.

Bernstein, A. *Hiking Oregon's Southern Cascades and Siskiyous.* Guilford, CT: Falcon-Guides, 2001.

Bernstein, A. *Native Trees of the Northwest.* Grants Pass, OR: Cloudcap Books, 1988.

Cranson, K. *Crater Lake: Gem of the Cascades.* Lansing, MI: KRC Press, 1982.

Grubbs, B. *Hiking the Central Oregon Cascades,* Helena, MT: FalconGuides, 1997.

Jackman, A., and A. Bernstein. *The Hip-Pocket Naturalist: A Guide to Oregon's Rogue River Basin.* Grants Pass, OR: Cloudcap Books, 1989.

Niehaus, T. *Pacific States Wildflowers. The Peterson's Field Guides Series.* Boston: Houghton Mifflin, 1976.

Randall, W. *Manual of Oregon Trees and Shrubs.* Corvallis, OR: OSU Bookstores, 1981.

Reyes, C. *The Table Rocks of Jackson County: Islands in the Sky.* Ashland, OR: Last Minute Publications, 1994.

APPENDIX C: FOR MORE INFORMATION

Bureau of Land Management

BLM—Medford District
3040 Biddle Rd.
Medford, OR 97504
(541) 770-2200
www.or.blm.gov/medford

BLM—Burns District Office
28910 Hwy 20 West
Hines, OR 97738
(541) 573-4400

BLM—Lakeview District
1301 S. "G" St.
Lakeview, OR 97630
(541) 947-2177

The Nature Conservancy

1150 Ashland St.
Ashland, OR 97520
www.tnc.org

National Park Service

Crater Lake National Park
Crater Lake, OR 97604
(541) 594-2211
crater.lake.national-park.com

Oregon Caves National Monument
19000 Caves Hwy.
Cave Junction, OR 97523
(541) 592-2100 (general)
(541) 592-2631 (recreation)
nps.gov/orca

Redwood National and State Parks
1111 Second St.
Crescent City, CA 95531
(707) 465-7335

US Army Corps of Engineers

Rogue Basin Project/Lost Creek Lake
100 Cole N. Rivers Dr.
Trail, OR 97541
(541) 878-2255

USDA Forest Service

Rogue River–Siskiyou National Forest
333 West Eighth St.
Medford, OR 97501
(541) 858-2200
www.fs.fed.us/r6/rogue

Six Rivers National Forest
1330 Bayshore Way
Eureka, CA 95501
(707) 442-1721

Umpqua National Forest
2900 NW Stewart Pkwy.
Roseburg, OR 97470
(541) 672-6601
www.fs.fed.us/r6/umpqua

Fremont-Winema National Forest
Klamath Ranger District
2819 Dahlia St.
Klamath Falls, OR 97601
(541) 883-6714
www.fs.fed.us/r6/winema

HIKE INDEX

Abbott Butte 117
Annie Creek Loop 137
Azalea Lake 228

Babyfoot Lake 282
Badger Lake 167
Bear Camp Prairie 267
Big Indian Gorge 27
Big Tree Loop 292
Black Butte 317
Blue Canyon Basin 162
Blue Lake 46
Boardman Scenic Corridor—Cape
    Ferrelo 313
Boardman Scenic Corridor—Indian
    Sands 310
Boundary Springs 126
Boy Scout Tree Trail 336
Briggs Creek 240

Cleetwood Cove 129
Cliff Lake / Grasshopper Mountain 108
Clover Creek 187
Coquille Falls 306
Crack in the Ground 36
Crater Lake Pinnacles 49

DeGarmo Canyon 39
Devil's Peak 158
Devil's Punchbowl 329
Dollar Mountain 246
Dread and Terror / Umpqua Hot
    Springs 83

Eagle Mountain 289
East Fork Illinois River 321

Fall Creek Falls 69
Fish Lake 111
Frog Pond 225

Garfield Peak 134
Gearhart Mountain 43
Golden Stairs 105
Grayback Mountain 251
Grizzly Peak 210

Hanging Rock Trail 272
Hatton Trail 339
Hobart Bluff / Pacific Crest Trail 206
Humbug Mountain 308

Illinois River—East 275
Illinois River—West 298

Kerby Peak 243

Lemolo Falls 86
Limpy Creek Botanical Loop 249
Little Blitzen Gorge 30
Little Falls Loop 279
Loeb State Park / Redwood Nature
    Loop 304
Lower Sky Lakes 176
Lower Table Rock 194

Magic Canyon 285
Middle Fork Rogue River 147
Mill Creek Falls 123
Miller to Maidu Lake 89
Mount Ashland Meadows / Pacific Crest
    Trail 212
Mount Bailey 55
Mount Bolivar 270

Mount McLoughlin 184
Mount Scott 131
Mount Thielsen 52

Nannie Creek / Puck Lake 173
National Creek Falls 96
Natural Bridge / Farewell Bend 98

Oregon Redwoods 315

Pike Creek Canyon 33
Pilot Rock 203
Pine Bench 75
Plaikni Falls 145

Rainie Falls 254
Raspberry Lake 325
Rattlesnake Mountain 114
Red Buttes / Pacific Crest Trail 232
Rogue River Greenway 200
Rogue River Trail—Grave Creek to
    Foster Bar 257
Rogue River Trail—Marial to Paradise
    Bar Lodge 263

Seven Lakes Basin—East 154
Seven Lakes Basin—West 150
Southeast Oregon 23

Squaw Lake 170
Stout Grove 332

Takelma Gorge 102
Tanner Lakes 221
Taylor Creek 236
Thielsen Creek Meadows 58
Toketee Falls 78
Tunnel Ridge / Sterling Mine Trail 215
Twin Lakes 72

Union Peak 141
Upper Rogue Canyon / Rough Rider
    Falls 92
Upper Sky Lakes 180
Upper Table Rock 197

Varney Creek 190
Viewpoint Mike 120
Vulcan Lake 295

Wagner Butte 218
Watson Falls 80
Wildhorse Lake 24
Windy Valley 301
Wolf Creek Falls 62

Yellowjacket Loop 65

About the Authors

Art Bernstein has written sixteen other nature and hiking books. His most recent FalconGuide was *Best Easy Day Hikes Eugene* (with his wife, Lynn Bernstein) and *Weird Hikes,* second edition. An avid hiker and naturalist with an MS in Natural Resources from the University of Michigan, Art grew up in Detroit but has lived in Grants Pass, Oregon, since 1970.

Zach Urness is an award-winning outdoors columnist and photographer who's been reporting on Oregon's wild spaces for six years. He covers the environment and recreation at the *Statesman Journal* newspaper in Salem, Oregon, and previously worked in Southern Oregon for the *Grants Pass Daily Courier.* A hiker, biker, whitewater kayaker, fly fisherman, and climber, Zach spends almost every outside-the-office moment rambling the Beaver State's forests, mountains, and rivers.

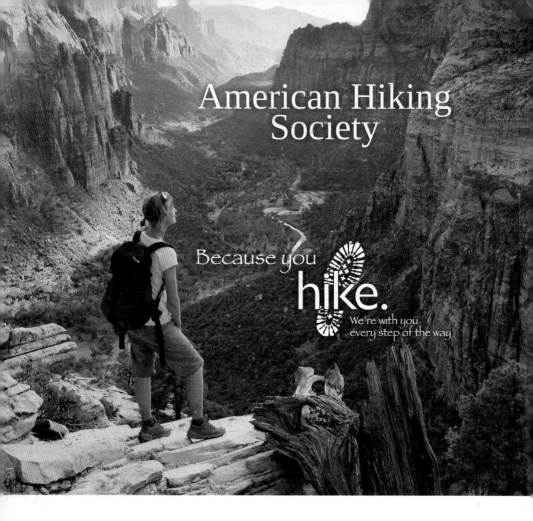

American Hiking Society

Because you

hike.

We're with you every step of the way

As a national voice for hikers, **American Hiking Society** works every day:

- Building and maintaining hiking trails
- Educating and supporting hikers by providing information and resources
- Supporting hiking and trail organizations nationwide
- Speaking for hikers in the halls of Congress and with federal land managers

Whether you're a casual hiker or a seasoned backpacker, become a member of American Hiking Society and join the national hiking community! You'll enjoy great member benefits and help preserve the nation's hiking trails, so tomorrow's hike is even better than today's. We invite you to join us now!

American Hiking Society

HILLSBORO PUBLIC LIBRARIES
Hillsboro, OR